Programming Microsoft Dynamics 365 Business Central

Build powerful, robust, and scalable extensions customized for your business requirements

Marije Brummel

Natalie Karolak

Christopher D. Studebaker

David Studebaker

Programming Microsoft Dynamics 365 Business Central

Group Product Manager: Aaron Tanna

Associate Publishing Product Manager: Uzma Sheerin

Senior Editor: Rounak Kulkarni

Technical Editor: Vidhisha Patidar

Copy Editor: Safis Editing

Book Project Manager: Prajakta Naik

Proofreader: Rounak Kulkarni

Indexer: Pratik Shirodkar

Production Designer: Aparna Bhagat

Business Development Executives: Saloni Garg

Cover picture credit: Elizabeth Studebaker

First edition: September 2007

Second edition: November 2009

Third edition: February 2013

Fourth edition: July 2015

Fifth edition: April 2017

Sixth edition: April 2019

Seventh edition: November 2024

Production reference: 1160924

Published by Packt Publishing Ltd.

Grosvenor House

11 St Paul's Square

Birmingham

B3 1RB, UK.

ISBN 978-1-80323-641-4

www.packtpub.com

To my father, David, whose authorship of the first editions of this book has been a guide to all that have come after, with many more to come.

– Christopher D. Studebaker

To the great Business Central community, which has always enriched me with both supportive and entertaining exchanges. May this book be the newcomers' first step toward their membership of the community as well.

– Natalie Karolak

Contributors

About the authors

Marije Brummel is a coach, author, programmer, consultant, project manager, presenter, evangelist, and trainer. Marije has received the Microsoft MVP and the NAVUG All-Star awards, among several other awards. She has chaired the Microsoft Dynamics Credentialing committee and has authored official Microsoft Exam materials. She's the go-to girl for performance troubleshooting and upgrade challenges. One of her biggest achievements was introducing Design Patterns into the Business Central community. Her books, blog articles, and YouTube videos have influenced almost everyone involved with Business Central. She is a mother of five, enjoys the outdoors with her dog, and loves spending time with her family.

Natalie Karolak works at COSMO CONSULT, a leading European provider of industry-specific business software and end-to-end IT solutions. As a product architect, she develops and maintains Business Central apps for Microsoft AppSource. Programming for NAV/BC partners since 2006, Natalie has always been passionate about knowledge gain and knowledge sharing. For her commitment to the German-speaking online community, she was presented with the MVP award from 2012 to 2016 and regained it in 2024. Today, she shares English-speaking news and information for AL programmers on X, and on her blog that is named after the title that the community gave her: The BC Docs Librarian.

Christopher D. Studebaker was a certified environmental consultant working with manufacturing facilities to meet national and state regulations before he started working with Business Central (then known as Navision) in 1999. After working on regulatory reporting, data analysis, project management, and subcontractor oversight, Chris has used those skills to sell, develop, and implement Business Central for more than 25 years. He has specialized in retail, manufacturing, job shop, and distribution implementations, mostly in high-user-count, high-data-volume applications. Chris serves as a technical consultant and trainer for customers and fellow Business Central professionals. He has a Bachelor of Science degree from Northern Illinois University and has done graduate work at Denmark Technical University.

David Studebaker has been designing and developing software since 1962 as a developer, consultant, manager, and business owner. In 1967, David co-authored the first general-purpose SPOOL system, an AT&T/IBM joint project. He has been a founding partner in several firms, most recently Studebaker Technology and Liberty Grove Software. David's publications include a decade of technical reviews for ACM Computing Reviews and a number of articles on shop floor data collection. David originated the Packt series of books on programming Microsoft Dynamics Business Central (aka Dynamics NAV). He holds a BS in mechanical engineering from Purdue University and an MBA from the University of Chicago. He is a life member of the Association for Computing Machinery.

About the reviewer

Brad Prendergast is a seasoned professional with over 20 years of experience with Microsoft Dynamics 365 Business Central (formerly Navision) and holds an undergraduate and master's degree in computer information systems. Over the years, Brad has worked on both sides of ERP implementations, providing him with a unique perspective as both a partner and an end user. His extensive experience includes architecting and developing solutions, with both process and technology, to increase efficiency. Brad is also an active member of the Business Central community, and co-host of the popular Dynamics Corner podcast, frequently sharing his insights and expertise online and at industry events and conferences. His passion for the application and the community is evident in his dedication to helping businesses achieve their goals through innovative ERP solutions.

Table of Contents

1

Introduction to Business Central   1

2

Tables   57

3

Data Types and Table Fields   109

4

Pages – The Interactive Interface   157

5

Reports and Queries   225

6

Introduction to AL 283

7

Intermediate AL 333

8

Extensibility beyond AL   387

Preface

Welcome to the worldwide community of Microsoft Dynamics 365 Business Central developers! This is a collegial environment populated by AL developers who readily and generously share their knowledge. There are formal and informal organizations of Business Central-focused users, developers, and vendor firms scattered throughout the globe and active on the web. Our community continues to grow and prosper, and it now includes over 200,000 user companies worldwide.

The information in this book will help you shorten your learning curve on how to program for the Business Central **Enterprise Resource Planning** (ERP) system using the AL language, the Visual Studio Code development environment, and their capabilities. We hope you will enjoy working with Business Central as much as we have.

A brief history of Business Central

Each new version of Microsoft Dynamics 365 Business Central is the result of inspiration and hard work, along with some good fortune and expert technical investment over the last 30 years.

The beginning

Three college friends, Jesper Balser, Torben Wind, and Peter Bang, from **Denmark Technical University** (**DTU**) founded their computer software business in 1984 when they were in their early twenties; that business was **PC Computing & Consulting** (**PC & C**), and its first product was called PC Plus.

Single-user PC Plus

PC Plus was released in 1985 with the primary goal of ease of use. An early employee said its functional design was inspired by the combination of a manual ledger journal, an Epson FX-80 printer, and a Canon calculator. Incidentally, Peter Bang is the grandson of one of the founders of Bang & Olufsen, the manufacturer of home entertainment systems par excellence.

PC Plus was a PC DOS-based, single-user system. PC Plus's design included the following features:

- An interface resembling the use of documents and calculators
- Online help
- Good exception handling
- Minimal reliance on computer resources

The PC Plus product was marketed through dealers in Denmark and Norway.

Multi-user Navigator

In 1987, PC & C released a new product, the multi-user Navigator, and a new corporate name, Navision. Navigator was quite a technological leap forward. It included the following features:

- Client/server technology
- A relational database
- Transaction-based processing
- Version management
- High-speed OLAP capabilities (SIFT technology)
- A screen painter tool
- A programmable report writer

In 1990, Navision was expanding its marketing and dealer recruitment efforts into Germany, Spain, and the United Kingdom. Also, in 1990, a third version of Navigator was released. Navigator V3 was still a character-based system, albeit a very sophisticated one. If you had the opportunity to study Navigator V3.x, you would instantly recognize the roots of today's Business Central product. By V3, the product included the following features:

- A design based on object-oriented concepts
- Integrated 4GL Table, Form, and Report Design tools (the IDE)
- Structured exception handling
- Built-in resource management
- The original programming language that became C/AL, which later changed to AL
- Function libraries
- The concept of regional or country-based localization

When Navigator V3.5 was released, it also included support for multiple platforms and multiple databases. Navigator V3.5 would run on both Unix and Windows NT networks. It supported Oracle and Informix databases, as well as those developed in-house.

At about this time, several major strategic efforts were initiated. On the technical side, the decision was made to develop a GUI-based product. The first prototype of Navision Financials (for Windows) was shown in 1992. At about the same time, a relationship was established that would take Navision into distribution in the United States. The initial release in the US in 1995 was V3.5 of the character-based product, rechristened Avista for US distribution.

Navision Financials for Windows

In 1995, Navision Financials V1.0 for Microsoft Windows was released. This product had many (but not all) of the features of Navigator V3.5. It was designed for complete look-and-feel compatibility with Windows 95. There was an effort to provide the same ease of use and flexibility of development in Microsoft Access. The new Navision Financials was very compatible with Microsoft Office and was thus sold as "being familiar to any Office user." Like any V1.0 product, it was quickly followed by a much-improved V1.1.

In the next few years, Navision continued to be improved and enhanced. Major new functionalities, such as the following, were added:

- **Customer Relation Management (CRM)**
- **Manufacturing (ERP)**
- **Advanced distribution** (including **Warehouse Management**)

Various Microsoft certifications were obtained, providing muscle to the marketing efforts. Geographic and dealer-based expansion continued apace. By 2000, according to the Navision Annual Report of that year, the product was represented by nearly 1,000 dealers (Navision Solution Centers) in 24 countries and used by 41,000 customers, located in 108 countries.

Growth and mergers

In 2000, Navision Software A/S and its primary Danish competitor, Damgaard A/S, merged. Product development and new releases continued for the primary products of both original firms (Navision and Axapta). In 2002, the now much larger Navision Software, with all of its products (Navision, Axapta, the smaller, older C5, and XAL) was purchased by Microsoft, becoming part of the Microsoft Business Systems division, along with the previously purchased Great Plains Software business and its several product lines. The Navision and Great Plains products all received a common rebranding to become the Dynamics product line. Navision was renamed Dynamics NAV and, later, Business Central.

As early as 2003, research began with the Dynamics NAV development team, planning moves to further enhance NAV and take advantage of various parts of the Microsoft product line. Goals were defined to increase integration with products such as Microsoft Office and Microsoft Outlook. Goals were also set to leverage the functional capabilities of Visual Studio Code and SQL Server, among others. Throughout this, there was a determination not to lose the strength and flexibility of the base product.

NAV 2009 was released in late 2008, NAV 2013 in late 2012, followed by NAV 2015 in late 2014. NAV 2017 was released in October 2016. The biggest hurdles to the new technologies have been cleared. A new user interface, the Role Tailored Client, was created as part of this renewal. NAV was tightly integrated with Microsoft's SQL Server and other Microsoft products, such as Office, Outlook, and SharePoint. Development is more integrated with Visual Studio Code and is more .NET-compliant. The product became more open and, at the same time, more sophisticated, supporting features such as web services access, web and tablet clients, integration of third-party controls, and RDLC and Word-based reporting.

Continuous enhancement

Business Central was made available from Microsoft as a cloud-based application in April 2018. Development changed from inline code changes to extensions. Extensions are a method of adding functionality to existing objects to modify a solution's behavior. Microsoft continues to invest in, enhance, and advance Business Central. More capabilities and functionality are added with every new release. Business Central continues to be one of the fastest-growing products within the Microsoft organization.

AL language roots

One of the first questions asked by people new to AL is often, "*What other programming language is it like?*" The best response is Pascal enhanced with C# features.

At the time, the three founders of Navision were attending classes at DTU, Pascal was widely used as a preferred language, not only on computer courses but also on other courses where computers were tools and software had to be written for data analyses. Some of the strengths of Pascal as a tool in an educational environment also made it an ideal model for Navision's business application development.

Perhaps coincidentally (or perhaps not), at the same time at DTU, a Pascal compiler called Blue Label Pascal was developed by Anders Hejlsberg. That compiler became the basis for what was Borland's Turbo Pascal, which was considered the everyman's compiler of the 1980s because of its low price. Anders went with his Pascal compiler to Borland. While he was there, Turbo Pascal morphed into the Delphi language and IDE tool set under his guidance.

Michael Nielsen, formerly of Navision and Microsoft, who developed the original C/AL compiler, runtime, and IDE, said that the design criteria provide an environment that can be used without the following tasks:

- Dealing with memory and other resource-handling
- Thinking about exception handling and state
- Thinking about database transactions and rollbacks
- Knowing about set operations (SQL)
- Knowing about OLAP (SIFT)

Paraphrasing some of Michael's additional comments, the goals of the language and IDE designs included the following:

- Allowing a developer to focus on design rather than coding but still allowing flexibility
- Providing a syntax based on Pascal stripped of complexities, especially relating to memory management
- Providing a limited set of predefined object types and reducing the complexity and learning curve

Implementing database versioning for a consistent and reliable view of the database

The basic principles of Michael's design for Navision still exist within the AL language and Visual Studio Code IDE for modern Business Central development.

Who this book is for

This book is for the following:

A business application designer or developer for whom the following is true:

- Wants to become productive in AL development within Visual Studio Code as quickly as possible
- Understands business applications and the type of software required to support those applications
- Has some programming experience
- Has access to a Microsoft-hosted cloud instance of Business Central
- Is willing to do exercises to get hands-on experience

The manager or executive (with technical experience) who wants a concise, in-depth view of Business Central's extension development tool sets.

The technically knowledgeable manager or executive of a firm using Business Central that is about to embark on a significant Business Central enhancement project

The technically knowledgeable manager or executive of a firm considering the purchase of Business Central as a flexible and extendable business applications platform

The experienced business analyst, consultant, or advanced student of application software development who wants to learn more about Business Central, as it is one of the most widely used, and most flexible, business application systems available

The reader of this book does not need the following:

- To be an expert in programming
- Previous experience with Business Central, AL, or Visual Studio Code

What this book covers

Chapter 1, Introduction to Business Central, starts with an overview of Business Central as a business application and functional terminology. It covers the basics of the base applications, 12 object types, and an introduction to Visual Studio Code **integrated development environment (IDE)**. After stepping through setting up an AL project in Visual Studio Code, the chapter closes with an extended hands-on experience in the over-arching exercise scenario.

Chapter 2, Tables, focuses on the foundation level of Business Central's data structure – tables and their components. This chapter covers properties, triggers (where AL business logic resides), field groups, table relations, and SumIndexFields. It will then present the hands-on creation and extension of several tables in support of an example application. The chapter will also review the types of tables found in Business Central applications.

Chapter 3, Data Types and Table Fields, will teach you about fields, the basic building blocks of Business Central's data structure. It will review the different data types in Business Central and cover all its field properties and triggers in detail, as well as the different field classes.

Chapter 4, Pages – The Interactive Interface, reviews the different types of pages, their structures (triggers and properties), and general usage. The chapter will encourage you to build several pages for an example application using snippets. It will also explore the different types of controls and actions that can be used on pages. Client tools for page development and user search functions will be covered.

Chapter 5, Reports and Queries, delves into the data reporting capabilities of Business Central with report and query objects. Report structure, data flow, properties, and triggers are covered in detail. Layout formats including SQL Report Layout, Word, and Excel are reviewed. The chapter also covers ways that report objects can process as well as output data. An in-depth example of creating a report from scratch with a multi-sheet Excel layout allows you to build upon your knowledge so far. Query object structure, properties, and triggers, as well as use cases, are explored in detail.

Chapter 6, Introduction to AL, shows the level of flexibility Business Central has in implementing custom business logic. AL syntax, naming conventions, variables, operators, and frequently used AL methods are covered in detail. Custom procedures and data validation are discussed, along with an example of creating a sample report with a Word layout.

Chapter 7, Intermediate AL, digs deeper into AL development and techniques. It will review some more advanced built-in methods, including those relating to dates and decimal calculations—both critical business application tools. This chapter will also explore AL methods that support process flow control functions, CRUD operations, and filtering, before reviewing methods of communication between objects. Multi-language support and debugging are covered in detail. Finally, this chapter offers the opportunity to practically enhance an example application.

Chapter 8, *Extensibility beyond AL*, shows that developing in AL is not limited to data and processes inside a Business Central application. The various API types offered as input/output interfaces are discussed, and hands-on examples are available for XML and JSON data. We discuss the structure, properties, and triggers of Pages, Queries, XMLports, and codeunits used as SOAP and OData web services, as well as RESTful API pages. The final example in the sample solution involves using AL to access and consume an external API.

To get the most out of this book

To get the maximum out of this book as a developer, the following should apply:

- You should be an experienced developer

- You should know at least one programming language

- You should have IDE experience

- You should be knowledgeable about business applications

- You should be good at self-directed study

If you have these attributes, this book will help you become productive with AL and Business Central much more rapidly.

Even though this book is targeted primarily at developers, it is also designed to be useful to executives, consultants, managers, business owners, and others who want to learn about the development technology and operational capabilities of Dynamics 365 Business Central.

If you fit into one of these, or similar, categories, start by studying *Chapter 1* for a good overview of Business Central and its tools. You should then consider reviewing sections of other chapters, where specific topics may apply to your specific areas of interest.

Software/hardware covered in the book	Operating system requirements
Visual Studio Code	Windows, macOS, or Linux
Microsoft Office 365	Windows, macOS, or Android
Microsoft SQL Report Builder	Windows with .NET Framework 4.6
Web browser	Microsoft Edge, Google Chrome (77.0 or later), or Mozilla Firefox (69.0 or later) for Windows Safari for macOS (12.0 or later)

This book's illustrations are from the CRONUS International database, Dynamics 365 Business Central v24, and Visual Studio Code v1.92 for Windows.

To sign up for a free trial of Microsoft Dynamics 365 Business Central, follow the instructions on the Microsoft website:

```
https://learn.microsoft.com/en-us/dynamics365/business-central/
trial-signup
```

To connect a Visual Studio Code AL project to an existing cloud sandbox environment, follow these instructions:

```
https://learn.microsoft.com/en-us/dynamics365/business-central/
dev-itpro/developer/devenv-troubleshoot-vscode-webclient
```

> **Note**
>
> If you are using the digital version of this book, we advise you to type the code yourself or access the code from the book's GitHub repository (a link is available in the next section). Doing so will help you avoid any potential errors related to the copying and pasting of code. Each chapter is available as a separate branch of the main repository.

Download the example code files

You can download the example code files for this book from GitHub at `https://github.com/PacktPublishing/Programming-Microsoft-Dynamics-365-Business-Central-Seventh-Edition`. If there's an update to the code, it will be updated in the GitHub repository.

We also have other code bundles from our rich catalog of books and videos available at `https://github.com/PacktPublishing/`. Check them out!

Conventions used

There are a number of text conventions used throughout this book.

`Code in text`: Indicates code words in text, database table names, folder names, filenames, file extensions, pathnames, dummy URLs, user input, and Twitter handles. Here is an example: "Right-click on the `RadioShows.xlsx` file and open it in Microsoft Excel"

A block of code is set as follows:

```
part(ControlName; PartPageName)
{
    <properties>
}
```

Bold: Indicates a new term, an important word, or words that you see on screen. For instance, words in menus or dialog boxes appear in **bold**. Here is an example: "The easiest way to create a table is by using **snippets**."

> **Tips or important notes**
> Appear like this.

Get in touch

Feedback from our readers is always welcome.

General feedback: If you have questions about any aspect of this book, email us at customercare@ packtpub.com and mention the book title in the subject of your message.

Errata: Although we have taken every care to ensure the accuracy of our content, mistakes do happen. If you have found a mistake in this book, we would be grateful if you would report this to us. Please visit www.packtpub.com/support/errata and fill in the form.

Piracy: If you come across any illegal copies of our works in any form on the internet, we would be grateful if you would provide us with the location address or website name. Please contact us at copyright@packt.com with a link to the material.

If you are interested in becoming an author: If there is a topic that you have expertise in and you are interested in either writing or contributing to a book, please visit authors.packtpub.com.

Share Your Thoughts

Once you've read *Programming Microsoft Dynamics 365 Business Central - seventh edition*, we'd love to hear your thoughts! Scan the QR code below to go straight to the Amazon review page for this book and share your feedback.

https://packt.link/r/1803236418

Your review is important to us and the tech community and will help us make sure we're delivering excellent quality content.

Download a free PDF copy of this book

Thanks for purchasing this book!

Do you like to read on the go but are unable to carry your print books everywhere?

Is your eBook purchase not compatible with the device of your choice?

Don't worry, now with every Packt book you get a DRM-free PDF version of that book at no cost.

Read anywhere, any place, on any device. Search, copy, and paste code from your favorite technical books directly into your application.

The perks don't stop there, you can get exclusive access to discounts, newsletters, and great free content in your inbox daily

Follow these simple steps to get the benefits:

1. Scan the QR code or visit the link below

https://packt.link/free-ebook/978-1-80323-641-4

2. Submit your proof of purchase
3. That's it! We'll send your free PDF and other benefits to your email directly

Introduction to Business Central

"Time changes all things; there is no reason why language should escape this universal law."

– Ferdinand de Saussure

"Computers are like Old Testament gods; lots of rules and no mercy."

– Joseph Campbell

Microsoft Dynamics 365 Business Central has one of the largest installed user bases of any **enterprise resource planning** (**ERP**) system, serving over two hundred thousand companies and millions of individual users, at the time of writing. The community of supporting organizations, consultants, implementers, and developers continues to grow and prosper. The capabilities of the off-the-shelf product increase with every release. Additionally, the selection of add-on products and services expands both in variety and depth.

The release of Microsoft Dynamics Business Central continues its 30-plus-year history of continuous product improvement. It provides more user options for access and output formatting. For new installations, Business Central includes tools for rapid implementation. For all installations, it provides enhanced business functionality and more support for ERP computing in the cloud, including integration with Microsoft Office 365 and the greater Azure cloud architecture, including Power Platform (Power Automate, Power Apps, Power BI, and Power Virtual Agents).

Our goal in this chapter is to gain a big-picture understanding of Business Central. Upon completing this chapter, you will be able to envision how Business Central can be used by owners and managers of an organization to help manage activities and resources, whether the organization is for-profit or not-for-profit. You will also be introduced to the technical side of Business Central from a developer's point of view.

In this chapter, we will take a look at Business Central by covering the following topics:

- A general overview of Business Central

- A technical overview of Business Central

- A hands-on introduction to **Visual Studio Code (VS Code)** development in Business Central

Technical requirements

Developing for Business Central requires access to a Business Central environment, as well as Visual Studio Code installed as the source code editor.

Business Central (hosted by Microsoft in the Azure cloud) can be accessed from a modern browser (Microsoft Edge, Google Chrome, and Mozilla Firefox for Windows or Safari for macOS). Having a subscription to Office 365 is strongly recommended for Word, Excel, and emailing functionality.

Visual Studio Code (VS Code) is a small download (< 200 MB) and has a disk footprint of < 500 MB. It's lightweight and should easily run on today's hardware.

For an on-premises installation of VS Code, the following is required:

1.6 GHz or faster processor

- 1 GB of RAM

- Windows 10 and 11 (64-bit)

- macOS (current and previous two versions)

- Linux (Debian): Ubuntu Desktop 20.04, Debian 10

Linux (Red Hat): Red Hat Enterprise Linux 8, Fedora 36A `https://github.com/PacktPublishing/Programming-Microsoft-Dynamics-365-Business-Central-Seventh-Edition`.

For a complete list of VS Code requirements, please visit `https://code.visualstudio.com/Docs/supporting/requirements`.

Installing VS Code will be covered later in this chapter, in the *The VS Code integrated development environment* section.

Business Central – an ERP system

Business Central is an integrated set of business applications that are designed to service a wide variety of business operations. Microsoft Dynamics 365 Business Central is an ERP system. An ERP system integrates internal and external data across a variety of functional areas, including manufacturing, accounting, supply chain management, customer relationships, service operations, and human resource management, as well as managing other valued resources and activities. By having many related applications well integrated, a fully featured ERP system provides an *enter data once, use many ways* information processing toolset.

Business Central ERP addresses the following functional areas:

- Financial Management (for example general ledger, accounts payable, and accounts receivable)
- Supply Chain Management (for example sales orders, purchase orders, shipping, inventory, and receiving)
- Relationship management (for example vendors, customers, prospects, employees, and contractors)
- Manufacturing (for example MRP, sales forecasting, and production forecasting)
- Other critical business areas (for example human resource management, project management, warehouse management, marketing, cash management, and fixed assets)
- A complete set of development tools that allow the application to be customized and expanded for specific industries, and even individual businesses.

These are not the only functional areas Business Central addresses, but the main ones. New areas are being added all the time, and many extensions are being produced that address more niche business needs.

A good ERP system, such as Business Central, is modular in design, which simplifies implementation, upgrading, modification, integration with third-party products, and expansion for different types of clients. All the modules in the system share a common database and, where appropriate, common data.

The following groupings of individual Business Central functions are based on the **Search** menu structure, which is supplemented by information from Microsoft marketing materials. The important thing to understand is the overall components that make up the Business Central ERP system:

Figure 1.1 – Fully integrated functional areas of Business Central

Business Central has a web browser role-tailored **user interface** (**UI**). In Business Central, there's a universal web-based client that can be used on personal computers, tablets, and other mobile devices.

As illustrated in *Figure 1.1*, Business Central is a fully integrated system that has multiple functional areas. Let's take a closer look at them.

Financial management

The foundation of any ERP system is financial management. Irrespective of the business, the money must be kept flowing and tracked. Business Central's financial management module contains tools that can help you manage the capital resources of a business. These include all or part of the following application functions:

- **General ledger**: Managing the overall finances of the firm
- **Cash management and banking**: Managing the inventory of financial assets
- **Accounts receivable**: Tracking the incoming revenue
- **Accounts payable**: Tracking outgoing funds
- **Analytical accounting**: Analyzing the various flows of funds

- **Inventory and fixed assets**: Managing inventories of goods and equipment
- **Multicurrency and multilingual**: For supporting international business activities

Business Central is not just a financial system – it is the basis for all other functional areas. The main areas related to inventory consist of making goods, moving goods, and servicing goods. Other areas that don't focus on inventory are project management, managing employees, customer communications, and internal reporting.

Manufacturing

Business Central manufacturing is general-purpose enough to be appropriate for **Make to Stock** (**MTS**), **Make to Order** (**MTO**), and **Assemble to Order** (**ATO**), as well as various subsets and combinations of those. Although Business Central is not particularly suitable for most process manufacturing and some of the very high-volume assembly line operations off the shelf, there are third-party extension enhancements available for those applications. As with most of the Business Central application functions, manufacturing can be implemented either in a basic mode or as a fully featured system. Business Central manufacturing includes the following functions:

- Product design (**Bills of Materials** [**BOMs**] and routings) for the structure management of product components and the flow management of manufacturing processes
- Capacity and supply requirement planning, for tracking the intangible and tangible manufacturing resources
- Production scheduling (infinite and finite), execution, and tracking quantities and costs, plus tracking manufacturing resources' planned use, both on a constrained and unconstrained basis

Supply chain management

Some of the functions that are categorized as part of Business Central's **supply chain management** (**SCM**), such as sales and purchasing, are actively used in almost every Business Central implementation. The supply chain applications in Business Central include all or parts of the following applications:

- **Sales order processing and pricing**: To support the heart of every business
- **Purchasing (including requisitions)**: For planning, entering, pricing, and processing purchase orders
- **Inventory management**: For managing inventories of goods and materials
- **Warehouse management including receiving and shipping**: For managing the receipt, storage, retrieval, and shipment of material and goods in warehouses

As a whole, these functions constitute the base components of a system that's appropriate for distribution operations, including those that operate on an ATO basis.

Business intelligence and reporting

Although Microsoft marketing materials identify **business intelligence** (**BI**) and reporting as though they're separate modules within Business Central, it's difficult to physically identify them as such. Most of the components that are used for BI and reporting purposes are (appropriately) scattered throughout various application areas. In the words of one Microsoft document, *business intelligence is a strategy, not a product*. The following functions within Business Central support a BI strategy:

- **Standard reports**: Distributed and ready to use by end users

- **Financial reporting and analysis reports**: A specialized report writer for general ledger data

- **Queries, XMLports, and reports**: The AL programming language supports the creation of a wide variety of report formats [**SQL Server Reporting Services** (**SSRS**), Microsoft Word, and Excel], queries, XML, and CSV files

- **Analysis by dimensions**: A capability embedded in many Business Central tools

- **Office 365 Interfaces**: Including communicating Excel data either into or out of Business Central

- **RDLC report viewer**: Allows you to present Business Central data in a variety of textual and graphic formats, including providing user interactive capabilities

- **Interface capabilities such as SOAP, ODATA, and REST web services**: Technologies to support interfaces between Business Central and external software products

- **Standard packages for Power BI**: Integrated in the role center as well as dashboards

Relationship management

Business Central's **relationship management** (**RM**) functionality is the *little sibling* of the fully featured standalone Microsoft CRM system and Dynamics 365 for Sales and Dynamics 365 for Marketing. The big advantage of Business Central RM is its tight integration with Business Central customer and sales data.

Also falling under the heading of the customer relationship module is the Business Central **service management** (**SM**) functionality. The following functionalities fall under RM and SM:

- **Relationship management**:

  - Marketing campaigns, to plan and manage promotions

  - Customer activity tracking, to analyze customer orders

  - To-do lists, to manage what is to be done and track what has been done

- **Service management**:

  - Service contracts, to support service operations

  - Warranty tracking for items and repair

  - Labor and part consumption tracking, to track resources that are consumed by the service business

  - Planning and dispatching, to manage service calls

Human resource management

The Business Central human resources module is very small, but it relates to a critical component of the business: employees. Basic employee data can be stored and reported via the master table (in fact, you can use the **human resources (HR)** module to manage data about individual contractors in addition to employees). A wide variety of individual employee attributes can be tracked through the use of tailorable dimension fields:

- **Employee tracking**: Maintain basic employee description data

- **Skills inventory**: Inventory of the capabilities of employees

- **Absence tracking**: Maintain basic attendance information

- **Employee statistics**: For tracking government and other required employee attribute data, such as age, gender, and length of service

Project management

The Business Central project management module consists of allocating, budgeting, and utilizing resources for projects that can be either short-term or long-term. They can be external (in other words, billable) or internal. This module is often used by third parties as the base for vertical market add-ons (such as construction or job-oriented manufacturing). This application area includes parts or all of the following functions:

- Budgeting and cost tracking, for managing project finances

- Scheduling, for planning project activities

- Resource requirements and usage tracking, for managing people and equipment

- Project accounting, for tracking the results

Now that we've learned about Business Central at a functional level, let's switch to a developer's perspective.

A developer's overview of Business Central

From the point of view of a developer, Business Central consists of a set of applications with thousands of potentially extensible, off-the-shelf program objects written in the AL programming language. **Visual Studio Code**, as the **integrated development environment** (IDE), in combination with the AL Language extension, allows us to work with existing objects and create new ones. Our AL code will compile into a `*.app` file as yet another application to publish and install.

> **Note**
>
> This book provides an overview of Business Central, including the basics, so that you have a quick hands-on start. To find the complete developer documentation, please refer to Microsoft Docs at `https://learn.microsoft.com/en-us/dynamics365/business-central/dev-itpro/#resources-for-a-developer`.

Business Central applications

As a developer, we need to be aware of the following applications that form the Business Central application. They have been listed in their dependency hierarchy from top to bottom:

- **Base Application**: This provides core business processes such as sales and purchasing, customer and vendor management, plus complex processes, such as assembly, manufacturing, service, and directed warehouse management – simply put, the business logic.

- **Business Foundation (since version 24)**: This serves as a foundation for developing business applications, such as No. series management or dimension management. The standard functionality is used globally and not tied to a specific area. Before version 24, the content resided in the Base Application.

- **System Application**: This contains objects to serve mere technical purposes, such as emailing, OAuth, and RegEx, and provides mathematical functions. These objects support the base application and its interaction with the platform and Microsoft ecosystem.

- **System**: This provides system objects and virtual tables. We will discuss some of these objects at the end of *Chapter 2*.

> **Tip**
>
> The Business Central source code is being developed at `https://github.com/microsoft/BCApps`. The repository is a contribution project. At the time of writing this book, the repository consisted of the System Application, the Business Foundation, and various tools. The Base Application will be added in the future. Please refer to the repository's README file for more current information.

Business Central object types

Let's start with basic definitions of the Business Central object types that will be covered in this book. This is meant to act as a rough overview – we will cover them later in this chapter again:

- **Table**: Tables serve both to define the data structure and to contain the data records.

- **Table extension**: Table extensions allow for the creation of companion tables that are linked to tables defined by Microsoft in the base product or by other solutions.

- **Page**: Pages are the way data is formatted and displayed appropriately for each of the client types and user roles.

- **Page extension**: Page extensions allow controls in existing pages to be added or hidden.

- **Report**: Reports are provided to display data to the user in hard copy format, computer file format (PDF, Microsoft Word, or Excel), on-screen (preview mode), or via a printing device. Report objects can also update data in processes with or without data display.

- **Report Extension**: Report extensions allow you to add columns to existing reports' datasets, add new data items, extend trigger logic, provide additional fields and logic to request pages, and define new layouts.

- **Codeunit**: Codeunits are containers for code that are utilized by other objects. Codeunits are always structured in code segments called procedures.

- **Query**: Queries support extracting data from one or more tables, making calculations, and outputting them in the form of a new data structure. Queries can output data directly into charts, Excel, XML, and OData. They can be used as an indirect source for pages and reports.

- **XMLport**: XMLports allow you to import and export data to/from external files. The external file structure can be in XML or other file formats.

- **Profile**: Profiles allow you to define Role Centers and group page customizations.

- **Enum**: Enums (enumerated lists) are extendable options that can be connected to tables and interfaces.

- **Enum extension**: Enum extensions are extra options that are added to Enums from either the Microsoft Business Central Base App or other extensions.

The Visual Studio Code integrated development environment

Business Central includes an extensive set of software development tools. These Business Central development tools can be accessed through Visual Studio Code and the **AL Language extension**. We will install the extension soon in the *Extensions* section, and we will learn about the AL Language extension in the *AL programming language* section.

The Visual Studio Code IDE is Microsoft's most popular free code editor and is available for Windows, Linux, and macOS. The images used in this book have been taken on a Windows system. You can download Visual Studio Code from `https://code.visualstudio.com/`:

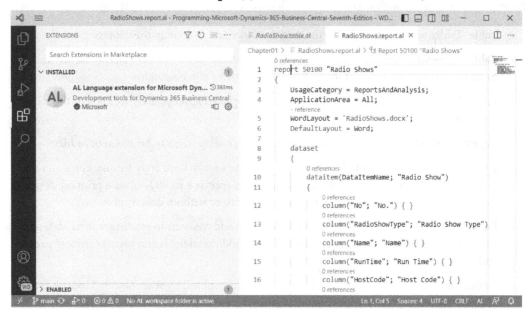

Figure 1.2 – Visual Studio (VS) Code with the AL Language extension installed

Let's explore its interface in more detail.

Visual Studio Code icons

When we open Visual Studio Code, we will see five icons. These icons appear on the left-hand side of the screen. They also determine the navigation part that appears on the left-hand side of your screen. If you click on an icon twice, the navigation part will be hidden and allow full-screen code editing. Let's see what each of these do in detail.

EXPLORER

The **EXPLORER** view is the default view when you open a project. It allows you to view the files in a project and select one or more files for editing. The **EXPLORER** view is shown in the following screenshot:

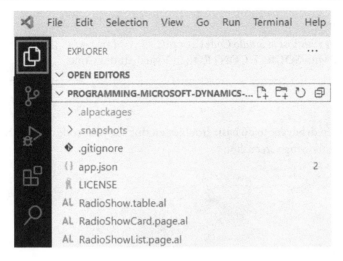

Figure 1.3 – EXPLORER in VS Code

While the list of files is fine for smaller projects, sometimes, it is necessary to locate a file in a larger list or even text within files.

> **Tip**
>
> We can use *Ctrl + P* to search files by name.

SOURCE CONTROL

VS Code provides access to a built-in connection to **SOURCE CONTROL**. When source control is activated, all changes that are made to files are automatically tracked and displayed in this window:

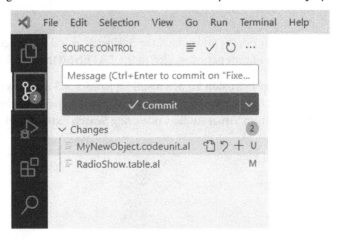

Figure 1.4 – SOURCE CONTROL in VS Code

> **Further reference**
>
> The video *Using Git with Visual Studio Code* (`https://youtu.be/i_23KUAEtUM`) explains how to get started with **SOURCE CONTROL** in Visual Studio Code.

Debugger

You can use the built-in debugger to do basic troubleshooting for your code. The **RUN AND DEBUG** view is shown in the following screenshot:

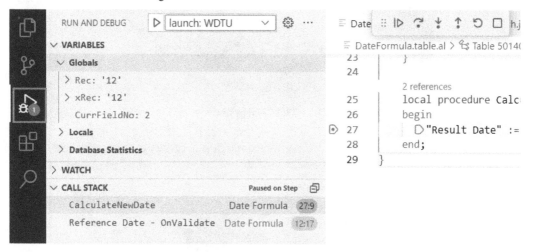

Figure 1.5 – The debugger in VS Code

We will learn more about debugging in Business Central in *Chapter 7, Intermediate AL*.

Extensions

Out of the box, Visual Studio Code doesn't understand the Business Central AL Language syntax. To activate the compiler, an extension needs to be installed in the **EXTENSIONS** window.

This extension, called **AL Language extension for Microsoft Dynamics 365 Business Central** (in this book, it will be referred to as **AL Language extension**), can be downloaded from the Visual Studio Marketplace or installed directly from Visual Studio Code using **Search Extensions in Marketplace**:

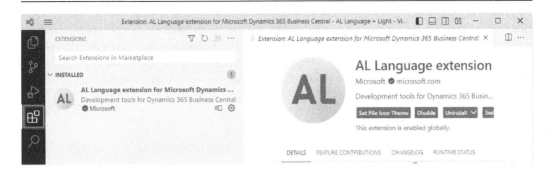

Figure 1.6 – The AL Language extension in VS Code

> **Note**
> The Visual Studio Code Marketplace can be found at `https://marketplace.visualstudio.com/`.

Microsoft does a monthly update of Business Central and the AL Language extension. Usually, you install and use the most current version released in the Marketplace. There is also a pre-release version available that allows early access to features that are being prepared for the next major version of Business Central.

SEARCH

The **SEARCH** view provides an advanced search and replace option within the files of your project. The **SEARCH** view is shown in the following screenshot:

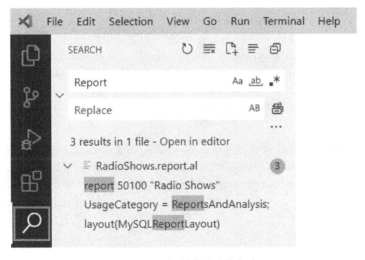

Figure 1.7 – SEARCH in VS Code

Visual Studio Code provides an easy-to-understand toolset that's used by many programmers. The AL compiler extension provides an entry point for you to extend and develop new areas in the Microsoft 365 Business Central application. Later, we will get into the additional benefits of its deep integration with Git and repositories to control code development between one and more developers.

AL programming language

The language in which Business Central is coded is AL. A small sample of AL code within Visual Studio Code is shown here:

```
local procedure SetCurrencyCode(AccType2: Enum "Gen. Journal Account Type"; AccNo2: Code[20]): Boolean
var
    Cust: Record Customer;
    Vend: Record Vendor;
    BankAcc: Record "Bank Account";
begin
    "Currency Code" := '';
    if AccNo2 <> '' then
        case AccType2 of
            AccType2::Customer:
                if Cust.Get(AccNo2) then
                    "Currency Code" := Cust."Currency Code";
            AccType2::Vendor:
                if Vend.Get(AccNo2) then
                    "Currency Code" := Vend."Currency Code";
            AccType2::"Bank Account":
                if BankAcc.Get(AccNo2) then
                    "Currency Code" := BankAcc."Currency Code";
        end;
    exit("Currency Code" <> '');
end;
```

Figure 1.8 – Example of AL code

AL syntax is similar to Pascal syntax. But other than Pascal, AL is not an object-oriented programming language but an object-based one. Code readability is always enhanced by careful programmer attention to structure and logical variable naming, as well as ensuring that the process flow is consistent with that of the code in the base product and that there is good documentation both inside and outside of the code.

Good software development focuses on design before coding and accomplishing design goals with a minimal amount of code. Dynamics Business Central facilitates that approach. In 2012, a team made up of Microsoft and Business Central community **members** began the NAV **design patterns** project. As defined by Wikipedia, a design pattern is a general reusable solution to a commonly occurring problem.

In 2022, long after the transition to Business Central and the AL language, the project was relaunched as Business Central design patterns and moved to another website: `https://alguidelines.dev/docs/`.

> **Note**
>
> One of the primary goals of this project is to document patterns that exist within Business Central. In addition, new best practice patterns have been suggested as ways to solve common issues we encounter during our customization efforts. Now, when we work on Business Central enhancements, we will be aided by references to the documentation of patterns within Business Central. This allows us to spend more of our time designing a good solution using existing, proven procedures (the documented patterns) and less time writing and debugging code. Please refer to the *Reusing Code* section of Business Central at `https://learn.microsoft.com/en-us/dynamics365/business-central/dev-itpro/developer/devenv-programming-in-al#reusing-code` for more information.

Much of our Business Central development work is done by assembling references to previously defined objects and procedures and adding new data structures where necessary. As the tools for Business Central design and development that are provided both by Microsoft and the Business Central community continue to mature, our development work becomes more oriented toward design and less toward coding. The result is that we are more productive and cost-effective on behalf of our customers. Everyone wins.

Business Central object elements

Here are some important terms that are used in Business Central:

- **Field**: An individual data item, defined either in a table or in the working storage (temporary storage) of an object.

- **Record**: A group of fields (data items) that are handled as a unit in many operations. Table data consists of rows (records) with columns (fields).

- **Control**: In **Microsoft Developer Network** (**MSDN**), a control is defined as a component that provides (or enables) UI capabilities.

- **Properties**: These are the attributes of the element, such as an object, field, record, or control, that define some aspect of its behavior or use. Example property attributes include display captions, relationships, size, position, and whether the element is editable or viewable.

- **Trigger**: These are mechanisms that initiate (fire) an action when an event occurs and is communicated to the application object. A trigger in an object is either empty or contains code that is executed when the associated event fires the trigger. Each object type, data field, control, and so on may have its own set of predefined triggers. The event trigger name begins with On – for example, `OnInsertRecord`, `OnOpenPage`, or `OnNextRecord`. Business

Central triggers have similarities to those in SQL, but they are not the same (*similarly named triggers may not even serve similar purposes*). Business Central triggers are locations within objects where a developer can place comments or AL code.

- **Procedures**: These can be defined by the developer. They are callable routines that can be accessed by other AL code from either inside or outside the object where the called procedure resides. Many procedures are provided as part of the standard product. As developers, we may add custom procedures as needed.

- **Attributes**: An attribute is a modifier on a procedure declaration that controls the procedure's use and behavior.

- **Object numbers and field numbers**: All objects of the same object type are assigned a number that's unique within the object type. All fields within a table object are assigned a number that's unique within the object (that is, the same field number may be repeated within many objects, regardless of whether it is referring to similar or different data). In this book, we will generally use comma notation for these numbers (fifty thousand is 50,000). In AL, no punctuation is used. The object numbers range from 1 (one) to 49,999 and those from 100,000 to 999,999 are reserved for use by Business Central as part of the base product. Numbers from 1,000,000 (one million) to 74,999,999 are reserved for partners. Field numbers in standard objects often start with one (1). Historically, object and field numbers from 50,000 to 99,999 are generally available to the rest of us for assignment as part of extensions that are developed. Field numbers from 90,000 to 99,999 should not be used for new fields that have been added to standard tables as those numbers are sometimes used in training materials. Microsoft allocates ranges of object and field numbers to **independent software vendor** (**ISV**) developers for their add-on enhancements. Some such objects (the 14 million range in North America, and other ranges for other geographic regions) can be accessed, modified, or deleted, but they can't be created using a normal development license. Others (such as in the 37 million range) can be executed but not viewed or modified with a typical development license. The following table summarizes this object numbering practice:

Object Number Range	Usage
1 – 9,999	Base application objects
10,000 – 49,999	Country-specific objects
50,000 – 99,999	Customer-specific objects
100,000 – 999,999	Localization-specific objects
1,000,000 – 74,999,999	Partner-created objects

Table 1.1 – BC object number ranges

- **Events**: Procedures can subscribe to events that are raised in the system. Business Central has both platform and manual events. Procedures can also be used to raise events.

- **Work date**: This is a date that's controlled by the user operator. It is used as the default date for many transaction entries. The system date is the date that's recognized by Windows. The work date that can be adjusted at any time by the user is specific to the workstation and can be set to any point in the future or the past. This is very convenient for procedures such as the ending sales order entry for one calendar day at the end of the first shift, and then the second shift entering sales orders dated to the next calendar day. Some settings allow you to limit the range of work dates allowed. The work date can be set by clicking on the cogwheel drop-down list next to the question mark icon and selecting the **My Settings** option:

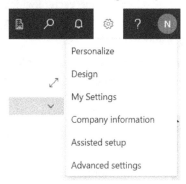

Figure 1.9 – Settings in the Business Central client

Clicking on **My Settings** in the dropdown displays the **My Settings** screen. Here, we can enter a new **Work Date** value:

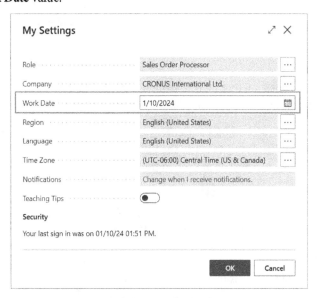

Figure 1.10 – Work Date on the My Settings screen

In addition to basic functionality, you will also encounter terminology that's used in the functional areas that are important to understand for development purposes.

Business Central functional terminology

For various application functions, Business Central uses terminology that's more similar to accounting than to traditional data processing terminology. Here are some examples:

- **Journal**: A table of unposted transaction entries, each of which represents an event, an entity, or an action to be processed. There are general journals for general accounting entries, item journals for inventory changes, and so on.

- **Ledger**: A detailed history of posted transaction entries that have been processed – for example, the general ledger, customer ledger, vendor ledger, and item ledger. Some ledgers have subordinate detail ledgers, typically providing a greater level of quantity and/or value detail. With minor exceptions, ledger entries cannot be edited. This maintains auditable data integrity. Business Central has a posting logic-driven data integrity that is founded on General Ledger Entries tying to all other ledgers.

- **Posting**: The process by which entries in a journal are validated, and then entered into one or more ledgers.

- **Batch**: A group of one or more journal entries, posted at the same time.

- **Register**: An audit trail showing a history, by entry number ranges, of posted journal batches.

- **Document**: A formatted page such as an invoice, a purchase order, or a payment check, typically one page for each primary transaction (a page may require display scrolling to be fully viewed).

UI

The Business Central UI is designed to be role-oriented (also called role-tailored). The term *role-oriented* means tailoring the available options to fit the user-specific job tasks and responsibilities.

The first page that a user will see is the Role Center page. The Role Center page provides the user with a view of work tasks to be done; it acts as the user's home page. The Role Center home page should be tailored to the job duties of each user so there are a variety of Role Center page formats for any installation.

Someone whose role focuses on order entry will probably see a different Role Center home page than the user whose role focuses on invoicing, even though both user roles are in what we generally think of as sales and receivables. The Business Central tailorable Role Center allows a great deal of flexibility for implementers, system administrators, managers, and individual users to configure and reconfigure screen layouts and the set of functions that are visible to a particular user.

The following screenshot is the out-of-the-box Role Center for a business manager:

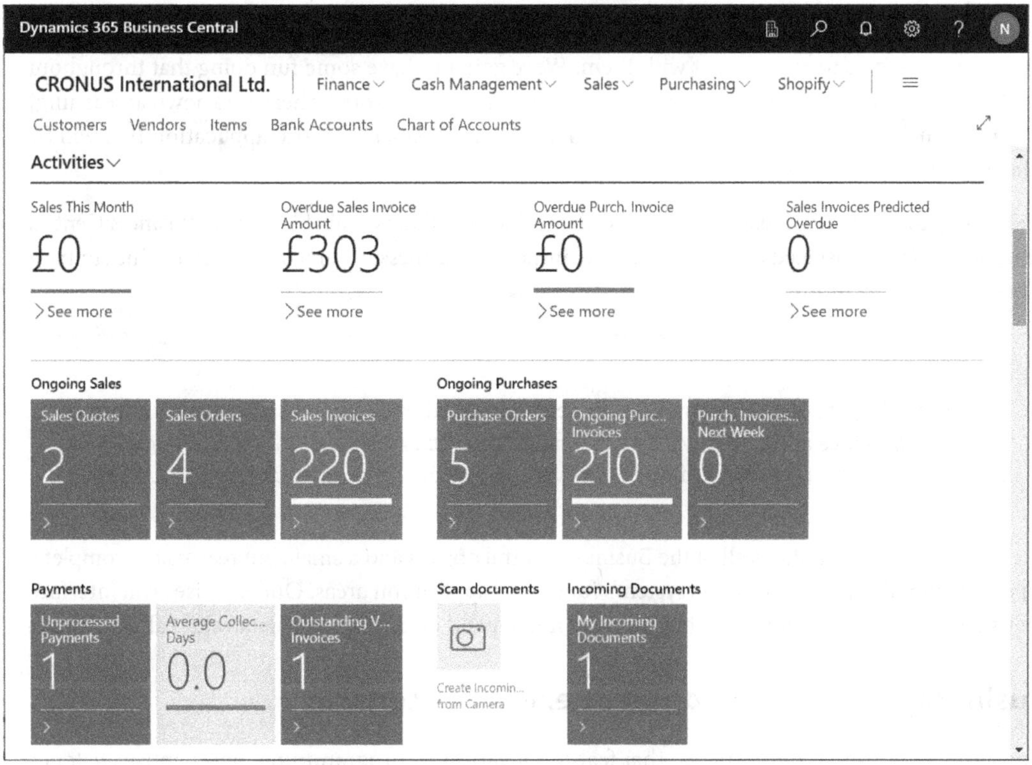

Figure 1.11 – Business Central – Role Center

The key to properly designing and implementing any system, especially a role-tailored system, is the quality of the user profile analysis that's done as the first step in requirements analysis. User profiles identify the day-to-day needs of each user's responsibilities, relative to accomplishing the business's goals. Each user's tasks must be mapped to individual Business Central functions or elements, identifying how those tasks will be supported by the system.

> **Important**
>
> A successful implementation requires the use of a proven methodology. The upfront work must be done and done well. The best programming cannot compensate for badly defined goals.

In our exercises, we will assume that the upfront work has been well done, so we will concentrate on addressing the requirements that have been defined by our project team.

Hands-on development in Business Central

One of the best ways to learn a new set of tools, such as those that make up a programming language and environment, is to experiment with them. We're going to have some fun doing that throughout this book. To do so, we're going to experiment where the cost of errors (otherwise known as learning) is small. Our development work will consist of a custom Business Central application that will be relatively simple but realistic.

We're going to do our work using the Cronus demo database that is available with all Business Central distributions and is installed by default when we install the Business Central demo system. The simplest way is to use the sandbox.

> **Note**
> You can find up-to-date information on getting started with Business Central sandboxes via Microsoft Docs at `https://learn.microsoft.com/en-us/dynamics365/` `business-central/dev-itpro/developer/devenv-sandbox-overview`.

The Cronus database contains all of the Business Central objects and a small, but reasonably complete, set of data populated in most of the system's functional application areas. Our exercises will interface very slightly with the Cronus data, but they will not depend on any specific data values already there.

Business Central development exercise scenario

Our business is a small radio station that features a variety of programming, news, music, listener call-ins, and other program types. Our station call letters are WDTU. Our broadcast materials come from several sources and in several formats: vinyl records, CDs, MP3s, and downloaded digital (usually MP3s). While our station has a large library, especially of recorded music, sometimes, our program hosts (also called **disc jockeys** or **DJs**) want to share material from other sources. For that reason, we need to be able to easily add items to our playlists (the list of what is to be broadcast) and also have an easy-to-access method for our DJs to preview MP3 material.

Like any business, we have accounting and activity tracking requirements. Our income is from selling advertisements. We must pay royalties for music played, fees for purchased materials, such as prepared text for news, sports, and weather information, and service charges for our streaming internet broadcast service. As part of our licensed access to the public airwaves, a radio station is required to broadcast public service programming at no charge. Often, this is in the form of **public service announcements** (**PSAs**), such as encouraging traffic safety or reduction in tobacco use.

Like all radio stations, we must plan what is to be broadcast (create schedules) and track what has been broadcast (such as advertisements, music, purchased programming, and PSAs) by date and time. We bill our customers for this advertising, pay our vendors their fees and royalties, and report our public service data to the appropriate government agency.

Getting started with application design

The design for our radio station will start with a `Radio Show` table, a `Radio Show Card` page, a `Radio Show List` page, and a simple `Radio Show List` report. Along the way, we will review the basics of each Business Central object type.

When we open Visual Studio, we need to create a new project folder. This can be done using the Command Palette via **View | Command Palette...** or *F1* or *Ctrl + Shift + P*. Then, type `AL:Go!`:

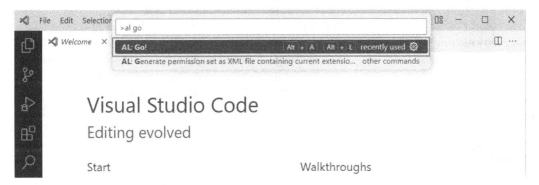

Figure 1.12 – Command Palette in VS Code

The project folder will default to your `Documents` folder if you run this on a Windows machine. We will call our project WDTU:

Figure 1.13 – Naming the project folder

Select the version with which you are working (the public cloud will always be the latest version; your on-premises version may be a different version):

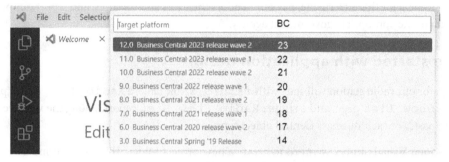

Figure 1.14 – Platform and corresponding BC major release

In the bottom right corner of VS Code, a notification about missing symbols will appear. Clicking on the **Download symbols** button, we now need to choose a server type to download the symbols from. Both provided options (own server or Microsoft-hosed SaaS, such as a sandbox) will create a launch.json file that we will deal with soon. But first, we must close the **Could not download symbols** error message that appeared together with the server selection prompt.

Now, let's inspect the folder structure that has been created.

Folder structure

A folder called WDTU has been created with some default files and subfolders. The HelloWorld.al file can be deleted immediately. This file is a page extension that will be explored more fully in *Chapter 4, Pages – The Interactive Interface*:

```al
// Welcome to your new AL extension.
// Remember that object names and IDs should be unique across al
// AL snippets start with t*, like tpageext - give them a try an

namespace DefaultPublisher.WDTU;

using Microsoft.Sales.Customer;

0 references
pageextension 50100 CustomerListExt extends "Customer List"
{
    0 references
    trigger OnOpenPage();
    begin
        Message('App published: Hello world');
    end;
}
```

Figure 1.15 – Folder structure after AL: Go

Let's dive a bit deeper into the folder structure.

> **Note**
>
> The json files that will be explained in the upcoming sections consist of more settings than this book is going to cover. We will only look at the mandatory or most used settings for now.
>
> All settings are explained at Microsoft Docs (`https://learn.microsoft.com/en-us/dynamics365/business-central/dev-itpro/developer/devenv-json-files`).

launch.json

Inside a subfolder called `.vscode`, a file is created called `launch.json` that defines the connection to all our Business Central target environments. Each connection is defined in a separate configuration object. We will soon use a configuration for downloading symbols, publishing our application, and debugging.

Let's take a moment to update the configuration that was recently created for us. The following settings apply to all configurations:

- `name`: For documentation purposes only. You can put the name of your project here. If more than one configuration is defined, VS Code uses the names to build a lookup list.

- `environmentType`: This specifies which environment to use to connect to Business Central. It must be set to `Sandbox` or `Production` in the cloud, and to `OnPrem` for on-premises. This field is mandatory.

- `startupObjectId`: This setting determines which object is executed when the project is published. Specifying any startup settings is optional.

- `startupObjectType`: This setting works alongside `startupObjectId` and specifies whether the object to open after publishing is a table, page, report, or query object. The default is `Page`.

- `startupCompany`: This specifies the name of the company to open after publishing. If specified, the `startupObjectId` and `startupObjectType` settings must also be defined.

For addressing cloud environments (production or sandbox), we will need to populate one additional setting:

- `environmentName`: This specifies which named environment to use in cases where multiple sandboxes are owned by the same tenant

The following settings are required for connecting to your own servers:

- `server`: This contains a URL to the development endpoint of your server.

- `port`: This optional setting specifies the port that's assigned to the development service. This is for on-premises installations only and is required if the default port is not used for the server instance you are connecting to.

- `serverInstance`: A server can have multiple instances.

- `authentication`: This can be `UserPassword`, `AAD`, or `Windows`. The default is `UserPassword`.

app.json

Located in the main folder, the `app.json` file contains properties about your extension, such as its name and version. These are mandatory fields; the others that are available are optional:

- `id`: This is a unique ID (GUID) for your extension and is autogenerated. *Never* change this value.

- `name`: The name of your extension as it will be displayed to the user.

- `publisher`: This usually contains the name of the company or individual who owns the intellectual property of the extension. It will be displayed to the user.

- `version`: Your extensions can be versioned using this property. You can use this when you create a new version of the extension to determine if upgrade code needs to be executed.

- `idRange`: This tells the compiler which object numbers are to be used for this extension. You must provide a range for application object IDs in `"idRanges": [{"from": 50100,"to": 50200},{"from": 50202,"to": 50300}]` format.

- `platform`, `application`, and `runtime`: These properties were automatically set when we ran `AL: Go!`. They determine the minimum version of Business Central (`platform`, `application`) and the minimum AL Language features (`runtime`) our application shall be compatible with.

Symbol files

Before we can start creating our extension, we need to do one more thing: download the **symbol files**. The compiler needs the symbol files to determine whether the dependencies are correct. The symbol files contain metadata about other extensions. To download the required Business Central applications from our development environment, we need to select **AL: Download symbols** from the Visual Studio Command Palette:

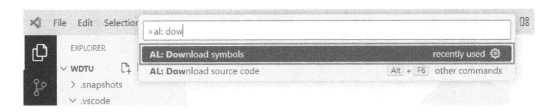

Figure 1.16 – The AL: Download symbols command

> **Note**
>
> When the symbol files are downloaded, by default, they'll be placed in the `./alpackages` folder of your project.

Later, in *Chapter 2*, in the *Non-Extensible Tables* section, and *Chapter 3*, in the *Data Structure Examples* section, we will use the **AL Explorer** in VS Code to inspect the symbol files.

Application tables

Table objects are the foundation of every Business Central application. Tables contain data structure definitions, as well as properties that describe the behavior of the data, including data validations and constraints.

More business logic is required in complex applications than in simple data type validation, and Business Central allows AL code to be put in the table to control the insertion, modification, and deletion of records, as well as logic at the field level.

> **Note**
>
> When the bulk of the business logic is coded at the table level, it is easier to develop, debug, support, modify, and even upgrade. Good design in Business Central requires that as much of the business logic as possible resides in the tables.

Having the business logic coded at the table level doesn't necessarily mean that the code resides in the table. The Business Central online documentation recommends the following guidelines for placing AL code:

- In general, put the code in codeunits instead of on the object on which it operates. This promotes a clean design and provides the ability to reuse code. It also helps enforce security. For example, typically, users do not have direct access to tables that contain sensitive data, such as the general ledger entry table, nor do they have permission to modify objects. If you put the code that operates on the general ledger in a `codeunit` object, give the `codeunit` object access to the table, and give the user permission to execute the `codeunit` object, then you will not compromise the security of the table and the user will be able to access the table.

- Outside codeunit objects, put the code as close as possible to the object on which it operates. For example, you should put code that modifies records in the triggers of the table fields.

Designing a simple table

Our primary master data table will be the `Radio Show` table. This table lists our inventory of shows that are available to be scheduled.

Each master table has a standard field for the primary key (a `Code` data type field of 20 characters called `No.`) and has standard information regarding the entity the master record represents (for example, `Name`, `Address`, and `City` for the `Customer` table, and `Description`, `Base Unit of Measure`, and `Unit Cost` for the `Item` table).

The `Radio Show` table will have the following field definitions (we may add more later on):

Field Names	Definitions
No.	20-character text (code)
Radio Show Type	10-character text (code)
Name	100-character text
Run Time	Duration
Host No.	20-character text (code)
Host Name	100-character text
Average Listeners	Decimal
Audience Share	Decimal
Advertising Revenue	Decimal
Royalty Cost	Decimal

Table 1.2 – The Radio Show table's field names and data types

In the preceding list, three of the fields are defined as `Code` fields, which are text fields that limit the alphanumeric characters to uppercase values. Such `Code` fields are used throughout Business Central for primary key values. They are used to reference or be referenced by other tables (foreign keys). `No.` will be the unique identifier in our table. We will utilize a set of standard internal Business Central procedures to assign a user-defined `No.` series range that will auto-increment the value on table insertion and possibly allow for user entry (so long as it is unique in the table) based on a setup value. Note that `Host No.` references the standard `Resource` table, while the `Radio Show Type` field will reference a custom table that we will create to allow for flexible `Type` values.

We must design and define the reference properties at the field level, as well as compile them before the validation will work. At this point, let's just get started with these field definitions and create the foundation for the `Radio Show` table.

Creating a simple table

The easiest way to create a table is by using **snippets**. Snippets are textual templates for a specific programming task, such as for creating a new table object. To use snippets, Visual Studio Code needs to understand that our file is written in the AL language. This can be done by saving the file with the .al extension.

To add a new AL file, right-click on the space below the app.json file and select **New File...** from the context menu. Name it RadioShow.table.al and press *Enter*:

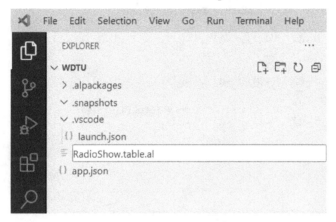

Figure 1.17 – Adding the Radio Show table

> **Note**
>
> As a best practice exemplified by Microsoft, always extend your AL filenames with the <object name>.<object type>.al pattern. You can change the <object name> part at any time later. Try to avoid spaces in filenames. Although using camel case is generally recommended, this book will continue using lowercase object types.

Now, we can use the snippet called ttable. If we type in the letters tt, IntelliSense will suggest this snippet:

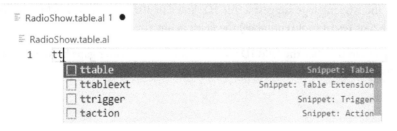

Figure 1.18 – Snippets in VS Code

Code snippets are templates in Visual Studio Code that are available in IntelliSense. Snippets make it easier to enter repeating code patterns and we can use them for object definition templates. This snippet creates content for our file and sets the cursor on the place where we need to define the object ID:

```
RadioShow.table.al 7  ●

RadioShow.table.al > ᵗ₃ Table 0 id
        0 references
1    table id MyTable
2    {
3        DataClassification = ToBeClassified;
4
5        fields
6        {
              1 reference
7            field(1;MyField; Integer)
8            {
9                DataClassification = ToBeClassified;
10
11           }
12       }
13
14       keys
15       {
              - reference
16           key(Key1; MyField)
17           {
18               Clustered = true;
```

Figure 1.19 – A snippet of the generated code structure

We will press *Backspace*, then *Ctrl* + spacebar, and finally *Enter* to select value 50100. Next, we must press the *Tab* key to go to the next field, which contains the object name, where we will type "Radio Show". The snippet has already created a field with the default ID of 1. The field name is MyField and its type is Integer. We will change the name to "No." and the type to Code[20].

The next field will be field number 2. Just like for the object ID we just created, you can use *Ctrl* + spacebar to let the AL language suggest a free ID. You can also place a new field, 3, between field numbers 1 and 2, or resort (not renumber) the fields at any time later.

Alternatively, you can number the field IDs manually, leaving smaller gaps between each field and larger gaps between sets of fields with a particular purpose.

Note

Once a table is referenced by other objects or contains any data, the field numbers of the previously defined fields should not be changed.

The following screenshot shows our new table definition in the .al file:

```
AL RadioShow.table.al  ✕

AL  RadioShow.table.al  >  ⅓ Table 50100 "Radio Show"
       3 references
  1    table 50100 "Radio Show"
  2    {
  3        fields
  4        {
           4 references
  5            field(1; "No."; Code[20]) { }
           3 references
  6            field(2; "Radio Show Type"; Code[10]) { }
           3 references
  7            field(3; "Name"; Text[100]) { }
           3 references
  8            field(4; "Run Time"; Duration) { }
           3 references
  9            field(5; "Host Code"; Code[20]) { }
           3 references
 10            field(6; "Host Name"; Text[100]) { }
           3 references
 11            field(7; "Average Listeners"; Decimal) { }
           3 references
 12            field(8; "Audience Share"; Decimal) { }
           3 references
 13            field(9; "Advertising Revenue"; Decimal) { }
           3 references
 14            field(10; "Royalty Cost"; Decimal) { }
 15        }
 16    }
```

Figure 1.20 – Radio Show table AL code

Note

You can remove anything that's automatically supplied that you don't need from this snippet. Here, we've removed the DataClassification and keys sections, variable declarations, and triggers. We will cover their usage and details in *Chapter 2, Tables*.

Pages

Pages provide views of data or processes that are designed for on-screen display (or exposure as web services and REST APIs) and also allow user data entry into the system. Pages act as containers for action items (menu options).

From a user perspective, there are several basic types of display/entry pages available in Business Central by default:

- List

- Card

- Document

- Journal/worksheet

We will review each page type here.

There are also page parts (they look and program like a page but aren't intended to stand alone), dialogs, as well as **user interfaces** (**UIs**) that display like pages, but are not page objects. The latter UIs are generated by various dialog methods. In addition, there are special page types, such as **Role Center** pages and wizards. All those will be covered later in *Chapter 4, Pages – The Interactive Interface*.

Standard elements of pages

A page consists of page properties and triggers, controls, and control properties. Data controls are generally either labels displaying constant text or graphics, or containers that display data or other controls. Controls can also be buttons, action items, and page parts. While there are a few instances where we must include AL code within page or page control triggers, it is good practice to minimize the amount of code that's embedded within pages. Any data-related AL code should be located in the table object rather than in the page object.

List pages

List pages display a simple list of any number of records in a single table. The **Customers** list page (with its associated FactBoxes) in the following screenshot shows a subset of the data for each customer displayed. List pages often do not allow you to enter or edit data:

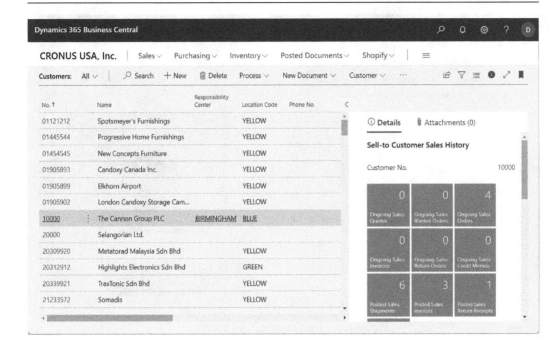

Figure 1.21 – The Customers list page

Card pages

Card pages display one record at a time. They are generally used for entering or displaying individual table records. Examples of frequently accessed card pages include **Customer Card** for customer data, **Item Card** for inventory items, and **G/L Account Card** for general ledger accounts.

Card pages have **FastTabs** (a FastTab consists of a group of controls, with each tab focusing on a different set of related customer data). FastTabs can be expanded or collapsed dynamically, allowing the data that's visible to be controlled by the user at any time. Important data elements can be promoted to be visible all the time, even when a FastTab is collapsed.

Card pages for master records display all the required data entry fields. If a field is set to ShowMandatory (a control property that we will discuss in *Chapter 4, Pages – The Interactive Interface*), a red asterisk will appear until the field is filled. Typically, card pages also display **FactBoxes**, which contain summary data about related activity. Thus, cards can be used as the primary inquiry point for master records. The following screenshot shows an example standard **Customer Card**:

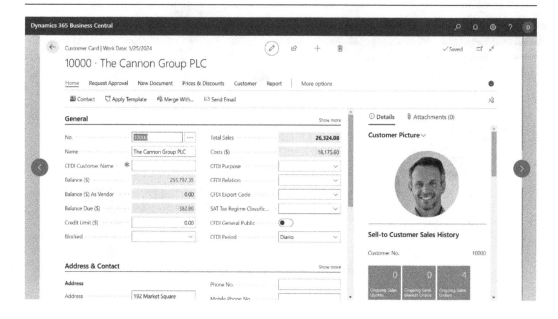

Figure 1.22 – The Customer Card page

Document pages

A document page looks like a card page with one tab containing a list part page. An example of a document page is the **Sales Order** page shown in the following screenshot. In this example, the first tab (**General**) and the last four (invisible) tabs are in card page format and show order data fields that have a single occurrence on the page (in other words, they do not occur in a repeating column).

The second tab from the top (**Lines**) is in a list part page format (all fields are in repeating columns) that shows the order line items. **Sales Order** line items may include products to be shipped, special charges, comments, and other pertinent order details.

The information to the right of the data entry area is related to data and computations (**FactBoxes**) that have been retrieved and formatted. The top FactBox (**Sell-to Customer Sales History**) counts and links various sales documents for the current customer:

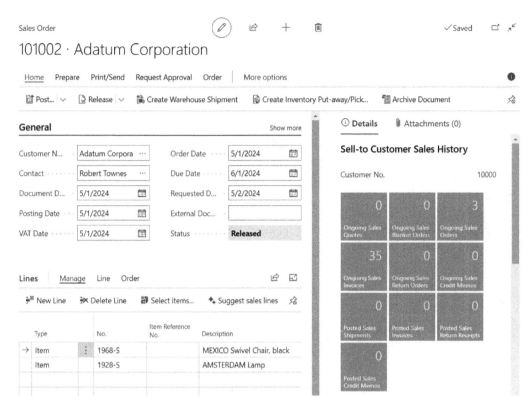

Figure 1.23 – The Sales Order document page

After the short introduction into pages, let's resume designing our WDTU application.

Journal/worksheet pages

Journal and worksheet pages look very much like list pages. They display a list of records in the body of the page. Many also have a section at the bottom that shows details about the selected line and/or totals for the displayed data. These pages may include a filter pane and perhaps a FactBox. The biggest difference between journal/worksheet pages and basic list pages is that journal and worksheet pages are designed to be used for data entry (though this may be a matter of personal or site preference).

An example of the **Payment Journals** page in finance is shown in the following screenshot:

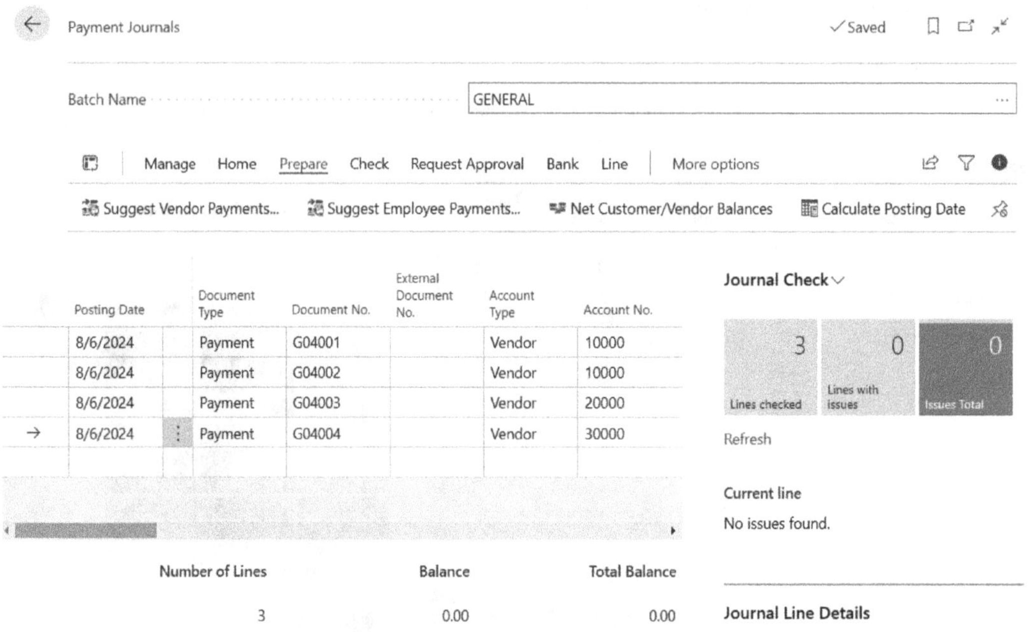

Figure 1.24 – The Payment Journals page

After the short introduction into pages, let's resume designing our WDTU application.

Creating a list page

Now, we will create a list page for the table we created earlier. A list page is the initial page that's displayed when a user initially accesses any data table for the first time. Since the AL language doesn't have wizards, we'll use snippets to create the framework for objects and procedures. Visual Studio Code allows you to create custom snippets if you have repeated patterns that are not available out of the box.

Our first list page will be the basis for viewing our Radio Show master records. From Visual Studio Code, add a new file and enter the name RadioShowList.page.al. Now, we can use the tpage snippet (choose the **Page of type List** entry):

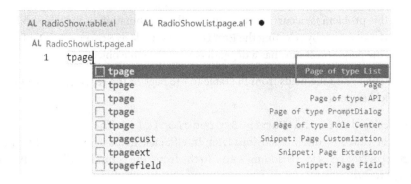

Figure 1.25 – A snippet page being used to generate a page template

Now, we will set the ID to 50100 and the name to "Radio Show List", as well as change SourceTable to "Radio Show", as shown in the following screenshot:

```al
page 50100 "Radio Show List"
{
    PageType = List;
    ApplicationArea = All;
    UsageCategory = Lists;
    SourceTable = "Radio Show";

    layout
    {
        area(Content)
        {
            repeater(GroupName)
            {
                field(Name; NameSource)
                {
                    ApplicationArea = All;
```

TERMINAL   PROBLEMS ①   DEBUG CONSOLE   ···   Filter (e.g. text, **/*.ts,...

∨ ≡ RadioShowList.page.al ①
   ⊗ The name 'NameSource' does not exist in the current context. AL(AL0118) [Ln 14, Col 29]

Figure 1.26 – Fill in the information as shown

After doing this, we can see that NameSource is highlighted as a problem, and the **PROBLEMS** window at the bottom of our screen tells us that NameSource does not exist in this context.

The reason why this problem is occurring is because of the combination of the table object and this page. We joined these objects by selecting the `Radio Show` table as `SourceTable` for this page. By joining them, the page object now has a dependency on the table object.

The next step will be to add the fields from the table to the page in the repeater. We will remove the `NameSource` field to do so.

Page fields are declared as `field(Name; Expression) { }`. The `Name` value can be freely chosen and can be called by other extensions later. IntelliSense helps us fill in the `Expression` value for a `SourceTable` field: By adding `Rec.` to the front, the compiler will identify it as a field from the current record.

After that, we can replace the snippet's `GroupName` with `Group`.

We should also remove everything we don't need, such as FactBoxes and actions:

```
RadioShow.table.al          RadioShowList.page.al ●

RadioShowList.page.al > Page 50100 "Radio Show List"
        0 references
 1      page 50100 "Radio Show List"
 2      {
 3          PageType = List;
 4          ApplicationArea = All;
 5          UsageCategory = Lists;
 6          SourceTable = "Radio Show";
 7
 8          layout
 9          {
                0 references
10              area(content)
11              {
                    0 references
12                  repeater(Group)
13                  {
                        0 references
14                      field("No."; Rec."No.") { }
                        0 references
15                      field("Radio Show Type"; Rec."Radio Show Type") { }
                        0 references
16                      field("Name"; Rec."Name") { }
                        0 references
17                      field("Run Time"; Rec."Run Time") { }
                        0 references
18                      field("Host Code"; Rec."Host Code") { }
                        0 references
19                      field("Host Name"; Rec."Host Name") { }
                        0 references
20                      field("Average Listeners"; Rec."Average Listeners") { }
                        0 references
21                      field("Audience Share"; Rec."Audience Share") { }
                        0 references
22                      field("Advertising Revenue"; Rec."Advertising Revenue") { }
                        0 references
23                      field("Royalty Cost"; Rec."Royalty Cost") { }
24                  }
25              }
26          }
27      }
```

Figure 1.27 – The completed Radio Show list page so far

We can view the page by modifying the `launch.json` file. Change `startupObjectId` to `50100` and select **AL: Publish without debugging** from the Command Palette, as shown in the following screenshot:

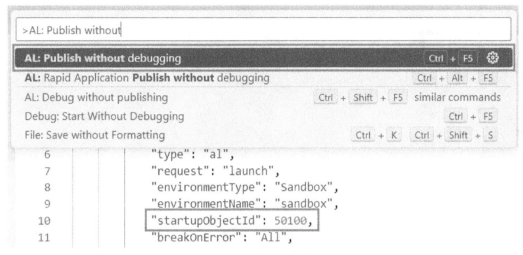

Figure 1.28 – Setting startupObjectId to the Radio Show list page's object number

This will launch the Business Central application with our newly created page as the startup object:

Figure 1.29 – The Radio Show list page in the Business Central client. Text readability
is not a requirement here; the intent is to show the empty Radio Show list

Because our table doesn't contain any data, we will only see a header that displays the name of our page.

Creating a card page

Now, let's create a card page. The process for a card page is almost the same as for a list page, but we use a different `tpage` snippet. Our page number will be `50101` and the name will be `Radio Show Card`:

```
≡ RadioShow.table.al        ≡ RadioShowList.page.al        ≡ RadioShowCard.page.al ●

≡ RadioShowCard.page.al > ⁤⁣ Page 50101 "Radio Show Card"
       0 references
  1    page 50101 "Radio Show Card"
  2    {
  3        PageType = Card;
  4        SourceTable = "Radio Show";
  5        ApplicationArea = All;
  6
  7        layout
  8        {
              0 references
  9            area(content)
 10            {
                  0 references
 11                group(General)
 12                {
                      0 references
 13                    field("No."; Rec."No.") { }
                      0 references
 14                    field("Radio Show Type"; Rec."Radio Show Type") { }
                      0 references
 15                    field("Name"; Rec."Name") { }
                      0 references
 16                    field("Run Time"; Rec."Run Time") { }
                      0 references
 17                    field("Host Code"; Rec."Host Code") { }
                      0 references
 18                    field("Host Name"; Rec."Host Name") { }
                      0 references
 19                    field("Average Listeners"; Rec."Average Listeners") { }
                      0 references
 20                    field("Audience Share"; Rec."Audience Share") { }
                      0 references
 21                    field("Advertising Revenue"; Rec."Advertising Revenue") { }
                      0 references
 22                    field("Royalty Cost"; Rec."Royalty Cost") { }
 23                }
 24            }
 25        }
 26    }
```

Figure 1.30 – Fill in the Radio Show card page as shown

As we don't want our card page to be searchable in the web client, we have removed `UsageCategory`. Additionally, we have renamed the snippet's `GroupName` to `General`; This will be displayed as a FastTab caption to the user.

Note

You can copy and paste most of the definitions from the list page file, or even use **File** and **Save As** in Visual Studio Code if you find that faster or easier to use.

Let's change the `launch.json` file to this new page and publish the extension again. We can view the page by modifying the `launch.json` file. Change `startupObjectId` to `50101` and select **AL: Publish without debugging** from the Command Palette. The page will look like this:

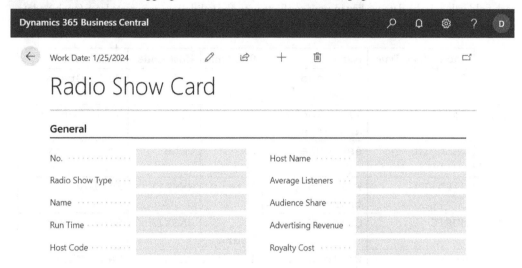

Figure 1.31 – The Radio Show card page in the Business Central client

Creating some sample data

Even though we haven't added all the bells and whistles to our `Radio Show` table and pages, we can still use them to enter sample data. The **Radio Show List** page will be the easiest to use for this.

We will now revert the `launch.json` file so that it runs the `50100` page, as originally defined, and then publish the extension. In the published window, click **New**; you'll see the following screen:

Figure 1.32 – Adding a new record to the Radio Show list page

Enter the data shown in the following table so that we can see what the page looks like when it contains data. Later, once we've added more capabilities to our table and pages, some fields will be validated, and some will be either automatically entered or available on a lookup basis. But for now, simply key in each field value. If the data we key in now conflicts with the validations we create later (such as data in referenced tables), we may have to delete this test data and enter new test data later:

No.	Radio Show Type	Name	Run Time	Host Code	Host Name
RS001	TALK	CeCe and Friends	2 hours	CECE	CeCe Grace
RS002	MUSIC	Alec Rocks and Bops	2 hours	ALEC	Alec Benito
RS003	CALL-IN	Ask Cole!	2 hours	COLE	Cole Henry
RS004	CALL-IN	What do you think?	1 hour	WESLEY	Wesley Ernest
RS005	MUSIC	Quiet Times	3 hours	SASKIA	Saskia Mae
RS006	NEWS	World News	1 hour	DAAN	Daan White
RS007	ROCK	Rock Classics	2 hours	JOSEPH	Josephine Black
RS008	TALK	Kristel's Babytalks	1 hour	KRIS	Kristel van Vugt

Table 1.3 – Test data

Creating a list report

To create a report, we will use the report snippet *treport* and create the 50100 Radio Shows report.

> **Note**
> Testing this report will result in an error message occurring if the sample data hasn't been created yet.

Type 50100 into the Id and Radio Shows into MyReport:

```
     0 references
1    report 50100 "Radio Shows"
2    {
3        UsageCategory = ReportsAndAnalysis;
4        ApplicationArea = All;
5        DefaultRenderingLayout = LayoutName;
6
7        dataset
8        {
             0 references
9            dataitem(DataItemName; SourceTableName)
10           {
                 0 references
11               column(ColumnName; SourceFieldName)
12               {
13
14               }
15           }
16       }
```

Figure 1.33 – Edited report template

If we want users to be able to execute our report from Business Central, we also need to enable a search so that they can find our report. We will do that using the UsageCategory and ApplicationArea properties. The UsageCategory property will determine where the report will be listed, while the ApplicationArea property will determine the access level a user requires to be able to execute the report:

```
1    report 50100 "Radio Shows"
2    {
3        UsageCategory = ReportsAndAnalysis;
4        ApplicationArea = All;
5
6        dataset
```

Figure 1.34 – Properties to show pages and reports in the search

> **Note**
>
> We will learn more about these properties later in *Chapter 4*, in the *Page Searchability* section.

The `SourceTableName` value (visible in *Figure 1.32*) for our report is the `Radio Show` table. The columns are the fields from this table. Spaces and special characters are not allowed in column names for reports.

After selecting the columns and removing any unnecessary elements (`requestpage` and `var`) from the snippet, our report code above `rendering` should look as follows:

```
1    report 50100 "Radio Shows"
2    {
3        UsageCategory = ReportsAndAnalysis;
4        ApplicationArea = All;
5        DefaultRenderingLayout = LayoutName;
6
7        dataset
8        {
             0 references
9            dataitem(DataItemName; "Radio Show")
10           {
                 0 references
11               column(No; "No.") { }
                 0 references
12               column(RadioShowType; "Radio Show Type") { }
                 0 references
13               column(Name; "Name") { }
                 0 references
14               column(RunTime; "Run Time") { }
                 0 references
15               column(HostCode; "Host Code") { }
                 0 references
16               column(HostName; "Host Name") { }
                 0 references
17               column(AverageListeners; "Average Listeners") { }
                 0 references
18               column(AudienceShare; "Audience Share") { }
                 0 references
19               column(AdvertisingRevenue; "Advertising Revenue") { }
                 0 references
20               column(RoyaltyCost; "Royalty Cost") { }
21           }
```

Figure 1.35 – Columns in the "Radio Shows" report

Generating the layout

Now that we've defined our dataset, we can create the layout. Business Central supports RDLC, which can be edited in Visual Studio, SQL Report Builder, Microsoft Excel, and Microsoft Word.

There is no limit to the number or variety of layouts that can be defined for each report, though a single rendering layout must be defined as the default using `DefaultRenderingLayout`. In our example, we will create one of each of the three available types (RDLC, Word, and Excel):

```
1    report 50100 "Radio Shows"
2    {
3        UsageCategory = ReportsAndAnalysis;
4        ApplicationArea = All;
5        DefaultRenderingLayout = MySQLReportLayout;
6
7  >     dataset ...
23
24       rendering
25       {
             1 reference
26           layout(MySQLReportLayout)
27           {
28               Type = RDLC;
29               LayoutFile = 'RadioShows.rdl';
30           }
             0 references
31           layout(MyWordLayout)
32           {
33               Type = Word;
34               LayoutFile = 'RadioShows.docx';
35           }
             0 references
36           layout(MyExcelLayout)
37           {
38               Type = Excel;
39               LayoutFile = 'RadioShows.xlsx';
40           }
41       }
42   }
```

Figure 1.36 – Rendering layouts

To generate the layouts, we need to package our application. We can do this from the Command Palette by running **AL: Package**:

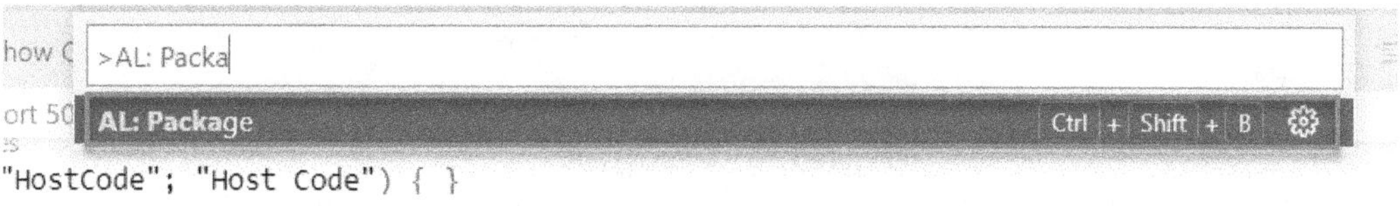

```
how C   > AL: Packa
ort 50  AL: Package                                    Ctrl + Shift + B  ⚙
es
"HostCode"; "Host Code") { }
```

Figure 1.37 – Building the package to generate the layout

This screenshot shows the generated RDLC, which is essentially similar to XML syntax:

Figure 1.38 – RDLC layout

Let's see if we can run our report. To do that, we will publish our extension without `startupObjectId`:

Figure 1.39 – launch.json

In the Business Central session, we will use the search box and type in the word `radio`, which will show our report:

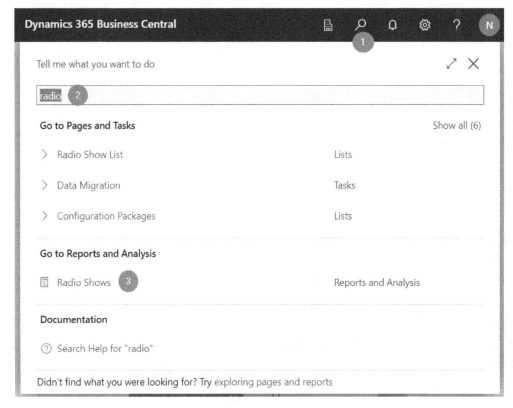

Figure 1.40 – Searching for our new report in the client

When you click on the report and select **Preview & Close**, you should see an empty layout.

Designing the layout

In this book, we will focus on Excel reports, so we will remove the RDLC and Word files and associated properties in the report. We will use the `DefaultRenderingLayout` property to make Excel the default report format choice. Follow these steps:

1.   Right-click on the `RadioShows.xlsx` file and open it in Microsoft Excel:

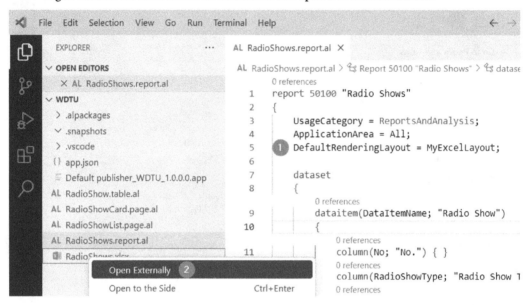

Figure 1.41 – Opening the Excel layout outside of VS Code

Excel will open; you should see the dataset of the Radio Shows report on a sheet labeled **Data**. Every Excel layout must include two elements: the datasheet and the data table. These elements form the basis of the layout by defining the flattened data generated by the report that you can work with. This data table is the basis of the calculations and visualizations that you will want to present on the other sheets. Don't change the name, add, modify, or delete the datasheet, data table, or columns as these are controlled by the report dataset definition.

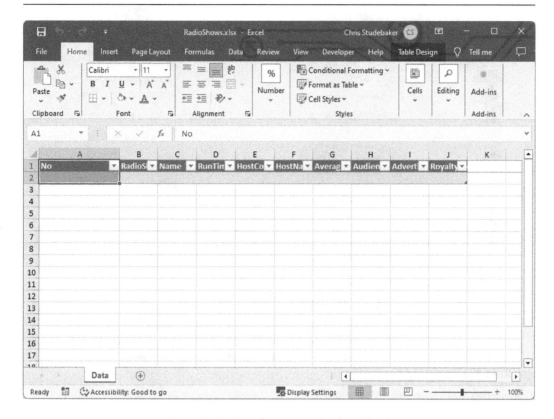

Figure 1.42 – Datasheet in our Excel workbook

2.   In Excel, click the **Insert** tab in the ribbon and choose **PivotTable**:

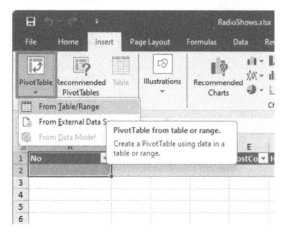

Figure 1.43 – The PivotTable button

3. Choose **From Table/Range** with the default options of **Data** and **New worksheet**. Then, click **OK**:

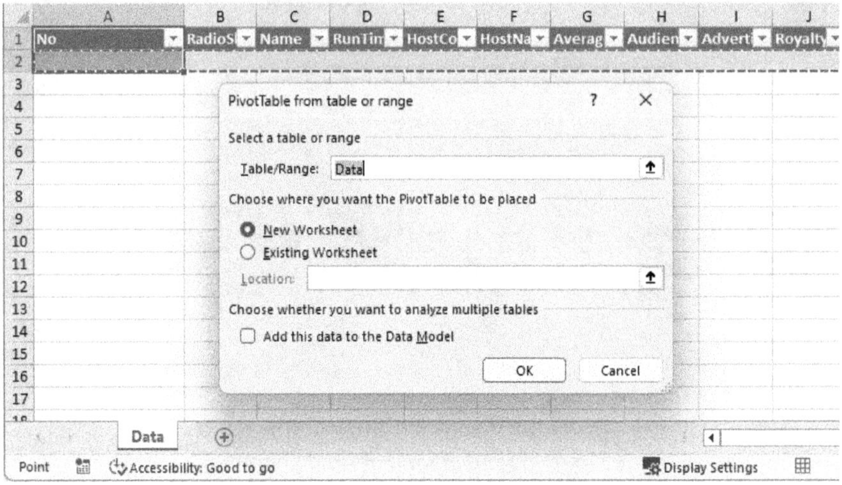

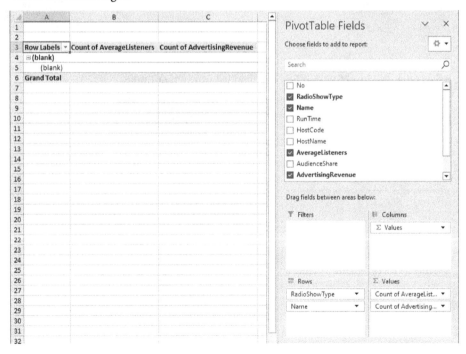

Figure 1.44 – Adding a PivotTable in Excel

4. Select the **RadioShowType**, **Name**, **AverageListeners**, and **AdvertisingRevenue** columns. Drag and drop **Count of AverageListeners** and **Count of AdvertisingRevenue** to **Values** from the **Rows** box on the right:

Figure 1.45 – Populating PivotTable Fields

5. After saving and closing the Microsoft Excel document, we can publish our extension, search for the report, and select **Download**:

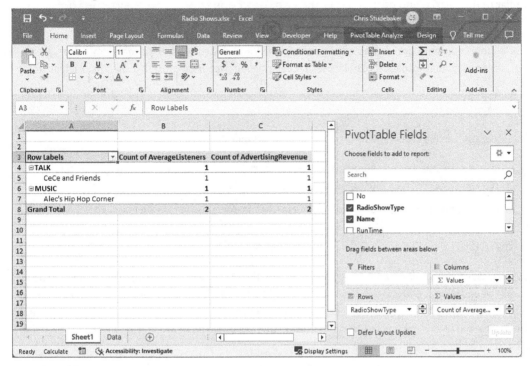

Figure 1.46 – Preview of the Pivot-style report in Excel

There is much more to come. All we've done so far is scratch the surface. But by now, you should have a pretty good overview of the development process for Business Central.

> **Note**
>
> You will be in especially good shape if you've been able to follow along on your system, doing a little experimenting along the way.

Other Business Central object types

We'll finish our introductory review by covering the Business Central object types that haven't been covered in detail yet.

Extension data types

Similar to the `table` and `page` objects, the `tableextension` and `pageextension` objects allow you to define additional fields in the database and display them to the user:

- Table extensions are connected to existing tables and share the same primary key values. Fields defined in table extensions can be used on any existing page and report that uses the original table.

- Page extensions allow developers to add new fields, tabs, actions, and FactBoxes to existing pages. You can also use this to hide controls.

Objects of the `report` and `enum` type can also be extended:

- `reportextension` objects allow developers to add new data items, fields, trigger logic, request page controls, and layouts to existing reports

- `enumextension` objects allow developers to add new values within their app-specific ID range

Codeunits

A `codeunit` object is a container for chunks of AL code to be called from other objects. These chunks of code are called procedures, also referred to as functions or methods. Procedures can be called from any of the other Business Central object types that can contain AL code. Codeunits can also be exposed (published) as web services. This allows the procedures within a published `codeunit` to be invoked by external routines.

Codeunits are suited structurally to contain only procedures. Even though procedures could be placed in other object types, the other object types have superstructures that relate to their designed primary use, such as pages and reports.

Codeunits act only as containers for AL-coded procedures. They have no auxiliary procedures, no method of direct user interaction, and no predefined processing. Even if we are creating only one or two procedures and they are closely related to the primary activity of a particular object, and if these procedures are needed from both inside and outside of the particular object, the best practice is still to locate the procedures in a `codeunit` object.

Several codeunits are delivered as part of the standard Business Central product and are just procedure libraries. These codeunits consist completely of utility routines and are generally organized on some functional basis (for example, associated with dimensions, some aspect of manufacturing, or some aspect of warehouse management). Many of these can be found by filtering the `codeunit` names on the `Management` and `Mgt` strings (the same could be said for some of the tables with the `Buffer` string in their name). When we customize a system, we should create procedure library codeunits to consolidate our customizations and make software maintenance easier. Some developers create libraries of their favorite special procedures and include a custom procedure library codeunit in the systems on which they work.

Queries

Queries are objects of the `query` type. Their purpose is to create extracted sets of data from the Business Central database and do so very efficiently. Business Central queries translate directly into T-SQL query statements and run on the SQL Server side rather than on the Business Central Service Tier. A query can extract data from a single table or multiple tables. In the process of extracting data, a query can make different types of joins (inner join, outer join, or cross join), filters, calculate FlowFields (special Business Central calculations that will be discussed in detail in *Chapter 3, Data Types and Table Fields*), sorts, and create sums and averages. Queries obey the Business Central data structure business logic.

Pages can open queries the very same way they would open other pages. A query is then rendered like a list page, providing a practical analysis view. Other than that, the output of a query can be a CSV file (useful for Excel charts), an XML file (for charts or external applications), or an OData file for a web service. Queries can be published for web service access, similar to pages and codeunits, and as RESTful APIs. The results of a query can also be viewed by pages (as described in *Chapter 5, Reports and Queries*), but they are especially powerful when output to charts. With a little creativity, a query can also be used to feed data to a report via the use of a temporary table to hold the query's results.

XMLports

XMLports are a tool for importing and exporting data. Objects of the `xmlport` type handle both XML structured data and other external text data formats. **XML (eXtensible Markup Language)** is the de facto standard format for exchanging data between dissimilar systems. For example, XMLports could be used to communicate between our Business Central ERP system and our accounting firm's financial analysis and tax preparation system.

XML is designed to be extensible, which means that we can create or extend the definition, so long as we communicate the defined XML format to our correspondents. There is a standard set of syntax rules to which XML formats must conform. Despite the rise of JSON, XML still finds applications in specific domains, such as web services communications.

The non-XML text data files handled by XMLports fall into two categories. One is known as **comma-separated value** or **comma-delimited** files (they usually have a `.csv` file extension). Of course, the delimiters don't have to be commas. The other category is fixed format, in which the length and relative position of each field are predefined.

XMLports can contain AL logic for any type of appropriate data manipulation, either when importing or exporting. Functions such as editing, validating, combining, and filtering can be applied to the data as it passes through an XMLport.

Development backups and documentation

As with any system where we can do development work, paying careful attention to documentation and backing up our work is very important. Visual Studio Code provides a variety of techniques for handling each of these tasks.

The first area where we can place documentation is in line with modified AL code. Individual **comment** lines can be created by starting the line with double forward slashes, //. Whole sections of comments (or commented-out code) can be created by enclosing the section with /* ... */. Depending on the type of object and the nature of the specific changes, we should generally annotate each change inline with forward slashes rather than wherever the code is touched so that all the changes can be easily identified by the next developer who will work on this code.

> **Tip**
> The easiest way to add – and remove – double forward slashes at the beginning of the current line or for a marked range of lines is to press *Ctrl + /* or *Ctrl + #*, depending on your environment's language.

The best documentation resides outside of our source code. Visual Studio Code has built-in support for **Git**, which means that we can use any source code control system that supports Git repositories, including, but not limited to, GitHub, GitLab, or Azure DevOps.

There are some great resources on how to get started with Git, such as the ones we mentioned earlier in this chapter. A good explanation of using Git source control in VS Code can be found at `https://code.visualstudio.com/docs/sourcecontrol/overview`.

In short, when doing development in Business Central VS Code, everything we have learned earlier about good documentation practices applies. This holds true, regardless of whether development involves new work or modifying existing logic.

Summary

In this chapter, we covered some basic definitions of terms related to Business Central and VS Code. We followed this by introducing 12 Business Central object types (tables, table extensions, pages, page extensions, reports, report extensions, profiles, codeunits, queries, enums, enum extensions, and XMLports). We introduced table, page, and report creation through review and hands-on use and began a Business Central application for managing Radio Show at WTDU. Finally, we briefly looked at the tools that we can use to integrate with external entities and discussed how different types of backups and documentation are handled in VisuVS Code.

Now that we've covered the basics, we can dive into primary object types in the next few chapters. In the next chapter, we will focus on tables – the foundation of any Business Central system.

Questions

Answer the following questions to test your knowledge of this chapter:

1. An ERP system such as Business Central includes several functional areas. Which of the following are part of Business Central? Choose four:

    *   Manufacturing

    *   Sales order processing

    *   Inventory

    *   **Computer-aided design (CAD)**

    *   Financial management

    ANSWER: Manufacturing, sales order processing, inventory, and financial management

2. Business Central development is done in Visual Studio Professional. True or false?

    ANSWER: False

3. Match the following page types and descriptions for Business Central:

Journal	Audit trail
Ledger	Validation process
Register	Invoice
Document	Transaction entries
Posting	History

    ANSWER: Journal – Transaction entries, Ledger – History, Register – Audit trail, Document – Invoice, Posting – Validation process

4. You can create extensions using VS Code in a Linux or macOS environment. True or false?

    ANSWER: True

5. Which of the following are Business Central applications? Choose three:

    *   System Application

    *   Core Application

    *   Sales and Distribution Application

    *   Base Application

    *   Business Foundation

    ANSWER: System Application, Base Application, and Business Foundation

6. Which of the following describes Business Central? Choose two:

    - Customizable

    - Includes a storefront module

    - Object-based

    - Azure .NET

    - Object-oriented

    ANSWER: Customizable and object-based

7. Which are the valid options for environment types that you can connect to in the `launch.json` file? Choose two:

    - Docker

    - Sandbox

    - Live

    - Production

    ANSWER: Sandbox and production

8. Symbols are `.app` files containing metadata for other extensions. True or false?

    ANSWER: True

9. When working with Excel report layouts, you can update the dataset from Business Central directly in the **Data** tab. True or false?

    ANSWER: False

10. Codeunits are the only Business Central objects that can contain procedures. True or false?

    ANSWER: False

11. Query output can be used as a data item for reports. True or false?

    ANSWERS: True

12. VS Code with the AL extension is required for Business Central development. True or false?

    ANSWER: True

13. Which object number range can be assigned to customer-specific objects?

    - 20 – 500

    - 17,000,000 – 37,000,000

    - 150,000 – 200,000

- 50,000 – 99,999

- 10,000 – 100,000

ANSWER: 50,000 – 99,999

14. XMLports can only process XML-formatted data. True or false?

ANSWER: False

15. The work date can only be changed by the system administrator. True or false?

ANSWER: False

16. A design pattern is which of the following? Choose two:

- Reusable code

- Stripes and plaid together

- A proven way to solve a common problem

- UI guidelines

ANSWER: Reusable code and a proven way to solve common problems

17. Business Central reports are often generated automatically through the use of a wizard. True or false?

ANSWER: False

2
Tables

Design is not just what it looks like and feels like. Design is how it works.

– Steve Jobs

The competent programmer is fully aware of the limited size of his own skull. He therefore approaches his task with full humility, and avoids clever tricks like the plague.

– Edsger Dijkstra

The foundation of any system is the data structure definition. In Business Central, the building blocks of this foundation are the tables and the individual data fields that the tables contain. Once the functional analysis and process definition have been completed, any new design work must begin with the data structure. For Business Central, that means the tables and their contents.

A Business Central table includes much more than just the data fields and keys. A Business Central table definition also includes data validation rules, processing rules, business rules, and logic to ensure referential integrity. These rules are in the form of properties and AL code.

> **Note**
> For object-oriented developers, a Dynamics Business Central table is best compared to a class with methods and properties that have been stored one-to-one as a table on SQL Server.

In this chapter, we will learn about the structure and creation of tables. Details regarding fields and the components of tables will be covered in the following chapter. In particular, we will cover the following topics:

- An overview of tables, including properties, triggers, keys, `SumIndexFields`, field groups, and temporary tables

- Enhancing our scenario application – creating and modifying tables

- Types of tables – extensible and non-extensible

An overview of tables

There is a distinction between the table (data definition and data container) and the data (the contents of a table). The **table definition** describes the identification information, data structure, validation rules, storage, and retrieval of the data that is stored in the table (container). This definition is defined by its design and can only be changed by a developer. The **table data** is the variable content that originates from user activities. The place where we can see the data being explicitly referenced, independent of the table as a definition of structure, is in **Permission Sets**. In the following screenshot, the data is formally referred to as **Table Data**:

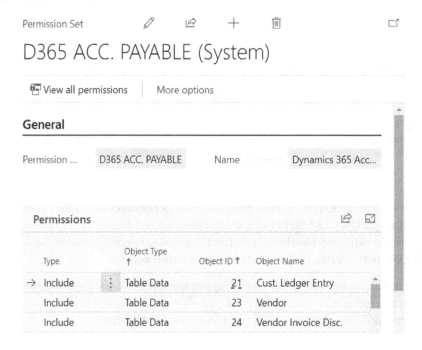

Figure 2.1 – Permission Set showing Table Data Object Type

The table is not the data – it is the definition of data contained in the table. Even so, we commonly refer to both the data and the table as if they were the same. That is what we will do in this book.

All permanent data must be stored in a table. All tables are defined by the developer working in Visual Studio Code. As much as possible, critical system design components should be embedded in the tables. Each table should include the code that controls what happens when records are added, changed, or deleted, as well as how data is validated when records are added or changed. This includes functions to maintain the aspects of referential integrity that are not automatically handled. The `table` object should also include the procedures that are commonly used to manipulate the table and its data, whether this be for database maintenance or in support of business logic. In the cases where the business logic is either a modification that's been applied to a standard (out-of-the-box) table or used elsewhere in the system, the code should reside in a `codeunit` procedure library and be called from the table.

Visual Studio Code provides snippets for the definition of the data structure within tables. We will explore these capabilities through examples and analysis of the structure of table objects. We find that the approach of embedding control and business logic within the table object has several advantages:

- Clarity of design

- Centralization of rules for data constraints

- More efficient development of logic

- Increased ease of debugging

- Easier upgrading

The basis of any database-driven system is the data, which is stored in tables. How you organize the data and the business logic driven by the data are all defined within the table object in Business Central.

To gain an overview of basic table design, we will now look further into table components, naming and numbering, properties, triggers and keys, `SumIndexFields` and **Nonclustered Columnstore Indexes**, field groups, and finally, temporary tables.

Components of a table

A table is made up of **Fields**, **Properties**, **Triggers** (some of which may contain AL code), and **Keys**. **Fields** also have **Properties** and **Triggers**. Keys also have Properties:

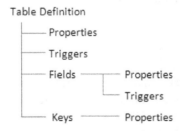

Figure 2.2 – Illustration of the components of a table

A table definition that takes full advantage of these capabilities reduces the effort that's required to construct other parts of the application. Good table design can significantly enhance the application's processing speed, efficiency, and flexibility.

A table can have the following components:

- Up to 500 fields

- A defined record size of up to 8,060 bytes (with each field sized at its maximum)

- Up to 40 different keys (including the primary)

A design consideration in Business Central that started in its earlier versions is to name the tables for what they contain.

Naming tables

There are standardized naming conventions for Business Central that we should follow. Names for tables and other objects should be as descriptive as possible while keeping to a reasonable length. This makes our work more self-documenting.

Table names should always be singular. The table containing data about customers should not be named `Customers`, but `Customer`. The table we created for our WDTU Radio Station Business Central enhancement was named `Radio Show`, even though it will contain data for all of WDTU's radio shows.

In general, we should always name a table so that it is easy to identify the relationship between the table and the data it contains. For example, two tables containing the transactions on which a document page is based should normally be referred to as a `Header` table (for the main portion of the page) and a `Line` table (for the line detail portion of the page). As an example, the tables underlying a **Sales Order** page are the `Sales Header` and `Sales Line` tables. The `Sales Header` table contains all of the data that occurs only once for a **Sales Order**, while the `Sales Line` table contains all of the lines for the order.

Table numbering

There are no hard and fast rules for table numbering, except that one must only use the table object numbers that they are licensed to use, and that are within the range specified in the `app.json` file. For Azure public cloud implementations of Business Central, the license holder is not limited to the number of objects by license but is limited to the number range from 50,000 to 99,999. Extension objects are considered a different object type to base objects so a table extension can share the same object number as a custom table.

It does not require considerable effort to renumber tables containing data. However, parts of the application – such as the Configuration Packages feature of Business Central – may refer to table numbers and would need an update to continue working.

Table properties

The first step in studying the internal construction of a table is to open one in Visual Studio Code. We will use the Radio Show table we created in *Chapter 1, Introduction to Business Central,* to show you this.

We now have the Radio Show table open in Visual Studio Code, as shown in the following screenshot:

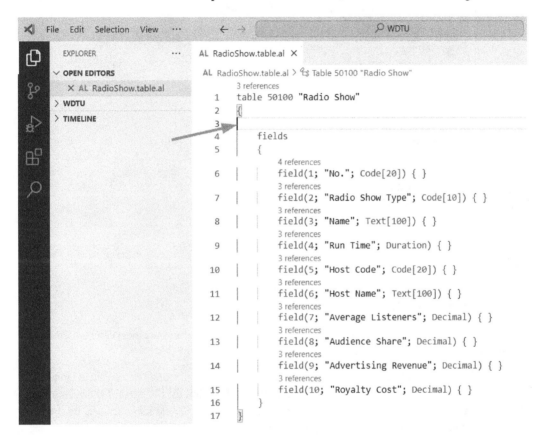

Figure 2.3 – The Radio Show table

We can access the properties of a table. Place the cursor on the empty line above the fields (as shown with the help of an arrow in the preceding screenshot) and click on *Ctrl* + the spacebar. If we hit *Ctrl* + the spacebar while the focus is on a filled field line, we will see the properties of that field (not the table).

The options you can see in Visual Studio Code should look as follows:

```
≡ RadioShow.table.al ✕

≡ RadioShow.table.al > ⚏ Table 50100 "Radio Show"
     3 references
 1   table 50100 "Radio Show"
 2   {
 3
 4   🔧 Access                                    Access property
 5   🔧 Caption
     🔧 CaptionML
 6   🔧 ColumnStoreIndex
     🔧 CompressionType
 7   🔧 DataCaptionFields
     🔧 DataClassification
 8   🔧 DataPerCompany
     🔧 Description
 9   🔧 DrillDownPageId
     🔧 Extensible
10   🔧 ExternalName
11          field(6; "Host Name"; Text[50]) { }
     3 references
```

Figure 2.4 – Table object properties

The most common table properties are as follows:

- Access: Sets the object accessibility level, which controls whether the object can be used from other code in your module or other modules.

- Caption and CaptionML set the table display name for the currently selected client language. If none is set, the table name will be displayed. If no translation for the current client language is available, then the caption defined for the English (United States) language will be shown. Multilanguage functionality for captions is controlled either by XLIFF (translation) files in the project (Caption), or by defining the translations directly in the table object (CaptionML). We will review the language capabilities later in *Chapter 7*, in the *Multi-language system* section.

- ColumnStoreIndex: Sets the fields that are added to the ColumnStore index inside SQL Server.

- CompressionType: Specifies the compression type used: Unspecified, None, Row, or Page. The TableType property must be set to normal and cannot be used in Table Extensions.

- DataCaptionFields: This allows us to define specific fields whose contents will be displayed as part of the caption. For the Customer table, No. and Name will be displayed in the title bar at the top of a page showing a customer record.

- `DataClassification`: This sets a default value for all table fields to help the users classify sensitive or personal data. In the Microsoft Docs, we can read more about data classification in the *Classifying data sensitivity fields* article (`https://learn.microsoft.com/en-us/dynamics365/business-central/admin-classifying-data-sensitivity`).

- `DataPerCompany`: This lets us define whether or not the data in this table is segregated by company (the default), or whether it is common (shared) across all of the companies in the database. The generated names of tables within SQL Server (not within Business Central) are affected by this choice.

- `Description`: This property is for optional documentation usage.

- `DrillDownPageID`: This allows us to define the default page for drilling down into the supporting detail for data that is displayed and summarized in this table.

- `Extensible`: By default, tables can be extended through other apps. If we don't want to allow that, we can set the value to `false`.

- `LookupPageID`: This allows us to define the default page for looking up data in this table.

- `ObsoleteState`: This can be used to indicate to developers this table will be removed in a future version.

- When the `ObsoleteState` property is used, `ObsoleteReason` and `ObsoleteTag` can be set to explain why the table has been discontinued or what will replace it, and in which extension version the discontinuation has been first announced.

- `PasteIsValid`: This property determines whether users are allowed to paste data into the table.

- `Permissions`: This allows us to grant users of this table different levels of access (r for read, i for insert, m for modify, and d for delete) to the table data in other table objects, for example, read-only tables such as ledgers.

- `TableType`: The `Temporary` value lets us store the table in memory only. No SQL table will ever be created. The other values (CRM and CDS) are rarely used. We will review temporary tables later in the *Temporary tables* section.

> **Tip**
> The Microsoft Docs list all table properties in the *Table, Table Fields, and Table Extension Properties* article (`https://learn.microsoft.com/en-us/dynamics365/business-central/dev-itpro/developer/properties/devenv-table-properties`).

As developers, we most frequently deal with the ID, Name, `LookupPageID`, `DrillDownPageID`, `Caption`/`CaptionML`, `DataCaptionFields`, `Permissions`, and `TableType` properties. When developing apps for AppSource, we additionally deal with `DataClassification`, `ObsoleteState`, `ObsoleteReason`, and `ObsoleteTag`. We rarely deal with the other properties.

Table triggers

To display the triggers with the table open in Visual Studio Code, enter the `trigger` keyword in the first line after the fields section, followed by *Ctrl* + spacebar. This is shown in the following screenshot:

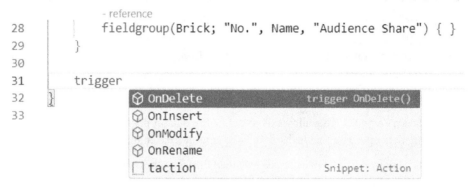

Figure 2.5 – Table level triggers

The code contained in `trigger` is executed prior to the event represented by `trigger`. In other words, the code in the `OnInsert()` trigger is executed before the record is inserted into the table. This allows the developer a final opportunity to perform validations and enforce data consistency, such as referential integrity. We can even abort the intended action if data inconsistencies or conflicts are found.

The triggers in the following bullet list are automatically invoked when record processing occurs as a result of user action. But when table data is changed by AL code or by a data import, the AL code or import process determines whether or not the code in the applicable trigger is executed:

- `OnInsert()`: This is executed when a new record is to be inserted in the table through the UI. (In general, new records are added when the last field of the **primary key** (**PK**) is completed and the focus leaves that field. See the property in *Chapter 4, Pages – The Interactive Interface.*)

- `OnModify()`: This is executed when a record is rewritten after the contents of any field other than a PK field have been changed. The change is determined by comparing xRec (the image of the record prior to being changed) to Rec (the current record copy). If we need to see what the *before* value of a record or field is, we can reference the contents of xRec and compare that to the equivalent portion of Rec. These variables (Rec and xRec) are system-defined variables.

- `OnDelete()`: This is executed before a record is to be deleted from the table.

- `OnRename()`: This is executed when some portion of the PK of the record is about to be changed. Changing any part of the PK is a rename action. This maintains a level of referential integrity. Unlike some other systems, Business Central allows the PK of any master record to be changed. This automatically maintains all of the affected foreign key references from other records.

> **Note**
>
> There is an internal inconsistency in the handling of data integrity by Business Central. On the one hand, the `Rename` trigger automatically maintains one level of referential integrity when any part of the PK is changed (that is, the record is renamed). This happens in a black box process, an internal process that we cannot see or touch.
>
> However, if we delete a record, Business Central doesn't automatically do anything to maintain referential integrity. For example, child records could be orphaned by a deletion, that is, left without any parent record. Or, if there are references in other records back to the deleted record, they could be left with no target. As developers, we are responsible for ensuring this part of referential integrity in our customizations.

When we write AL code in one object that updates data in another (table) object, we can control whether or not the applicable table update trigger fires (executes). For example, if we were adding a record to our `Radio Show` table and used the following AL code, the `OnInsert ()` trigger would fire:

```
RadioShow.Insert(true);
```

However, say we were to use either of the following AL code options:

```
RadioShow.Insert(false); or RadioShow.Insert;
```

then the `OnInsert ()` trigger will not fire and none of the logic inside the trigger will be executed. The automatic black box logic enforcing PK uniqueness will happen regardless of whether the `OnInsert ()` trigger is fired.

Keys

Table keys are used to identify records and to speed up filtering and sorting. Having too few keys may result in painfully slow inquiries and reports. However, each key incurs a processing cost, because the index containing the key must be updated every time information in a key field changes. Key cost is measured primarily in terms of increased index maintenance processing. There is also additional cost in terms of disk storage space (usually not significant) and additional backup/recovery time for the increased database size (sometimes important).

When a system is optimized for processing speed, it is critical to analyze the SQL Server indexes that are active because that is where the updating and retrieval time are determined. The determination of the proper number and design of keys and indexes for a table requires a thorough understanding of the types and frequencies of inquiries, reports, and other processing for that table.

Every Business Central table must have at least one key: the PK. The PK is always the first key in the key list. By default, the PK is made up of the first field that's defined in the table. In many of the reference tables, there is only one field in the PK, and the only key is the PK.

Our `Radio Show` table does not have an explicit key defined, which means that Business Central defaults to the first field. If we were to explicitly define this key, we would have to declare it, as shown in the following screenshot:

```
14              field(120; "Advertising Revenue"; Decimal) { }
                3 references
15              field(130; "Royalty Cost"; Decimal) { }
16          }
17
18      keys
19      {
            - reference
20          key(PK; "No.") {}
21      }
22
```

Figure 2.6 – PK

The PK must have a unique value in each table record. We can change the PK to be any field or a combination of up to 16 fields totaling up to 900 bytes, but the uniqueness requirement must be met. It will automatically be enforced by Business Central because Business Central will not allow us to add a record with a duplicate PK to a table.

When we add other keys, the first key remains the SQL clustered index key and other keys become secondary. Let's now add the following keys to our `Radio Show` table:

```
    }
    keys
    {
        - reference
        key(PK; "No.") { }
        - reference
        key(Name; Name) { }
        - reference
        key(HostName; "Host Name") { }
    }
```

Figure 2.7 – Secondary keys

All keys except the PK are secondary ones. There is no required uniqueness constraint on secondary keys, though they do support the `Unique` property, which will put a unique constraint on the SQL table. There is no requirement to have any secondary keys. If we want a secondary key not to have duplicate values, and SQL is not enforcing via the `Unique` property, our AL code must check for duplication before completing the new entry.

Behind the scenes, each secondary key has the PK appended to the backend. A maximum of 40 keys are allowed per table.

> **Note**
>
> Database maintenance performance is faster with fewer fields in keys and fewer keys, especially the PK. This must be balanced against improved performance in processes by having the optimum key contents and choices.

Other significant key attributes include key groups and SQL Server-specific properties:

- Several SQL Server-specific key-related parameters have been added to Business Central. These key properties can be accessed by using *Ctrl* + the spacebar inside the curly braces in a key.

- The `IncludedFields` property is used to add columns on the index leaf nodes (logical data location based on the tree index model). Included columns do not count against the 16-field maximum in a key definition and require less I/O on the database, increasing performance.

The `MaintainSqlIndex` and `MaintainSiftIndex` properties allow the developer and/or system administrator to determine whether or not a particular key or **SumIndexField Technology** (**SIFT**) field will be continuously maintained. Indexes that are not maintained minimize record update time but require longer processing time to dynamically create the indexes when they are used. This level of control is useful for managing indexes that are only needed occasionally. For example, a key or SIFT index that is used only for monthly reports can be disabled, and no index maintenance processing will be done day to day.

```
28        keys
29        {
             - reference
30           key(PK; "No.") {}
31        }
32
33    }
34
```
```
 Clustered                          Clustered property
 Description
 Enabled
 IncludedFields
 MaintainSiftIndex
 MaintainSqlIndex
 ObsoleteReason
 ObsoleteState
 ObsoleteTag
 SqlIndex
 SumIndexFields
 Unique
```

Figure 2.8 – Key properties

Each key has settings that allow you to manage FlowFields, how the index is created in SQL, and many other useful properties that we will discuss next.

SumIndexFields

Dynamics Business Central has a unique capability called the **SIFT** feature. These fields serve as the basis for FlowFields (automatically accumulating totals) and are unique to Business Central. This feature allows Business Central to provide almost instantaneous responses to user inquiries for summed data, which are calculated on the fly at runtime and are related to `SumIndexFields`. The cost is primarily that of the time required to maintain the SIFT indexes when a table is updated.

Business Central maintains SIFT totals using SQL Server-indexed views. An **indexed view** is a view that has been preprocessed and stored. Business Central creates one indexed view for each enabled **SIFT key**. SIFT keys are enabled and disabled through the `MaintainSiftIndex` property. SQL Server maintains the contents of the view when any changes are made to the base table unless the `MaintainSiftIndex` property is set to `false`. When the property is `false`, SQL calculates the view on the fly every time the value is needed, potentially consuming greater processing resources.

`SumIndexFields` are accumulated sums of individual fields (columns) in tables. When the totals are automatically pre-calculated, they are easy to use and provide very high-speed access for inquiries. If users need to know the total of the `Amount` values in a `Ledger` table, the `Amount` field can be attached as `SumIndexField` to the appropriate keys. In another table, such as `Customer`, FlowFields can be defined as display fields that take advantage of `SumIndexFields`. This gives users a very rapid response for calculating a total balance amount inquiry, based on detailed ledger amounts tied to those keys. We will discuss the various data field types and FlowFields in more detail in *Chapter 3, Data Types and Table Fields*.

In a typical ERP system, many thousands, millions, or even hundreds of millions of records might have to be processed to give such results, which would take considerable time. In Business Central, only a few records need to be accessed to provide the requested results. Processing is very fast and programming is greatly simplified.

SQL Server SIFT values are maintained through the use of SQL-indexed views. By using the key property, `MaintainSiftIndex`, we can control whether or not the SIFT index is maintained dynamically (faster response) or only created when needed (less ongoing system performance load). The AL code is the same, regardless of whether the SIFT is maintained dynamically or not.

Having too many keys or SIFT fields can negatively affect system performance for two reasons. The first, which we have already discussed, is the index maintenance processing load. The second is the table locking interference that can occur when multiple threads are requesting update access to a set of records that update SIFT values.

Conversely, a lack of necessary keys or SIFT definitions can also cause performance problems. Having unnecessary data fields in a SIFT key creates many extra entries, which affects performance. `Integer` fields usually create an especially large number of unique SIFT index values, and `Option` or `Enum` fields create a relatively small number of index values.

> **Important**
>
> The best design for a SIFT index is where the fields that will be used most frequently in queries are positioned on the left-hand side of the index, in order of descending frequency of use. In a nutshell, we should be careful when designing keys and SIFT fields. While a system is in production, applicable SQL Server statistics should be monitored regularly and appropriate maintenance actions should be taken. Business Central automatically maintains a count for all SIFT indexes, thus speeding up all `Count` and `Average FlowField` calculations.

Nonclustered Columnstore Indexes

In an effort to increase SQL performance and still keep the core functionality of FlowFields in Business Central, **Nonclustered Columnstore Indexes** (**NCCI**) was included in table definitions. A NCCI is always associated with a table, and there can only be one defined per table. The indexes for SIFT defined on keys must be maintained for each insert, update, and delete transaction to a table. This maintenance causes overhead on SQL, though the amount of overhead depends on the number of keys defined and the volume data for each table. Unlike SIFT indexes, NCCI is not stored in the database and all queries are executed at runtime. A major advantage of not maintaining indexes is that it does not matter to the developer which keys or in what order the fields are defined. To replace SIFT keys with an NCCI, just add all fields from the key and `SumIndexFields` to the definition of the `ColumnStoreIndex` property and remove the SIFT keys.

Here is an example of two secondary keys each with `SumIndexField` defined for `Fee Amount` being condensed into a single `ColumnStoreIndex` definition. The involved table is new for us, as we are going to create it later in the *New tables for our WDTU project* section:

```
1    table 50105 "Radio Show Entry"
2    {
3        ColumnStoreIndex = "Radio Show No.", Type, "No.", Date, "Fee Amount";
4
5  >     fields ···
20       keys
21       {
             0 references
22           key(PK; "Entry No.") { Clustered = true; }
             0 references
23           key(Reporting; "Radio Show No.", Date) { SumIndexFields = "Fee Amount"; }
             0 references
24           key(Reporting2; Type, "No.", Date) { SumIndexFields = "Fee Amount"; }
25       }
26   }
```

Figure 2.9 – NonClustered Columnstore example

Keep in mind that SIFT and NCCI are mutually exclusive in a table definition and only one should be defined.

Field groups

When a user starts to enter data in a field where the choices are constrained to existing data (for example, an Item No., a **Salesperson Code**, a **Unit of Measure Code**, a **Customer No.**, and so on), good design dictates that the system will help the user by displaying the universe of acceptable choices. Put simply, a **lookup** list of choices should be displayed.

In the web client, the lookup display (a drop-down control) is generated dynamically when its display is requested by the user's effort to enter data in a field that references a table through the `TableRelation` property (which will be discussed in more detail in the next chapter). The format of the drop-down control is a basic list. The fields that are included in that list and their left-to-right display sequence are either defined by default or by an entry in the `fieldgroups` control.

The `fieldgroups` control is part of the Business Central table definition, much like the list of keys. In fact, the `fieldgroups` control is accessed very similarly to the list of keys, that is, via *Ctrl* + spacebar, as shown in the following screenshot:

Figure 2.10 – The fieldgroups control

If we add the `fieldgroups` control for the `Radio Show` table, we can create two field groups, which both are declared with the `fieldgroup` keyword and must be named `DropDown` (without a hyphen) and `Brick`:

```
fieldgroups
{
    fieldgroup(DropDown; "No.", Name, "Host Name") { }
    fieldgroup(Brick; "No.", Name, "Audience Share") { }
}
```

Next, let's inspect how drop-downs and bricks appear in the web client.

Dropdowns

The drop-down display created by this particular field group is shown in the following screenshot on the **Sales Order** page. It contains fields that are in the same order of appearance as they are in the field group definition:

Type	No.	Item Reference No.	Description		Location Code	Quantity	Qty
→ Item	1920-S ⌄		ANTWERP Conference Table		RED	4	

	No. ↑	Description	Base Unit of Measure	Unit Price
→	1920-S	ANTWERP Conference Table	PCS	647.80
	1924-W	CHAMONIX Base Storage Unit	PCS	210.20
	1925-W	Conference Bundle 1-6	PCS	188.80
	1928-S	AMSTERDAM Lamp	PCS	54.90
	1928-W	ST.MORITZ Storage Unit/Draw...	PCS	527.20

Subtotal Excl. Tax (USD)	2,461.64
Inv. Discount Amount...	172.31
Invoice Discount % + New Select from full list	2,633.95

Figure 2.11– Drop-down list using fieldgroup

If no field group is defined for a table, the system defaults to using the PK plus the Description field (or the Name field). Field groups are not the only way to display data concisely in Business Central.

Bricks

In addition to the DropDown field group, we can also define a brick. The brick for the **Customer** table is rendered as follows:

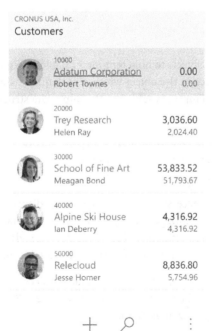

Figure 2.12 – Brick on the Customers phone app page

The same brick is rendered differently in the web client, as displayed in the following screenshot:

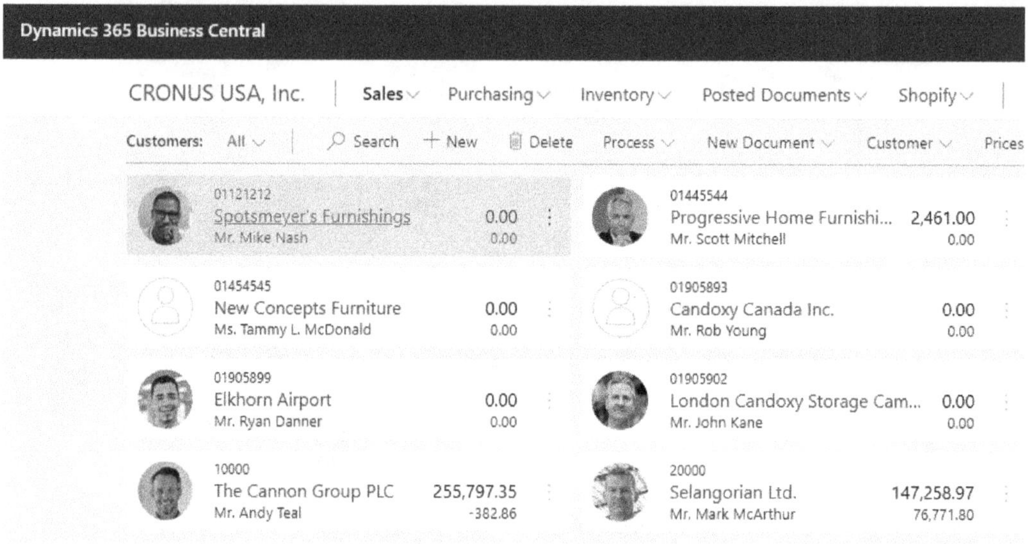

Figure 2.13 – Brick on the Customers web client page

We can enhance and configure Business Central utilizing many properties available throughout the table architecture.

Temporary tables

A temporary table is used within objects to hold temporary data in memory only. A temporary table does not exist outside the instance of the object where it is defined using a permanent table as the source of the table definition. A temporary table has the same data structure as the permanent table after which it is modeled.

Temporary tables are created empty when the parent object execution initiates, and they disappear along with their data contents when the parent object execution terminates (that is, when the temporary table variable goes out of scope).

Temporary tables are not generally accessible to users, except on a display-only basis. They can directly be the target of reports, pages, and XML ports. In general, temporary tables are intended to be work areas, and as such, are containers of temporary (or work) data. The definition of a temporary table can only be changed by changing the definition of the permanent table on which it has been modeled.

Using the `TableType = Temporary` property in a table object definition, that table will never be created on a database level. On the other hand, we can use every `Normal` table that is stored in the SQL Server to work as a temporary table in our code.

We won't use temporary tables in our sample application, but you can review some code samples in the Microsoft Docs, at `https://learn.microsoft.com/en-us/dynamics365/business-central/dev-itpro/developer/devenv-temporary-tables`.

Enhancing our sample application

Now, we can take our knowledge of tables and expand our WDTU application. Our base `Radio Show` table needs to be added to and modified. We also need to create and reference additional tables.

Although we want to have a realistic design in our sample application, we will focus on changes that illustrate features in the Business Central table design that this book's authors feel are among the most important. If there are capabilities or functionalities that you feel are missing, feel free to add them. Adjust the examples as much as you wish to make them more meaningful to you.

Creating and modifying tables

In *Chapter 1*, *Introduction to Business Central*, we created the `Radio Show` table for the WDTU application. At that time, we used the minimum fields that allowed us to usefully define a master record. Now, let's set properties on existing data fields, add more data fields, and create an additional data table to which the `Radio Show` table can refer.

Our new data fields are shown in the following layout table:

Field no.	Field name	Description
11	Frequency	An `Option` data type (`Hourly`, `Daily`, `Weekly`, or `Monthly`) is used for the frequency of a show; `Hourly` should be used for a show segment, such as news, sports, or weather, that is scheduled every hour. At WDTU, the default value is hourly, so it is the first index in the option list.
		If we wanted to leave the option field empty by default, we could have used a space/blank as the first option instead.
12	PSAs Required	Are **Public Service Announcements (PSAs)** to be played per show? (A Boolean.)
13	Ads Required	Are advertisements to be played per show? (A Boolean.)
14	News Required	Is headline news required to be broadcast during the show? (A Boolean.)
15	News Duration	This is the duration (stored as `Duration`) of the news program that's embedded within the show.

Field no.	Field name	Description
16	Sports Required	Is sports news required to be broadcast during the show? (A Boolean.)
17	Sports Duration	This is the duration (stored as Duration) of the sports program that's embedded within the show.
18	Weather Required	Is weather news required to be broadcast during the show? (A Boolean.)
19	Weather Duration	This is the duration (stored as Duration) of the weather program that's embedded within the show.
20	Date Filter	This is the date FlowFilter (stored as the Date data type and the FieldClass FlowFilter) that will change the calculations of the flow fields based on the date filter that's applied. We will cover FlowFilters in more detail in *Chapter 3, Data Types and Table Fields*.

Table 2.1 – Layout for new Radio Show table fields

After we have completed our Radio Show table, it will look like this:

```
table 50100 "Radio Show"
{

    fields
    {
        field(1; "No."; Code[20]) { }
        field(2; "Radio Show Type"; Code[10]) { }
        field(3; "Name"; Text[100]) { }
        field(4; "Run Time"; Duration) { }
        field(5; "Host Code"; Code[20]) { }
        field(6; "Host Name"; Text[100]) { }
        field(7; "Average Listeners"; Decimal) { }
        field(8; "Audience Share"; Decimal) { }
        field(9; "Advertising Revenue"; Decimal) { }
        field(10; "Royalty Cost"; Decimal) { }
        field(11; Frequency; Option) { }
        field(12; "PSAs Required"; Boolean) { }
        field(13; "Ads Required"; Boolean) { }
        field(14; "News Required"; Boolean) { }
        field(15; "News Duration"; Duration) { }
        field(16; "Sports Required"; Boolean) { }
        field(17; "Sports Duration"; Duration) { }
        field(18; "Weather Required"; Boolean) { }
        field(19; "Weather Duration"; Duration) { }
        field(20; "Date Filter"; Date) { FieldClass = FlowFilter; }
    }
}
```

Figure 2.14 – Additional fields (ignore the error indicated on the Frequency field, it will be addressed next)

Next, we need to fill the `OptionMembers` property for the `Option` field called `Frequency`. This is done between the curly braces, as shown in the following screenshot:

```
field(10; "Royalty Cost"; Decimal) { }
0 references
field(11; Frequency; Option) { OptionMembers = Hourly,Daily,Weekly,Monthly; }
0 references
field(12; "PSAs Required"; Boolean) { }
```

Figure 2.15 – Filling in the Options values

Next, we want to define the reference table we are going to tie to the `Radio Show Type` field. The table will contain a list of the available `Radio Show` types, such as `Music`, `Talk`, and `Sports`. We will keep this table very simple, with `Code` as the unique key field and `Description` as the text field. Both fields will be of the default length, as shown in the following layout. Create the new table and save it as `RadioShowType.table.al` with the name of `Radio Show Type`:

```
1    table 50101 "Radio Show Type"
2    {
3        fields
4        {
             2 references
5            field(1; Code; Code[20]) { }
             2 references
6            field(2; Description; Text[100]) { }
7        }
8    }
```

Figure 2.16 – The Radio Show Type table with only two fields

Before we can use this table as a reference from the `Radio Station` table, we need to create a list page that will be used for both data entry and data selection for the table. We will use a snippet to create a List page. We should be able to do this pretty quickly. Create a new file in Visual Studio Code called `RadioShowTypes.page.al` and start typing `tp`, then click on **Page of type List**:

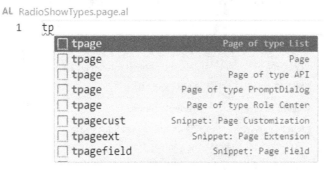

Figure 2.17 – Page snippets

Populate the page properties with both (all) of the fields from the Radio Show Type table. Our designed page should look as follows:

```
1    page 50102 "Radio Show Types"
2    {
3        PageType = List;
4        SourceTable = "Radio Show Type";
5        ApplicationArea = All;
6        UsageCategory = Administration;
7
8        layout
9        {
             0 references
10           area(Content)
11           {
                 0 references
12               repeater(Group)
13               {
                     0 references
14                   field(Code; Rec.Code) { }
                     0 references
15                   field(Description; Rec.Description) { }
16               }
17           }
18       }
19   }
```

Figure 2.18 – The Radio Show Types page

Publish your solution and search for the **Radio Show Types** page. The new page will be displayed. While the page is open, enter some data (by clicking on **New**), as shown in the following screenshot:

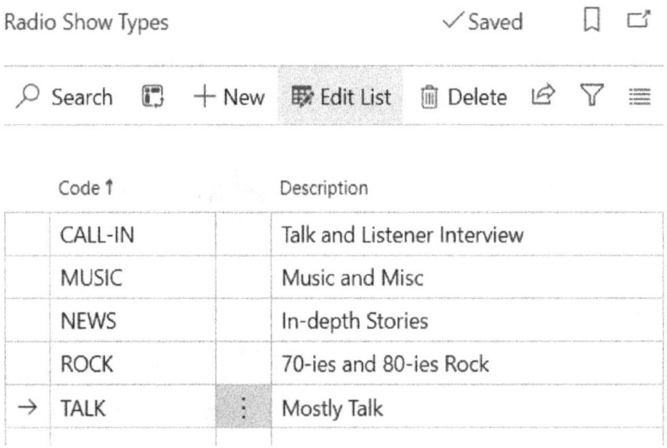

Code ↑	Description
CALL-IN	Talk and Listener Interview
MUSIC	Music and Misc
NEWS	In-depth Stories
ROCK	70-ies and 80-ies Rock
TALK	Mostly Talk

Figure 2.19 – Radio Show Types page in the web client

Now, we'll return to the Radio Show Type table and set the table's properties for LookupPageID and DrillDownPageID to point to the new page we have just created:

```
1    table 50101 "Radio Show Type"
2    {
3        LookupPageId = "Radio Show Types";
4        DrillDownPageId = "Radio Show Types";
5
6        fields
7        {
            2 references
8            field(1; Code; Code[20]) { }
            2 references
9            field(2; Description; Text[100]) { }
10        }
11    }
```

Figure 2.20 – Lookup and DrillDown page properties on the table

Next, we need to relate the Radio Show Type table to our field using a foreign key relationship.

Assigning a table relation property

We will open the Radio Show table again. This time, add the TableRelation property between the curly braces of the Radio Show Type field. Connect it to our new Radio Show Type table:

```
1    table 50100 "Radio Show"
2    {
3
4        fields
5        {
            2 references
6            field(1; "No."; Code[20]) { }
            2 references
7            field(2; "Radio Show Type"; Code[10]) { TableRelation = "Radio Show Type"; }
            2 references
8            field(3; "Name"; Text[100]) { }
```

Figure 2.21 – TableRelation is a foreign key relationship

To check that the TableRelation property is working properly, we can publish and run the **Radio Show List** page again. After clicking on **Edit List**, we should highlight the **Radio Show Type** field and click on the drop-down arrow to view the list of available entries. The following screenshot is of our **Radio Show List** page:

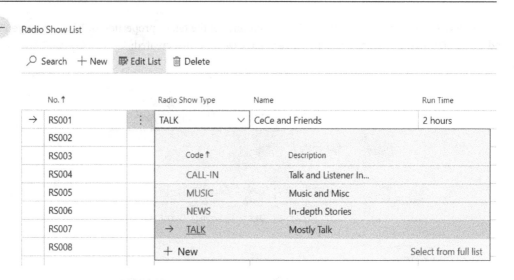

Figure 2.22 – Drilling down to the table relationship

Next, we are going to implement default field values.

Assigning an InitValue property

Another property we can define for several of the `Radio Show` fields is `InitValue`. WDTU has a standard policy that states that news, sports, and weather should be broadcast for a few minutes at the beginning of every hour of the day. We want the `Boolean (true/false)` fields, `News Required`, `Sports Required`, and `Weather Required` to default to `true`.

Setting the default for a field to a specific value simply requires setting the `InitValue` property to the desired value. In the case of the required Boolean fields, that value is set to `true`:

```
0 references
field(14; "News Required"; Boolean) { InitValue = true; }
0 references
field(15; "News Duration"; Duration) { }
0 references
field(16; "Sports Required"; Boolean) { InitValue = true; }
0 references
field(17; "Sports Duration"; Duration) { }
0 references
field(18; "Weather Required"; Boolean) { InitValue = true; }
0 references
field(19; "Weather Duration"; Duration) { }
```

Figure 2.23 – Initialize Boolean field value

Now, let's leave the `Radio Show` table for a while and figure out what tables we want to create next.

Adding a few activity-tracking tables

Our WDTU organization is a profitable and productive radio station. We track historical information about our advertisers, royalties owed, and listenership. We track the music that is played, the rates we charge for advertisements based on the time of day, and we provide a public service by broadcasting a variety of government and other public service announcements.

We aren't going to cover all of these features and functions in the following detailed exercises. However, it's always good to have a complete view of the system that we are working on, even if we are only working on one or two components. In this case, the parts of the system that aren't covered in detail in our exercises will be opportunities for you to extend your studies and practice on your own.

Any system development should start with a design document that completely spells out the goals and the functional design details. Neither system design nor project management will be covered in this book, *but when we begin working on production projects, proper attention to both of these areas will be critical to success.* The use of a proven project management methodology can make a project much more likely to be on time and within budget.

Based on the requirements our analysts have given us, we need to expand our application design. We started with a `Radio Show` table, one reference table (`Radio Show Type`), and pages for each of them. Earlier, we entered some test data and added a few additional fields to the `Radio Show` table (which we will not add to our pages here).

Now, we will add a supplemental table, document (header and line) tables, plus a ledger (activity history) table relating to playlist activities. Following this, we will also create some pages for our new data structures.

Our WDTU application will now include the following tables:

- `Radio Show`: This is a master list of all programs broadcast by our station.
- `Radio Show Type`: This is a reference list of possible types of radio shows.
- `Playlist Header`: This is a single instance of `Radio Show` with child data in the form of playlist lines.
- `Playlist Line`: Each line represents one of a list of items and/or duration per `Radio Show`.
- `Playlist Item Rate`: This is a list of rates for items that are played during a show, as determined by our advertising sales staff or the royalty organization we use.
- `Radio Show Entry`: This is a detailed history of all of the time spent and items played during the show, with any related royalties owed or advertisement revenue expected.
- `Listenership Entry`: This is a detailed history of estimated listenership provided by the ratings organization to which we subscribe.

- Publisher: This is a reference list of the publishers of content that we use. This will include music distributors, news wires, sports, and weather sources, as well as WDTU (we use material that we publish).

Remember, one purpose of this example system is for you to follow along on a hands-on basis in your own system. You may want to try different data structures and other object features. For example, you could add functionality to track volunteer activity, perhaps even detailing the type of support the volunteers provide.

For the best learning experience, you should be creating each of these objects in your development system to learn by experimenting. During these exercises, it will be good if you make some mistakes and see some new error messages. That's part of the learning experience. A test system is the best place to learn from mistakes with the minimum cost.

New tables for our WDTU project

First, we need to create a Playlist Header table (table number 50102), which will contain one record for each scheduled Radio Show:

```
1    table 50102 "Playlist Header"
2    {
3        fields
4        {
             0 references
5            field(1; "No."; Code[20]) { }
             0 references
6            field(2; "Radio Show No."; Code[20]) { }
             0 references
7            field(3; Description; Text[100]) { }
             0 references
8            field(4; "Broadcast Date"; Date) { }
             0 references
9            field(5; Duration; Duration) { }
             0 references
10           field(6; "Start Time"; Time) { }
             0 references
11           field(7; "End Time"; Time) { }
12       }
13   }
```

Figure 2.24 – The Playlist Header table

Then, we will create the associated Playlist Line table (table number 50103). This table will contain child records for the Playlist Header table. Each Playlist Line record represents one scheduled piece of music, advertisement, public service announcement, or embedded show within the scheduled Radio Show that's defined in the Playlist Header table. In the lines, we have two fields that are dropdowns, one of which may need to be extended to include new values as music formats change. We do this by making the DataType of the Data Format as Enum. Enum is a separate object that has a list defined for each dropdown. Enums are extensible (unless they have the property of Extensible = false) at any point in the future allowing for greater flexibility.

First, we will create an enum object called Playlist Data Format using the tenum snippet:

```
1  ∨ enum 50100 "Playlist Data Format"
2    {
3        Extensible = true;
4
5        value(0; "") { }
     0 references
6        value(1; Vinyl) { }
     0 references
7        value(2; CD) { }
     0 references
8        value(3; MP3) { }
     0 references
9        value(4; PSA) { }
     0 references
10        value(5; Advertisement) { }
11   }
```

Figure 2.25 – Playlist Header

This allows us to create the `Playlist Line` table as follows:

```
1    table 50103 "Playlist Line"
2    {
3        fields
4        {
             1 reference
5            field(1; "Document No."; Code[20]) { }
             1 reference
6            field(2; "Line No."; Integer) { }
             0 references
7            field(3; Type; Option) { OptionMembers = ,Resource,Show,Item; }
             0 references
8            field(4; "No."; Code[20]) { }
             0 references
9            field(5; "Data Format"; Enum "Playlist Data Format") { }
             0 references
10           field(6; "Publisher Code"; Code[10]) { }
             0 references
11           field(7; Description; Text[100]) { }
             0 references
12           field(8; Duration; Duration) { }
             0 references
13           field(9; "Start Time"; Time) { }
             0 references
14           field(10; "End Time"; Time) { }
15       }
```

Figure 2.26 – Playlist Line table

Now, we'll create our `Playlist Item Rate` table. These rates include both what we charge for advertising time and what we must pay in royalties for the material we broadcast:

```
1  ∨ table 50104 "Playlist Item Rate"
2    {
3  ∨    fields
4        {
             0 references
5            field(1; "Source Type"; Option) { OptionMembers = Vendor,Customer; }
             0 references
6            field(2; "Source No."; Code[20]) { }
             0 references
             field(3; "Item No."; Code[20]) { }
             0 references
8            field(4; "Start Time"; Time) { }
             0 references
9            field(5; "End Time"; Time) { }
             0 references
10           field(6; "Rate Amount"; Decimal) { }
             0 references
11           field(7; "Publisher Code"; Code[10]) { }
12       }
13   }
```

Figure 2.27 – Playlist Item Rate table

An entry table contains the detailed history of processed activity records. In this case, the data is a detailed history of all of the Playlist Line records for previously broadcast shows:

```
1    table 50105 "Radio Show Entry"
2    {
3        fields
4        {
                0 references
5            field(1; "Entry No."; Integer) { }
                0 references
6            field(2; "Radio Show No."; Code[20]) { }
                0 references
7            field(3; Type; Option) { OptionMembers = ,Resource,Show,Item; }
                0 references
8            field(4; "No."; Code[20]) { }
                0 references
9            field(5; "Data Format"; Enum "Playlist Data Format") { }
                0 references
10           field(6; Description; Text[100]) { }
                0 references
11           field(7; Date; Date) { }
                0 references
12           field(8; Time; Time) { }
                0 references
13           field(9; Duration; Duration) { }
                0 references
14           field(10; "Fee Amount"; Decimal) { }
                0 references
15           field(11; "ACSAP ID"; Integer) { }
                0 references
16           field(12; "Publisher Code"; Code[10]) { }
17       }
18   }
```

Figure 2.28 – The Radio Show Entry table

Now, we'll create the `Listenership Entry` table (50106) to retain data we receive from the listenership rating service:

```
1    table 50106 "Listenership Entry"
2    {
3        fields
4        {
             1 reference
5            field(1; "Entry No."; Integer) { }
             1 reference
6            field(2; "Ratings Source Entry No."; Integer) { }
             1 reference
7            field(3; Date; Date) { }
             1 reference
8            field(4; "Start Time"; Time) { }
             1 reference
9            field(5; "End Time"; Time) { }
             1 reference
10           field(6; "Radio Show No."; Code[20]) { }
             0 references
11           field(7; "Listener Count"; Decimal) { }
             1 reference
12           field(8; "Audience Share"; Decimal) { }
             1 reference
13           field(9; "Age Demographic"; Option)
14           {
15               OptionMembers = ,"0-12","13-18","19-34","35-50","51+";
16           }
17       }
18   }
```

Figure 2.29 – The Listenership Entry table

Finally, we'll add the last new table definition for now, which is our `Publisher` table:

```
1    table 50107 Publisher
2    {
3        fields
4        {
5            field(1; Code; Code[10]) { }
6            field(2; Description; Text[100]) { }
7        }
8    }
```

Figure 2.30 – The Publisher table

Let's now add pages for all the tables that we have just created.

New list pages for our WDTU project

Each of the new tables we have created should be supported with an appropriately named list page. As part of our WDTU project work, we should create the following pages (please refer to the *Creating a list page* section in *Chapter 1* for how to create list pages):

- 50103: Playlist Document List
- 50105: Playlist Item Rates
- 50106: Radio Show Entries
- 50107: Listenership Entries
- 50108: Publishers

Keys, SumIndexFields, and table relations in our examples

So far, we have created basic table definitions and associated pages for the WDTU project. The next step is to flesh out those definitions with additional keys, SIFT field definitions, table relations, and so on. The purpose of this is to make our data easier and faster to access, to take advantage of the special features of Business Central to create data totals, and to facilitate relationships between various data elements.

Secondary keys and SumIndexFields

The Playlist Line table's default PK was Document No.. For the PK to be unique for each record, another field is needed. For a Line table, the additional field is the Line No. field, which is incremented via AL code for each record. So, we'll change the key for table 50003 accordingly:

```
16    keys
17    {
        - reference
18        key(PK; "Document No.", "Line No.")
19        {
20            Clustered = true;
21        }
22    }
```

Figure 2.31 – Compound PK

We know that a lot of reporting will be done based on the historical data to be stored in Radio Show Entry. We also know that we want to do reporting on data by Radio Show and by the type of entry (individual song, specific advertisement, and so on). So, we will add secondary keys for each of those, including a Date field so that we can rapidly filter the data by Date. The financial reporting will need totals of the Fee Amount field, so we'll put that in the SumIndexFields column for our new keys:

```
18        keys
19        {
              - reference
20        |   key(PK; "Entry No.") { Clustered = true; }
              - reference
21        |   key(Reporting; "Radio Show No.", Date) { SumIndexFields = "Fee Amount"; }
              - reference
22        |   key(Reporting2; Type, "No.", Date) { SumIndexFields = "Fee Amount"; }
23        }
```

Figure 2.32 – Additional keys used for reporting

We know that to do the necessary listenership analysis, the Listenership Entry table needs an additional key, combined with SumIndexFields for totaling listener statistics:

```
keys
{
    - reference
    key(PK; "Entry No.") { Clustered = true; }
    - reference
    key(Reporting; "Radio Show No.", Date, "Start Time", "Age Demographic")
    {
        SumIndexFields = "Listener Count", "Audience Share";
    }
}
```

Figure 2.33 – Additional keys used for reporting

To utilize the SumIndexFields column we have just defined, we will need to define corresponding FlowFields in other tables. We will leave that part of the development effort for the next chapter, where we are going to discuss fields, FlowFields, and FlowFilters in detail.

Table relations

For the tables where we defined fields that are intended to refer to data in other tables for lookups and validation, we must define their relationships in the referring tables. Sometimes, these relationships are complicated and are dependent on other values within the record.

In table 50103, Playlist Line, we have the No. field. If the Type field contains Resource, then the No. field should contain Resource No.. If the Type field contains Show, then the No. field should contain Radio Show No.. Finally, if the Type field contains Item, the No. field should contain Item No.. The pseudocode (approximate syntax) for that logic can be written as follows:

```
if Type = 'Resource' then No. := Resource.No. else if Type = 'Show'
then No. := Radio Show.No. else if Type = 'Item' then No. := Item.No.
```

The syntax to put in Visual Studio Code is displayed in the following screenshot:

```
8          field(4; "No."; Code[20])
9          {
10             TableRelation = if (Type = const(Resource)) Resource."No."
11             else
12             if (Type = const(Show)) "Radio Show"."No."
13             else
14             if (Type = const(Item)) Item."No.";
15         }
```

Figure 2.34 – Conditional foreign key using the TableRelation property

Table 50004, Playlist Item Rate, has a similar TableRelation requirement for the Source No. field in that table. In this case, if Source Type = Vendor, then the Source No. field will refer to Vendor No., and if Source Type = Customer, then the Source No. field will refer to Customer No.:

```
6          field(2; "Source No."; Code[20])
7          {
8              TableRelation =
9              if ("Source Type" = const(Vendor)) Vendor."No."
10             else
11             if ("Source Type" = const(Customer)) Customer."No.";
12         }
```

Figure 2.35 – Conditional foreign key using the TableRelation property

Now that we have learned how to enhance table objects in general, let's find out what we can do to enhance Business Central standard tables.

Extending an original Business Central table

One of the big advantages of the Business Central system development environment is the fact that we are allowed to enhance the tables that are part of the original standard product. Many software packages do not provide this flexibility. Nevertheless, with privilege comes responsibility. When we modify a standard Business Central table, we must do so carefully.

Only tables that have a property of Extensible equals to true (the default value) allow for extension. Extending Business Central tables means we can do one or more of the following to existing tables:

- Add or change certain table-level properties
- Modify certain field properties
- Add new fields, and write trigger code for those new fields
- Create new keys

Keys in table extension objects can contain the new fields from the extension or fields from the base table object. A key can contain fields exclusively either from the extension or from the base object, but a single key cannot contain fields from both the extension and base object. Existing keys cannot be extended, nor can you assign a new PK.

In our system, we are going to use the standard Item table – table 27 – to store data about recordings, such as music and advertisements, and PSAs that we have available for broadcast. To do this, we will create a table extension, as described in *Chapter 1, Introduction to Business Central*. One of the new fields will be an Enum field. Another will refer to the Publisher table we created earlier. When the modifications for the Item extension table design are completed, they will look as follows:

```
      0 references
 1 ∨ tableextension 50100 Item extends Item
 2   {
 3 ∨     fields
 4       {
          0 references
 5         field(50100; "Publisher Code"; Code[10]) { TableRelation = Publisher.Code; }
          0 references
 6         field(50101; "ACSAP ID"; Integer) { }
          0 references
 7         field(50102; Duration; Duration) { }
          0 references
 8         field(50103; "Data Format"; Enum "Playlist Data Format") { }
          0 references
 9         field(50104; "MP3 Location"; Text[250]) { }
10       }
11   }
```

Figure 2.36 – Table Extension to add custom fields to a standard Business Central table

To close this chapter, let's focus again on the functional aspects of Business Central, and learn about some functional table types and their representation in the web client.

Functional table types

For this discussion, we will first divide tables into two parent categories, depending on whether they are extensible by code, or not. Let's take a closer look.

Extensible tables

As developers, we can change both the definition and the contents of extensible tables. Those tables reside in the **Base Application**, **Business Foundation** and **System Application** modules of Business Central.

The following table types are included in the extensible tables category, and are part of the Base Application module:

- Master data
- Journal

- Template
- Entry tables
- Subsidiary (supplementary) tables
- Register
- Posted document
- Singleton
- Temporary

Let's look at these in detail.

Master data

The master data table type contains primary data (such as customers, vendors, items, and employees). In any enhancement project, these are the tables that should be designed first because everything else will be based on these tables. When working on a modification, necessary changes to master data tables should be defined first. Master data tables always use card pages as their primary user input method. The **Customer** page is a master data table. A customer record is shown in the following screenshot:

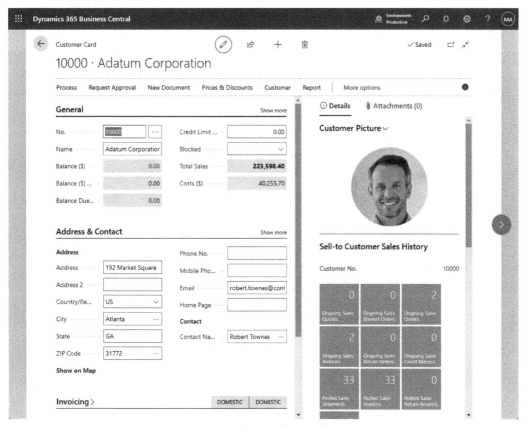

Figure 2.37 – Master data card page

The preceding screenshot shows how the card page segregates the data into categories on different **FastTabs** (such as **General**, **Address & Contact**, and **Invoicing**), and includes primary data fields (for example, **Name** and **Address**) and a FlowField (**Balance (LCY)**).

Journal

The journal table type contains unposted activity details, which are data that other systems refer to as transactions. Journals are where the most repetitive data entry occurs in Business Central. In the standard system, all journal tables are matched with corresponding template tables (one template table for each journal table). The standard system includes journals for **Sales**, **Cash Receipts**, **General Journal** entries, **Physical Inventory**, **Purchases**, **Fixed Assets**, and **Warehouse Activity**, among others.

The transactions in a journal can be segregated into batches for entry, edit review, and processing purposes. Journal tables always use worksheet pages as their primary user input method. The following screenshots show two journal entry screens. They both use the Gen. Journal Line table, but each is slightly different in appearance and is based on different pages and different templates:

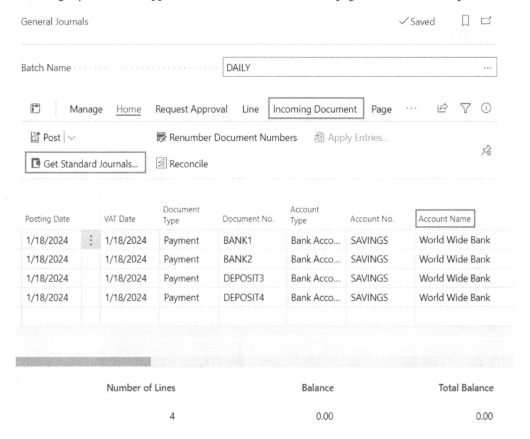

Figure 2.38 – Journal page

By comparing *Figure 2.38* and *Figure 2.39*, we can see the differences highlighted:

Sales Journals | Work Date: 1/22/2026

| Batch Name | DEFAULT | ... |

Manage   Home   Request Approval   Line   Page   More options

Post ∨   Renumber Document Numbers   Reconcile   Apply Entries...

Posting Date	VAT Date	Document Type	Document No.	Account Type	Account No.	Customer Name
1/22/2026	1/22/2026		G01001	G/L Account		

Number of Lines	Balance	Total Balance
0	0.00	0.00

Figure 2.39 – Journal page

Template

The template table type operates behind the scenes, providing control information for a journal, which operates in the foreground. By using a template, multiple instances of a journal can each be tailored for different purposes. Control information that's contained in a template includes the following:

- The default type of accounts to be updated (for example, **Customer**, **Vendor**, **Bank**, and **General Ledger**)
- The specific account numbers to be used as defaults, including balancing accounts
- What transaction numbering series will be used
- The default encoding to be applied to transactions for the journal (for example, **Source Code** and **Reason Code**)
- Specific pages and reports to be used for data entry, processing of both edits, and posting runs

For example, **General Journal Templates** allows the Gen. Journal Line table to be tailored so that it can display fields and perform validations that are specific to the entry of particular transaction categories, such as **Cash Receipts**, **Payments**, **Sales**, and other transaction entry types. Template tables always use tabular pages for user input. The following screenshot shows a listing of the various General Journal Templates that are defined in the Cronus International Ltd. demonstration database:

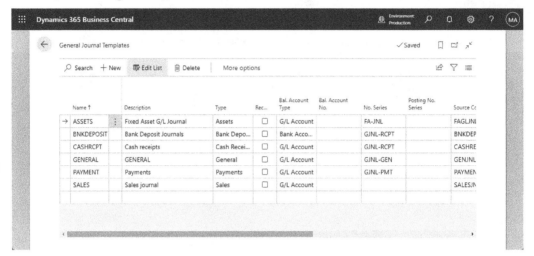

Figure 2.40 – Journal page

In addition to these templates, there are batch tables, which allow us to set up any number of batches of data under each journal template. The batch, template, and journal line structure provide a great deal of flexibility in the data organization and definition of required fields while utilizing a common underlying table definition (**General Journal**).

Entry tables

The entry table type contains posted activity details, which is the data other systems call history. Business Central data flows from a journal table through a posting routine into an entry table. A significant advantage of Business Central entry design is the fact that Business Central allows you to retain all transaction details indefinitely. While there are routines that support the compression of the entry data (when that's feasible), if storage space and processing times allow, we should retain the full historical detail of all activities. This allows users to have total flexibility for historical, comparative, or trend data analysis.

> **Important note**
> Entry data is considered accounting data in Business Central. We are not allowed to directly enter data into an entry or change existing data in an entry; instead, we must post to an entry. Posting is done by creating journal lines, validating the data as necessary, and then posting those journal lines into the appropriate posted entry table. Although we can physically force data into an entry with our developer tools, we shouldn't do so.

When used with accounting, an entry is called a **ledger entry**.

When ledger entry data is accounting data, we are not permitted to delete this data from an entry table. Corrections are done by posting adjustments or reversing entries. We can compress or summarize some entry data (very carefully), which eliminates detail, but we should not change anything that would affect accounting totals for money or quantities. You can always correct accounting information by posting additional correction entries, but never by modifying a ledger entry.

User views of entry data are generally done through the use of list pages. The following screenshots show a **Customer Ledger Entries** list (financially oriented data) and an **Item Ledger Entries** list (quantity oriented data). In each case, the data represents historical activity details with accounting significance. There are other data fields in addition to what is shown in the following screenshots, but the fields that are shown are representative. First, we will look at the **Customer Ledger Entries** list:

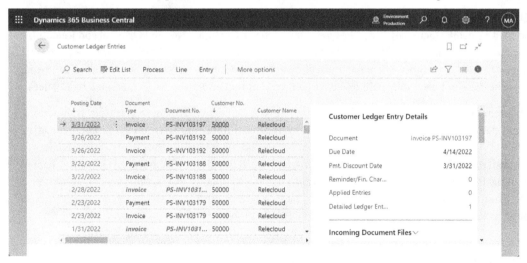

Figure 2.41 – Customer Ledger Entries

Then, we have the **Item Ledger Entries** list:

Posting Date	Entry Type	Document Type	Document No.	Item No.	Description	Department Code	Customergro... Code	Locatio
5/30/2021	Sale	Sales Ship...	S-SHPT102...	1896-S		SALES	LARGE	
5/29/2021	Sale	Sales Ship...	S-SHPT102...	1900-S		SALES	MEDIUM	
5/27/2021	Sale	Sales Ship...	S-SHPT102...	1980-S		SALES	SMALL	
5/27/2021	Sale	Sales Ship...	S-SHPT102...	1968-S		SALES	SMALL	
5/27/2021	Sale	Sales Ship...	S-SHPT102...	1920-S		SALES	SMALL	
5/27/2021	Sale	Sales Ship...	S-SHPT102...	1908-S		SALES	SMALL	
5/27/2021	Sale	Sales Ship...	S-SHPT102...	1928-S	Red Swivel Lamp	SALES	LARGE	
5/26/2021	Sale	Sales Ship...	S-SHPT102...	1906-S		SALES	MEDIUM	

Figure 2.42 – Customer Ledger Entries

The **Customer Ledger Entries** page displays critical information, such as **Posting Date** (the effective accounting date), **Document Type** (the type of transaction), **Customer No.**, and **Original** and **Remaining Amount** of the transaction. The record also contains **Entry No.**, which uniquely identifies each record. The open entries are those where the transaction amount has not been fully applied, such as an invoice amount that's not been fully paid or a payment amount that's not been fully consumed by invoices.

The **Item Ledger Entries** page displays similar information that's pertinent to inventory transactions. As we described previously, **Posting Date**, **Entry Type**, and **Item No.**, as well as the assigned **Location Code** for the item, control the meaning of each transaction. Item Ledger Entries are expressed both in **Quantity** and **Amount (Value)**. The open entries here are tied to the **Remaining Quantity**, such as material that has been received but is still available in stock. In other words, the open entries represent the current inventory. Both the Customer Ledger Entry and Item Ledger Entry tables have underlying tables that provide additional details for entries affecting values.

Users can utilize page-customization tools (which we will discuss in *Chapter 4, Pages – The Interactive Interface*, to create personalized page displays in a wide variety of ways.

Subsidiary (supplementary) tables

The subsidiary (also called **supplementary**) table type contains lists of codes, descriptions, or other validation data. Subsidiary table examples are postal zone codes, country codes, currency codes, currency exchange rates, and so on. Subsidiary tables are often accessed by means of one of the setup menu options because they must be set up prior to being used for reference purposes by other tables. In our WDTU example, the `50101 Radio Show Type` and `50107 Publisher` tables are subsidiary tables.

The following screenshots show some sample subsidiary tables for location, country/region, and payment terms. Each table contains data elements that are appropriate for use as a subsidiary table, as well as, in some cases, fields that control the effect of referencing a particular entry. These data elements are usually entered as part of a setup process and then updated over time as appropriate:

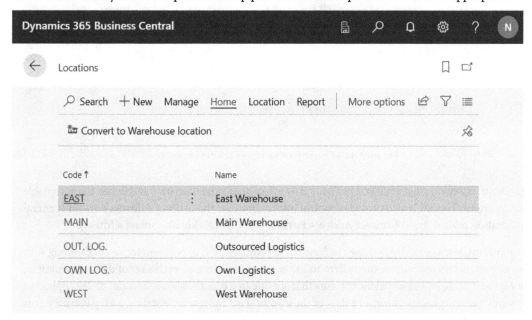

Figure 2.43 – The Locations list page

The **Locations** list page in the preceding screenshot is a simple validation list of the locations for this implementation. Usually, they represent physical sites, but depending on the implementation, they can also be used to segregate types of inventory. For example, locations could be refrigerated versus unrefrigerated, or there could be locations for awaiting inspection, passed inspection, and failed inspection:

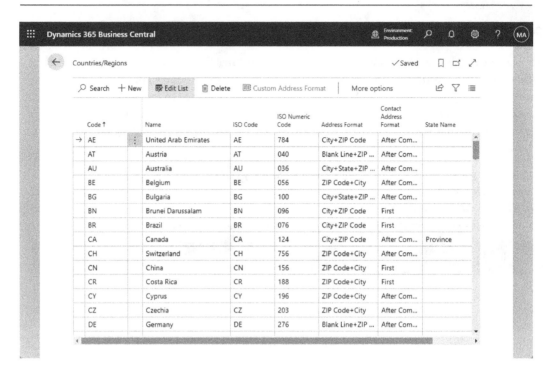

Figure 2.44 – Country table stores address format

The countries/regions that are listed in *Figure 2.44* are used as validation data and define the acceptable country codes. This table also provides control information for the mailing **Address Format** (general organization address) and **Contact Address Format** (for an individual's contact address).

The **Payment Terms** page that's shown in *Figure 2.45* provides a list of payment terms codes, along with a set of parameters that allows the system to calculate specific terms. In this set of data, for example, the 1M(8D) code will yield payment terms that are due in a month, with a discount of 2% applied to payments that are processed within 8 days of the invoice date. In another instance, 14D payment terms will calculate the payment as being due in 14 days from the date of invoice with no discount available:

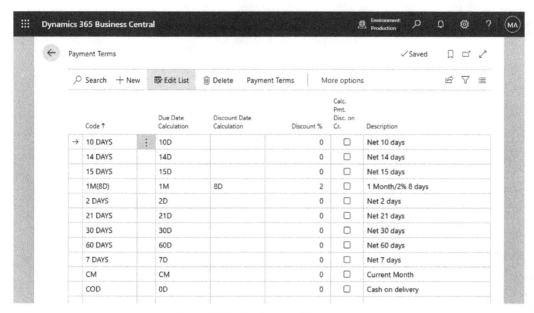

Figure 2.45 – The Payment Terms page

Register

The register table type contains a record of the range of transaction ID numbers for each batch of posted Ledger Entries. Register data provides an audit trail of the physical timing and sequence of postings. This, combined with the full details that are retained in the Ledger Entry, makes Business Central a very auditable system because we can see exactly what activity was done and when it was done:

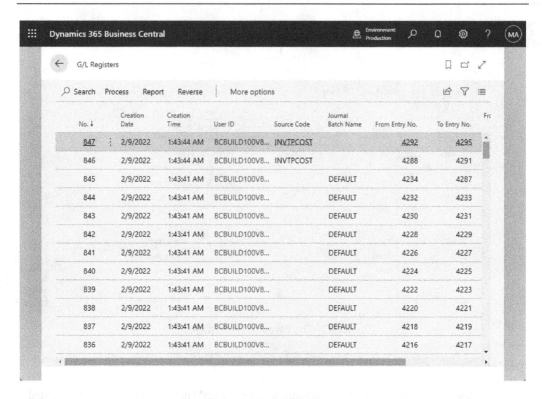

Figure 2.46 – Register page

The user views the register through a tabular page, as shown in the previous screenshot. We can see that each register entry has **Creation Date**, **Source Code**, **Journal Batch Name**, and the identifying entry number range for all of the entries in that batch.

> **Note**
>
> Another Business Central feature, the **Find entries** function, which we will discuss in detail in *Chapter 4*, *Pages – The Interactive Interface*, provides an additional very useful auditing tool.
>
> The **Find entries** function allows the user (who may be a developer doing testing) to highlight a single Ledger Entry and find all of the other ledger entries and related records that resulted from the posting that created that highlighted entry.

Posted document

The posted document type contains the history version of the original documents for a variety of data types, such as **Sales Invoices**, **Purchase Invoices**, **Sales Shipments**, and **Purchase Receipts**. Posted documents are designed to provide an easy reference to the historical data in a format similar to what would have been stored in paper files. A posted document looks very similar to the original source document. For example, **Posted Sales Invoice** will look very similar to the original **Sales Orders** or **Sales Invoices**. The posted documents are included in the **Find entries** function.

The following screenshots show a **Sales Orders** document before posting and the resulting **Posted Sales Invoice** document. Both documents are in a header/detail format, where the information in the header applies to the whole order and the information in the detail is specific to the individual order line. As part of the **Sales Orders** page, there is information being displayed to the right of the actual order, as highlighted in the following screenshot:

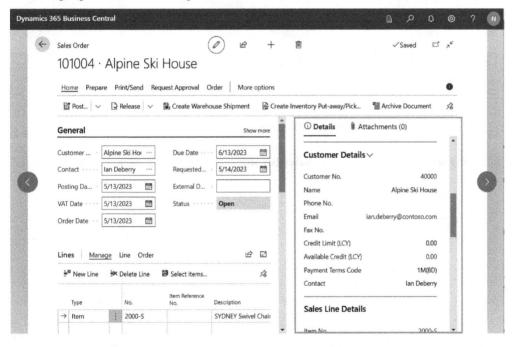

Figure 2.47 – The FactBox area on the Sales Order page

This is designed to make the user's life easier by providing related information without requiring a separate lookup action.

Concentrating next on the **Lines** area on the lower-left part of the page, we can see that the **Sales Orders** document is ready to be posted, as it has all the necessary information, such as the item number, quantity, and total price:

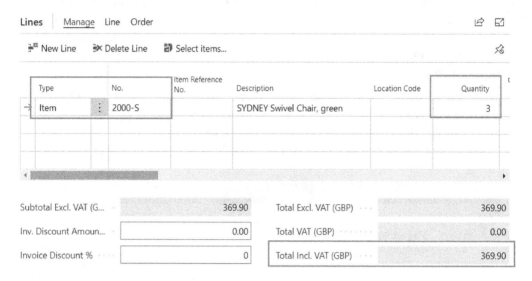

Figure 2.48 – Unposted sales order lines

The following screenshot is that of the **Sales Invoice** lines after the invoice was posted for the shipped goods:

Figure 2.49 – Posted Sales Invoice lines

Setup

The setup table type contains system or functional application control information. There is one setup table per functional application area, for example, one for **Sales & Receivables**, one for **Purchases & Payables**, one for **General Ledger**, and one for **Inventory**. As a setup table contains only a single record, it can have a PK field that has no value assigned to it (this is how all of the standard Business Central setup tables are designed). Ensuring to keep only a single record is also referred to as the **singleton** pattern, hence setup tables can be also referred to as singleton tables.

> **Note**
>
> The singleton table design pattern can be found at `https://alguidelines.dev/docs/navpatterns/patterns/singleton/singleton-table/`. Though the content was originally written for NAV (C/AL), the concept still applies to Business Central.

The **Inventory Setup** page is as follows:

Figure 2.50 – Singletons are setup tables with a single record

Non-extensible tables

As their name suggests, we cannot change the definition of non-extensible tables. Though we can define non-extensible tables ourselves, only those provided by the **System** module of Business Central are referred to as system or virtual tables and are the subject of this section. Their table ID numbers are above 2,000,000,000.

> **Caution**
>
> Do not confuse the System module with the System Application module.

We can inspect all tables (even virtual tables) as part of our downloaded symbols, by opening **AL Explorer** from the Visual Studio Code Command Palette (*F1*) and selecting the **System** module, as indicated in the following screenshot:

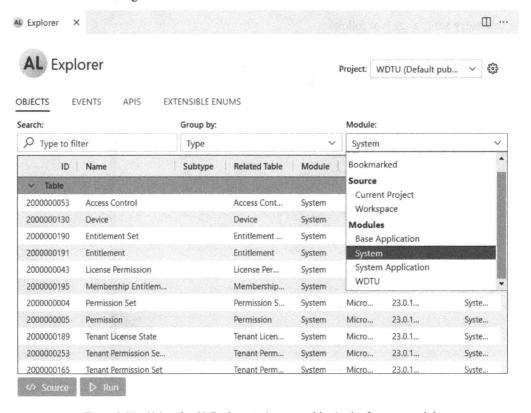

Figure 2.51 – Using the AL Explorer to inspect tables in the System module

Some non-extensible tables still allow the change of data (system tables), while others are read-only (virtual tables). Unfortunately, even with the help of the AL Explorer, we cannot easily determine whether a System module table is read-only, or not. Instead, let's inspect a few examples.

System tables

The system table type contains user-maintainable information that pertains to the management or administration of the Business Central application system. An example of a system table type is the User table, which contains user login information. Other system tables contain data on record links, tenant media sets, API web services, and so on. The following are examples of system tables in which content can be modified. The first three relate to system security functions:

- User: The table of identified users and their security information

- Tenant Permission Set: The table containing a list of all of the permission sets in the database

- Tenant Permission: The table defining what individual permission sets are allowed to do, based on object permission assignments

- Access Control: The table of the security roles that are assigned to each Windows login

The following tables are used to track a variety of system data or control structures:

- Company: The companies in this database. Most Business Central data is automatically segregated by company.

- Web Service: This lists the pages, queries, and code units that have been published as **Simple Object Access Protocol (SOAP)** and **Open Data Protocol (OData)** web services.

- User Personalization: Despite its name, this table does not contain information about user personalization that has occurred. Instead, this table contains the link between the user ID and the profile ID, and the language, company, and debugger controls. (Personalization are changes in page definition by a user such as adding or removing fields, page parts, restructuring menus, resizing columns, and so on. This information can be found in the User Page Metadata table.)

The following tables contain information about various system internals. As developers, we cannot extract human-readable data from these, nor can we change the data without compromising the application. Their detailed description is beyond the scope of this book:

- Send-to Program

- Style Sheet

- User Default Style Sheet

- Record Link

- `Object Metadata`
- `All Profile`
- `User Page Metadata`

Virtual tables

The virtual table type is computed at runtime by the system. A virtual table contains data and is accessed like other tables, but we cannot modify either the definition or the contents of a virtual table. We can think of virtual tables as system data that's presented in the form of a table so that it is readily available to AL code. Some of these tables (such as `Database`, `File`, and `Drive` (on-premise only) tables) provide access to information about the computing environment. Other virtual tables (such as the `Table Information`, `Field`, and `Session` tables) provide information about the internal structure and operating activities of our database. A good way to learn more about any of these tables is to create and run a list page that's bound to the table of interest. We can then view the field data contents of the target virtual table.

Some virtual tables (such as `Date` and `Integer`) provide tools that can be used in our application routines. The `Date` table provides a list of calendar periods (such as days, weeks, months, quarters, and years) to make it much easier to manage various types of accounting and managerial data handling. The `Integer` table provides a list of integers from -1,000,000,000 to 1,000,000,000. As we explore standard Business Central reports, we will frequently see the `Integer` table being used to supply a sequential count to facilitate a reporting sequence (often in a limited numeric range, such as 1 or 1 to 10).

We can only access virtual tables as targets for pages, reports, or variables in AL code. Knowledge of the existence, contents, and usage of these virtual tables isn't useful to an end user. However, as developers, we will regularly use some of these virtual tables. There is educational value in studying the structure and contents of these tables, as well as having the ability to create valuable tools using one or more virtual tables.

Summary

In this chapter, we focused on the foundation level of Business Central data structure: tables and their internal structure. We worked our way through the hands-on creation of a number of tables and their data definitions in support of our WDTU application. We briefly discussed field groups and how they are used. We also discussed how we used pages to view and maintain the data stored in tables. We will discuss pages in more detail in *Chapter 4*.

We identified essential table structure elements, including properties, object numbers, triggers, keys, and `SumIndexFields`. Finally, we reviewed the various categories of tables that can be found in Business Central. Now, you can identify what tables are used in standard functionality, locate what properties and AL procedures are used to accomplish business logic and start to create your own.

In the next chapter, we will dig deeper into the Business Central data structure to understand how fields and their attributes are assembled to make up tables. We will also focus on what can be done with triggers. Then, we will explore how other object types use tables so that we can work toward developing a fully featured Business Central development toolkit.

Questions

1. Which of the following is a correct description of a table in Business Central? Choose two:

    *   A Business Central table is the definition of data structure
    *   A Business Central table includes a built-in data entry page
    *   A Business Central table can contain AL code, but that should be avoided
    *   A Business Central table should implement many of the business rules of a system

    ANSWER: A Business Central table is the definition of data structure, and a Business Central table should implement many of the business rules of a system

2. All PKs should contain only one data field. True or false?

    ANSWER: False

3. System tables cannot be extended. True or false?

    ANSWER: True

4. Which of the following are table triggers? Choose two:

    *   OnInsert
    *   OnChange
    *   OnNewKey
    *   OnRename

    ANSWER: OnInsert and OnRename

5. In a table extension, a single key can contain fields from both the base and extension object. True or false?

    ANSWER: False

6. Because setup tables only contain one record, they do not need to have a PK. True or false?

    ANSWER: False

7. Table numbers that are intended to be used for customized table objects should only range between 5,000 to 9,999. True or false?

ANSWER: False; the correct range is 50,000 to 99,000

8. Only the clustered index (PK) forces a unique key value in records in Business Central. True or false?

    ANSWER: False; secondary keys can be defined as `Unique = true` for that purpose

9. The drop-down display on a field lookup can be changed by modifying the source table's field groups. True or false?

    ANSWER: True

10. Temporary table data can be saved in a special database storage area. True or false?

    ANSWER: False

11. Which of the following virtual tables are commonly used in Business Central development projects? Choose two:

    * `Date`

    * `GPS Location`

    * `Integer`

    * `Object Metadata`

    ANSWER: `Date` and `Integer`

12. `SumIndexFields` can be used to calculate totals. True or false?

    ANSWER: True

13. Table permissions (for access to another table's data) include which of the following permissions? Choose three:

    * Read

    * Sort

    * Delete

    * Modify

    ANSWER: Read, Delete, and Modify

14. The table relation property allows a field in one table to reference data in another table. True or false?

    ANSWER: True

15. Tables can be created or deleted dynamically. True or false?

    ANSWER: False, except with a very advanced technical method

16. Only tables have triggers and only fields have properties. True or false?

    ANSWER: False

17. Ledger Entry data in Business Central can be freely updated through either posting routines or direct data entry. True or false?

    ANSWER: False

18. SQL Server for Business Central supports SIFT by which mechanism? Choose one:

    - SQL SIFT indexes

    - SQL dynamic indexes

    - SQL indexed views

    - SIFT is not supported in SQL

    ANSWER: SQL indexed views

19. Reference tables and virtual tables are simply two different names for the same type of tables. True or false?

    ANSWER: False

3
Data Types and Table Fields

Do little things now; so shall big things come to thee by and by asking to be done.

- Persian Proverb

Design must reflect the partial and aesthetic in business but above all...good design must primarily serve people.

- Thomas J. Watson, Sr.

The design of an application should begin at the simplest level; that is, with the design of the data elements. The type of data our development tool supports has a significant effect on our design. Because Business Central is designed for financially oriented business applications, Business Central data types are financially and business-oriented.

In this chapter, we will cover many of the data types that we will use within Business Central. For each data type, we will cover some of the more frequently modified field properties and how particular properties, such as `FieldClass`, are used to support application functionality. In particular, we will be covering the following topics:

- Basic definitions
- Table fields
- Data types
- `FieldClass` property options
- Filtering

Basic definitions

First, let's review some basic terminology:

- **Data type**: This defines the kind of data that can be held in a field, whether it be numeric (such as integer or decimal), text, a table `RecordID` property, time, date, Boolean, and so forth. The data type defines what constraints can be placed on the contents of a field, determines the procedures in which the data element can be used (not all data types are supported by all procedures), and defines what the results of certain procedures will be.

- **Simple data type**: This is a simple, single-component structure consisting of a single value at any point in time—for example, a number, a string, or a Boolean value.

- **Complex data type**: This is a structure that's made up of or relates to simple data types—for example, records, program objects, such as pages or reports, **Binary Large OBjects** (**BLOBs**), external files, and indirect reference variables, such as the `Media` data type for table fields.

- **Data element**: This is an instance of a data type that may be a constant or a variable.

- **Constant**: This is a data element that's explicitly defined in the code by a literal value. Constants are only modifiable during execution by a developer. All of the simple data types can be represented by constants. Examples include `MAIN` (code or text), `12.34` (decimal), and `+01-312-444-5555` (text).

- **Variable**: This is a data element that can have a value assigned to it dynamically during execution. Except for special cases, a variable will be of a single, unchanging, specific data type.

- **System field**: With all records in Business Central, the following fields are automatically added by the application: `SystemId`, `SystemCreatedAt/By`, `SystemModifiedAt/By`, and `SystemRowVersion`. These fields are immutable and store references that will not break.

Table fields

A field is the basic element of data definition in Business Central—the atom in the structure of a system. It consists of an elemental definition and a set of properties and the **application language** (**AL**) code contained in its triggers. Let us explore the following aspects of a table field:

- Field definition
- Field properties
- Field triggers
- Field events
- Data structure examples
- Field numbering
- Field and variable naming

Field definition

The elemental definition of a field consists of the `field` keyword, its `Number` value, its `Name` value, and its data `Type` value:

```
field(Number; Name; Type) { <properties> }
```

Within each declaring table (including all its extensions), each `Number` and `Name` value must be unique.

The AL language references fields by their `Name` value. A name can consist of up to 30 characters and should be defined in the English language. The name can be changed by a developer at any time by clicking on it and then running the **Rename Symbol** (*F2*) Visual Studio Code command, and Visual Studio Code will automatically ripple that change throughout the application.

The `Type` value defines what type of data format applies to this field (for example, `Integer`, `Date`, `Code`, `Text`, `Decimal`, `Option`, `Enum`, and `Boolean`).

Field numbering

We can easily change a field number when we are initially defining a table layout, but after other objects, such as `pages`, `reports`, or `codeunit` objects, reference the fields in a table, it becomes difficult to change the number of referenced fields. Deleting a field and reusing its field number for a different purpose is not a good idea and can easily lead to programming confusion and processing errors.

> **Note**
>
> We cannot safely change the definition of, re-number, or delete a field that has data present in the database. The same can be said for reducing the defined size of a field to less than the largest size of the data that's already present in that field. However, if we force the change, that will override the system's built-in safeguards. This action can truncate or delete data.

When we add new fields to standard Business Central product tables (those shipped with the product) by using table extensions, the new field numbers must be in the 50,000 to 99,999 number range unless we have been explicitly licensed for another number range that is defined in the `app.json` file. Field numbers for fields in new tables that we create may be anything from 1 to 1,999,999,999. Field numbers 2,000,000,000 and above are reserved for system fields.

When a field representing the same data element appears in related tables (for example, `Table 37 Sales Line` and `Table 113 Sales Invoice Line`), the same field number should be assigned to that data element for each of the tables. Not only is this consistent approach easier for reference and maintenance, but it also supports the `TransferFields` method. The `TransferFields` method permits the copying of data from one table's record instance to another table's record instance by doing record-to-record mapping based on the field numbers.

Field and variable naming

In general, the rules for naming fields (data elements in a table) and variables (data elements within the working storage of an object) are the same, and we will discuss them on that basis. Information on this can be found in the released *Best Practices for AL* at `https://learn.microsoft.com/en-us/dynamics365/business-central/dev-itpro/compliance/apptest-bestpracticesforalcode`.

Variables in Business Central can either be protected (accessible from extension objects), global (with a scope across the breadth of an object), or local (with a scope only within a single procedure). Variable names should be unique within the sphere of their scope. Per object, we should avoid using the same variable name in protected/global and local scopes at one time.

Uniqueness includes not duplicating reserved words or system variables. For example, we shouldn't use the words `Page` or `Boolean` as variable names. A much better naming would be `ItemCard` or `IsEditable`. Variable names in Business Central are not case-sensitive. There is a 120-character length limit on variable names (but still a 30-character length limit on field names in tables). Variable names can contain all ASCII characters, except for control characters (ASCII values 0 to 31 and 255) and the double quote (ASCII value 34), as well as some Unicode characters that are used in languages other than English. Characters outside the standard ASCII set (0-127) may display differently on different systems.

> **Note**
>
> The compiler won't tell us that an asterisk (`*`, ASCII value 42) cannot be used in a variable name. However, because both the asterisk and the question mark (`?`, ASCII value 63) can be used as wildcards in many expressions, especially filtering, neither one should be used in a variable name.

The first character of a variable name must be a letter from *A* to *Z* (upper- or lowercase) or an underscore (`_`, ASCII value 95); that is, unless the variable name is enclosed in double quotes when it is referenced in code (and such names should be avoided except for table field names). If we use any characters other than the *A-Z* alphabet, numerals, and underscore, we must surround our variable name with double quotes each time we use it in AL code (for example, `Cust List`, which contains an embedded space, or `No.`, which contains a period, both require double quotes).

Typically, variable names consisting of more than one word are written in `PascalCase`, whereas field names are written in `"Double Quotes"`.

Field properties

The specific properties that can be defined for a field depend on the data type. There is a minimum set of universal properties, which we will review first. Then, we will review the rest of the more frequently used properties, some of which are data-dependent and some not. Check out the remaining properties by using *Microsoft Docs* at `https://learn.microsoft.com/en-us/dynamics365/` `business-central/dev-itpro/developer/properties/devenv-table-properties`.

We can access the properties of a field while clicking inside the curly braces right next to the field definition and pressing *Ctrl* + spacebar, which is the **IntelliSense** shortcut. All of the property screenshots in this section were obtained in this way for fields within the `Radio Show` table. As we review various field properties, you will learn more if you follow along in your Business Central system using Visual Studio Code. Explore different properties and the values they can have. Use *Microsoft Docs* liberally for additional information and examples.

> **Note**
>
> When a property value is not explicitly set, the default value is used. It is considered a best practice to not set a property if the default value applies.

All of the fields, of any data type, have the following properties:

- `Caption` or `CaptionML`: This contains the defined caption for different languages, including English. If no `Caption` value has been defined, the field name is used as the default caption when data from this field is displayed. Whereas we should not change field names once our application has been deployed outside our development environment, we can easily adjust captions as often as needed. Refer to *Chapter 7's Multi-language system* section for more details.

- `Description`: This is an optional-use property for our internal documentation.

- `Enabled`: This determines whether you can store data in the field. The property defaults to `true` and is rarely changed.

- `AccessByPermission`: This determines the permission mask that's required for a user to access this field in pages or in the **user interface** (**UI**).

The following screenshot shows the properties for a field of the `Blob` data type:

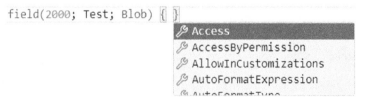

Figure 3.1 – Blob data type properties

The set of properties shown for a `Blob` data type field is the simplest set of field properties. After the properties that are shared by all of the data types are given, the `Blob`-specific properties are shown; that is, `Subtype` and `Compressed`:

- `Subtype`: This defines the type of data stored in `Blob` and sets a filter in the import/export function for the field. The four subtype choices are `Bitmap` (for bitmap graphics), `Json` (for Json data), `Memo` (for text data), and `UserDefined` (for anything else). The `UserDefined` property is the default value.

- `Compressed`: This defines whether the data stored in `Blob` is stored in a compressed format. If we want to access `Blob` data with an external tool (from outside Business Central), this property must be set to `false`.

The properties of `Code` and `Text` data type fields are quite similar to one another. This is logical since both represent types of textual data. Some of the available properties are shown in the following screenshot:

```
field(2000; Test; Code[30])
{
    InitValue = '';
    CaptionClass = '1,1';
    Editable = true;
    NotBlank = true;
    Numeric = true;
    CharAllowed = '';
    DateFormula = false;
    ValuesAllowed = '';
    SqlDataType = Varchar;
    TableRelation = Customer;
    ExtendedDatatype = Masked;
}
```

Figure 3.2 – Text and Code data type properties

The following are some common properties between the `Code` and `Text` data types:

- `InitValue`: This is the value that the system will supply as a default when the field is initialized.

- `CaptionClass`: This can be set up by the developer to dynamically change the field caption. The `CaptionClass` property defaults to `empty`. This is used in base Business Central in dimensions fields.

- `Editable`: This is set to `false` when we don't want to allow a field to be edited—for example, if it is a computed or assigned value field that the user should not change. The `Editable` property defaults to `true`.

- `NotBlank`, `Numeric`, `CharAllowed`, `DateFormula`, and `ValuesAllowed`: Each of these allows us to place constraints on the data that can be entered into this field by a user. They do not affect data updates that are driven by application AL code.

- `SqlDataType`: This applies to `Code` fields only. The `SqlDataType` property defines what data type will be allowed in this particular `Code` field and how it will be mapped to a SQL Server data type. This controls sorting and display. Options include `Varchar`, `Integer`, `BigInteger`, or `Variant`. The `Varchar` option is the default and causes all of the data to be treated as text. The `Integer` and `BigInteger` options allow only numeric data to be entered. The `Variant` option can contain any of a wide range of Business Central data types. In general, once set, this property should not be changed. These settings should not affect data handling that's done in SQL Server external to Business Central, but the conservative approach is not to make changes here.

- `TableRelation`: This is used to specify a relationship to data in the specified target table. The target table field must be in the primary key. The relationship can be conditional and/or filtered. The relationship can be used for validation, lookups, and data-change propagation.

- `ValidateTableRelation`: If `TableRelation` is specified, this property is set to `true` by default to validate the relation when data is entered or changed (in other words, confirm that the entered data exists in the target table). If `TableRelation` is defined and this property is set to `false`, the automatic table referential integrity will not be maintained.

> **Caution**
> Application code can be written that will bypass this validation.

- `ExtendedDatatype`: This property allows for the optional designation of an extended data type, which automatically receives special formatting and validation. Type options include an email address, URL, phone number, masked entry (as dots), **rich text** style, or **barcode** entry points for phone and tablet clients. For phone numbers, email addresses, and URLs, a link is displayed whenever the page is not editable, as shown in the following screenshot:

Figure 3.3 – A phone number linked by the ExtendedDatatype property

Let's take a look at the properties of two more data types, `Decimal` and `Integer`, especially those properties related to numeric content:

- `DecimalPlaces`: This sets the minimum and maximum number of decimal places (`min:max`) for storage and for display in a `Decimal` data item. The default is 2 <2:2>, the minimum is 0, and the maximum is 18.

- `BlankNumbers` and `BlankZero`: These can be used to control the formatting and display of the data field on a page. The `BlankNumbers` and `BlankZero` properties mean that all fields of the chosen values are to be displayed as blank.

- `MinValue` and `MaxValue`: When set, these constrain the range of data values that are allowed for user entry. The range that's available depends on the field data type.

- `AutoIncrement`: This allows for the definition of one `Integer` or `BigInteger` field in a table to automatically increment for each record that's entered. When this is used, which is not often, it is almost always to support the automatic updating of a field that's used as the last field in a primary key, hence enabling the creation of a unique key. The use of this feature does not ensure a contiguous number sequence, and it is not supported within temporary tables. When the property is set to `true`, the automatic functionality should not be overridden in code:

```
field(2000; Test; Decimal)
{
    DecimalPlaces = 0;
    BlankNumbers = DontBlank;
    BlankZero = true;
    MinValue = 0;
    MaxValue = 10;
    AutoIncrement = true;
}
```

Figure 3.4 – Decimal data type properties

The properties of an `Option` data type are similar to those of other numeric data types. This is reasonable because `Option` is stored as an integer, starting with position 0, 1, 2, and so on, but there are also `Option`-specific properties:

- `OptionMembers`: This details the names for each of the stored integer values contained in an `Option` field. The value names are separated by a comma, whereas the first value is internally translated as 0, the second as 1, and so on.

- `OptionCaption` or `OptionCaptionML`: These serve the same captioning and multi-language purposes as caption properties for other data types.

The OptionMembers and OptionCaption properties are shown in the following screenshot:

```
field(2000; Test; Option)
{
    OptionMembers = Hourly,Daily,Weekly,Monthly;
    OptionCaption = 'Hourly,Daily,Weekly,Monthly';
}
```

Figure 3.5 – Option data type properties

Other than Option fields, fields of the Enum data type do not have any specialized properties, hence just as for Option fields, all numeric field properties can be used. Worth mentioning in this context is the ValuesAllowed field property, which allows us to present only a subset of available Option or Enum values to the user. We will elaborate more on Option and Enum data types later in this chapter, in the *Numeric data* section.

After having elaborated on field properties, it's time to take a closer look at field triggers.

Field triggers

To view field triggers, let's look at our 50100 "Radio Show" table. Add the following triggers to the No. field within the curly braces:

```
1    table 50100 "Radio Show"
2    {
3
4        fields
5        {
             6 references
6            field(1; "No."; Code[20])
7            {
                 0 references
8                trigger OnValidate()
9                begin
10
11               end;
12
                 0 references
13               trigger OnLookup()
14               begin
15
16               end;
17           }
```

Figure 3.6 – Field-level triggers

Each field has two triggers, the `OnValidate()` trigger and the `OnLookup()` trigger, which function as follows:

- `OnValidate()`: The AL code in this trigger is executed whenever an entry is made by the user. The intended use is to validate that the entry conforms to the design parameters for the field. It can also be executed under program control through the use of the `Validate` method (which we will discuss later).

- `OnLookup()`: Lookup behavior can be triggered by clicking on the dropdown in a field, as shown in the following screenshot:

Figure 3.7 – Field dropdown to related data

- If the field's `TableRelation` property refers to a table, then the default behavior is to display a drop-down list to allow for the selection of a table entry to be stored in this field. The list will be based on the `DropDown` field group that has been defined for the table. We may choose to override that behavior by coding different behavior for a special case. *We must be careful, because any entry whatsoever in the body of an* `OnLookup()` *trigger, even a comment line, will eliminate the default behavior of this trigger.*

Field events

Subscribing to field events is required to make modifications to objects that are shipped by Microsoft, as we cannot place code directly in their fields. For each field, we can subscribe to the `OnBeforeValidate` event and the `OnAfterValidate` event. These events are triggered, as their name suggests, before and after the code we place in the `OnValidate` trigger.

> **Note**
>
> More information about events in Dynamics Business Central can be found in *Microsoft Docs* at https://learn.microsoft.com/en-us/dynamics365/business-central/ dev-itpro/developer/devenv-events-in-al.

Data structure examples

As of today, in order to let us inspect Business Central standard objects, Microsoft has not yet published its Base Application module to a public repository. However, we can inspect the downloaded symbols in our repository, either by temporarily declaring the object to inspect as a variable and then calling **Go to Definition** in the Visual Studio Code context menu or by using the **AL Explorer** opened from the Visual Studio Code Command Palette (*F1*).

Within the AL Explorer, we can search for any object either by its number or by its name. The following screenshot demonstrates a search by object number:

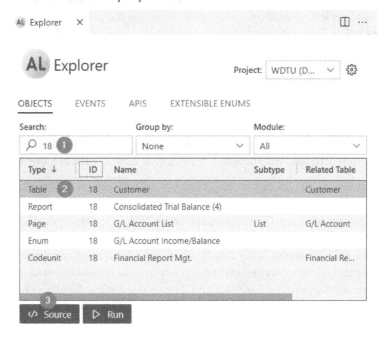

Figure 3.8 – Using the AL Explorer to inspect table number 18

Some good examples of tables in the standard product to review for particular features are as follows:

- `Table 18 Customer` has a variety of data types and field classes. This table contains some fairly complex examples of AL code in the `trigger` sections. A wide variety of field property variations can be seen in this table as well.

- `Table 14 Location` and `Table 91 User Setup` both have good examples of `OnValidate` trigger AL code, as do all of the primary master tables (`Customer`, `Vendor`, `Item`, `Job`, and so on).

Let's close the table fields topic for now, in favor of exploring data types.

Data types

In this section, we are going to segregate data types into several groups. First, we will look at simple data types and then complex data types.

> **Note**
>
> The data types to be introduced in the next sections are just a selection for us as a starting point. In order to review all available data types, especially the complex ones, refer to the *Microsoft Docs* article *Data Types and Methods in AL* at `https://learn.microsoft.com/en-us/dynamics365/business-central/dev-itpro/developer/methods-auto/library`.

Simple data types

Simple data types are the basic components from which complex data types are formed. They are grouped into numeric, string, and date/time data types. Let us explore each in more detail.

Numeric data

Just as with other systems, Business Central supports several numeric data types. The specifications for each Business Central data type are defined for Business Central, independent of the supporting SQL Server database rules. However, some data types are stored and handled somewhat differently from a SQL Server point of view than the way they appear to us as Business Central developers and users. Our discussion will focus on the Business Central representation and handling of each data type.

The various numeric data types are as follows:

- `Integer`: This is an integer number ranging from -2,147,483,647 to +2,147,483,647.

- `Decimal`: This is a decimal number in the range of +/-999,999,999,999,999.99. Although it is possible to construct larger numbers, errors such as overflow, truncation, or loss of precision might occur. In addition, there is no facility to display or edit larger numbers.

- `Option/Enum`: This is a special instance of an integer, stored as an integer number ranging from 0 to +2,147,483,647. An `Option` or Enum data type is normally represented in the body of our AL code as an option string or as an `Enum` object, respectively. We will inspect both types separately at the end of this listing. Though their declaration is different, the way we use them in AL code is identical, as we will see later in *Chapter 6*, in the *Operators* section.

- `Boolean`: A `Boolean` variable is stored as `1` or `0`, which in AL code is programmatically referred to as `true` or `false`. Variables of type `Boolean` may be displayed as `Yes` or `No` (language dependent) or as a toggle control in the web client.

- `BigInteger`: This is an 8-byte integer as opposed to a 4-byte integer. Variables of type `BigInteger` are for very big numbers (from -9,223,372,036,854,775,807 to +9,223,372,036,854,775,807).

- Char: This is a numeric code between 0 and 65,535 (hexadecimal FFFF) representing a single 16-bit Unicode character. Variables of type Char can operate either as text or as numbers. Numeric operations can be done on Char variables. Variables of type Char variables can also be defined with individual text character values. Variables of type Char cannot be defined as permanent variables in a table, only as working storage variables within AL objects.

- Byte: A single 8-bit ASCII character with a value of 0 to 255. Byte variables can operate either as text or as numbers. Numeric operations can be done on Byte variables. Variables of type Byte can also be defined with individual text character values. Variables of type Byte cannot be defined as permanent variables in a table, only as working storage variables within AL objects.

- Action: This is a variable that's returned from a page RunModal method that specifies what action a user performs on a page. Possible values are OK, Cancel, LookupOK, LookupCancel, Yes, No, RunObject, and RunSystem.

- ExecutionMode: This specifies the mode in which a session is running. Possible values are Debug and Standard.

Option

We can compare an Option data type to an integer in AL rather than using the option string, but that's not good practice because it eliminates the self-documenting aspect of an option field. The option string is declared by using the OptionMembers property, and it is a set of choices listed in a comma-separated string, one of which is chosen and stored as the current option. The currently selected choice within the set of options is stored in the option field as the ordinal position of that option within the set. For example, the selection of an entry from the option string of red, yellow, and blue would result in the storing of 0 (red), 1 (yellow), and 2 (blue). If red were selected, 0 would be stored in the variable, and if blue were selected, 2 would be stored.

Quite often, an option string starts with a blank to allow an effective choice if none has been chosen. An example of this (blank, Hourly, Daily, Weekly, Monthly) is as follows:

```
field(2000; Test; Option)
{
    OptionMembers = " ",Hourly,Daily,Weekly,Monthly;
    OptionCaption = ' ,Hourly,Daily,Weekly,Monthly';
}
```

Because options are not extensible or reusable, they are rarely used. However, we still find them often in unchanged Business Central Base Application code. Both will be shown in the book's examples, with options being used more for brevity than extensibility.

Enum

Just as for `Option` values, `Enum` values are stored as integers but are translated within the UI and AL code into a human-readable format. Designed for extensibility and flexibility, their declaration differs a lot from the one for options.

To demonstrate the difference, let's build the same example as at the end of the preceding *Option* section. As a first step, we declare an `Enum` object with the values blank, `Hourly`, `Daily`, `Weekly`, `Monthly`, representing the integers 0 to 4, and each with a caption:

```
enum 50100 TestEnum
{
    value(0; " ") { Caption = ' '; }
    value(1; Hourly) { Caption = 'Hourly'; }
    value(2; Daily) { Caption = 'Daily'; }
    value(3; Weekly) { Caption = 'Weekly'; }
    value(4; Monthly) { Caption = 'Monthly'; }
}
```

Note that the Enum object would allow us to freely choose other positive integer values, and also switching of value lines is allowed. Their order determines the order in which they will be represented to the users when they activate a value dropdown.

Enums are not extensible by default, but we can declare them individually as such, by setting the `Extensible` property to `true`.

Using the `TestEnum` enum as the data type for our new `Test` field would look like this:

```
field(2000; Test; Enum TestEnum)
{
}
```

> **Note the difference**
>
> Whereas `Option` members need to be defined for each field and updated throughout if changed, every field referencing an Enum member automatically inherits its updated Enum values.

Let's now close the topic of numeric data types and continue with string data instead.

String data

The following are data types that are included in string data:

- `Text`: This contains any string of alphanumeric characters. In a table, a `Text` field can be from 1 to 2,048 characters long. In working storage within an object, a `Text` variable can be any length if there is no maximum length defined. When calculating the length of a record for design purposes (relative to the maximum record length of 8,060 bytes), the fully defined field length should be counted.

- `Code`: All of the letters are automatically converted into uppercase when data is entered into a `Code` variable; any leading or trailing spaces are removed.

- `TextBuilder`: Allows for easy string manipulation, such as `Append`, `Replace`, and `Length`. Using `TextBuilder` instead of `Text` can boost performance when concatenating many strings together in a loop.

> **Note**
>
> You can find more details on the `TextBuilder` class at *Microsoft Docs*: https://learn.microsoft.com/en-us/dynamics365/business-central/dev-itpro/developer/methods-auto/textbuilder/textbuilder-data-type

Date/time data

Date/time data display is region-specific; in other words, the data is displayed according to local standards for date and time display. The following are data types that are included in date/time data:

- `Date`
- `Time`
- `DateTime`
- `Duration`

Let's take a closer look.

Date

Variables of type `Date` contain an integer number, which is interpreted as a date ranging from January 1, 1754 to December 31, 9999. A `0D` (numeral zero, letter D) instance in AL code represents an undefined date (stored as a SQL Server `DATETIME` field), which is interpreted as January 1, 1753. A **date constant** can be written as the letter D, preceded by eight digits as *YYYYMMDD* (where *Y* is for year, *M* for month, and *D* for day). For example, `20240119D` represents January 19, 2024. Later, in `DateFormula`, we will find D interpreted as day, but here, the trailing D is interpreted as the date (data type) constant. Business Central also defines a special date called a **closing date**, which represents the point in time between one day and the next. The purpose of a closing date is to provide a point at the end of a day after all real date- and time-sensitive activity is recorded; that is, the point when accounting closing entries can be recorded.

Closing entries are recorded, in effect, at the stroke of midnight between two dates—this is the date of closing of accounting books and has been designed like this so that you can include or not include, at the user's choosing, closing entries in various reports. When sorted by date, the closing date entries will get sorted after all of the normal entries for a day. For example, the normal date entry for December 31, 2024 would display as **12/31/24** (depending on the date format masking), and the closing date entry would display as **C12/31/24**. All of the **C12/31/24** ledger entries would appear after all normal **12/31/24** ledger entries.

The following screenshot shows three 2022 closing date entries mixed with normal entries from January 1, 2023. The 2022 closing entries have an **Opening Entry** description showing that these were the first entries for the data in the respective accounts. This is not a normal set of production data:

Posting Date ↑	Document Type	Document No.	G/L Account No. ↑	Description
C12/31/2022		START	2910	Opening Entry
C12/31/2022		START	2920	Opening Entry
C12/31/2022		START	2930	Opening Entry
1/1/2023	Invoice	108018	1220	Order 10618
1/1/2023	Payment	10817	1220	Order 106015
1/1/2023		2023-1	1220	Entries, January 2023

Figure 3.9 – Closing dates

Time

Variables of type Time contain an integer number, which is interpreted on a 24-hour clock, in milliseconds plus 1, from 00:00:00 to 23:59:59:999. A 0T (numeral zero, letter T) instance in AL code represents an undefined time and is stored as 1/1/1753 00:00:00.000.

DateTime

Variables of type DateTime represent a combined date and time, stored in **Coordinated Universal Time (UTC)**, and always display local time (that is, the local time on our system). Fields of type DateTime do not support Business Central closing dates. A DateTime field is helpful for an application that needs to support multiple time zones simultaneously.

Values of type DateTime can range from January 1, 1754 00:00:00.000 to December 31, 9999 23:59:59.999, but dates earlier than January 1, 1754 cannot be entered (don't test with dates late in 9999 as an intended advance to the year 10000 won't work). Assigning a date of 0DT yields an undefined or blank DateTime value.

Duration

A variable of type `Duration` represents the positive or negative difference between two `DateTime` values, in milliseconds, stored as `BigInteger`. Durations are automatically output in the following text format: *DDD days HH hours MM minutes SS seconds.*

Now that we've got to know the fundamental data types, let's review the complex ones.

Complex data types

Each complex data type consists of multiple data elements. For ease of reference, we will categorize them into several groups of similar types.

Records

A `Record` type refers to a single data row within a Business Central table that consists of individual fields. Quite often, multiple variable instances of a record (table) are defined in working storage to support a validation process, allowing access to different records within the table at one time in the same procedure.

Objects

Variables of type `Page`, `Report`, `Codeunit`, `Query`, `Enum`, and `XMLport` each represent an object data type. Object data types are used when there is a need for a reference to an object or a procedure in another object. Tables are referenced as `Record`. Some examples of object reference are as follows:

- Invoking a report or an `XMLport` property from a page
- Calling a trigger for data validation or processing is coded as a procedure in a table or a `Codeunit` property

Lists

Think of a `List` variable as a single dimension, a single simple data type, or an unbounded array.

Variables of type `List` are strongly typed groups of ordered data that can accessed by an index beginning with 1. Unlike the `array` data type, the `List` type is unbounded and does not need to have a limited dimension value predefined.

Variables of type `List` must be made of simple data types, meaning you can only have a list of `Integer`, `Decimal`, `Boolean`, `Text`, `Date`, `DateTime`, `Time`, `Char`, and `DateFormula`, but not `Blob`, `Record`, `Page`, `Codeunit`, `Report`, nor `Variant`.

`List` variables are more efficient than `array` or temporary `Record` variables and exist as a performance enhancement for Business Central developers.

Dictionaries

In Business Central, a `Dictionary` variable is an unordered collection of keys and values, optimized for fast lookup of values. The main performance benefit of `Dictionary` variables is the replacement of reliance on temporary tables. While you can only have simple data types as elements in a `Dictionary` variable, you can mix your data types and even include embedded `Dictionary` variables as elements to create complex data structures:

```
var
    DictionaryOne: Dictionary of [Integer, Text];
    DictionaryTwo: Dictionary of [Code[20], Decimal];
    DictionaryThree: Dictionary of [Guid, DateTime];
```

Figure 3.10 – Examples of Dictionary variables

An example of how you can utilize this data type in replacing temporary records would be to create a `Dictionary` variable inside another `Dictionary` variable. If we wanted to create a simple list of customers' addresses and manipulate them in code without repeated database access, we could retrieve the values from the record and put them in a set of `Dictionary` variables. The first `Dictionary` variable has a key of `Integer` and a value of `Text` to store address information. The second (larger) `Dictionary` variable has a key of type `Code` for the customer number, and the value will be the `Dictionary` address:

```
0 references
local procedure FillCustomerDictionary()
var
    Cust: Record Customer;
    DictionaryAddress: Dictionary of [Integer, Text];
    DictionaryCustomer: Dictionary of [Code[20], Dictionary of [Integer, Text]];
begin
    //Fill Dictionary
    if Cust.FindSet() then
        repeat
            DictionaryAddress.Add(1, Cust.Name);
            DictionaryAddress.Add(2, Cust.Address);
            DictionaryAddress.Add(3, Cust.City);
            DictionaryAddress.Add(4, Cust."Post Code");
            DictionaryAddress.Add(5, Cust."Country/Region Code");

            DictionaryCustomer.Add(Cust."No.", DictionaryAddress);
            Clear(DictionaryAddress);
        until Cust.Next() = 0;
end;
```

Figure 3.11 – Populating a dictionary with customer address information

The data will look something like this:

DictionaryCustomer	DictionaryAddress	
01121212	1	Spotsmeyer's Furnishings
	2	612 South Sunset Drive
	3	Miami
	4	37125
	5	US
	DictionaryAddress	
01445544	1	Progressive Home Furnishings
	2	3000 Roosevelt Blvd.
	3	Chicago
	4	61236
	5	US

Figure 3.12 – Data structure with embedded dictionary

Web services

To work with web services, Business Central supports a set of HTTP, XML, and JSON variables. Documentation on these types can be found at *Microsoft Docs*: `https://learn.microsoft. com/en-us/dynamics365/business-central/dev-itpro/developer/devenv- restapi-overview`.

Input/output

The following are input/output data types:

- `Dialog`: This supports the definition of a simple UI window without the use of a page object. Typically, `Dialog` windows are used to communicate processing progress or to allow a brief user response to a go/no-go question, although the latter could result in bad performance due to locking. There are other user communication tools as well, but they do not use a `Dialog`-type data item.

- `InStream` and `OutStream`: These allow you to read from and write to files and BLOBs.

DateFormula

The `DateFormula` type provides the definition and storage of a simple, but clever, set of constructs to support the calculation of runtime-sensitive dates. The `DateFormula` type is stored in a non-language dependent format, hence supporting multi-language functionality. The `DateFormula` type is a combination of the following:

- Numeric multipliers (for example, *1*, *2*, *3*, *4*, and so on, whereas the maximum is *9999*)
- Alpha time units (all must be uppercase)

- *D* for a day

- *W* for a week

- *WD* for the day of the week—that is, day 1 through day 7 (either in the future or in the past, not today); Monday is day 1, and Sunday is day 7

- *M* for a calendar month

- *Y* for year

- *CM* for the current month, *CY* for the current year, and *CW* for the current week

- Math symbols interpretation: + (plus)—that is, *CM + 10D*—means the current month end plus 10 days (in other words, the 10th of next month), and - (minus) —that is, -*WD3*—means the date of the previous Wednesday (the third day of the past week)

- Positional notation (*D15* means the 15th day of the month and *15D* means 15 days)

Payment terms for invoices support the full use of `DateFormula`. All `DateFormula` results are expressed as a date based on a reference date. The default reference date is the system date, not the work date.

Here are some sample `DateFormula` types and their interpretations (displayed dates are based on the US calendar), with a reference date of July 5, 2024, a Friday:

- *CM* or *+CM*: The last day of the current month, 07/31/24.

- *-CM*: The first day of the current month, 07/01/24.

- *CM + 10D*: The 10th of next month, 08/10/24.

- *WD6*: The next sixth day of the week, 07/12/24.

- *WD5*: The next fifth day of the week, 07/11/24.

- *CM - M + 2D*: The end of the current month minus 1 month plus 2 days, 07/02/24. We could also write it as –*CM + 1D*.

- *CM - 5M*: The end of the current month minus 5 months, 02/29/24.

Let's take the opportunity to use the `DateFormula` data type to learn a few Business Central development basics. We will do so by experimenting with some hands-on evaluations of several `DateFormula` values. We will create a table to calculate dates using `DateFormula` and reference dates.

Create a new file called `DateFormula.table.al`. Type in `ttable` (with two ts) and give the table an ID of `50140` and a name of `Date Formula`. After we've finished this test, we will save the table for later testing:

```
1    table 50140 "Date Formula"
2    {
3        DataClassification = CustomerContent;
4
5        fields
6        {
             0 references
7            field(1; "Primary Key"; Code[10]) { }
             0 references
8            field(2; "Reference Date"; Date) { }
             0 references
9            field(3; "Date Formula"; DateFormula) { }
             0 references
10           field(4; "Result Date"; Date) { }
11       }
12   }
```

Figure 3.13 – Date Formula table

Now, we will add some simple AL code to our table so that when we enter or change either the Reference Date or Date Formula fields, we can calculate a new Result Date value.

At the bottom of the file, we delete the triggers that were generated by the snippet and create a new procedure. The name of the procedure is CalculateNewDate:

```
local procedure CalculateNewDate()
begin
    "Result Date" := CalcDate("Date Formula", "Reference Date");
end;
```

Figure 3.14 – New CalculateNewDate procedure

Notice that our new procedure was defined as a local procedure. This means that it cannot be accessed from another object unless we change it to a global or internal procedure.

Because our goal now is to focus on experimenting with DateFormula, we will not go into detail explaining the logic we are creating.

The logic we're going to code follows: when an entry is made (new or changed) in either the Reference Date field or in the Date Formula field, invoke the CalculateNewDate procedure to calculate a new Result Date value based on the entered data.

First, we will create the logic within our new procedure, CalculateNewDate, to evaluate and store Result Date based on the Date Formula and Reference Date fields that we enter into the table.

Just copy the AL code exactly, as shown in the following screenshot, and save the table:

```
fields
{
    0 references
    field(1; "Primary Key"; Code[10]) { }
    1 reference
    field(2; "Reference Date"; Date)
    {
        trigger OnValidate()
        begin
            CalculateNewDate();
        end;
    }
    1 reference
    field(3; "Date Formula"; DateFormula)
    {
        trigger OnValidate()
        begin
            CalculateNewDate();
        end;
    }
    1 reference
    field(4; "Result Date"; Date) { }
}
```

Figure 3.15 – OnValidate() triggers

This code will cause the `CalculateNewDate` procedure to be called via the `OnValidate` trigger when an entry is made in either the `Reference Date` or `Date Formula` fields. The procedure will place the result in the `Result Date` field. The use of an integer value in the redundantly named primary key field allows us to enter any number of records into the table (by manually numbering them 1, 2, 3, and so forth).

Let's experiment with several different date and date formula combinations. We will access the table via a simple page, as shown in the following screenshot:

```
1    page 50140 "Date Formula"
2    {
3        PageType = List;
4        ApplicationArea = All;
5        UsageCategory = Administration;
6        SourceTable = "Date Formula";
7
8        layout
9        {
             0 references
10           area(Content)
11           {
                 0 references
12               repeater(GroupName)
13               {
                     0 references
14                   field("Primary Key"; Rec."Primary Key") { }
                     0 references
15                   field("Reference Date"; Rec."Reference Date") { }
                     0 references
16                   field("Date Formula"; Rec."Date Formula") { }
                     0 references
17                   field("Result Date"; Rec."Result Date") { }
18               }
19           }
20       }
21   }
```

Figure 3.16 – Date Formula page

If we build and publish the extension, we can run the page from the search option.

> **Note**
>
> In order to be able to apply the same alpha time units as mentioned next, switch the client language to English. If you prefer testing in another language than English, translate the time unit names into your language, and then use the first letter in the unit.

Enter a primary key value of 01 (zero and one). In **Reference Date**, enter either an uppercase or lowercase T for today, the system date. The same date will appear in the **Result Date** field because, at this point, no **Date Formula** value has been entered. Now, enter 1D (numeral 1 followed by uppercase or lowercase letter D; the application will take care of making it uppercase) in the **Date Formula** field. We will see that the contents of the **Result Date** field have changed to be 1 day beyond the date in the **Reference Date** field.

Now, for another test entry—let's start with 02 in the primary key field. Again, enter the letter T (for today) in the **Reference Date** field, and enter the letter W (for week) in the **Date Formula** field. We will get an error message telling us that our formulas should include a number. Make the system happy and enter 1W. We'll now see a date in the **Result Date** field that is 1 week beyond our system date.

Set the system's work date to a date in the middle of a month (remember—we discussed setting the work date in *Chapter 1, Introduction to Business Central*). Start another line with the number 03 as the primary key, followed by W (for work date) in the **Reference Date** field. Enter cm (or CM, cM, or Cm—it doesn't matter) in the **Date Formula** field. Our **Result Date** value will be the last day of our work date month. Now, enter another line using the work date, but enter a formula of -cm (the same as before, but with a minus sign). This time, our **Result Date** value will be the first day of our work date month. Notice that the DateFormula logic handles month-end dates correctly, even including leap years. Try starting with a date in the middle of February 2024 to confirm that:

← Date Formula			✓ Saved 🔖 ▢ ↗
🔍 Search + New ▣ Edit List 🗑 Delete			↩ ▽ ≡
Primary Key ↑	**Reference Date**	**Date Formula**	**Result Date**
01	2/1/2024	1D	2/2/2024
02	2/1/2024	1W	2/8/2024
03	12/15/2024	CM	12/31/2024
04	12/15/2024	-CM	12/1/2024
→ 05	2/11/2024	CM	2/29/2024

Figure 3.17 – Date Formula page in client

Enter another line with a new primary key. Skip over the **Reference Date** field and just enter 1D in the **Date Formula** field. What happens? We get an error message stating, **You cannot base a date calculation on an undefined date**. In other words, Business Central cannot make the requested calculation without a reference date. Before we put this function into production, we want our code to check for a **Reference Date** value before calculating. We could default an empty date to the system date or the work date and avoid this particular error.

The preceding and following screenshots show different sample calculations. Build on these sample calculations and then experiment more on your own:

Primary Key ↑	Reference Date	Date Formula	Result Date
01	2/1/2024	1D	2/2/2024
02	2/1/2024	1W	2/8/2024
03	12/15/2024	CM	12/31/2024
04	12/15/2024	-CM	12/1/2024
05	2/11/2024	CM	2/29/2024
06	11/15/2025	CM	11/30/2025
07	1/3/2025	-1W-1D	12/26/2024
08	1/3/2025	1W+1D	1/11/2025
09	12/12/2024	-CM-1D	11/30/2024
10	12/12/2024	CM+1D	1/1/2025
11	1/1/2025	-1Y-CM	1/1/2024

Figure 3.18 – Date formulas to test

We can create a variety of different algebraic date formulas and get some very interesting and useful results. One Business Central user business has due dates for all invoices of the 10th of the next month. The invoices are dated on the dates they are actually printed, at various times throughout the month. But by using a **Date Formula** value of *CM + 10D*, each invoice due date is always automatically calculated to be the 10th of the next month.

Don't forget to test with WD (weekday), Q (quarter), and Y (year), as well as D (day), W (week), and M (month).

> **Note**
>
> For our code to be language-independent, we should enter the date formulas with < > delimiters around them (for example, <1D+1W>). Business Central will translate the formula into the correct language codes using the installed language layer.

Although our focus for the work we just completed was the DateFormula data type, we've accomplished a lot more than simply learning about that one data type:

- We created a new table just for the purpose of experimenting with an AL feature that we might use. This is a technique that comes in handy when we are learning a new feature, trying to decide how it works or how we might use it.

- We put some critical `OnValidate` logic into the table. When data is entered in one area, the entry is validated and, if valid, the defined processing is done instantly.

- We created a common routine as a new `local` procedure. That procedure is then called from all places to which it applies.

- Finally, and most specifically, we saw how Business Central tools make a variety of relative date calculations easy. These are very useful in business applications, many aspects of which are date-centered.

App information

You might want to expose app internals, such as the current app version, to the user, or handle upgrade scenarios. For such cases, AL offers you a variety of data types:

- `NavApp`: Use this data type to connect to installed apps or to determine whether the app is being installed.

- `ModuleInfo`: This is used to return properties of any installed extension at runtime, such as (but not limited to) the name and version. Use `NavApp.GetCurrentModuleInfo` to bind the variable to your app.

- `Version`: This represents a version matching the format *Major.Minor.Build.Revision*. This is especially useful for comparing two versions.

References and other data types

The following data types are used for advanced functionality in Business Central:

- `RecordID`: This contains the object number and primary key of a table.

- `RecordRef`: This identifies a record/row in an arbitrary table. The `RecordRef` type can be used to obtain information about a table, a record, fields in a record, and currently active filters on a table.

- `FieldRef`: This identifies a field in a table, hence allowing access to the contents of that field.

- `KeyRef`: This identifies a key in a table and the fields in that key.

> **Note**
>
> Since the specific record, field, and key references are assigned at runtime, `RecordRef`, `FieldRef`, and `KeyRef` are used to support logic that can run on tables that aren't specified at design time. This means that one routine built on these data types can be created to perform a common function for a variety of different tables and table formats.

- `Variant`: Represents an AL variable object. The `variant` data type can contain many AL data types. We might use it for passing arbitrary field values without the need to declare a separate procedure per field data type.

- `TransactionType`: This property has optional values of `UpdateNoLocks`, `Update`, `Snapshot`, `Browse`, and `Report`, which define SQL Server behavior for a Business Central report or XMLport transaction from the beginning of the transaction.

- `Blob`: This can contain either specially formatted text, a graphic in the form of a bitmap, or other developer-defined binary data that's up to 2 GB in size. **Binary Large Objects (BLOBs)** BLOBs can only be included in tables; they cannot be used to define working storage variables. See *Microsoft Docs* for additional information.

- `BigText`: This can contain large chunks of text up to 2 GB in size. Variables of type `BigText` can only be defined in the working storage within an object but are not included in tables. Variables of type `BigText` cannot be directly displayed or seen in the debugger. There is a group of special methods that can be used to handle `BigText` data. See *Microsoft Docs* for additional information: `https://learn.microsoft.com/en-us/dynamics365/business-central/dev-itpro/developer/methods-auto/bigtext/bigtext-data-type`.

- `Media`: This data type enables you to import a media file (such as image `.jpg` and `.png` files) to the application database and reference the file from records, making it possible to display the media file in the client UI. You can also export media from the database to files and streams, but you cannot use it as a variable or parameter.

> **Tip**
>
> To learn more about the different methods of storing and displaying media, such as images, refer to the *Working With Media on Records* article at *Microsoft Docs*: `https://learn.microsoft.com/en-us/dynamics365/business-central/dev-itpro/developer/devenv-working-with-media-on-records`

- `Guid`: This is used to assign a unique identifying number. A **Globally Unique Identifier (GUID)** is a 16-byte binary data type that is used for the unique global identification of records, apps, and so on. The GUID is generated by an algorithm that was developed by Microsoft.

- `TestPage`: This is used to store a test page that is a logical representation of a page that does not display a UI. Test pages are used only for automated testing in Business Central. Automated testing is not covered in this book.

Data type usage

Just a minority of all data types can be used to define data that's stored in tables. The majority can only be used for working storage data definitions (that is, in a global or local variable within an object).

The `Blob`, `Media`, and `MediaSet` data types can only be used to define table-stored data, but not working storage data.

FieldClass property options

Almost all data fields have a `FieldClass` property. The `FieldClass` property has as much effect on the content and usage of a data field as the data type does and, in some instances, more. In the next chapter, we'll cover most of the field properties, but we'll discuss `FieldClass` property options now.

FieldClass – Normal

When `FieldClass` is `Normal`, the field will contain the type of application data that's typically stored in a table, which is the content we would expect based on the data type and various properties.

FieldClass – FlowField

Properties of type `FlowField` must be dynamically calculated. Properties of type `FlowField` are virtual fields that are stored as metadata; they do not contain data in the conventional sense. A `FlowField` property contains the definition of how to calculate (at runtime) the data that the field represents and a place to store the result of that calculation. It is strongly recommended that the `Editable` property for `FlowField` be set to `false`.

Depending on the `CalcFormula` property, this could be a value, a reference lookup, or a `Boolean` value. When the `CalcFormula` property is `Sum`, `FieldClass` connects a data field to a field in the table defined in `CalcFormula`. There are two kinds of indexes used by Business Central to quickly calculate `FlowField` sums: the **nonclustered columnstore index** (**NCCI**) and legacy **SumIndexField Technology** (**SIFT**). NCCI is seen as the successor to SIFT as it has both development and performance improvements. SIFT needs to be assigned to individual indexes, which incurs performance overhead from SQL. NCCI is defined once per table, and so only a single index needs to be maintained.

A `FlowField` value is always 0, blank, or `false` unless it has been calculated. If a `FlowField` value is displayed directly on a page, it is calculated automatically when the page is rendered. Values of the `FlowField` type are also automatically calculated when they are the subject of predefined filters as part of the properties of a data item in an object (this will be explained in more detail in *Chapter 4, Pages – The Interactive Interface*, when we talk about reports, and *Chapter 8, Extensibility beyond AL*, when we talk about XMLports). In all other cases, `FlowField` must be forced to calculate using the AL `RecordName.CalcFields(FlowField1, [FlowField2],...)` method or by using the `SetAutoCalcFields` method. This is also true if the underlying data is changed after the initial display of a page (that is, `FlowField` must be recalculated to take a data change into account).

> **Note**
>
> Because a `FlowField` property does not contain actual data, it cannot be used as a field in a key; in other words, we cannot include a `FlowField` property as part of a key. Also, we cannot define a `FlowField` property that is based on another `FlowField` property, except in special circumstances.

When a field has its `FieldClass` value set to `FlowField`, another directly associated property becomes available—`CalcFormula`. The `CalcFormula` property is the place where we can define the formula for calculating `FlowField`. On the `CalcFormula` property line, we define the calculation as the average `Listener Count` value where the `Radio Show No.` value on the entry is the same as the primary key value of the record we are on:

```
field(7; "Average Listeners"; Decimal)
{
    FieldClass = FlowField;
    CalcFormula = average("Listernership Entry"."Listener Count"
    where("Radio Show No." = field("No.")));
}
```

Figure 3.19 – FlowField FieldClass type example

Use *Ctrl* + spacebar to show the seven `FlowField` methods:

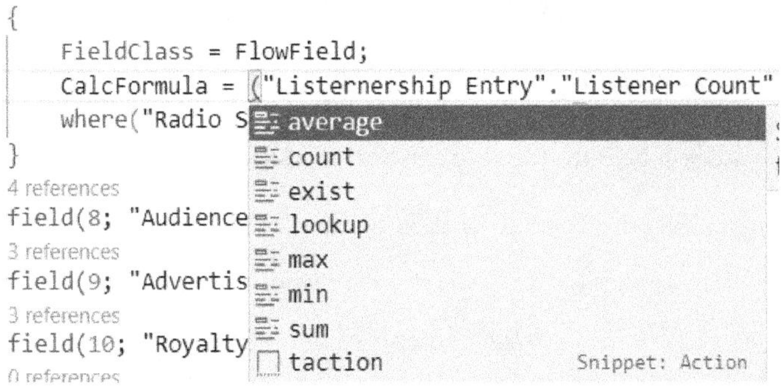

Figure 3.20 – FlowField calculation types

The seven `FlowField` types are described in the following table:

Calculation type	Field data type	Description
Sum	Numeric	The sum total
Average	Numeric	The average value (the sum divided by the row count)
Exist	Boolean	Yes or no/ true or false—does an entry exist?
Count	Integer	The number of entries that exist

Calculation type	Field data type	Description
Min	Any	The smallest value of any entry
Max	Any	The largest value of any entry
Lookup	Any	The value of the specified entry

Table 3.1 – The seven FlowField types

We can negate Exist, Sum, and Average values by prefixing the respective keyword with a minus sign.

The last but by no means the least significant component of the FlowField calculation formula is the table filter in the where clause:

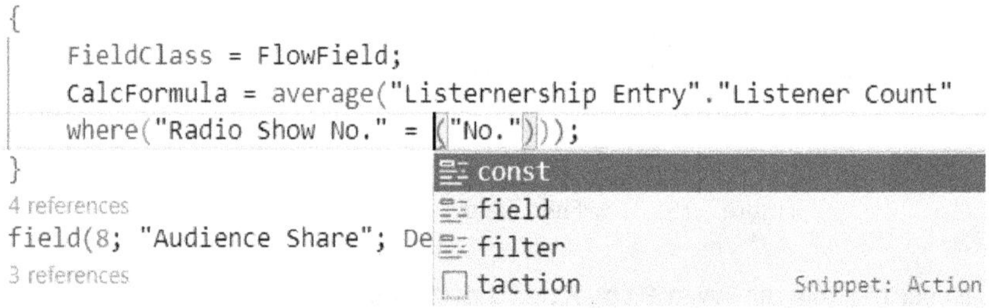

```
{
    FieldClass = FlowField;
    CalcFormula = average("Listernership Entry"."Listener Count"
    where("Radio Show No." = ("No.")));
}                          const
4 references               field
field(8; "Audience Share"; De  filter
3 references               taction        Snippet: Action
```

Figure 3.21 – FlowField filter types

The left part of the where clause contains a field in the linked table whereby the right part links to a field type in this table, const, or filter. These choices are described in the following list (note that FlowFilter fields will be introduced in the next section):

- const(Value): Uses the Value constant to filter for equally valued entries.

- filter(Value): Applies the Value filter expression.

- field(NormalField): Uses the contents of the specified NormalField property to filter for equally valued entries.

- field(FlowFilterField): Uses the contents of the specified FlowFilterField property as a filter expression. For an example, see the 31 - Balance at Date field in the 15 - G/L Account table on the Business Unit Filter field.

- field(upperlimit(FlowFilterField)): Applies the FlowFilterField range as a filter, but on the basis of only having the upper limit; that is, having no bottom limit. This is useful for the date filters for balance sheet data. For an example, see the 31 - Balance at Date field in the 15 - G/L Account table on the Date Filter field.

- `field(filter(NormalField))`: Causes the contents of the specified `NormalField` property to be interpreted as a filter. For an example, see the `31 - Balance at Date` field in the `15 - G/L Account` table on the `Totaling` field.

- `field(upperlimit(filter(NormalField)))`: Causes the contents of the specified `NormalField` property to be interpreted as a filter, but applying only the upper limit.

FieldClass – FlowFilter

Properties of type `FlowFilter` control the calculation of `FlowField` properties in the table (when the `FlowFilter` properties are included in the `CalcFormula` property). Properties of type `FlowFilter` do not contain permanent data but instead contain filters on a per-user basis, with the information stored in that user's instance of the code being executed. A `FlowFilter` field allows a filter to be entered at a parent record level by the user (for example, G/L account) and applied (through the use of `FlowField` formulas, for example) to constrain what child data (for example, G/L entry records) is selected.

A `FlowFilter` property allows us to provide flexible data selection functions to users. The user does not need to have a full understanding of the data structure that's used to apply filtering in intuitive ways to both the primary data table and also to subordinate data. Based on our AL code design, `FlowFilter` properties can be used to apply filtering on multiple tables, whether this be from a subordinate to a parent table. Of course, it is our responsibility as developers to make good use of this tool. As with many AL capabilities, a good way to learn more is by studying standard code, as designed by the Microsoft developers of Business Central, and then experimenting.

A number of good examples of the use of `FlowFilter` properties can be found in the `Customer` (table 18) and `Item` (table 27) tables. In the `Customer` table, some of the `FlowField` properties that are using `FlowFilter` properties are `Balance`, `Balance (LCY)`, `Net Change`, `Net Change (LCY)`, `Sales (LCY)`, and `Profit (LCY)`, where **LCY** stands for **Local Currency**. The `Balance Due FlowFilter` usage is shown in the following screenshot:

```
field(66; "Balance Due"; Decimal)
{
    AutoFormatExpression = "Currency Code";
    AutoFormatType = 1;
    CalcFormula = Sum("Detailed Cust. Ledg. Entry".Amount
    WHERE("Customer No." = FIELD("No."),
          "Initial Entry Due Date" = FIELD(UPPERLIMIT("Date Filter")),
          "Initial Entry Global Dim. 1" = FIELD("Global Dimension 1 Filter"),
          "Initial Entry Global Dim. 2" = FIELD("Global Dimension 2 Filter"),
          "Currency Code" = FIELD("Currency Filter")));
    Caption = 'Balance Due';
    Editable = false;
    FieldClass = FlowField;
}
```

Figure 3.22 – Balance Due FlowField customer table

Similarly constructed `FlowField` properties that use `FlowFilter` properties in the `Item` table include `Inventory`, `Net Invoiced Qty.`, `Net Change`, and `Purchases (Qty.)`, as well as others.

Throughout the standard code, there are `FlowFilter` properties in most of the master table definitions, which include date filters and global dimension filters (global dimensions are user-defined codes that facilitate the segregation of accounting data by groupings such as divisions, departments, projects, customer type, and so on). Other `FlowFilter` properties that are widely used in the standard code are related to inventory activity such as `Location Filter`, `Lot No. Filter`, `Serial No. Filter`, and `Bin Filter`.

The following screenshot shows two fields from the `Customer` table, both with a data type of `Date`. The first field in the screenshot is the `Last Date Modified` field (`FieldClass` is not defined, hence it is `Normal`), while the last field in the screenshot is the `Date Filter` field (`FieldClass` value of `FlowFilter`):

```
field(54; "Last Date Modified"; Date)
{
    Caption = 'Last Date Modified';
    Editable = false;
}
field(55; "Date Filter"; Date)
{
    Caption = 'Date Filter';
    FieldClass = FlowFilter;
}
```

Figure 3.23 – FlowFilter example

FlowField and FlowFilter properties for our application

In our application, we have decided to have several `FlowField` and `FlowFilter` properties in the `50100 Radio Show` table. The reason for these fields is to provide instant analysis for individual shows based on the detailed data stored in subordinate tables. In *Chapter 2*, *Tables*, we showed table `50100` with fields 7 through 10 and 20 but didn't provide any information on how those fields should be constructed. Let's go through that construction process now. Here's how fields 7 through 10 and 20 should look when we open table `50100` in Visual Studio Code. If you didn't add these fields as described in *Chapter 2*, *Tables*, in the *Creating and modifying tables* section, do that now:

```
field(1; "No."; Code[20]) { }
3 references
field(2; "Radio Show Type"; Code[10]) { TableRelation = "Radio Show Type"; }
6 references
field(3; "Name"; Text[100]) { }
3 references
field(4; "Run Time"; Duration) { }
3 references
field(5; "Host Code"; Code[20]) { }
5 references
field(6; "Host Name"; Text[100]) { }
3 references
field(7; "Average Listeners"; Decimal) { }
4 references
field(8; "Audience Share"; Decimal) { }
3 references
field(9; "Advertising Revenue"; Decimal) { }
3 references
field(10; "Royalty Cost"; Decimal) { }
0 references
field(11; Frequency; Option) { OptionMembers = Hourly,Daily,Weekly,Monthly; }
```

Figure 3.24 – 50100 Radio Show table

The following five fields will be used for statistical analysis for each radio show:

- Field 7—Average Listeners: The average number of listeners, as reported by the ratings agency

- Field 8—Audience Share: The percentage of the station's total estimated listening audience per time slot

- Field 9—Advertising Revenue: The sum total of the advertising revenue generated by the show

- Field 10—Royalty Cost: The sum total of the royalties incurred by the show by playing copyrighted material

- Field 20—Date Filter: A filter to restrict the data that's calculated for the preceding four fields

To begin with, we will set the calculation properties for the first `FlowField` property, `Average Listeners`:

```
field(7; "Average Listeners"; Decimal)
{
    Editable = false;
    FieldClass = FlowField;
    CalcFormula = average("Listenership Entry"."Listener Count"
    where("Radio Show No." = field("No."), Date = field("Date Filter")));
}
```

Figure 3.25 – Average Listeners FlowField property

> **Tip**
> Set the `Editable` property to `false`.

The following fields will be used for statistical analysis:

- For field 8, `Audience Share`, repeat the procedure we just went through, but for `field`, select `Audience Share` from the `Listenership Entry` field list. Our result should be as follows:

```
field(8; "Audience Share"; Decimal)
{
    Editable = false;
    FieldClass = FlowField;
    CalcFormula = average("Listenership Entry"."Audience Share"
    where("Radio Show No." = field("No."), Date = field("Date Filter")));
}
```

Figure 3.26 – Audience Share FlowField property

- For fields 9, `Advertising Revenue`, and 10, `Royalty Cost`, the `FlowField` property calculation is a sum with multiple fields that have filters applied.

- For `Advertising Revenue`, make the method `Sum`; for `table`, enter `Radio Show Entry`; and set `field` to `Fee Amount`:

```
field(9; "Advertising Revenue"; Decimal)
{
    Editable = false;
    FieldClass = FlowField;
    CalcFormula = sum("Radio Show Entry"."Fee Amount"
    where(
        "Radio Show No." = field("No."),
        "Data Format" = filter(Advertisement)
        ));
}
```

Figure 3.27 – Advertising Revenue FlowField property

- The Advertisement value is an available value of the Data Format field (the Playlist Data Format data type enum created in *Chapter 2*, in the *NewTables for Our WDTU Project* section). If in Radio Show Entry we had typed a value that was not declared in the Enum object, such as Commercial, an error message would have displayed:

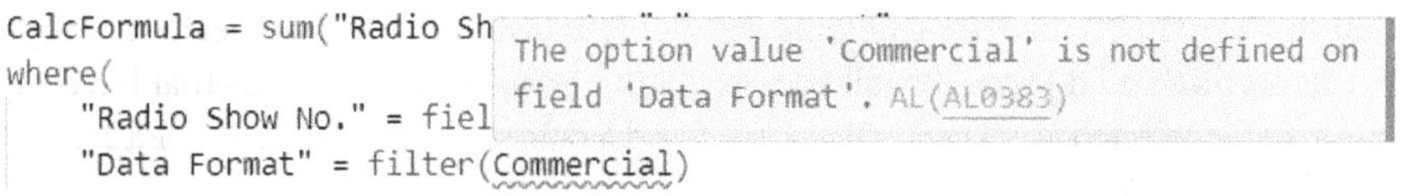

```
CalcFormula = sum("Radio Sh
                            The option value 'Commercial' is not defined on
where(
                            field 'Data Format'. AL(AL0383)
    "Radio Show No." = fiel
    "Data Format" = filter(Commercial)
```

Figure 3.28 – Error message for an invalid Enum value

As for all Option or Enum fields, we can use *Ctrl* + spacebar to get a list of all available values, as shown in the following screenshot:

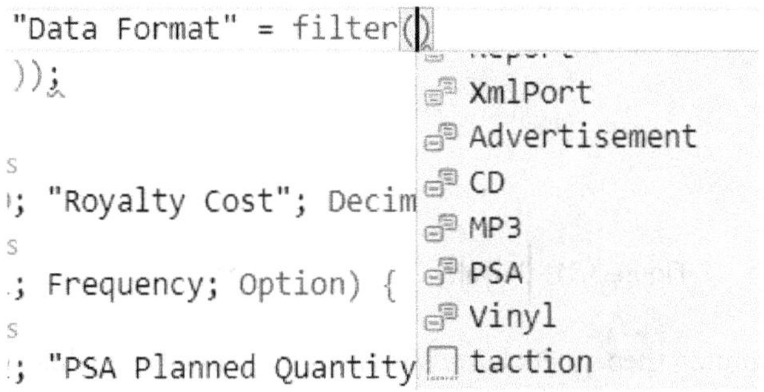

```
"Data Format" = filter()
));

S
; "Royalty Cost"; Decim

S
; Frequency; Option) {

S
; "PSA Planned Quantity
```

XmlPort
Advertisement
CD
MP3
PSA
Vinyl
taction

Figure 3.29 – Ctrl + spacebar to get a list of enum values

Let's create a FlowField property with a complex filter:

1. Start Royalty Cost with the same properties as Advertising Revenue for Editable and FieldClass.

2. For CalcFormula, make sure the method is Sum and use the Radio Show Entry table field named Fee Amount.

3. For the where clause, set Radio Show No. equal to the current record.

4. Next, set the Date value of the Radio Show Entry table equal to the Date Filter filter set on the Radio Show table:

```
field(20; "Date Filter"; Date) { FieldClass = FlowFilter; }
```

Figure 3.30 – Date Filter FlowFilter property

Finally, set the Data Format value to type filter. In the parentheses, set the value to Vinyl | CD | MP3. This means that we will filter for all records where the Data Format property contains a value equal to Vinyl, CD, or MP3 (the pipe symbol is translated to the Boolean OR property). As a result, this FlowField property will sum up all the Fee Amount values that have a Data Format enum value selected as Vinyl, CD, or MP3 and a date satisfying the Date Filter value that was specified on the Radio Show table:

```
field(10; "Royalty Cost"; Decimal)
{
    Editable = false;
    FieldClass = FlowField;
    CalcFormula = sum("Radio Show Entry"."Fee Amount"
    where(
        "Radio Show No." = field("No."),
        Date = field("Date Filter"),
        "Data Format" = filter(Vinyl | CD | MP3)
        ));
}
```

Figure 3.31 – Royalty Cost FlowField property

After so much programming theory, let's leave Visual Studio Code for a while, to learn about and play with filters.

Filtering

Filtering is one of the most powerful tools within Business Central. Filtering is the application of defined limits on the data that is to be considered in a process. When we apply a filter to a Normal data field, we only view or process records where the filtered data field satisfies the limits defined by the filter. When we apply a filter to a `FlowField` property, the calculated value for that field will only consider data that satisfies the limits defined by the filter.

Filter structures can be applied in at least three different ways, depending on the design of the process:

- The first way is for the developer to fully define the filter structure and the value of the filter. This might be done in a report that's designed to show information on only a selected group of customers, such as those with an unpaid balance. The `Customer` table would be filtered to report only on customers who have an outstanding balance greater than zero.

- The second way is for the developer to define the filter structure but allow the user to fill in the specific value to be applied. This approach would be appropriate in an accounting report that has to be tied to specific accounting periods. The user would be allowed to define what periods are to be considered for each report run.

- The third way is the ad hoc definition of a filter structure and value by the user. This approach is often used for the general analysis of ledger data, where the developer wants to give the user total flexibility in how they slice and dice the available data.

It is common to use a combination of the different filtering types. For example, the report we previously mentioned that lists only customers with an open balance (via a developer-defined filter) could also allow the user to define additional filter criteria. If the user wants to see only Euro currency customers, they will also filter on the customer currency code field.

Filters are an integral part of the implementation of both `FlowField` and `FlowFilter` properties. These flexible, powerful tools allow the Business Central developer to create pages, reports, and other processes that can be used in a wide variety of circumstances. In most competitive systems, standard user inquiries and processes are quite specific. The Business Central AL toolset allows us to have relatively generic user inquiries and processes and then allows the user to apply filtering to generate results that fit their specific needs.

The user will see `FlowFilter` filtering referred to as **Filter totals by:** on screen, whereas normal field filtering appears on screen as **Filter list by:** on list pages and as **Filter:** on request pages. A good set of examples of filtering options and syntax can be found at *Microsoft Docs* on the page titled *Entering Criteria in Filters*: `https://learn.microsoft.com/en-us/dynamics365/business-central/dev-itpro/developer/devenv-entering-criteria-in-filters`.

Experimenting with filters

Now, it's time to do some experimenting with filters. We want to accomplish a couple of things through our experimentation. First, we want to get more comfortable with how filters are entered; and second, we want to see the effects of different types of filter structures and combinations. If we had a database with a large volume of data, we could also test the speed of filtering on fields in keys and on fields not in keys. However, the amount of data in the basic CRONUS database is small, so any speed differences will be difficult to see in these tests.

We could experiment on any report that allows filtering. A good report for this experimentation is the **Customer/Item Sales** report, which lists which customer purchased what items. It can be accessed by using the global **Search** functionality (**Tell Me**, *Alt + Q*). When we initially run **Customer/Item Sales**, we will see just three data fields listed for the entry of filters on the Customer table and the Value Entry table, as shown in the following screenshot:

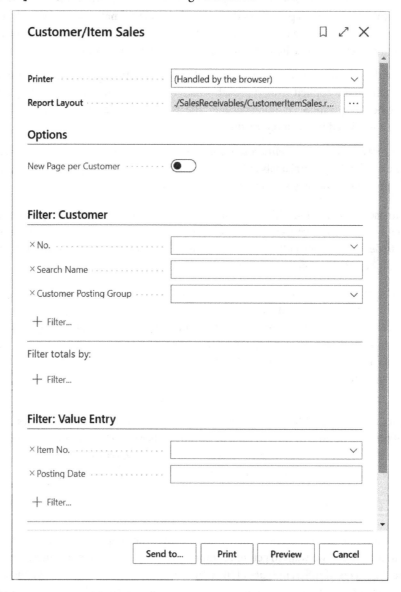

Figure 3.32 – Customer/Item Sales request page with filters

For both **Customer** and **Value Entry**, these are the fields that the developer of this report determined should be emphasized. If we run the report without entering any filter constraints at all and just use the standard CRONUS data, the first page of the report will resemble the following:

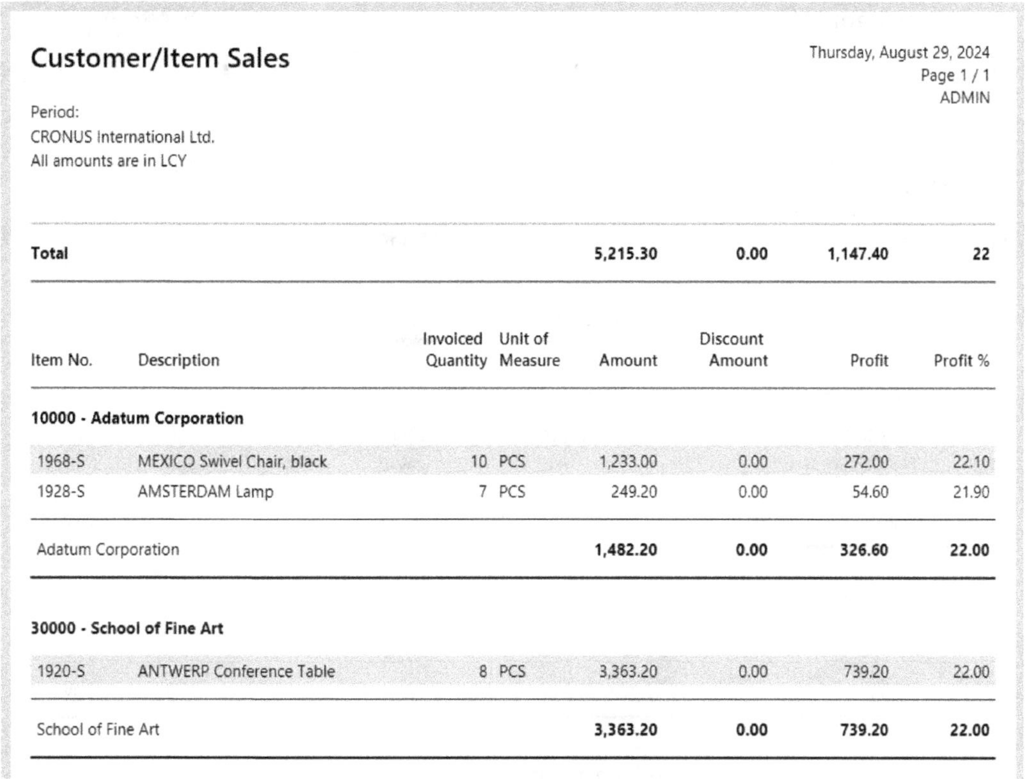

Customer/Item Sales

Thursday, August 29, 2024
Page 1 / 1
ADMIN

Period:
CRONUS International Ltd.
All amounts are in LCY

				Amount	Discount Amount	Profit	Profit %
Total				**5,215.30**	**0.00**	**1,147.40**	**22**

Item No.	Description	Invoiced Quantity	Unit of Measure	Amount	Discount Amount	Profit	Profit %
10000 - Adatum Corporation							
1968-S	MEXICO Swivel Chair, black	10	PCS	1,233.00	0.00	272.00	22.10
1928-S	AMSTERDAM Lamp	7	PCS	249.20	0.00	54.60	21.90
Adatum Corporation				**1,482.20**	**0.00**	**326.60**	**22.00**
30000 - School of Fine Art							
1920-S	ANTWERP Conference Table	8	PCS	3,363.20	0.00	739.20	22.00
School of Fine Art				**3,363.20**	**0.00**	**739.20**	**22.00**

Figure 3.33 – Customer/Item Sales report output

If we want to print information only for customers whose names begin with the letter A, our filter will be very simple and similar to the following screenshot:

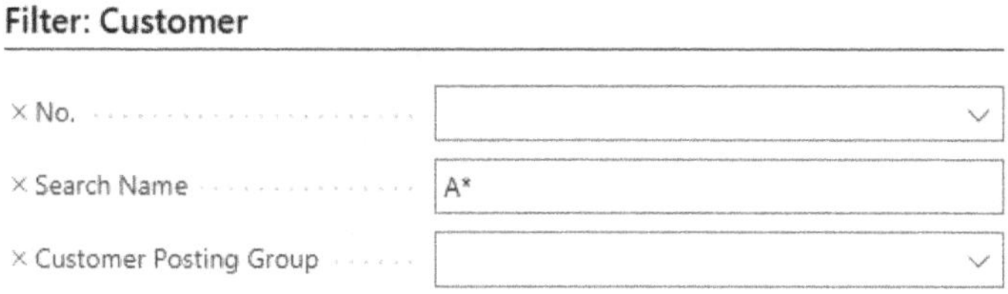

Filter: Customer

× No. .... [⌄]

× Search Name .... [A*   ]

× Customer Posting Group ..... [⌄]

Figure 3.34 – Request page filter A with * wildcard

The resulting report will be similar to the following screenshot, showing only data for the two customers on file whose names begin with the letter A:

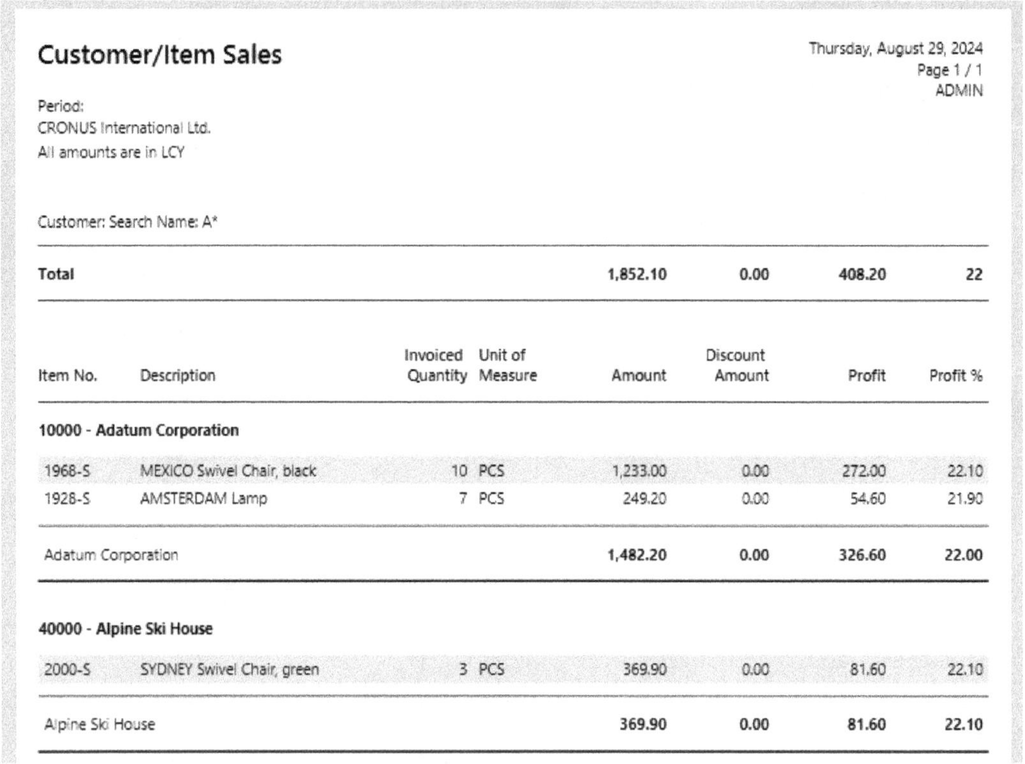

Customer/Item Sales

Thursday, August 29, 2024
Page 1 / 1
ADMIN

Period:
CRONUS International Ltd.
All amounts are in LCY

Customer: Search Name: A*

Total				1,852.10	0.00	408.20	22

Item No.	Description	Invoiced Quantity	Unit of Measure	Amount	Discount Amount	Profit	Profit %
10000 - Adatum Corporation							
1968-S	MEXICO Swivel Chair, black	10	PCS	1,233.00	0.00	272.00	22.10
1928-S	AMSTERDAM Lamp	7	PCS	249.20	0.00	54.60	21.90
Adatum Corporation				1,482.20	0.00	326.60	22.00
40000 - Alpine Ski House							
2000-S	SYDNEY Swivel Chair, green	3	PCS	369.90	0.00	81.60	22.10
Alpine Ski House				369.90	0.00	81.60	22.10

Figure 3.35 – Filtered output

If we want to expand the customer fields so that we can apply filters, we can access a full list of other fields in the `customer` table by clicking on the **+Filter...** button to add a new filter field with drop-down list access. Notice that the lists are in alphabetical order, based on their field names:

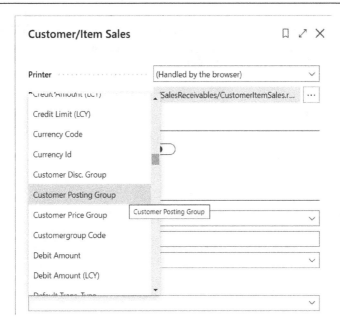

Figure 3.36 – Adding a new filter to a request page

From these lists, we can choose one or more fields and then enter filters on those fields. If we chose **Territory Code**, for example, then the request page would look similar to what's shown in the following screenshot. If we clicked on the lookup arrow in the **Filter** column, a screen would pop up, allowing us to choose from data items in the related table, which, in this case, is Territories:

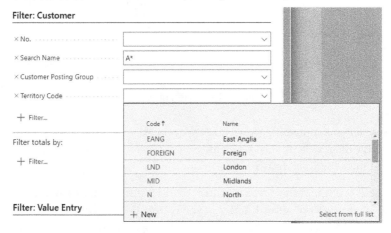

Figure 3.37 – Drop-down selection

This request page has FastTabs for each of the two primary tables in the report. Click on the **Value Entry** FastTab to filter on item-related data. If we filter on **Item No.** for item numbers that contain the letter W, the report will look similar to the following:

Customer/Item Sales

Thursday, August 29, 2024
Page 1 / 1
ADMIN

Period:
CRONUS International Ltd.
All amounts are in LCY

Customer: Search Name: A*
Value Entry: Item No.: *W*

| Total | | | | | 2,170.90 | 0.00 | 2,170.90 | 100 |

Item No.	Description	Invoiced Quantity	Unit of Measure	Amount	Discount Amount	Profit	Profit %
10000 - Adatum Corporation							
1965-W	Conference Bundle 2-8	7	PCS	1,061.90	0.00	1,061.90	100.00
1969-W	Conference Package 1	5	PCS	1,109.00	0.00	1,109.00	100.00
Adatum Corporation				2,170.90	0.00	2,170.90	100.00
Total				2,170.90	0.00	2,170.90	100

Figure 3.38 – Filtered output

If we want to see all items containing either the letter W or the letter S, our filter would be *W* | *S*. If we made the filter, W | S, then we would only get entries that are exactly equal to W or to S because we didn't include any wildcards.

You should go back over the various types of filters we discussed and try each one and try them in combination. Get creative! Try some things that you're not sure will work and see what happens. Explore a variety of reports or list pages in the system by applying filters to see the results of your experiments. A good page to apply filters on is the **Customers** list page. This filtering experimentation process is safe (you can't hurt anything or anyone) and is a great learning experience.

Accessing filter controls

When a page such as the **Customers** list page is opened, the filter section at the top of the page looks as follows. On the upper-left corner is a place to enter multiple-field filters. This is called **Search**, but the result will be a multi-column filter:

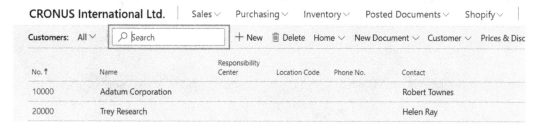

Figure 3.39 – Search

If we click on the **All** button in the upper-left corner, followed by **Show filter pane**, the result will look similar to the following. This filter display includes two additional filtering capabilities, **Filter list by:** and **Filter totals by::**

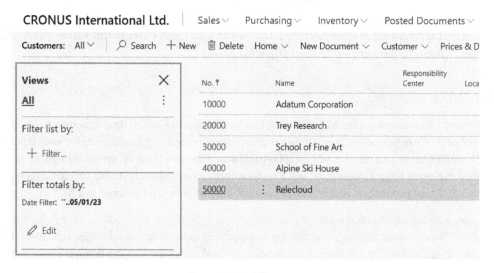

Figure 3.40 – Filter pane

If we apply a filter, the traditional filter icon (a funnel) will appear on the column with a filter, as shown in the following screenshot:

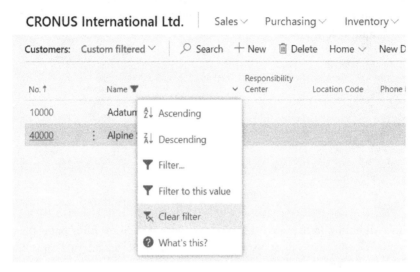

Figure 3.41 – Clear filter

If we click on the filter icon, we can clear the filter. We can also select **Filter to this value**, which will set the field filter with the value of the currently selected row.

Summary

In this chapter, we focused on the basic building blocks of Business Central data structure: fields and their attributes. We reviewed the types of data fields, properties, and trigger elements for each type of field. We walked through a number of examples to illustrate most of these elements, though we have postponed exploring triggers until later when we have more knowledge of AL. We covered data type and `FieldClass` properties, which determine what kind of data can be stored in a field.

We reviewed and experimented with the date calculation tool, which gives AL an edge in business applications. We discussed filtering, how filtering is considered as we design our database structure, and how users will access data. Finally, more of our Business Central Radio Show application was constructed.

In the next chapter, we will look at the many different types of pages in more detail. We'll put some of that knowledge to use to further expand our example Business Central application.

Questions

1. The maximum length for an AL field name or variable name is 250 characters. True or false?

    ANSWER: False. It is 30 for field names and 120 for variable names.

2. The `TableRelation` property defines the reference of a data field to a table. The related table data field must be one of the following:

    I.   In any key in the related table

    II.   Defined in the related table, but not in a key

    III.   In the primary key in the related table

    IV.   The first field in the primary key in the related table

    ANSWER: You can define a relationship only to a field that is a member of the primary key group

3. How many of the following field data types support storing application data such as names and amounts—1, 2, 3, or 4?

    I.   `FlowFilter`

    II.   `Editable`

    III.   `Normal`

    IV.   `FlowField`

    ANSWER: Only one—`Normal`

4. The `ExtendedDataType` property supports the designation of all but one of the following data types for displaying an appropriate action icon (choose the one that isn't supported):

    I.   Email address

    II.   Website URL

    III.   GPS location

    IV.   Telephone number

    V.   Masked entry

    ANSWER: GPS location

5. Which of the following is not a `FlowField` method (choose one)?

    I.   `Median`

    II.   `Count`

    III.   `Max`

IV.   Exist

V.   Average

ANSWER: Median

6.   It is important to have a consistent, well-planned approach to field numbers if the application will use the `TransferFields` function. True or false?

ANSWER: True

7.   When extending an existing table field in Business Central, what events can be subscribed to?

I.   OnAfterLookup

II.   OnBeforeValidate

III.   OnValidate

IV.   OnAfterValidate

ANSWER: OnBeforeValidate and OnAfterValidate

8.   Which properties are used to support the multi-language feature of Business Central, and how (choose two)?

I.   Name

II.   CaptionML

III.   Caption

IV.   LanguageRef

ANSWER: CaptionML by declaring the translated values within the Caption property by working with translation files

9.   Which of the following are field triggers (choose two)?

I.   OnEntry

II.   OnValidate

III.   OnDeletion

IV.   OnLookup

ANSWER: OnValidate and OnLookup

10. Which of the following are complex data types (choose three)?

I.   Records

II.   Strings of text

III.   DateFormula

IV.   `DateTime`

V.   Objects

ANSWER: Records, `DateFormula`, objects

11. Both `Option` and `Enum` data types appear to the user as fixed selectable dropdowns, but only Enum types are extensible (added to) in AL. True or false?

ANSWER: True

12. `Text` and `Code` variables can be any length in the following:

I.   In a memory variable (working storage)—true or false? ANSWER: True for `Text`, false for `Code`

II.   In a table field—true or false? ANSWER: False for both. The maximum is 2048.

13. `FlowField` results are not stored in the Business Central table data. True or false?

ANSWER: True

14. The following two filters are equivalent. True or false?

- (*W50?|I?5|D*)

- (I?5) OR (D*) OR (*W50?)

ANSWER: True

15. Limit totals apply to `FlowFilter` properties. True or false?

ANSWER: True

16. Dictionaries can be used to manipulate data with greater performance than temporary tables. True or false?

ANSWER: True

17. `DateFormula` alpha time (English) units include which of the following (choose two)?

I.   *C* for century

II.   *W* for week

III. *H* for holiday

IV.   *CM* for the current month

ANSWER: *W* and *CM*

18. `FlowFilter` data is stored in the database. True or false?

    ANSWER: False

19. `Option` and `Enum` data is stored as alphanumeric data strings. True or false?

    ANSWER: False. It is stored as integers.

20. Which of the following are numeric data types in Business Central (choose two)?

    I.   `Decimal`

    II.   `Enum`

    III.   `Hexadecimal`

    IV.   `Blob`

    ANSWER: `Decimal` and `Enum`

21. Which of the following act as wildcards in Business Central (choose two)?

    I.   Decimal point (.)

    II.   Question mark (?)

    III.   Asterisk (*)

    IV.   Hash mark (#)

    ANSWER: Question mark and asterisks

4

Pages – The Interactive Interface

"Design is not just what it looks like and feels like. Design is how it works."

– Steve Jobs

"True interactivity is not about clicking on icons or downloading files, it's about encouraging communication."

– Ed Schlossberg

Pages are Business Central's object type for interactively presenting information. The page rendering routines that paint the page on the target display handle much of the data presentation details. This allows a variety of clients to be created by Microsoft, such as a web browser resident client, the legacy Windows **Role-Tailored Client** (**RTC**), and a universal client that can be used on all devices, such as phones, tablets, and other platforms (iPad, Android, and Windows). **Independent Software Vendors** (**ISVs**) have created mobile clients and even clients targeted by devices other than video displays.

One of the benefits of page technology is the focus on the user experience rather than the underlying data structure. As always, the designer/developer has the responsibility of using the tools to their best effect. Another advantage of Business Central pages is the flexibility they provide the user for personalization, allowing them to tailor what is displayed and how it is organized.

In this chapter, we will explore the various types of pages offered by Business Central. We will review many options for format, data access, and tailoring pages. We will also learn about the inner structures of pages, their layout and actions, and more tools and resources.

We will cover the following topics:

- Page design and structure overview
- Types of pages
- Page components
- Page layout
- Page actions
- Page searchability
- Client tools for page development
- WDTU page enhancement exercises

Page design and structure overview

Pages serve the purpose of input, output, and control. They are views of data or process information designed for onscreen display only. They are also user data entry vehicles.

Pages are made up of various combinations of controls, properties, actions, triggers, and AL code, which are briefly explained here:

- **Controls**: These provide the users with ways to view, enter, and edit data; choose options or commands; initiate actions; and view status.
- **Properties**: These are attributes or characteristics of an object that define its state, appearance, or value.
- **Actions**: These are menu items that may contain icons. Actions are typically used for tasks relevant to the current page, such as running calculations or opening another page.
- **Triggers**: These are predefined functions that are executed when certain actions or events occur.

Business Central page structure

Let's look at what makes up a typical page in the Business Central web client. We can identify four main areas: (**1**) the navigation area, (**2**) the page header, (**3**) the content area, and (**4**) the FactBox area:

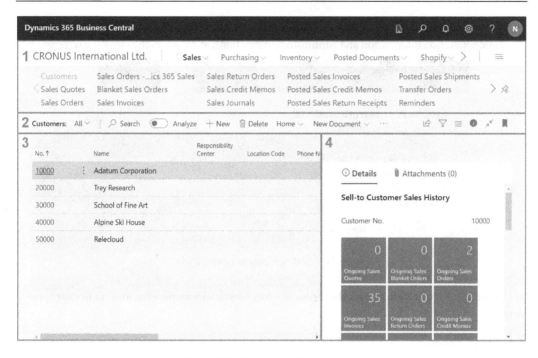

Figure 4.1 – The four main page areas

The black row at the very top is the **application bar**. Although the application bar is not a part of the page structure itself, we should get familiar with two of its items now:

Figure 4.2 – Application bar in Business Central

- The **Tell me** feature (**1**), also accessible by pressing *Alt* + *Q*, allows users to search for and run pages or reports, regardless of the role center they are using, and to find actions on the currently opened page. The **Tell me** search is based on object or action captions and names (full or partial), or sometimes on additionally defined search terms:

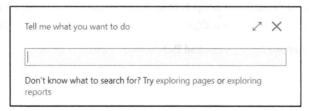

Figure 4.3 – Tell me window

- The **settings button** (**2**) provides access to a general set of menu options. It provides access to some basic application information and administration functions, as shown in the following screenshot:

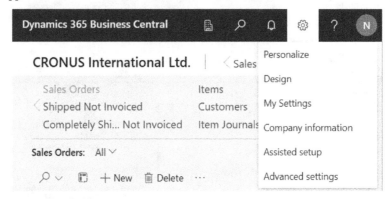

Figure 4.4 – Settings button options

That's all about the application bar for the moment – let's now finally inspect the four main page areas in detail.

Navigation area

The navigation area contains menu options based on the active Role Center, which is tied to the user's login. Consequently, the navigation area appears only on pages opened from the Role Center.

In the navigation area, we can identify three sub-areas:

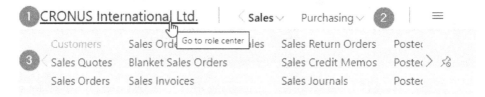

Figure 4.5 – Navigation area

- The **company name** (**1**) acts as a home button. It allows the user to navigate to the Role Center (**Go to role center**) or to refresh it depending on where the user is using the link.

- The **navigation menus** (**2**, here **Sales** and **Purchasing**) expand to display links to other pages (**3**).

Page header

The page header consists of multiple parts, as we can see in the following screenshot:

Figure 4.6 – Page header

While there are numerous system-generated items, only the following header items will be directly influenced by our page design:

- The **title** (1) displays the page caption.
- The **Views menu button** (2) is where the user controls the filtering to be applied to the page display. If we click on the down-facing arrowheads in the filter button, we always see the options **All** and **Show filter pane** in a drop-down list. The list can additionally contain programmed child menu options (called **views**, for example, **Unpaid**, **Paid**, and **Canceled**), as shown in the following screenshot:

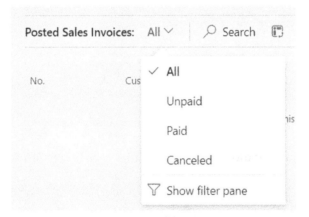

Figure 4.7 – Views menu button drop-down list

- The **action bar** (5) contains actions embedded in a menu structure, partly promoting actions on the left side of the bar. We will talk about designing actions later in the *Page actions* section.

Let us now quickly inspect other – but not AL-controllable – elements in the page header:

- The **Search** icon (3) is available on lists only. It provides users with a quick and easy way to reduce the records in a list and display only those records that contain the data that they are interested in seeing.

- The **Analyze toggle switch** (**4**) toggles **data analysis mode** in Business Central. It is provided only on list pages and queries. In older versions of Business Central, the switch changes its appearance depending on the page size.

- The **Filter pane toggle** (**6**) is available on all list pages, and just like the **Show filter pane** menu item previously shown in *Figure 4.7*, it is used to toggle the **filter pane** on and off. The filter pane enables users to apply filters on one or more fields in the list to limit the records that are displayed:

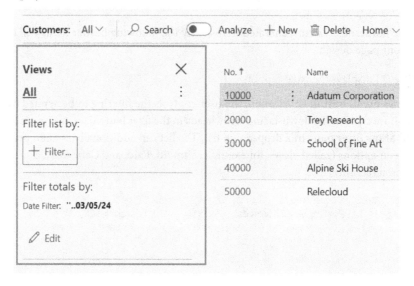

Figure 4.8 – Filter pane shown on the Customers page

- The **FactBox toggle** (**7**) is used to toggle the FactBox pane (or FactBox area) on and off.

Content area

The content area is the focus of the page. It is structured and rendered differently depending on the page type. We will investigate the different page types right after finishing this section about the page structure, in the *Types of pages* section.

FactBox area

The FactBox area (or FactBox pane) can appear on the right side of certain page types, and it is divided into one or more parts that are arranged vertically. FactBoxes can provide no-click and one-click access to related information about the relevant data in the content area.

In the following screenshot, we see a FactBox area consisting of two FactBoxes (**Resource Statistics** and **Resource Details**) grouped in a **Details** tab, and the **Attachments** tab (containing the FactBoxes Attachments and Notes, but they are not visible in the screenshot):

ⓘ **Details**   📎 Attachments (0)

Resource Statistics

Resource No.	KATHERINE
Capacity	0
Unused Capacity	0
Invoiced	0.00
Invoiced %	0.0
Usage (Cost)	0.00
Profit	0.00
Profit %	0.0

Resource Details

Resource No.	KATHERINE
Prices	0
Costs	0

Figure 4.9 – FactBox area with multiple FactBoxes

Now that we know about the four main Business Central page areas, it's about time to inspect the different types of pages that will influence the layout of the content area.

Types of pages

In addition to the very basic pages described from a user perspective in *Chapter 1, Pages section*, let's now review more types of pages available for use in an application. Then, we will create several examples for our WDTU Radio Station extension.

Each time we work on an application design, we will need to carefully consider which page type is best to use for the functionality we are creating. Types of pages presented in this section include RoleCenter, HeadlinePart, List, Card, Document, ListPlus, Worksheet, ConfirmationDialog, StandardDialog, NavigatePage, CardPart, and ListPart.

A complete list can be found in the Microsoft docs *Page types and layouts* article (https://learn. microsoft.com/en-us/dynamics365/business-central/dev-itpro/developer/ devenv-page-types-and-layouts).

Furthermore, we will investigate request pages, bound and unbound pages, and type-related page naming standards.

Pages can be created and modified by the developer and can be personalized by an administrator, superuser, or user.

RoleCenter page type

Users are each assigned a Role Center page as their home page in Business Central—the page where they land when first logging into Business Central. The purpose of a `RoleCenter` page is to provide a task-oriented home base that focuses on the tasks that the user typically needs in order to do their job on a day-to-day basis. Common tasks for any user should be no more than one or two clicks away.

The standard Business Central distribution includes predefined Role Center pages, including generic roles such as the bookkeeper, sales manager, and production planner. Some of the provided Role Centers are richly featured and have been heavily tailored by Microsoft as illustrations of what is possible. On the other hand, some of the provided Role Centers are only skeletons, essentially acting as placeholders.

> **Note**
>
> It is critical to understand that the provided Role Center pages are intended to be templates, not final deliverables.

Central to each Role Center page is the **Activities area**. The **Activities** area provides the user with a visual overview of their primary tasks. Within the **Activities** area are the cues, which are called **tiles** in the UI. Each dark tile (containing a number) represents a filtered list of documents in a particular status, indicating the amount of work to be handled by the user. The grey tiles display a calculated value.

The following screenshot shows the **Activities** area for the user role profile of a sales order processor:

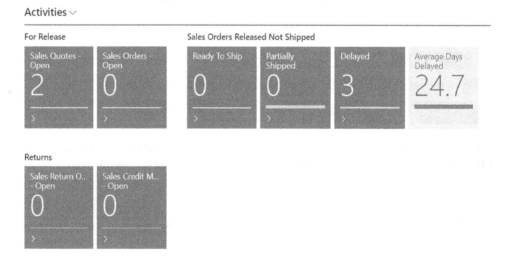

Figure 4.10 – Activities area on a Role Center page

HeadlinePart page type

HeadlinePart pages are embedded in the Role Center similar to activities. **Headlines** are designed to give the user insight into how the company is performing using the most important **Key Performance Indicators (KPIs)**, or to provide productivity tips or links to resources:

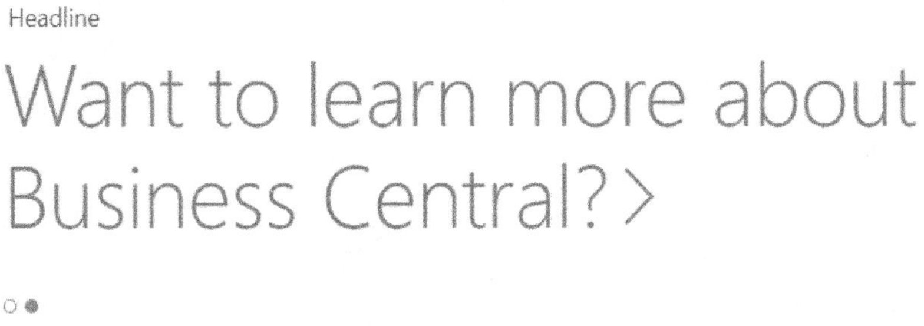

Headline

Want to learn more about Business Central? >

Figure 4.11 – Headline on a Role Center page

As indicated by the dots at the bottom of the previous screenshot, one HeadlinePart page can contain multiple headlines that are displayed one after the other.

List page type

List pages are the first pages accessed when choosing any menu option to access data. This includes all of the entries under the buttons on the navigation pane. A List page displays a list of records (rows), one line per record, with each displayed data field in a column.

When a list page is initially selected, it is not editable. To edit data, we either open an editable Card page by double-clicking on the row or click on **Edit List**. Examples of this latter behavior include the reference table pages, such as **Post Codes**, **Territories**, and **Languages**. A List page can also be used to show a list of master records to allow the user to visually scan through the list of records or to easily choose a record on which to focus.

List pages may optionally include one or more FactBoxes. Some Business Central list pages, such as **Customer Ledger Entries**, allow editing of some fields (for example, invoice due dates) and not other fields.

The following screenshot shows a typical List page—the **Items** list page:

CRONUS International Ltd. | ‹ Sales ⌄   Purchasing ⌄   **Inventory** ⌄   Posted Docu › | ≡

| Items: All ⌄ | | 🔍 📋 | + New \| ⌄ | 🗑 Delete | Home ⌄ | Item ⌄ | ··· | | ⬆ 🔽 ≣ ⓘ 🔖 |

No. ↑		Description	Inventory	Substi... Exist
1896-S	⋮	ATHENS Desk	0	No
1900-S		PARIS Guest Chair, black	0	No
1906-S		ATHENS Mobile Pedestal	0	No
1908-S		LONDON Swivel Chair, blue	0	No
1920-S		ANTWERP Conference Table	0	No
1925-W		Conference Bundle 1-6	0	No
1928-S		AMSTERDAM Lamp	0	No

ⓘ **Details**   📎 Attachments (0)

Item Details - Invoicing

Item No.	1896-S
Costing Method	FIFO
Cost is Adjusted	Yes
Cost is Posted to G/L	Yes
Standard Cost	0.00

Figure 4.12 – List page

The **No.** field values on the far left are linked: clicking them will open the **Item Card** page.

Card page type

Card pages display and allow updating of a single record at a time. Card pages are used for master tables and setup data. Complex cards can contain multiple FastTabs (explained soon, within the *Document page type* section that follows) and FactBoxes, as well as display data from subordinate tables. For example, a Card page image for the **Customer Card**, page **21**, follows, with the **General** and **Shipping** FastTabs expanded and the other FastTabs (**Address & Contact**, **Invoicing**, and **Payments**) collapsed:

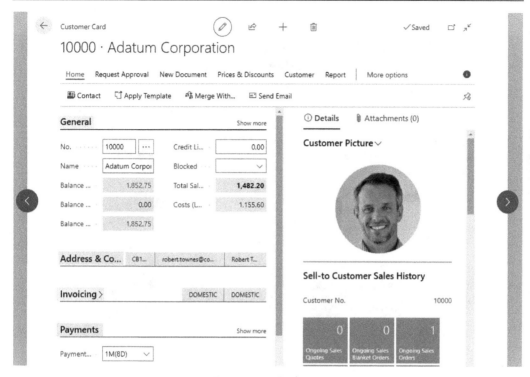

Figure 4.13 – Card page

Document page type

Document (task) pages have at least two FastTabs in a header/detail format. The FastTab at the top (usually named **General**) contains the header fields in a card-style format, followed by a FastTab containing multiple records in a list-style format (a ListPart page). Some examples are **Sales Orders**, **Sales Invoices**, **Purchase Orders**, **Purchase Invoices**, and **Production Orders**. The **Document** page type is appropriate whenever we have a parent record tied to subordinate child records in a one-to-many relationship. A Document page may also have FactBoxes. An example, the **Sales Order** document page, follows, with all FastTabs but one (**Lines**) collapsed:

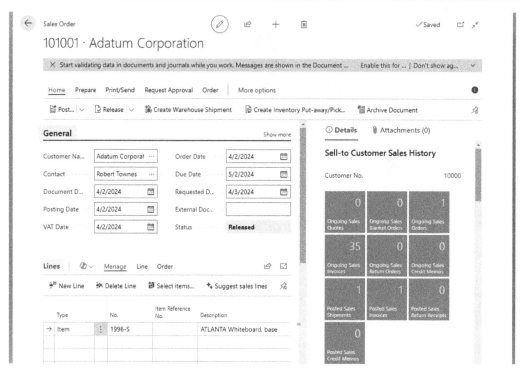

Figure 4.14 – Document page

FastTabs

FastTabs, as shown in the preceding **Customer Card** and **Sales Order** screenshots, are collapsible/expandable groups. FastTabs are often used to segregate data by subject area on a card page or a document page. In the preceding screenshot, the **Lines** FastTab is expanded and the remaining FastTabs are collapsed. Individually important fields can be promoted so that they display on the FastTab header when the tab is collapsed, allowing the user to see this data with minimal effort. Examples appear on the **Sales Orders** collapsed **Invoice Details** and **Prepayment** FastTabs. Promoted field displays disappear from the FastTab header when the FastTab is expanded.

ListPlus page type

A ListPlus page is similar in layout to a Document page as it will have at least one FastTab with fields in a card-type format and one FastTab with a List page format. Unlike a Document page, a ListPlus page may have more than one FastTab with card format fields and one or more FastTabs with a list page format, while a Document page can only have a single list-style subpage. The card format portion of a ListPlus page often contains control information determining what data is displayed in the associated list, such as on page **113**, **Budget**, which is shown in the following screenshot:

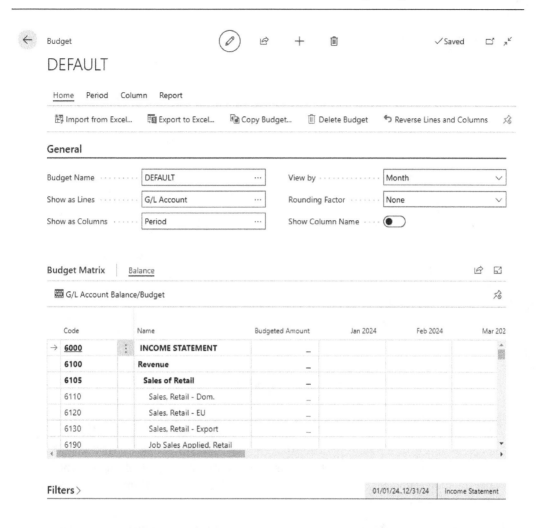

Figure 4.15 – ListPlus page with fields in card type format

A `ListPlus` page may also have FactBoxes. Other examples of `ListPlus` pages are page **155**, **Customer Sales**, and page **157**, **Item Availability by Periods**.

Worksheet page type

`Worksheet` pages are widely used in Business Central to enter transactions. The `worksheet` page format consists of a `List` page style section showing multiple record lines in the content area, followed by a section containing either additional detail fields for the line in focus or containing totals. All of the journals in Business Central use `Worksheet` pages. Data is usually entered into a journal/ worksheet by keyboard entry, but in some cases, it's entered via a batch process.

The following screenshot shows a Worksheet page, **Sales Journals**—page **253**:

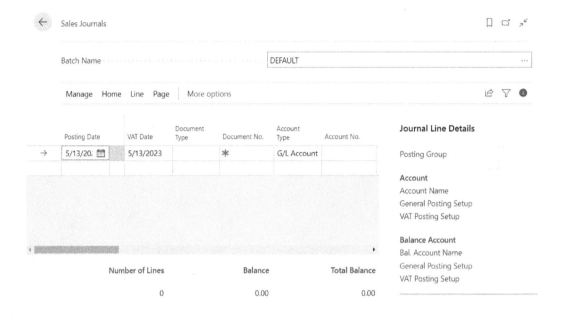

Figure 4.16 – Worksheet page

Find entries function

The **Find entries function**, formerly known as the **Navigate function**, has been a very powerful and unique feature of Business Central since the 1990s. Somewhat confusingly, in Business Central, the find entries function is implemented using the Worksheet page type, not the NavigatePage page type, which was used in early Business Central releases.

The **Find entries** page (page **344**) allows the user, who may be a developer operating in user mode, to view a summary of the number and type of posted entries having the same document number and posting date as a related entry or as a user-entered value. The user can drill down to examine the individual entries. **Find entries** is a terrific tool for tracking down related posted entries. It can be productively used by a user, an auditor, or even a developer. A sample **Find entries** page is shown in the following screenshot:

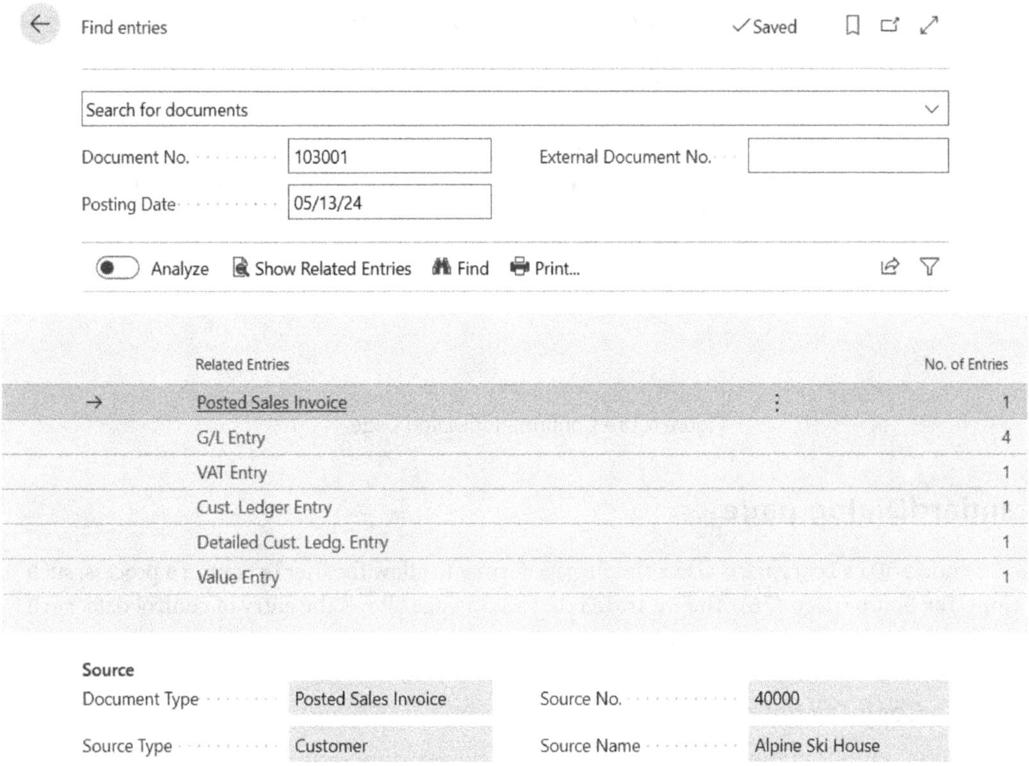

Figure 4.17 – Find entries page

ConfirmationDialog page

This is a simple display page embedded in a process. It is used to allow a user to control the flow of a process by clicking **Yes** or **No**. A sample ConfirmationDialog page is shown in the following screenshot:

Figure 4.18 – ConfirmationDialog page

StandardDialog page

The `StandardDialog` page is also a simple page format to allow the user to control a process, such as **Copy Tax Setup** (page **476**). The `StandardDialog` page allows the entry of control data, such as that shown in the following screenshot:

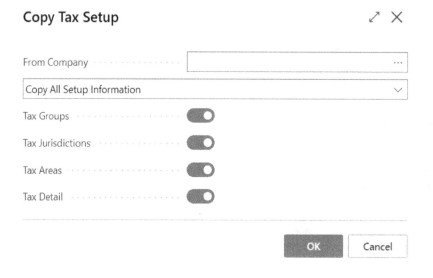

Figure 4.19 – StandardDialog page

NavigatePage page type

The primary use of the `NavigatePage` page type in Business Central is as the basis for multi-step wizards. The **Assisted Setup** page in Business Central uses many lists and wizards. A `NavigatePage` page consists of multiple user data entry screens linked together to provide a series of steps necessary to complete a task. The following screenshot shows the **Set Up Email** page:

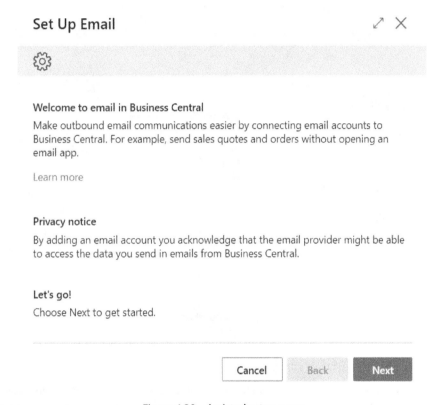

Figure 4.20 – Assisted setup page

Request page

A **request page** is a simple page that allows the user to enter information to control the execution of a `report` or `xmlport` object. Request pages can have multiple FastTabs. All request page designs will be similar to the following screenshot for the **VAT Register** (report **13**) request page:

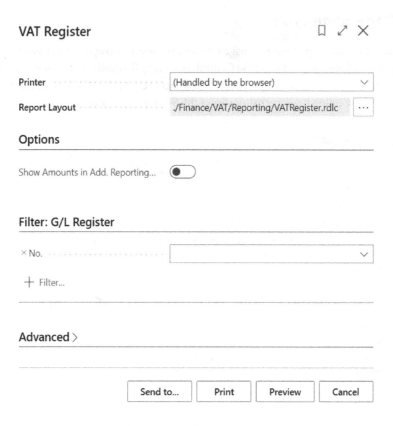

Figure 4.21 – Request page

Page parts

Several of the page types we have reviewed so far contain multiple panes, with each pane including special-purpose parts. Let's look at some of the component page parts available to the developer: the CardPart and ListPart page types.

> **Note**
>
> Some page parts compute the displayed data on the fly, taking advantage of **FlowFields** that may require considerable system resources to process the FlowField calculations. As developers, we must be careful about causing performance problems through the overuse of such displays.

CardPart page type

CardPart pages are used for mostly FactBoxes that don't require a list. CardPart pages typically display fields or perhaps a picture control. An example of the **Customer Statistics** FactBox (page **9082**) is shown in the following screenshot:

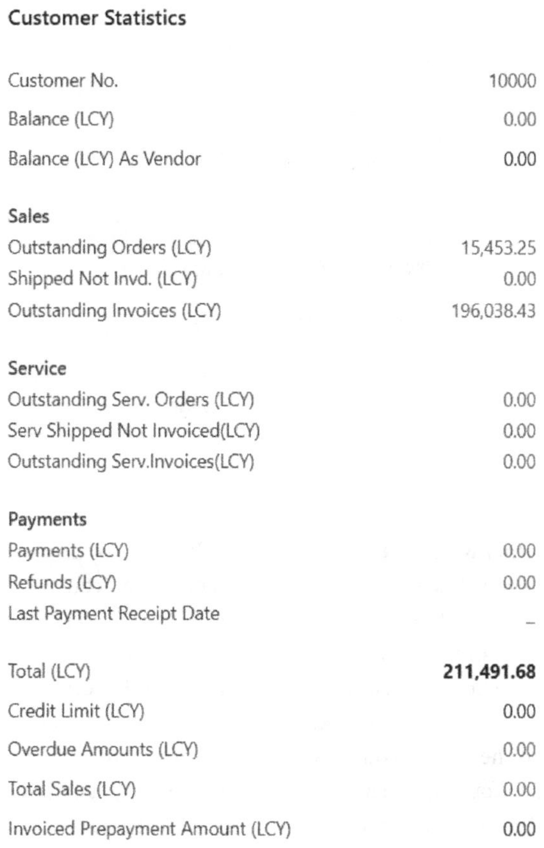

Customer Statistics

Customer No.	10000
Balance (LCY)	0.00
Balance (LCY) As Vendor	0.00
Sales	
Outstanding Orders (LCY)	15,453.25
Shipped Not Invd. (LCY)	0.00
Outstanding Invoices (LCY)	196,038.43
Service	
Outstanding Serv. Orders (LCY)	0.00
Serv Shipped Not Invoiced(LCY)	0.00
Outstanding Serv.Invoices(LCY)	0.00
Payments	
Payments (LCY)	0.00
Refunds (LCY)	0.00
Last Payment Receipt Date	–
Total (LCY)	**211,491.68**
Credit Limit (LCY)	0.00
Overdue Amounts (LCY)	0.00
Total Sales (LCY)	0.00
Invoiced Prepayment Amount (LCY)	0.00

Figure 4.22 – CardPart page

ListPart page type

A ListPart page is a type of page part used to display a list of records embedded within another page. It can be contained in Role Centers, in the FactBox and content area of other pages, in a tabular step in a Wizard, and as a subpage in a Document page.

A list is defined as columns of repeated data. No more than two or three columns should appear in a FactBox list. The following screenshot shows the three-column **My Items** FactBox (page **9152**):

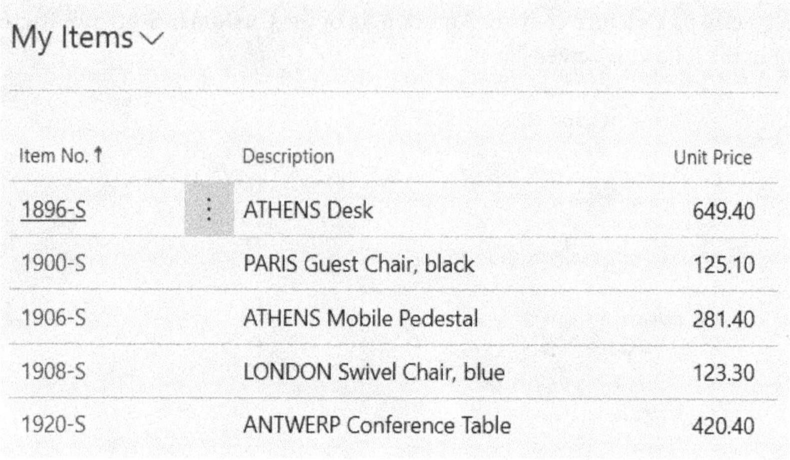

Item No. ↑		Description	Unit Price
1896-S	⋮	ATHENS Desk	649.40
1900-S		PARIS Guest Chair, black	125.10
1906-S		ATHENS Mobile Pedestal	281.40
1908-S		LONDON Swivel Chair, blue	123.30
1920-S		ANTWERP Conference Table	420.40

Figure 4.23 – ListPart page

Power BI

Business Central works together with the **Power BI service**. Reports for displaying in Business Central page parts are stored in a Power BI service. In Business Central, you can switch the report displayed in the Power BI part to any Power BI report available in your Power BI service. The **Power BI Reports Selection** page shows a list of all the Power BI reports that you have access to. This list is retrieved from any workspaces that have been shared with you in the Power BI service. Dynamics 365 Business Central includes a Power BI FactBox on several key list pages, hidden by default. This FactBox provides extra insight into the data in the list. As you move between rows in the list, the report is updated and filtered for the selected entry. You can add a Power BI report to any page by adding a Power BI report page part. The main object for displaying a Power BI report part on role centers and other pages is `page 6325 "Power BI Embedded Report Part"`. There are several parts you can add based on the type of page you are developing in (Role Center, `List`, `Card`, and so on). The code is detailed in the article that follows:

```
https://learn.microsoft.com/en-us/dynamics365/business-central/
dev-itpro/developer/devenv-power-bi-report-parts
```

Financial Dashboard

Gross Margin & Operating Margin % Change by Date

● Gross Margin % ● Operating Margin %

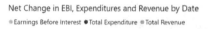

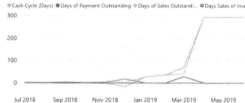

Net Change in EBI, Expenditures and Revenue by Date

● Earnings Before Interest ● Total Expenditure ● Total Revenue

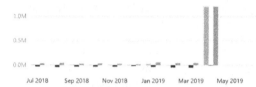

Mini Trial Balance

KPI_Code	KPI_Name	Net_Change_Actual	
30	Gross Margin		1,273,026.30
40	Gross Margin %		280.71
90	Income before Interest and Tax		1,255,016.30
50	Operating Expenses		18,000.00
60	Operating Margin		1,255,026.30
70	Operating Margin %		230.17
80	Other Expenses		10.00
20	Total Cost		275,258.80
10	Total Revenue		1,548,285.10

Figure 4.24 – Examples of Power BI reports

If you have **Power BI Desktop**, you can also create new Power BI reports. Then, once those reports are published to your Power BI workspace, they will appear on the **Power BI Reports Selection** page in Business Central. You can follow the instructions on how to use Power BI Desktop to connect to Business Central APIs at `https://learn.microsoft.com/en-us/dynamics365/business-central/across-how-use-financials-data-source-powerbi`.

Bound and unbound pages

Pages can be created as **bound** (associated with a specific table, using the `SourceTable` page property) or **unbound** (not specifically associated with any table). Typically, a `Card` or `List` page will be bound, but the `RoleCenter`, `StandardDialog`, and `NavigationPage` pages will be unbound. Unbound pages may be used to communicate status information or initiate a process. Examples of unbound pages are page **476—Copy Tax Setup** and page **1040—Copy Job**, both of which have a `PageType` property of `StandardDialog`. Other instances of unbound pages are rare.

Page names

Page naming is based on the page type being used.

`Card` pages are named similarly to the table with which they are associated, with the addition of the word `Card`. Examples include `Customer` table and **Customer Card**, `Item` table and **Item Card**, and `Vendor` table and **Vendor Card**.

List pages are named similarly to the table with which they are associated. List pages that are simple not-editable lists have the word List associated with the table name. Examples include Customer List, Item List, and Vendor List. For each of these, the table also has an associated Card page.

Where the table has no associated Card page, the list pages are named after the tables, but in the plural format. Examples include the Customer Ledger Entry table and **Customer Ledger Entries** page, Check Ledger Entry table and **Check Ledger Entries** page, Country/Region table and **Countries/Regions** page, and Production Forecast Name table and **Production Forecast Names** page.

The single-record setup tables that are used for application control information throughout Business Central are named after their functional area, with the addition of the word Setup. The associated Card page should also be, and generally is, named similarly to the table, for example, the General Ledger Setup table and **General Ledger Setup** page, the Manufacturing Setup table and **Manufacturing Setup** page, and so on.

Journal entry (Worksheet) pages are given names tied to their purpose, with the addition of the word Journal. In the standard product, several journal pages for different purposes are associated with the same table. For example, **Sales Journal**, **Cash Receipts Journal**, **Purchases Journal**, and **Payments Journal** all use the General Journal Line table as their source table (they are different pages all tied to the same table).

If there is a header and line table associated with a data category, such as **Sales Orders**, the related page and subpage should ideally be named to describe the relationship between the tables and the pages. However, in some cases, it's better to tie the page names directly to the function they perform rather than the underlying tables. An example is the two pages making up the display called by the **Sales Order** menu entry—the **Sales Orders** page is tied to the Sales Header table, and the Sales Order Subform page is tied to the Sales Line table. The same tables are involved for the **Sales Invoice** page and Sales Invoice Subform page.

> **Note**
>
> The use of the word *subform* rather than *subpage*, as in Sales Invoice Subform, is a leftover from previous versions of Business Central, which had forms rather than pages.
>
> Sometimes, while naming pages, we will have a conflict between naming pages based on the associated tables and naming them based on the use of the data. For example, the **Contacts** menu entry invokes a main page/subpage named **Contact Card** and Contact Card Subform. The respective tables are the Contact table and the Contact Profile Answer table. The context usage should take precedence in the page naming as was done here.

Before continuing with our WDTU example, we need to review the common components of pages: triggers, properties, layout controls, and actions.

Page components

All pages are made up of certain common components. The basic elements of a page object are the page triggers, page properties, page layout controls with their triggers and properties, and page actions.

In this section, we will first focus on page triggers and properties, and apply our knowledge to update our WDTU Radio Show extension. After that, we will continue with page layout controls, then update the extension once again, and finally look at page actions.

Page triggers

The following screenshot shows page triggers. Note that the OnQueryClosePage trigger isn't related to any query object action:

Figure 4.25 – Page triggers

> **Tip**
> The Microsoft docs do not provide an overview article about page triggers. An easy way of looking up any individual page trigger from Visual Studio Code is to select its name through IntelliSense, then hover over the pasted trigger name and press **Get help**.

In general, according to best practices, we should minimize the AL code placed in page triggers, putting code in a table or field trigger or calling a codeunit library procedure instead. However, many standard pages include a modest amount of code supporting page-specific filter or display functions. When we develop a new page, it's always a good idea to look for similar pages in the standard product and be guided by how those pages operate internally. Sometimes, special display requirements result in complex code being required within a page. It is important that the code in a page be used only to manage the data display, not for data modification.

Page properties

We will now look at the properties of the **Radio Show List** page we created earlier. The list of available page properties is the same for all page types. The values of those properties vary considerably from one page to another, even more from one page type to another. The following screenshot shows a subset of the possible properties using *Ctrl + spacebar* on our Radio Show List page (page **50100**):

```
1    page 50100 "Radio Show List"
2    {
3        PageType = List;
4        ApplicationArea = All;
5        UsageCategory = Lists;
6        SourceTable = "Radio Show";
7
8          DataCaptionExpression
9          DataCaptionFields
10         DelayedInsert
           DeleteAllowed
11         Description
12         Editable
           Extensible
13         HelpLink
14         InherentEntitlements
           InherentPermissions
15         InsertAllowed
                        0 references
```

Figure 4.26 – Page properties

We can see that many of these properties are still in their default condition (they are not explicitly defined, which means that the default value is used). The following are the properties with which we are most likely to be concerned:

- Caption and CaptionML: This is the page name to be displayed and to be searched by using Tell me, depending on the language option in use.

- Editable: This determines whether or not the controls in the page can be edited (assuming the table's editable properties are also set to true). If this property is set to true, the page allows the individual control to determine the appropriate editable property value.

- Description: This is for internal documentation only.

- Permissions: This is used to instruct the system to allow the users of this page to have certain levels of access (r to read, i to insert, m to modify, and d to delete) to the table data in the specified table objects. For example, users of page **499** (**Available – Sales Lines**) are only allowed to read or modify (permissions for Sales Line are equal to rm) the data in the Sales Line table.

- **PageType**: This specifies how this page will be displayed using one of the available page types, for example, **List**.

- **CardPageID**: This is the ID of the card page that should be launched when the user double-clicks on an entry in the list. This is only used on **List** pages. Despite the property name, we should always enter the page name instead.

- **RefreshOnActivate**: When this is set to **true**, it causes the page to refresh when the page is activated.

- **SourceTable**: This is the name of the table to which the page is bound. Only a few page types do not support having a source table.

- **SourceTableView**: This can be utilized to automatically apply defined filters and/or open the page with a key other than the primary key.

- **ShowFilter**: This is set to **false** to not let the filter pane be shown by default. The user can still make the filter pane visible.

- **DelayedInsert**: This delays the insertion of a new record until the user moves focus away from the new line being entered. If this value is **false**, then a new record will automatically be inserted into the table as soon as the primary key fields are completed. This property is generally set to **true** when **AutoSplitKey** (see the following) is set to **true**. It allows complex new data records to be entered with all of the necessary fields completed.

- **MultipleNewLines**: When it is set to **true**, this property allows the insertion of multiple new lines between existing records.

- **SaveValues**: If it is set to **true**, this causes user-specific entered control values to be retained and redisplayed when the page is invoked another time.

- **AutoSplitKey**: This allows for the automatic assignment of a primary key, provided the last field in the primary key is of the **Integer**, **BigInteger**, **Guid**, or **Decimal** data type, and provided the page is sorted by the primary key. This feature enables each new entry to be assigned a key so it will remain sequenced in the table following the record appearing above it. Note that **AutoSplitKey** and **DelayedInsert** are generally used jointly. On a new entry, at the end of a list of entries, the trailing integer portion of the primary key, often named **Line No.**, is automatically incremented by 10,000 (the increment value cannot be changed). When a new entry is inserted between two previously existing entries, their current key-terminating integer values are summed and divided by two (hence the term **AutoSplitKey**) with the resultant value being used for the new entry key-terminating integer value. Since 10,000 (the automatic increment) can only be divided by two and rounded to a non-zero integer result 13 times, only 13 new automatically numbered entries can be inserted between two previously recorded entries by the **AutoSplitKey** property.

- `SourceTableTemporary`: This allows the use of a temporary table as the source table for the page. This can be very useful where there is a need to display data based on the structure of a table, but not using the table data as it persists in the database. Examples of such application usage include page **634—Chart of Accounts Overview** and page **6510—Item Tracking Lines**. Note that the temporary instance of the source table is empty when the page opens up, so our code must populate the temporary table in memory.

Now that we have covered the most important properties, we need to understand how and when they impact the user experience through inheritance.

Inheritance

One of the attributes of an object-oriented system is the inheritance of properties. While Business Central is object-based rather than object-oriented, the properties that affect data validation are inherited. Properties such as decimal formatting are also inherited. If a property is explicitly defined in the table, it cannot be less restrictively defined elsewhere.

Controls that are bound to a table field will inherit the settings of the properties that are common to both the field definition and the control definition. This basic concept applies to the inheritance of data properties, beginning from fields in tables to pages and reports, and then from pages and reports to controls within pages and reports. Inherited property settings that involve data validation cannot be overridden, but all others can be changed. This is another example of why it is generally best to define the properties in the table for consistency and ease of maintenance, rather than defining them for each instance of use in a page or a report.

WDTU page enhancement – part 1

Before we move on to learn about controls and actions, let's do some basic enhancement work on our `WDTU Radio Show` application. In *Chapter 1*, in the *Getting started with application design* section, we created several minimal pages, and later in *Chapter 2*, in the *Enhancing our sample application section*, we added new fields to our `Radio Show` master table (table `50100`). We'll now check which fields to add to the Radio Show list and card pages.

Let's do a quick evaluation to help us to make our decision. First, let's take a look at the existing **Radio Show List** page:

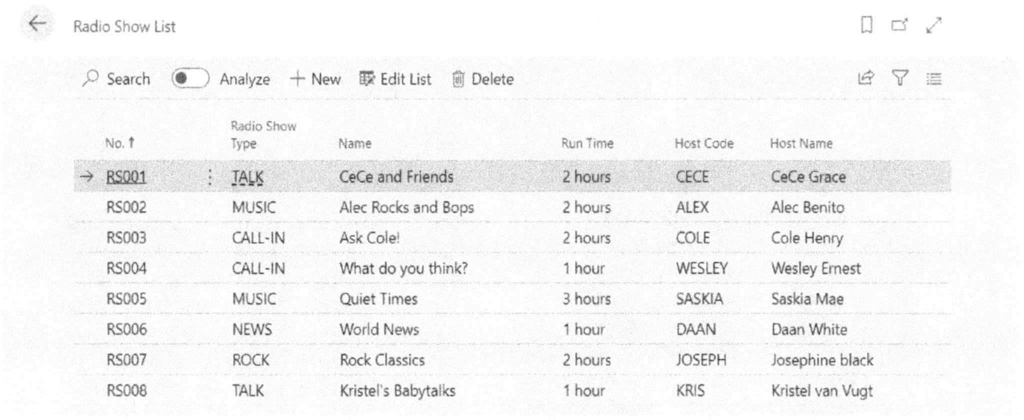

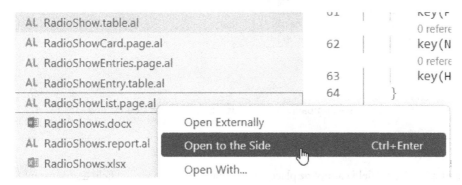

Figure 4.27 – Radio Show List page

To find out which fields are missing, we want to compare the list of fields that exist in the source table (Radio Show—50100) to what we see on the page. To do so, we open the table file first, and then use the **Open to the Side** option in the list available from the drop-down menu when clicking on the page file in Visual Studio Code, as shown in the following screenshot:

Figure 4.28 – Open to the Side in Visual Studio Code

This allows us to compare the table fields and page fields side-by-side and examine which fields are missing:

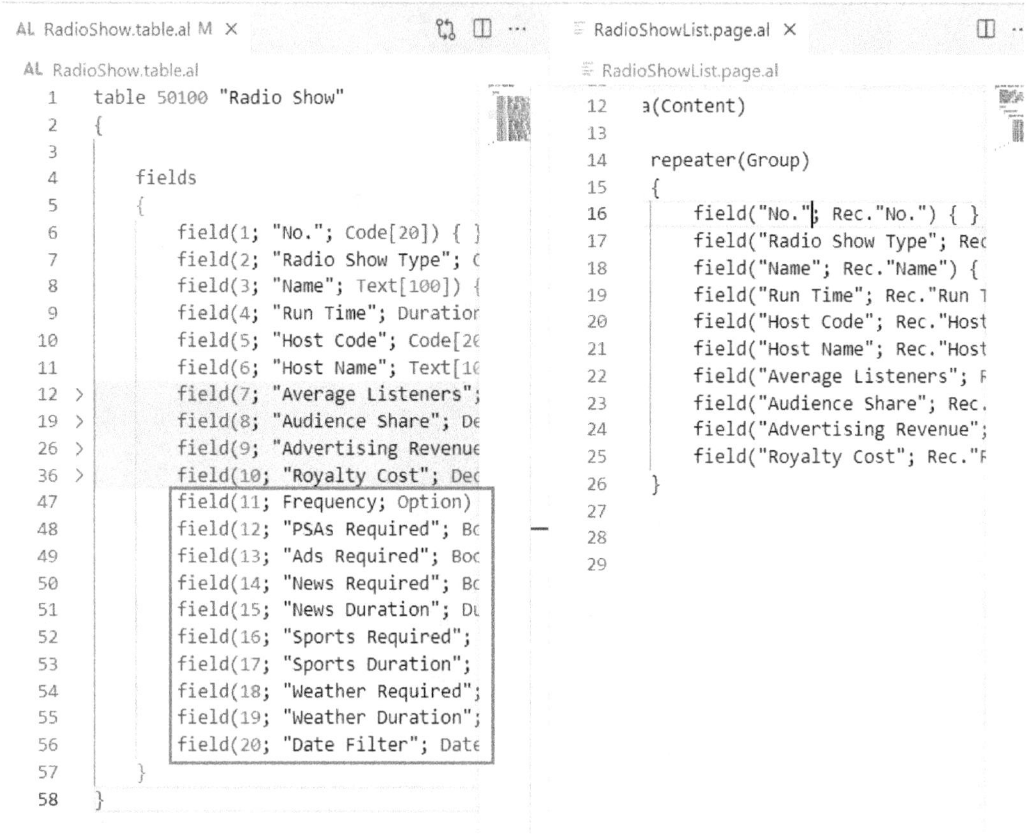

Figure 4.29 – Comparing table fields and page fields side-by-side

> **Note**
> The Date Filter field cannot be placed on the page. This is a virtual field that is meant for users to limit totals by using the filter pane.

After the examination, we decide that the missing fields are not relevant enough to add them to the list page. We will add them to the card page only.

Next, we want to create a new layout for **Radio Show Card**. When we review the data fields, we decide that we should have three FastTabs: **General**, **Requirements**, and **Statistics**. As before, the **Date Filter** field should not be on the page. We want our page to look like this:

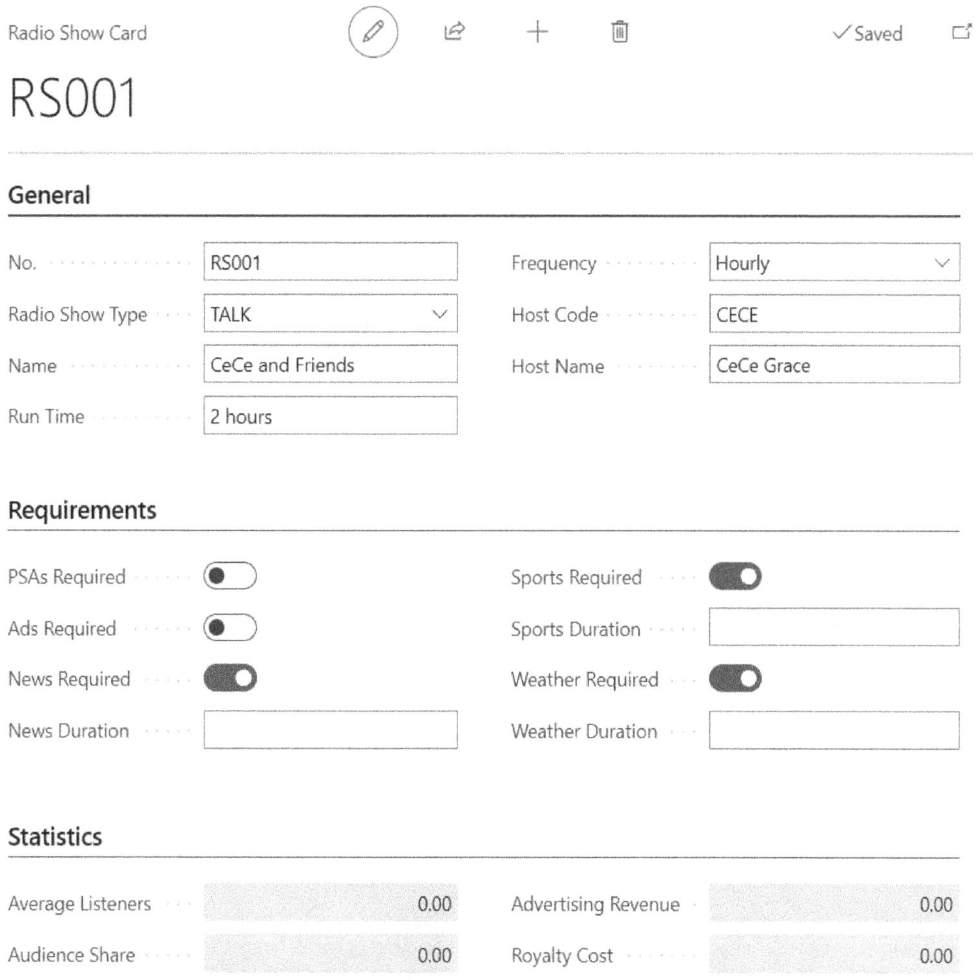

Figure 4.30 – Radio Show Card page with three FastTabs

To achieve this by code, we create a Requirements and Statistics group under – but still on the same indentation level as – the General group. Then we distribute the fields to the respective groups and save the file. To test it, we set the startupObjectID in our launch.json file to 50101 and publish the application. After successful testing, we reset startObjectID to the list page, 50100.

Our final step at this point is to connect the **Radio Show Card** to the **Radio Show List** page, so that when the user double-clicks on a list entry, the card page will be invoked, showing the list-selected entry. This is a simple matter of adding `CardPageId` to the list of properties. Fill in that property with the name of the target card (`Radio Show Card`):

```
1    page 50100 "Radio Show List"
2    {
3        PageType = List;
4        ApplicationArea = All;
5        UsageCategory = Lists;
6        SourceTable = "Radio Show";
7        CardPageId = "Radio Show Card";
8
9        layout
10       {
```

Figure 4.31 – Adding a CardPageID to the Radio Show List definition

> **Note**
>
> Entering the object ID (`50101`) instead of the object name is possible, but it is a bad practice: it lacks readability and support for **Find References** in Visual Studio Code. Furthermore, if we renumbered the object at any later point, we would need to update all its numeric references manually as well.

Next, save, publish, and run the page. We should see both **Edit** and **Edit List**, as shown in the following screenshot:

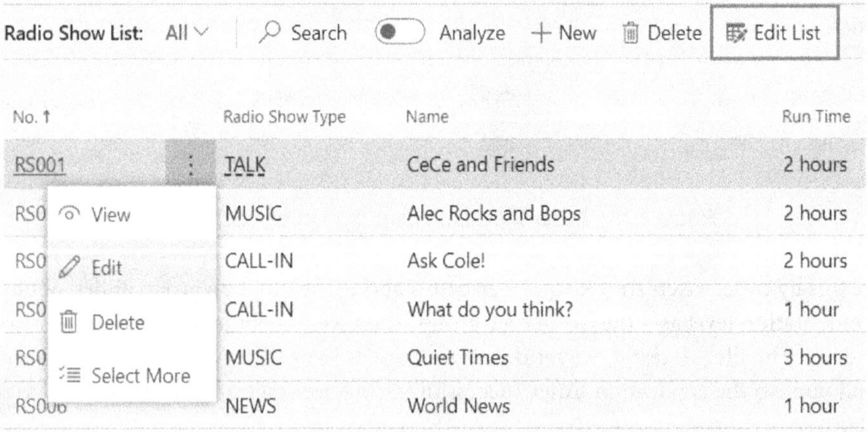

Figure 4.32 – Radio Show List with actions to edit

Clicking on **Edit** will bring up **Radio Show Card**. Clicking on **Edit List** will make the whole list editable. If we don't want the user to be able to edit within the list, we should set the `List` page's `Editable` property to `False`. That way, the **Edit List** action will not be available, as shown in the following screenshot:

Radio Show List: All ∨		Search ● Analyze + New 🗑 Delete	
No. ↑	Radio Show Type	Name	Run Time
RS001 ⋮	TALK	CeCe and Friends	2 hours
RS002	MUSIC	Alec Rocks and Bops	2 hours

Figure 4.33 – Radio Show List being non-editable

After our first page enhancement for the `WDTU Radio Show` extension, we now return to the page components and look at page controls.

Page layout

The page layout determines what the page will look like and is specified in the `layout` section. The layout contains one or more `area` sections that define a certain placement on the page.

Page layout controls are placed inside `area` sections and serve a variety of purposes. Some controls display information on pages. This can be data from the database, static material, pictures, or the results of an AL expression. Grouping controls make it easy for the developer to handle a set of contained controls as a group.

> **Tip**
> The Microsoft docs *Pages overview* site (https://learn.microsoft.com/en-us/dynamics365/business-central/dev-itpro/developer/devenv-pages-overview) provides good background guidance on the organization of controls within page types for Business Central.

Let's inspect the `area` section and the most commonly used page layout controls in detail, and then close with an example from standard Business Central.

Layout area section

Area sections define the root-level primary structures within a page layout. Every page layout, no matter the page type, starts with an area control. An `area` section can be one of three subtypes: `Content`, `FactBoxes`, or `RoleCenter`. The `RoleCenter` area section can only be used on a `RoleCenter` page type. A page can only have one instance of each area subtype, but different areas per page, for example, both `Content` and `FactBoxes`.

Until now, each page within the WDTU application was created with an `area` section of the `Content` subtype:

```
layout
{
    area(Content)
    {
        ...
    }
}
```

On closer inspection, we can see that the names of the `Content` and `FactBoxes` areas exactly reflect the page structure terms that we have learned at the very beginning of this chapter in the *Business Central page structure* section.

Within each `area` section, we can place grouping controls, parts, or fields.

Grouping controls

The `repeater`, `group`, `grid`, `fixed`, and `cuegroup` keywords define a new group of the controls on the page. Some grouping controls are reserved for certain page types.

Overall, more than 20 properties are available for any kind of grouping controls. Three of them are particularly significant because of their effect on all of the fields within the group:

- `Visible`: This can be `true` or `false`, defaulting to `true`. The `Visible` property can be assigned a Boolean expression, which can be evaluated during processing. This allows users to dynamically change the visibility of a group of fields during the processing, based on some variable conditions (dynamic processing must occur in the `OnInit`, `OnOpenPage`, or `OnAfterGetCurrRecord` trigger).

- `Enabled`: This can be `true` or `false`, defaulting to `true`. The `Enabled` property can be assigned a Boolean expression to allow dynamically changing the enabling of a group of fields.

- `Editable`: This can be `true` or `false`, defaulting to `true`. The `Editable` property can be assigned a Boolean expression to allow dynamically changing the editability of a group of fields.

Let's take a closer look at the available grouping controls.

repeater control

With the help of a `repeater` control in `List`-type pages, page fields are grouped and displayed as repeated rows. We use them on `tabular` type-looking pages. The layout of all WDTU `List` pages, such as the `Radio Show Types` page, was defined using the `repeater` control:

```
layout
{
    area(Content)

    {
        repeater(Group)
        {
            <field controls>
        }
    }
}
```

The following `repeater`-specific control properties are particularly worth mentioning:

- `IndentationColumn` and `IndentationControls`: These properties allow a group to be defined in which fields will be indented, as shown in the following screenshot of the **Chart of Accounts** page. Examples of other pages that utilize the indentation properties include page **16—Chart of Accounts** and page **18—G/L Account List**:

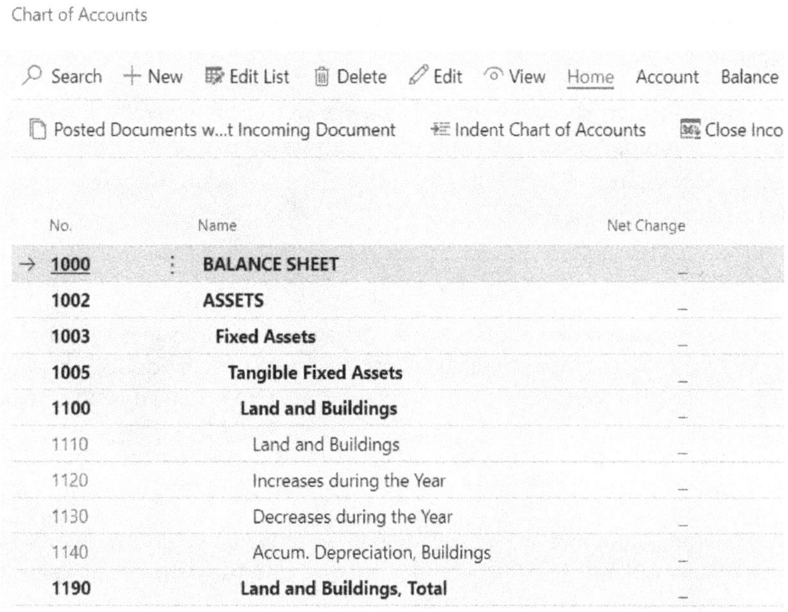

Chart of Accounts

No.	Name	Net Change
→ 1000	**BALANCE SHEET**	—
1002	**ASSETS**	—
1003	**Fixed Assets**	—
1005	**Tangible Fixed Assets**	—
1100	**Land and Buildings**	—
1110	Land and Buildings	—
1120	Increases during the Year	—
1130	Decreases during the Year	—
1140	Accum. Depreciation, Buildings	—
1190	**Land and Buildings, Total**	—

Figure 4.34 – Indented column

> **Note**
>
> For more information, see the Microsoft docs *Designing Indented Hierarchy Lists* article: `https://learn.microsoft.com/en-us/dynamics365/business-central/dev-itpro/developer/devenv-indented-hierarchy-lists`.

- `FreezeColumn`: This freezes the identified column and all of the columns to the left, so they remain in a fixed position while the columns to the right can scroll horizontally. This is like freezing a pane in an Excel worksheet. Users can also freeze columns as part of the personalization.

- `ShowAsTree`: This works together with the `IndentationColumn` property. `ShowAsTree` allows an indented set of rows to be expanded or collapsed dynamically by the user for easier viewing. Example pages that use this property are page **634—Chart of Accounts Overview**, and page **5522—Order Planning**.

group control

Using a `group` control, we can arrange and control a set of fields on page types that display only one record at a time, for example, on a `Card` page. The control can be placed in `area` sections and within `group` controls, but not in `repeater` controls.

Only `group` controls defined directly under the `area` section are rendered as a FastTab. In our WDTU application, the `Radio Show Card` was defined with three FastTabs.

A FastTab control also makes it easy for the user to consider a set of controls as a group. The user can make all of the controls on FastTabs visible or invisible by expanding or collapsing the FastTabs. The user also has the option to show, or not to show, a particular FastTab as a part of the page customizing capability.

A FastTab may contain further `group` controls. While the web client generally distributes all fields equally between two columns, we can put fields into a sub-group to display them automatically in one column only. Furthermore, a sub-group is useful whenever we want to apply properties to only a subset of fields within a page or a FastTab.

> **Tip**
>
> The Microsoft docs provide a dedicated help page for designing FastTabs named *Field Arrangement on FastTabs* (`https://learn.microsoft.com/en-us/dynamics365/business-central/dev-itpro/developer/devenv-arranging-fields-on-fasttab`).

grid control

A `grid` control provides additional formatting capabilities to layout fields, row by row, column by column, spanning rows or columns, and hiding or showing captions. Page **970—Time Sheet Allocation** contains an example of `grid` control use.

To learn more about `grid` control use, search the Microsoft docs for *Arranging Fields in Rows and Columns Using the Grid Control*.

fixed control

The `fixed` control is used at the bottom of `list` pages, following a `repeater` group. The `fixed` group typically contains totals or additional line-related detail fields. Many journal pages, such as page **39—General Journal**, page **40—Item Journal**, and page **201—Job Journal**, have `fixed` groups. The **Item Journal** `fixed` group only shows `Item Description`, which is also available in a repeater column, but can easily display other fields as well. A `fixed` group can also display a lookup or calculated value, such as many of the statistics pages, for example, page **151—Customer Statistics** and page **152—Vendor Statistics**.

To learn more about `fixed` control use, find *Arranging Fields in Rows and Columns Using a fixed Control* in the Microsoft docs.

cuegroup control

`cuegroup` controls are used for `RoleCenter` pages as the structure for the actions that are the primary focus of a user's workday. Cuegroups are found in page parts, typically having the word `Activities` in their name. They are included in Role Center page definitions. The following screenshot shows four `cuegroup` instances defined:

```
page 9060 "SO Processor Activities"
{
  layout
  {
    area(Content)
    {
      cuegroup("For Release")
      { ...
      }
      cuegroup("Sales Orders Released Not Shipped")
      { ...
      }
      cuegroup(Returns)
      { ...
      }
      cuegroup("Document Exchange Service")
```

Figure 4.35 – Cuegroups in code

The first three `cuegroup` instances are shown displayed in the following Role Center screenshot:

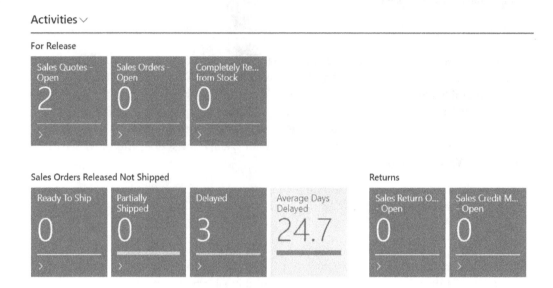

Figure 4.36 – Cuegroups in the web client

field control

The `area` section and all previously mentioned grouping controls serve as containers for `field` controls. For each single value to be displayed, regardless of its data type, one `field` control has to be placed. The page `field` control syntax is as follows:

```
field(ControlName; SourceExpr)
{
    <properties>
}
```

The `ControlName` has to be chosen by us; it is used for addressing the field in page extensions. The `SourceExpr` is the place to define the value to display. This is a table field in most cases, but we can also use variables or expressions. All of the `field` control properties are listed for each field, but individual properties only apply to the data type for which they make sense. For example, the `DecimalPlaces` property only applies to fields where the data type is decimal. The following is a subset screenshot of the properties for `field` controls, as revealed by IntelliSense:

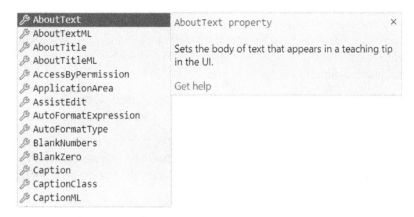

Figure 4.37 – field control properties

We'll review the `field` control properties that are more frequently used or that are more significant in terms of effect, as follows:

- `Visible`, `Enabled`, and `Editable`: These have the same functionality as the identically named grouping controls, but they only apply to individual fields. If the grouping control is set to `false`, either statically (in the control definition within the page) or dynamically by an expression evaluated during processing, the grouping control's `false` condition will take precedence over the equivalent field control setting. Precedence applies in the same way at the next, higher levels of identically named properties at the page level, and then at the table level. For example, if a data field is set to non-editable in the table, that setting will take precedence over (override) other settings in a page, control group, or control.

- `HideValue`: This allows the value of a field to be optionally displayed or hidden, based on an expression that evaluates to `true` or `false`.

- `Caption` or `CaptionML`: These define the caption that will be displayed for the field (in English or the current system language if that is not English). If no caption is defined using one of these properties, then the page will display the control name as `caption`.

- `ShowCaption`: This is set to `true` or `false`; it determines whether or not the caption is displayed.

- `MultiLine`: This must be set to `true` if the field is to display multiple lines of text.

- `OptionCaption` or `OptionCaptionML`: These set the text string options that are displayed to the user. The captions that are set as page field properties will override those defined in the equivalent table field property. The default captions are those defined in the table.

- `DecimalPlaces`: This applies to decimal fields only. If the number of decimal places defined on the page is smaller than that defined in the table, the display is rounded accordingly. If the field definition is the smaller number, it controls the display. In other words, the smaller number of decimal places defined is what is displayed.

- `Width`: This property works only on `field` controls that are placed inside a `repeater` control. It allows setting a specific field display width—a number of characters.

- `ShowMandatory`: This shows a red asterisk in the field display to indicate a required (mandatory) data field. `ShowManadatory` can be based on an expression that evaluates to `true` or `false`. This property does not enforce any validation of the field. Validation is left to the developer.

- `ApplicationArea`: This allows us to hide controls based on the Application Area feature. The `ApplicationArea` value is specified only if it differs from the value on the page object level. It must be specified on every page extension field. We will come to that again later in the *Visibility and searchability* section.

- `QuickEntry`: This allows the field to optionally receive focus or be skipped, based on an expression that evaluates to `true` or `false`.

- `AccessByPermission`: This determines the permission mask required for a user to view or access this field.

- `Importance`: This controls the display of a field. This property only applies to individual (non-repeating) fields located within a FastTab. Importance can be set to `Standard` (the default), `Promoted`, or `Additional`, which are briefly described here:

  - `Standard`: This is the normal display.

  - `Promoted`: If the FastTab is collapsed, the field value will be displayed in the header of the FastTab. If the FastTab is expanded, the field will display normally.

  - `Additional`: If the property is set to `Additional` and the FastTab is collapsed, there is no effect on the display. If the FastTab is expanded, then the user can determine whether or not the field is displayed by clicking on the **Show more** or **Show less** display controls in the upper-right corner of the expanded FastTab.

- `ExtendedDatatype`: This allows a text field to be categorized as a special data type that affects the layout and behavior on a page. The default value is `None`. If `ExtendedDatatype` is selected, it can be any one of the following data types:

  - `PhoneNo`: This displays a hyperlinked phone number whenever the field is not editable. Activating the hyperlink will launch the default dialing app on our device.

  - `URL`: This displays a formatted hyperlink whenever the field is not editable. Activating the hyperlink will open the URL using the default browser on our device.

- EMail: This displays a hyperlinked email address whenever the field is not editable. Activating the hyperlink will launch the default mail app on our device.

- Masked: This fills the field with bold dots in order to mask the actual entry. The number of masking characters displayed is independent of the actual field contents. The contents of a masked field cannot be copied.

- Person: This allows rendering an image of a person in the signature rounded styling.

- Barcode: This provides the option to set the field value using a barcode scanner on phone and tablet clients.

- RichContent: For a field within a FastTab that has the MultiLine property set to true, this enables the display of **rich text**.

- Image: This allows the display of an image on a cue for a field control in a cuegroup control. It only applies to a cuegroup field of an integer data type.

There are six triggers for each field control. The following screenshot shows field control triggers:

Figure 4.38 – Field control triggers

The guideline for the use of these triggers is the same as the guideline for page triggers—if there is a choice, don't put AL code in a control trigger. Not only will this make our code easier to upgrade in the future but it will also make it easier to debug, and it will be easier for the developer following us to decipher our changes.

Page part controls

Page parts are used for FactBoxes and subpages. We embed subpages with a part control using the following syntax:

```
part(ControlName; PartPageName)
{
    <properties>
}
```

Parts placed directly in an `area(Content)` control are rendered as a FastTab.

System parts are system-predefined controls to display links or record links attached to the current record. We declare a `systempart` control as follows:

```
systempart(ControlName; SystemPartType)
{
    <properties>
}
```

As `SystemPartType`, we can choose between `Links` and `Notes`. Other values offered by IntelliSense are ignored in the web client.

Many of the properties of page parts are similar to the properties of other Business Central components and operate essentially the same way in a page part as they operate elsewhere. Those properties include `Visible`, `Enabled`, `Editable`, `Caption`, `CaptionML`, `ToolTip`, `ToolTipML`, and `Description`.

Other properties that are specific to the page part controls are as follows:

- `SubPageView`: This defines the table view, hence the sort order and filters, that apply to named `Subpage` as shown in the following screenshot of `part`:

```
part(Subpage; "Example Document Subpage")
{
    SubPageView = sorting("Document No.", "Line No.");
    SubPageLink = "Document No." = field("No.");
}
```

Figure 4.39 – Setting SubPageView and SubPageLink for a page part

- `SubPageLink`: This defines the fields that link to the subpage and the link that is based on a constant, a filter, or another field. This is also shown in the preceding screenshot.

- `UpdatePropagation`: This allows us to update the parent page from the child (subordinate) page. A value of `SubPart` updates the subpage only. A value of `Both` will cause the parent page to be updated and refreshed at the same time as the subpage.

- `Provider`: This contains the name of another page `part` control within the current page. This enables us to link a subordinate part to a controlling parent part other than the current page. For example, page **42—Sales Order** uses this property to update `Sales Line FactBox` by linking it to the `SalesLines` part.

Layout example

The following (simplified) screenshot from page **5600—Fixed Asset Card**, with all of the grouping controls collapsed, shows two `area` sections. The content area consists of four FastTabs (three `group` controls and one `part` control), whereas the FactBox area consists of one page part (`part` control):

```
page 5600 "Fixed Asset Card"
{
  layout
  {
    area(Content)
    {
      group(General)
      { …
      }
      group("Depreciation Book")
      { …
      }
      part(DepreciationBook;"FA Depreciation Books Subform")
      {
      }
      group(Maintenance)
      { …
      }
    }
    area(FactBoxes)
    {
      part(FixedAssetPicture;"Fixed Asset Picture")
```

Figure 4.40 – Grouping controls

The resulting **Fixed Asset Card** page layout in the client, including the action bar that we will inspect at a later point, is displayed in the following screenshot:

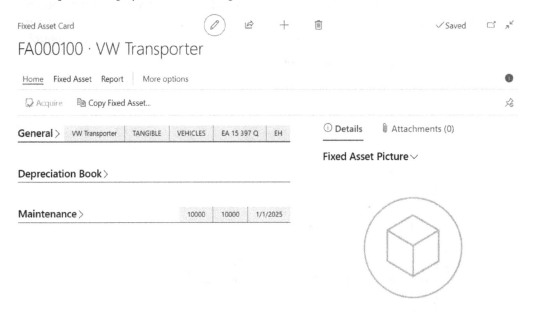

Figure 4.41 – Fixed Asset Card page in the client

The reason for seeing only three FastTabs instead of four is that due to their `Visible` property, either the `group` or `part` control is shown as **Depreciation Book**. Now that we have an additional understanding of page structures, let's do a little more enhancing of our WDTU application pages.

WDTU page enhancement – part 2

We've decided that it will be useful to keep track of specific listener contacts: a fan list. First, we will need to create a table of fan information that we will save as a table with the `50110` ID and name it `Radio Show Fan`, which will look like the following screenshot:

```
1    table 50110 "Radio Show Fan"
2    {
3        fields
4        {
             0 references
5            field(1; "No."; Code[20]) { }
             1 reference
6            field(2; "Radio Show No."; Code[20]) { }
             0 references
7            field(3; Name; Text[100]) { }
             0 references
8            field(4; "E-Mail"; Text[80]) { }
             0 references
9            field(5; "Last Contacted"; Date) { }
10       }
11   }
```

Figure 4.42 – Radio Show Fan table definition

We want to be able to review the fan list as we scan the **Radio Show List**. This requires adding a FactBox area to the `Radio Show List` page. In turn, that requires a page part that will be displayed in the FactBox. The logical sequence is to create the page part first, then add the FactBox to the `Radio Show List` page. We just want a simple list part with three columns, including just the `Name`, `Email`, and `Last Contacted` fields, which we will save as page **50110 – Radio Show Fan Factbox**. The following screenshot shows the new page in Visual Studio code:

```
1    page 50110 "Radio Show Fan Factbox"
2    {
3        PageType = ListPart;
4        ApplicationArea = All;
5        SourceTable = "Radio Show Fan";
6
7        layout
8        {
             0 references
9            area(Content)
10           {
                 0 references
11               repeater(Group)
12               {
                     0 references
13                   field(Name; Rec.Name) { }
                     0 references
14                   field("E-Mail"; Rec."E-Mail") { }
                     0 references
15                   field("Last Contacted"; Rec."Last Contacted") { }
16               }
17           }
18       }
19   }
```

Figure 4.43 – Radio Show Fan Factbox page definition

Next, we will add a `FactBoxes` area to the **Radio Show List** page, populate it with our page part (the `Radio Show Fan Factbox` page), and set the properties for the page part to link to the highlighted record in the **Radio Show List** page, as shown in the following screenshot:

```
25                          |        field("Royalty Cost"; Rec."Royalty Cost") { }
26                          }
27                      }
28
                    0 references
29                  area(FactBoxes)
30                  {
                        0 references
31                      part(Fans; "Radio Show Fan Factbox")
32                      {
33                          SubPageLink = "Radio Show No." = field("No.");
34                      }
35                  }
36              }
37          }
```

Figure 4.44 – Linking the Radio Show Fan FactBox

If we run the **Radio Show List** and press the **FactBox pane** toggle, we should see something like the following screenshot:

Figure 4.45 – Testing the Radio Show Fan Factbox

Before finishing this part of our enhancement effort, we will create a list page that we can use to view and maintain the data in the `Radio Show Fan` table in the future (assign it as the **50111** page— **Radio Show Fans**).

One other enhancement we can make now is to promote some fields in the `Radio Show Card` object so they can be seen when FastTabs are collapsed. All we have to do is choose the fields we want to promote and then change the field control property of `Importance` to `Promoted`. If we choose the fields and promote `No.`, `Radio Show Type`, `Name`, and `Average Listeners`, our card with collapsed FastTabs will look like the following screenshot; we don't have any listenership entry data for the **Statistics** FastTab yet:

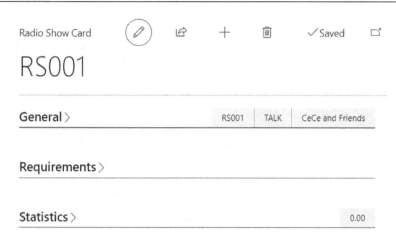

Figure 4.46 – Promoted fields on the Radio Show Card

After having gained practice with page layout controls, it is now time to learn about page action controls.

Page actions

Actions are the menu items of Business Central. Action menus can be found in several locations. The primary location is the action bar appearing at the top of most pages. Other locations for actions are the navigation pane, Role Center, cuegroups, and the action menu on FactBox page parts. The following image displays the action bar of the **Fixed Asset Card** page:

Figure 4.47 – Action bar structure on the Fixed Asset Card

On the right side (**1**), we find several clickable action menus containing actions and action groups. Where the **Related** and **Reports** menus have been added by AL code, the **Automate** menu is added by the platform. Other available action menu types, though not visible on the **Fixed Asset Card** page, are **Actions** and **New**.

To provide users quick access to the actions they need the most, we can promote actions, which will move them to the **promoted actions area** (**2**) on the left side of the action bar. Apart from **Home**, all promoted action menus can be named by the developer. Clicking on a promoted action menu will display actions in a separate line (**3**).

The action bar is defined in the `actions` section, sharing the same level as the `layout` section, just placed below it. Inside the `actions` section, we must define one or more action areas to place `action` or `group` controls. Let's review these one by one.

Action area section

Action area sections define where within the action bar actions will be placed. An `area` section can be one of five subtypes for usual pages: `Creation`, `Navigation`, `Processing`, `Promoted`, or `Reporting`. Those areas are displayed in different action menus as follows:

- Actions in `Reporting` will appear in a **Reports** action menu
- Actions in `Navigation` will appear in a **Related** action menu
- Actions in `Processing` will appear in an **Actions** action menu
- Actions in `Creation` will appear in a **New** action menu
- Actions in `Promoted` will appear on the left side of the action bar

Only on Role Center pages can we additionally select from action areas `Sections` and `Embedding`, as we will cover later in the *Navigation area actions* section.

A page can only have one instance of each area subtype, but different areas per page, for example, both `Navigation` and `Processing`.

Looking at the `Fixed Asset Card` page code (page `5600`), we find the following action areas:

```
actions
{
    area(Navigation)
    { ...
    }
    area(Processing)
    { ...
    }
    area(Reporting)
    { ...
    }
    area(Promoted)
    { ...
    }
}
```

As all actions inside the `Processing` area are promoted (that is, they are also included in the `Promoted` area), the **Actions** action menu is not displayed on the **Fixed Asset Card** page.

Within each `area` section, we can place `group` controls and `action` controls.

Action group control

Action groups provide a submenu grouping of actions within the assigned action menu. An action group is defined using a named group control. The following screenshot compares four action groups defined in the Business Central code with the same groups in the client view:

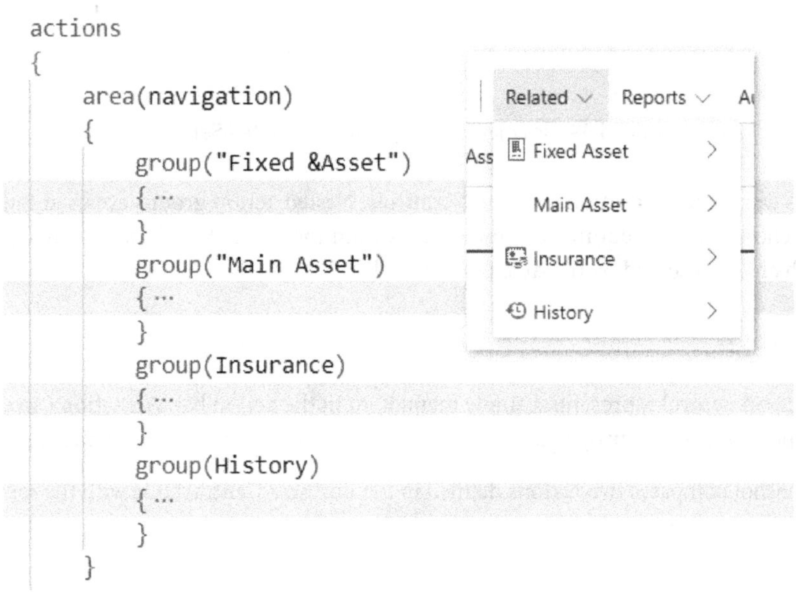

Figure 4.48 – Action groups in code and client

The following are the most frequently used group properties:

- Caption or CaptionML: This is the action name displayed, depending on the language option in use.

- Visible and Enabled: These are true or false, defaulting to true. These properties can be assigned Boolean expressions, which can be evaluated during processing.

- ToolTip or ToolTipML: This is for a helpful display for the user.

- Description: This is for internal documentation.

- Image: This can be used to assign an icon to be displayed. During design time, IntelliSense allows us to preview each image value individually (press *Ctrl* + *spacebar* again if the highlighted box is missing). Note that the image preview does not exactly match the image in the client:

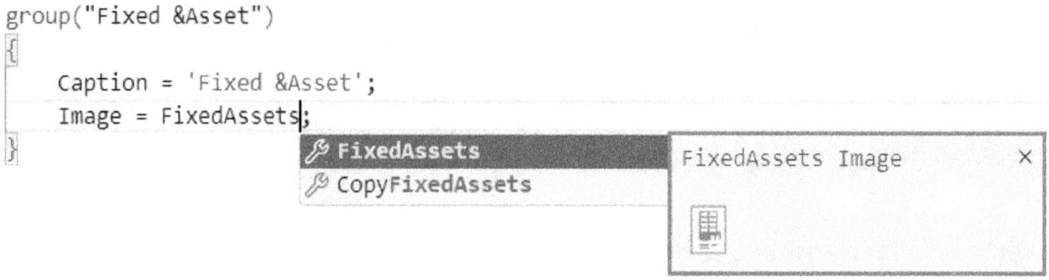
group("Fixed &Asset")
{
Caption = 'Fixed &Asset';
Image = FixedAssets;
}
FixedAssets
CopyFixedAssets
FixedAssets Image

Figure 4.49 – Image preview provided by IntelliSense

Action groups can contain additional `group` controls. Nested action groups are used rather rarely in Business Central, as they require additional clicks from the users. Mostly, action groups contain actions, which are represented by the `action` control

action control

A named `action` control represents a single menu item in the action bar. An action can either run an object by specifying action properties or by executing custom code inside the `OnAction` trigger.

The next screenshot compares two actions defined in the Business Central code with the same actions in the client view:

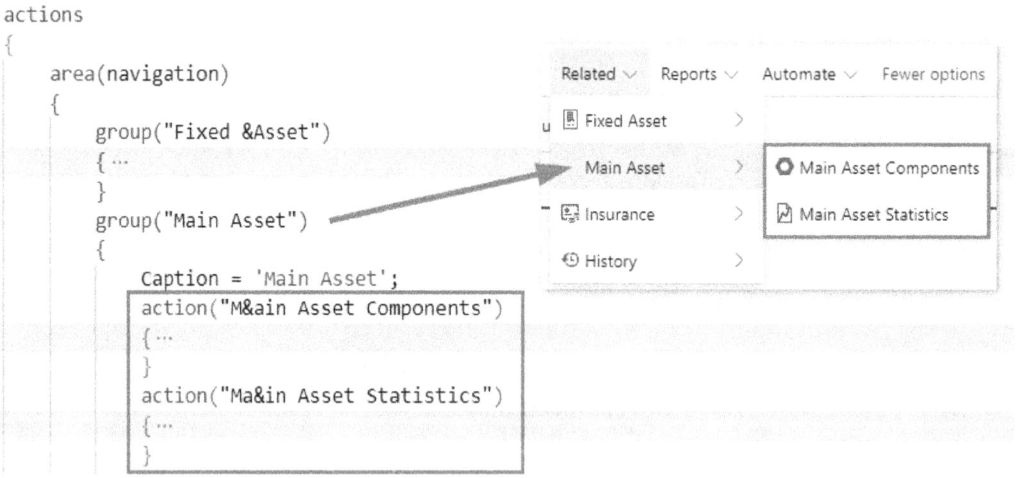
actions
{
area(navigation)
{
group("Fixed &Asset")
{...
}
group("Main Asset")
{
Caption = 'Main Asset';
action("M&ain Asset Components")
{...
}
action("Ma&in Asset Statistics")
{...
}
Related
Reports
Automate
Fewer options
Fixed Asset
Main Asset
Insurance
History
Main Asset Components
Main Asset Statistics

Figure 4.50 – Actions in code and client

The following are the most important action properties:

- `Caption` or `CaptionML`: This is the action name displayed, depending on the language option in use.

- `Visible` and `Enabled`: These are `true` or `false`, defaulting to `true`. These properties can be assigned Boolean expressions, which can be evaluated during processing.

- `RunPageMode`: This sets the mode in which the page is run. This can be `View` (no modification), `Edit` (the default), or `Create` (new). The page can then be changed to other modes based on the permissions of the user.

- `ToolTip` or `ToolTipML`: These are for a helpful display for the user.

- `Description`: This is for internal documentation.

- `ApplicationArea`: This allows us to hide controls based on the Application Area feature introduced in Business Central.

- `Image`: This can be used to assign an icon to be displayed. As mentioned earlier for action groups, we can use IntelliSense to get a rough idea of the image layout.

- `Ellipsis`: If `true`, this displays an ellipsis (...) after the caption. An ellipsis tells the user that other choices will appear. For example, the **Post** action on the **Sales Order** page is followed by the three choices: **Ship**, **Invoice**, and **Ship and Invoice**.

- `ShortcutKey`: This provides a shortcut key combination for this action.

- `RunObject`: This defines which object to run to accomplish the action.

- `RunPageView`: This defines the table view for the page being run.

- `RunPageLink`: This defines the field link for the object being run.

- `RunPageOnRec`: This defines a linkage for the run object to the current record.

- `InFooterBar`: This places the action icon in the page footer bar. This only works on pages with a `PageType` of `NavigatePage`.

- `Gesture`: This specifies a gesture that runs the action on a device with a touch interface, such as the phone client. Available values are `LeftSwipe`, `RightSwipe`, and `ContextMenu`.

Actions can be promoted and put in the navigation bar. The following sub-sections will briefly teach us how.

Promoting actions

Individual actions can be moved to the promoted actions area by referencing them in the `Promoted` area section using an `actionref` control:

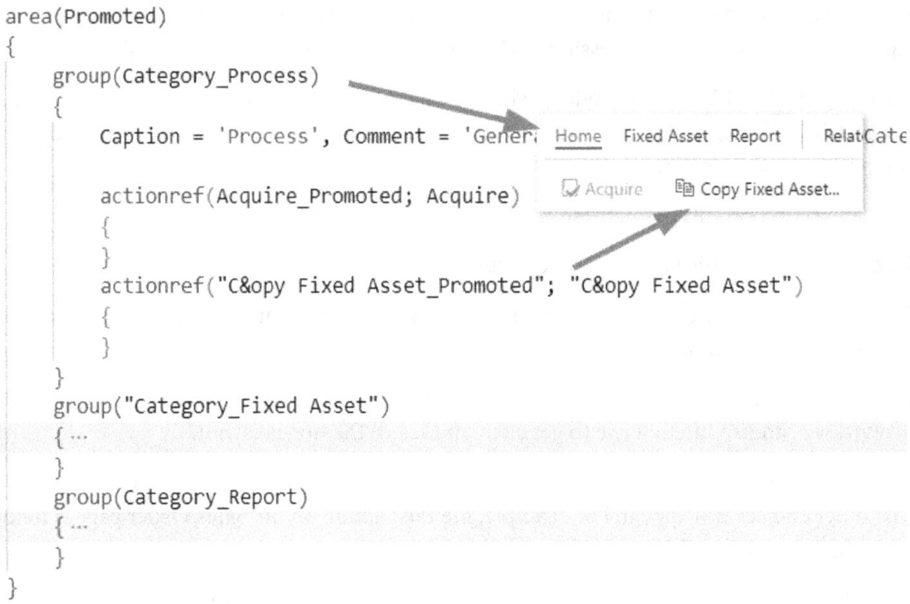
area(Promoted)
{
group(Category_Process)
{
Caption = 'Process', Comment = 'Gener
actionref(Acquire_Promoted; Acquire)
{
}
actionref("C&opy Fixed Asset_Promoted"; "C&opy Fixed Asset")
{
}
}
group("Category_Fixed Asset")
{...
}
group(Category_Report)
{...
}
}
Home
Fixed Asset
Report
Relat
Cate
Acquire
Copy Fixed Asset...

Figure 4.51 – Promoted actions in code and client

An `actionref` control definition consists of an individual control name, and of the name of the `action` control to refer to. `Actionref` controls can be placed only inside the `Promoted` area section, either directly or indirectly inside a promoted action group.

As we can derive from the preceding figure, actions originally defined inside the `Processing` area will be put into the **Home** action menu, regardless of the promoted `Caption` action group being `Process`. **Home** will always appear as the outermost-left action menu, whereas the other promoted action groups appear in the same order as they are defined in the code.

On the **Sales Order** page, we can find an example of how promoted actions sharing the same action group can be also displayed as a **split button**:

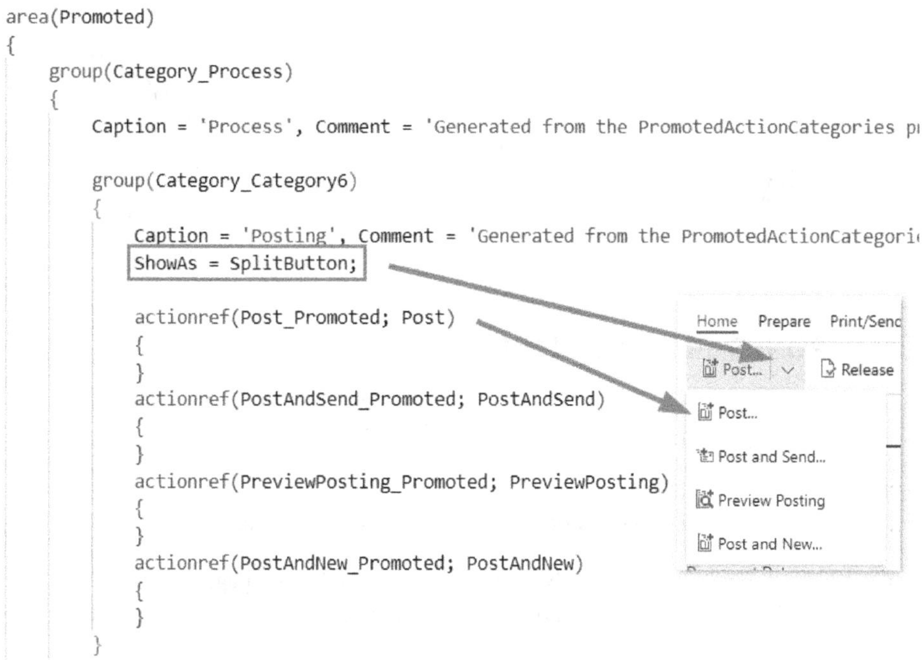
area(Promoted)
{
group(Category_Process)
{
Caption = 'Process', Comment = 'Generated from the PromotedActionCategories pı
group(Category_Category6)
{
Caption = 'Posting', Comment = 'Generated from the PromotedActionCategori
ShowAs = SplitButton;
actionref(Post_Promoted; Post)
{
}
actionref(PostAndSend_Promoted; PostAndSend)
{
}
actionref(PreviewPosting_Promoted; PreviewPosting)
{
}
actionref(PostAndNew_Promoted; PostAndNew)
{
}
}
Home
Prepare
Print/Senc
Post...
Release
Post...
Post and Send...
Preview Posting
Post and New...

Figure 4.52 – Split buttons for actions in code and client

> **Tip**
>
> The Microsoft docs *Common Promoted Action Groups* article (`https://learn.microsoft.com/en-us/dynamics365/business-central/dev-itpro/developer/devenv-common-promoted-action-groups`) provides good guidance on typical promoted action groups in Business Central and whether they are defined as split buttons or not.

Navigation area actions

When defining the actions in a Role Center page, we can include a group of actions in an `area` section with `Embedding`. These actions will be displayed in the navigation bar:

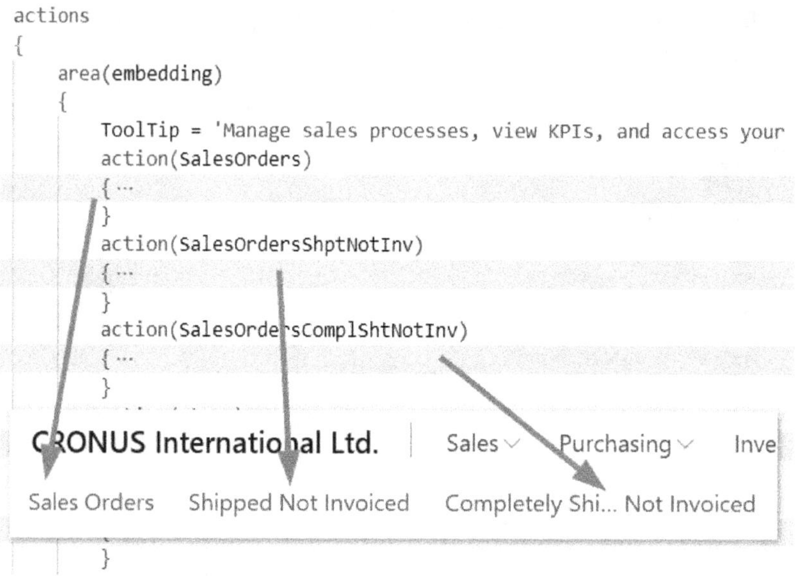

```
actions
{
    area(embedding)
    {
        ToolTip = 'Manage sales processes, view KPIs, and access your
        action(SalesOrders)
        { … }
        action(SalesOrdersShptNotInv)
        { … }
        action(SalesOrdersComplShtNotInv)
        { … }
```

CRONUS International Ltd. | Sales ⌄   Purchasing ⌄   Inve

Sales Orders   Shipped Not Invoiced   Completely Shi... Not Invoiced

```
    }
```

Figure 4.53 – Navigation bar actions in code and client

Additional navigation menus can also easily be defined in a Role Center page action list. First, define an area section with the Sections subtype. Each group defined within this area will define a new navigation menu:

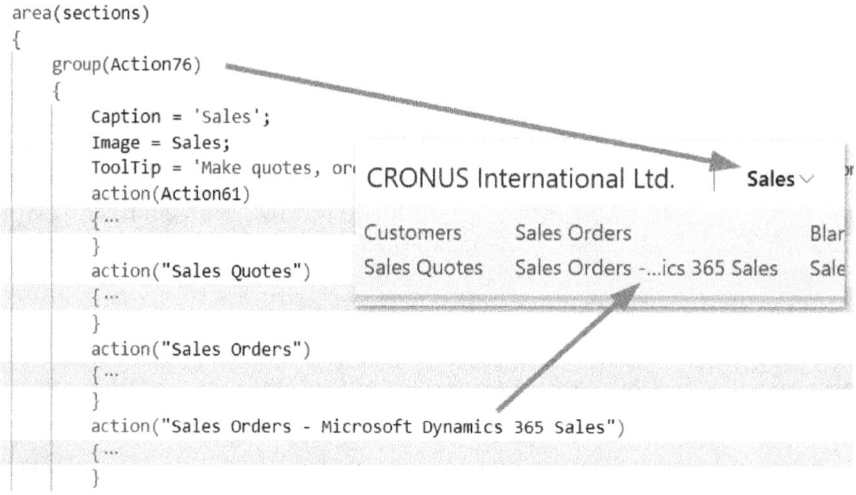

```
area(sections)
{
    group(Action76)
    {
        Caption = 'Sales';
        Image = Sales;
        ToolTip = 'Make quotes, or
        action(Action61)
        { … }
        action("Sales Quotes")
        { … }
        action("Sales Orders")
        { … }
        action("Sales Orders - Microsoft Dynamics 365 Sales")
        { … }
    }
```

CRONUS International Ltd. | Sales ⌄

Customers   Sales Orders   Blar
Sales Quotes   Sales Orders -...ics 365 Sales   Sale

Figure 4.54 – Navigation menu actions in code and client

Actions that allow the user to accomplish their tasks need to be placed in as logical an area as possible, be that in the regular action menu, promoted to be visible first on a page, or on the Role Center.

Actions summary

The primary location where each user's job role-based actions should appear is the navigation area. Detailed page- or task-specific actions should be located in the action bar at the top of each page.

As mentioned earlier, a key design criterion for the Business Central web client is for a user to have access to the actions they need to get their job done; in other words, to tailor the system to the individual user roles. Our job as developers is to take full advantage of all of these options and make life easier for the user. In general, it's better to go overboard in providing access to useful capabilities than to make the user search for the right tool or use several steps in order to get to it. The challenge is to not clutter up the first-level display with too many things, but still have the important user tools no more than one click away.

Furthermore, it is important to follow some other basic guidelines:

- Maintain the look and feel of the standard product wherever feasible and appropriate

- Be consistent in organizing actions, especially between a list page and its corresponding card page

After all these page control details, we will now discuss what's needed to make a page searchable through Tell me. This will help us to learn something about application areas.

Page searchability

The Tell me feature introduced in *Chapter 3, Data Types and Table Fields*, in the *Experimenting with filters* section, does not automatically cover every page object. Instead, for pages to be included in Tell me, we need to specify a `UsageCategory` property. Additionally, we can specify the `ApplicationArea` to ensure that the page is found only with a certain user experience being enabled.

Everything mentioned about page searchability also applies to report objects, as we already practiced in *Chapter 1, Introduction to Business Central*, in the *Creating a list report* section.

UsageCategory property

The `UsageCategory` property is available on the object level only, and it must have one of the following values: `None`, `Lists`, `Tasks`, `ReportsAndAnalysis`, `Documents`, `History`, or `Administration`.

> **Note**
> A `UsgeCategory` value that is different than `None` is required for a page to appear in Tell me.

The property also serves other purposes: It sets the department column in Tell me, it enables users to bookmark a link to the page, and it categorizes objects in the **role explorer** of the client.

ApplicationArea property

Business Central consists of essential features, such as sales and inventory management, and premium features, such as manufacturing and service management. If only the essential experience tier is available, all UI elements displaying premium features are automatically hidden. To achieve that, the standard application provides a set of application areas defined as tags, which are assigned by code to all controls using the `ApplicationArea` property. Our own apps can add custom application areas, which is a topic that is too advanced for this book. We can review all available tags on the **Application Area** page:

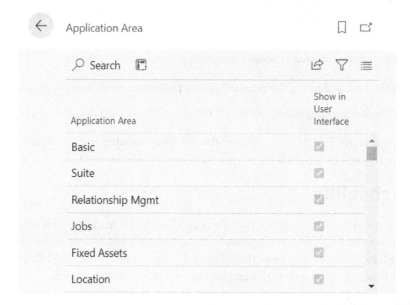

Figure 4.55 – Application Area page

The **Show in User Interface** column tells us which application areas are currently enabled.

In environments with additional application areas being used, pages without any `ApplicationArea` property defined are not only unknown to Tell me but also appear empty if opened directly. That's why it's good practice to always set the `ApplicationArea` property together with `UsageCategory`. Standard values are `All`, `Basic`, `Suite`, and `Advanced`. The `All` value does not appear on the **Application Area** page, but setting it ensures that the UI element is always visible.

> **Note**
>
> More information on `ApplicationArea` can be found in the Microsoft docs at `https://learn.microsoft.com/en-us/dynamics365/business-central/dev-itpro/developer/properties/devenv-applicationarea-property`.
>
> In most cases, we will use `ApplicationArea = All;`.

The `ApplicationArea` property is available on the page level and on the control level, hence for every field, page part, and so on. The page property acts as a default for the page controls. We specify it on the control level only if the value needs to be different than on the page level, and in extension objects.

Advanced content

The Microsoft docs provide articles with advanced topics:

- *Add pages and reports to Tell me* (`https://learn.microsoft.com/en-us/dynamics365/business-central/dev-itpro/developer/devenv-al-menusuite-functionality`) for adding search terms to pages and learning more about the `UsageCategory` property

- *Change which features are displayed* (`https://learn.microsoft.com/en-US/dynamics365/business-central/ui-experiences`) to learn more about the different **experience tiers** and how to switch them

- *Extending Application Areas* (`https://learn.microsoft.com/en-us/dynamics365/business-central/dev-itpro/developer/devenv-extending-application-areas`) for adding custom application areas

- *Finding pages and reports with the role explorer* (`https://learn.microsoft.com/en-us/dynamics365/business-central/ui-role-explorer`) for learning more about the role explorer

Now, let's leave the theoretical topics behind a bit, and let's try out some hands-on tools instead.

Client tools for page development

The Business Central web client provides us with two tools that come in handy for inspecting or extending pages. The first one, **Page Inspection**, is an important tool for identifying pages, whereas the second, **Designer**, can be helpful for writing our very first page extensions. Let's investigate these two.

Page inspection

The page inspection feature, also referred to as the **Page Inspector**, enables us to get details about a page, such as the page type, most page fields, and the source behind the data it displays. Furthermore, we can inspect which apps are extending the page, and which filters are being applied. We can inspect any page that we can view. This feature is a useful tool for developers, consultants, and users requesting support.

To inspect an opened page, we choose the question mark (**?**) in the black application bar, choose **Help & Support**, and then choose **Inspect pages and data**. Or we can just use the keyboard shortcut *Ctrl + Alt + F1*.

The **Page Inspection** pane opens on the side. Here, we are offered many possibilities. Let's open, for example, the page inspection for the **Sales Order** page:

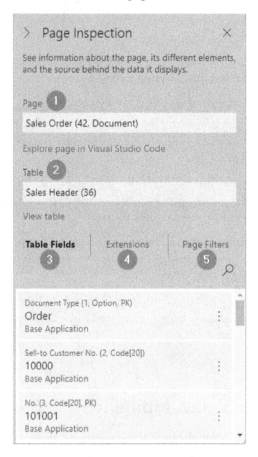

Figure 4.56 – Page Inspection pane

Let's explore the elements seen in the preceding figure:

- In the **Page** section (**1**), we can look up important page object parameters: page name, ID, and the PageType property. Using the **Explore page in Visual Studio Code** link, we can explore the code behind the page.

- In the **Table** section (**2**), we can see the SourceTable name and ID. The **View table** link opens the table in a separate browser window in a read-only view, so we can see all records and fields in the table.

- The **Table Fields** tab (**3**) displays information about all fields in the source table for the current record, including fields that don't appear on the page. To find where a field is used on a page, select it in the **Table Fields** tab. If it's used on the page, it's highlighted by an orange border.

- The **Extensions** tab (**4**) displays installed extensions that affect the selected page or its source table. It also includes two performance values.

- The **Page Filters** tab (**5**) displays the current filters used on the current page.

All these features are described in detail in the Microsoft docs on the *Inspecting and troubleshooting pages* page (`https://learn.microsoft.com/en-us/dynamics365/business-central//dev-itpro/developer/devenv-inspecting-pages`).

> **Note**
>
> The page inspection will initially only load the data from the main page object. To inspect an embedded page object, such as a FactBox or a sub-page, we need to click on it or use the keyboard to move the focus to it after the page inspection pane has been loaded. A border will highlight the focused area.

Designer

Designer is a tool accessed in sandbox environments from within the web client, through **Settings | Design**. Designer enables us to modify the layout of pages simply by drag and drop. The changes will be saved in a new AL extension to download. Using Designer together with Visual Studio Code is a great way to learn the technical notation (syntax) for page extensions.

> **Caution**
>
> Each Designer run creates and installs a new extension (with a dependency on previous Designer extensions), which will apply your changes permanently and for all users in the environment. Hence, we should remove any Designer extension right after downloading and immediately incorporate the changes from Designer into our own, single extension.

The page designer can be opened from anywhere in the application, but its use may be limited in some areas:

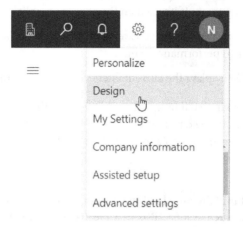

Figure 4.57 – Starting Designer

When we are in design mode and click on any part, it will highlight the section, as you can see in the following screenshot:

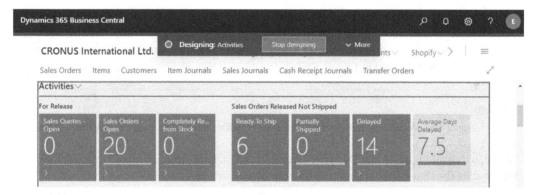

Figure 4.58 – Designer highlighting a section

We can proceed to select a specific control within the section and choose to hide or remove it:

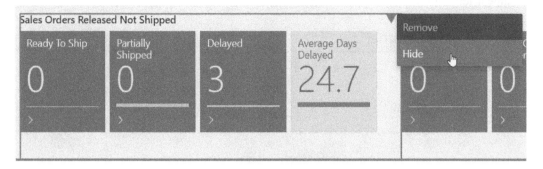

Figure 4.59 – Hiding a section in Designer

If we select a FastTab, we can change the name, for example, to **Customer**.

When we click on the **More** button in Designer and select **+ Field**, we will get a list of controls that can be added to the page, which we can drag and drop into the page:

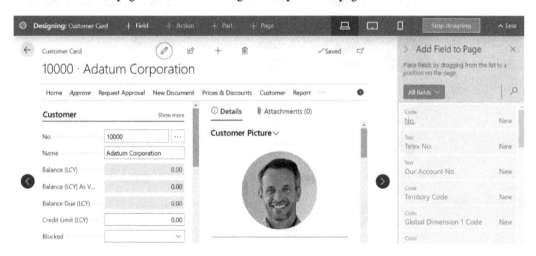

Figure 4.60 – Field list in Designer

When we move the **Name 2** field into the newly renamed **Customer** tab, we can drop it right under the **Name** field:

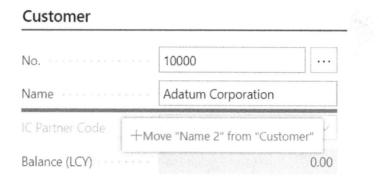

Figure 4.61 – Dropping a field in Designer

Once we have done all of the work that is feasible within Designer, we will click on **Stop designing**. Designer will ask for an **Extension Name** and **Publisher**. We will select **Download Code** and click **Save**, as shown in the following screenshot:

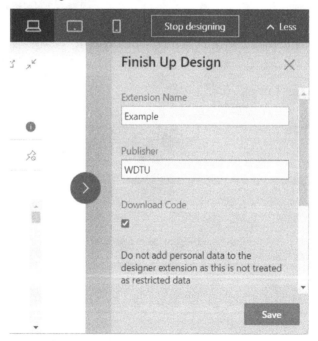

Figure 4.62 – Finishing Designer

> **Caution**
>
> Pressing the **X** button will not cancel creating and installing the Designer extension. Only the download will be canceled.

In the web browser (in our case, Google Chrome), a downloaded ZIP file will pop up that we must save somewhere on our local computer.

The next step is to unzip the file into a folder and look at the contents. With a little bit of luck, you will recognize the structure as an extension that we can open in Visual Studio Code:

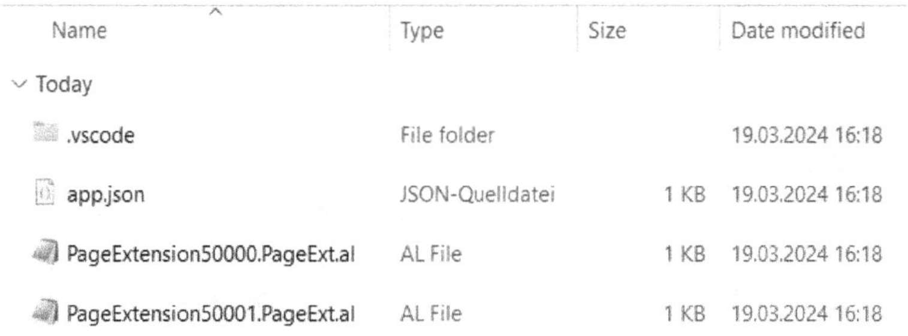

Name	Type	Size	Date modified
∨ Today			
.vscode	File folder		19.03.2024 16:18
app.json	JSON-Quelldatei	1 KB	19.03.2024 16:18
PageExtension50000.PageExt.al	AL File	1 KB	19.03.2024 16:18
PageExtension50001.PageExt.al	AL File	1 KB	19.03.2024 16:18

Figure 4.63 – Unzipped Designer extension files

When we open the `Example_WDTU_1.0.0.0` folder with Visual Studio Code, we see that each page we changed using Designer has a file. If we open the file that is related to the **Customer Card**, in our case, `PageExtension50001.al`, we can see exactly what we did. We can see the modification of the `General` tab, the moving of the hidden `Name 2` field, and how we finally made it visible:

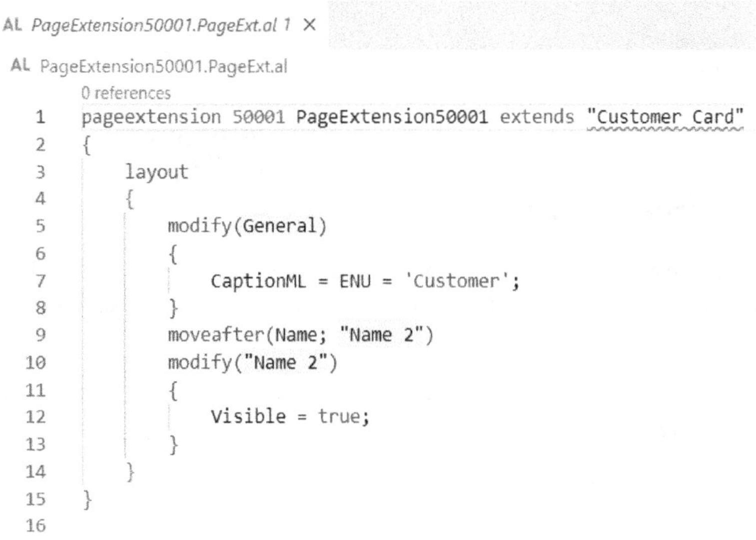

```al
pageextension 50001 PageExtension50001 extends "Customer Card"
{
    layout
    {
        modify(General)
        {
            CaptionML = ENU = 'Customer';
        }
        moveafter(Name; "Name 2")
        modify("Name 2")
        {
            Visible = true;
        }
    }
}
```

Figure 4.64 – Inspecting a page extension file

Let's not forget about the Designer extension still lingering in our environment: using Tell me (*Alt + Q*), open the **Extension Management** page, locate, uninstall, and then unpublish the **Example** extension.

Name ↑		Publisher	Version	Is Inst...	Published As
Essential Business Headlines		Microsoft	v. 23.4.15643.16709	☑	Global
EU 3-Party Trade Purchase		Microsoft	v. 23.4.15643.16709	☑	Global
Example	⋮	WDTU	v. 1.0.0.0	☐	Dev
Finnish lang	Manage	Microsoft	v. 23.4.15643.16709	☐	Global
French lang	📥 Install	Microsoft	v. 23.4.15643.16709	☐	Global
French lang	📤 Uninstall	Microsoft	v. 23.4.15643.16709	☐	Global
French lang	📤 Unpublish	Microsoft	v. 23.4.15643.16709	☐	Global
French lang	🖥 Set up	Microsoft	v. 23.4.15643.16709	☐	Global
German lan	📥 Download Source	Microsoft	v. 23.4.15643.16709	☐	Global
German lan	☰ Select More	Microsoft	v. 23.4.15643.16709	☐	Global
German lan		Microsoft	v. 23.4.15643.16709	☐	Global

Figure 4.65 – Unpublishing a Designer extension

Though the authors of this book wish it were the complete compilation of all knowledge that is programming AL, we realize that cannot be so. The following are some additional resources we feel are important.

Learning more

The following section gives a description of several excellent ways to learn more about pages and beyond.

Patterns and creative plagiarism

When we want to create new functionality, the first task is obviously to create functional specifications. Once those are in hand, we should look for guidelines to follow. Some of the sources that are readily available are listed here:

- Guidelines and patterns for development for Microsoft Dynamics 365 Business Central, community-run and Microsoft endorsed (`https://alguidelines.dev/docs/`)

- Blogs and other materials available in the **Microsoft Dynamics 365 Business Central community** (`https://community.dynamics.com/forums/thread/?partialUrl=business`)

- The **Business Central source code** distributed by Microsoft (`https://github.com/microsoft/BCApps`)

It's always good to start with an existing pattern or object that has capabilities similar to our requirements and study the existing logic and the code. In many lines of work, the term plagiarism is a nasty one. However, when it comes to modifying an existing system, copying existing code is a very effective research and design tool. This approach allows us to build on the hard work of the many skilled and knowledgeable people who have contributed to the Business Central product. In addition, this is working software. This eliminates at least some of the errors we would make if we were starting from scratch.

When designing modifications for Business Central, studying how the existing objects work and interact is often the fastest way to create new working models. We should allocate some time both for studying the material on `alguidelines.dev` and for exploring the Business Central standard code.

Search through the **CRONUS demonstration system** (or an available production system) in order to find one or more pages that have the feature we want to emulate (or a similar feature). If there are both complex and simple instances of pages that contain this feature, we should concentrate our research on the simple instance first. Make a test copy of the page. Read the code. Run the page. Make a minor modification. Run it again. Continue this process until our ability to predict the results of changes eliminates surprises or confusion.

Experimenting on your own

If you have followed along with the exercises in this book so far, it's time for you to do some experimenting on your own now. No matter how much information someone else describes, there is no substitute for personal hands-on experience. You will combine things in a new way from what was described here. You will either discover a new capability that you would not have learned otherwise, or you will have an interesting problem to solve. Either way, the result will be significantly more knowledge about pages in Business Central.

Don't forget to make liberal use of the Microsoft docs (`https://learn.microsoft.com/en-us/dynamics365/business-central/dev-itpro/`) while you are experimenting. Some of the help material is a bit sparse, but it is being updated on a frequent basis. In fact, if you find something missing or something that you think is incorrect, please use the **Feedback** link available at the top of every documentation page. The Microsoft docs team pays close attention to the feedback they receive and uses it to improve the documentation. Hence, we will all benefit from your feedback.

Experimentation

Start with the blank slate approach because that allows you to focus on specific features and functions. Since we've already gone through the mechanical procedures of creating new pages of the card and list types, adding controls, and modifying control properties, we won't detail those steps here. However, as you move the focus for experimentation from one feature to another, you may want to review what was covered in this chapter.

Let's walk through some examples of experiments you could do now, then build on them as you get more adventuresome. Each of the objects you create at this point should be assigned to an object number range that you are reserving for testing in the `app.json` file. Follow these steps:

1. Create a new table for testing playlist item rates. Do this by opening the `Playlist Item Rate` table in Visual Studio Code, changing it to `50050 Playlist Item Rate Test`, and then saving it as `PlaylistItemRateTest.table.al`.

2. Create a `List` page for the `Playlist Item Rate Test` table with at least three or four fields.

3. Run the test page and enter a few test records into it, such as `Source Type`, `Source No.`, `Item No.`, and `Rate Amount`.

4. Change the `Visible` property of a field by setting it to `false`.

5. Save and run the page.

6. Confirm that the page looks as expected. Go into edit mode on the page. See whether the field is still invisible.

7. Use the Designer feature to add the invisible field; also, remove a field that was previously visible. Exit Designer. View the page in various modes, such as view, edit, new, and so on.

8. Go back into Visual Studio Code and design the page again.

9. One or two at a time, experiment with setting `Editable`, `Caption`, `ToolTip`, and other control properties.

10. Don't just focus on text fields. Experiment with other data types as well. Create a text field that is 200 characters long. Try out the `MultiLine` property.

11. After you get comfortable with the effect of changing individual properties, try changing multiple properties to see how they interact.

When you feel you have thoroughly explored individual field properties in a list, try similar tests on a card page. You will find that some of the properties have one effect in a list, while they may have a different (or no) effect in the context of a card (or vice versa). Test enough to find out. If you have some *Aha!* experiences, it means that you are really learning.

The next logical step is to begin experimenting with the group-level controls. Add one or two to the test page, then begin setting the properties for that control, again experimenting with only one or two at a time, in order to understand very specifically what each one does. Do some experimenting to find out which properties at the group level override the properties at the field level and which ones do not override them.

Once you've done group controls, do part controls. Build some FactBoxes using a variety of the different components that are available. Use the system components and some chart parts as well. There is a wealth of prebuilt parts that come with the system. Even if the parts that are supplied aren't exactly right for the application, they can often be used as a model for the construction of custom parts. Remember that using a model can significantly reduce both the design and the debugging work when doing custom development.

After you feel that you have a grasp of the different types of controls in the context of cards and lists, consider checking out some of the other page types. Some of those won't require too much in the way of new concepts. Examples of these are the `ListPlus`, `ListPart`, `CardPart`, and, to a lesser extent, even `Document` pages.

You may now decide to learn by studying samples of the page objects that are part of the standard product. You could start by copying object code from the AL Explorer, such as page 22—**Customer List**, to another object number in your testing range and then begin to analyze how it is put together and how it operates. Again, you should tweak various controls and control properties in order to see how that affects the page. It's a good idea to back up your work one way or another before making additional changes. An easy way to back up individual objects is to use Git and create multiple branches. The restore method is to go back to a previous branch.

Another excellent learning option is to choose one of the patterns that have a relationship with the area about which you want more knowledge. If, for example, you are going to create an application that has a new type of document, such as a radio program schedule, you should study the document pattern. You might also want to study create data from a templates pattern. At this point, it has become obvious that there are a variety of sources and approaches to supplement the material in this text.

Summary

You should now be relatively comfortable with the navigation of Business Central and the use of Visual Studio Code. You should be able to use the page snippets as an advanced beginner. If you have taken full advantage of the various opportunities to create tables and pages, both with our guidance and experimentally on your own, you are beginning to become a Business Central developer.

We reviewed different types of pages and worked with some of them in this chapter. We reviewed all of the controls that can be used in pages and have worked with several of them. We also lightly reviewed page and control triggers. We had a good introduction to page designing and a significant insight into the structure of some types of pages. With the knowledge gained in this chapter, we expanded our WDTU application system, enhancing our pages for data maintenance and inquiry.

In the next chapter, we will learn about two of the reporting objects in AL: Reports and Queries. We will dig into the definition of datasets, layout options, and data processing capabilities. For the report object layout, we will focus on using Microsoft Excel, as well as discuss other toolsets, such as SQL Report Builder and Microsoft Word. Queries, which approximate direct SQL statements to the database, can extract data more quickly and efficiently than variable or looping mechanisms. We will demonstrate how to create and display a potentially resource-heavy query quickly and efficiently.

In the next chapter, we will learn about designing Business Central reports and queries, which are two primary ways to extract (and even process) data. We will dig into the flow, triggers, and controls that make up the report data design. After defining the data output, we will review the display options and even build an Excel layout. Additionally, we will dig into the very powerful Query object for quick data extraction.

Questions

1. Once a page has been developed using the Page Snippet, the developer has very little flexibility in the layout of the page. True or false?

    ANSWER: False

2. Actions appear on the Role Center screen in several places. Choose two:

    *   Address bar
    *   Action bar
    *   Filter pane
    *   Navigation pane
    *   Command bar

    ANSWER: Action bar and Navigation pane

3. A user can choose their Role Center when they log in. True or false?

    ANSWER: False

4. An action can only appear in one place in the action bar or in the navigation pane. True or false?

    ANSWER: True

5. Which of the following are only available in a List page?

    *   FactBox
    *   Document attachments
    *   Analyze Toggle Switch
    *   Links

    ANSWER: Analyze Toggle Switch

6. All page design and development is done within Visual Studio Code. True or false?

    ANSWER: False – page personalization and design can create page extensions as well

7. Document pages are for word processing. True or false?

    ANSWER: False

8. The **Filter** pane includes **Filter list by** and **Filter totals by** options. True or false?

    ANSWER: True

9. The AL code placed in pages should only be to control display characteristics, not to modify data. True or false?

    ANSWER: True

10. Inheritance is the passing of property definition defaults from one level of object to another. If a field property is explicitly defined in a table, it cannot be less restrictively defined for that field displayed on a page. True or false?

    ANSWER: True

11. Which of the following is true about the control property importance? Choose two:

    - Applies only to `Card` and `CardPart` pages

    - Can affect FastTab displays

    - Has three possible values: `Standard`, `Promoted`, and `Additional`

    - Applies to decimal fields only

    ANSWER: Can affect FastTab displays; has three possible values: `Standard`, `Promoted`, and `Additional`

12. FactBoxes are delivered as part of the standard product. They cannot be modified, nor can new FactBoxes be created. True or False?

    ANSWER: False

13. All pages must be bound to an underlying table. True or False?

    ANSWER: False

14. Some field control properties can be changed dynamically as the object executes. Which ones are they? Choose three:

    - `Visible`

    - `HideValue`

    - `Editable`

- `Multiline`
- `DecimalPlaces`

ANSWER: `Visible, HideValue, Editable`

15. Which property is normally used in combination with the `AutoSplitKey` property? Choose one:

- `SaveValues`
- `SplitIncrement`
- `DelayedInsert`
- `MultipleNewLines`

ANSWER: `DelayedInsert`

16. Inheritance between tables and pages operates in two ways—tables can inherit attributes from pages and pages can inherit from tables. True or false?

ANSWER: False

17. For the purpose of testing, pages can be run directly from Visual Studio Code using `AL : Explorer`. True or false?

ANSWER: True

5
Reports and Queries

"Data helps solve problems."

– Anne Wojcicki

"The greatest value of a picture is when it forces us to notice what we never expected to see."

– John Tukey

In Microsoft Dynamics 365 Business Central, reports and queries are two ways to extract and output data for the purpose of presentation to a user (reports can also modify data). The user also has the ability to run Analysis Mode from list pages, but this is not something that developers can customize. Each of these objects uses tools and processes that are Business Central-based and work on data extraction. An example of this is XMLports, which can also extract and modify data. XMLports will be covered in *Chapter 8, Extensibility beyond AL*). In this chapter, we will focus on understanding the strengths of each of these tools and when and how they might be used. We will cover the Business Central side of both queries and reports in detail to describe how to obtain the data we need to present to our users. We will cover output formatting and consumption of that data in less detail. There are currently no wizards available for either query building or report building, and therefore we must do this step by step using programming tools and our skills as designers and developers.

We will cover the following topics in this chapter:

- Reports
- Report components—overview
- Report data flow
- Report components—detail
- Creating and modifying reports
- Queries

Reports

Some consider the standard library of reports that's provided in the Business Central product distribution from Microsoft to be relatively simple in design and limited in its features. Others feel that the provided reports satisfy most needs because they are simple but flexible. Their basic structure is easy to use. They are made much more powerful and flexible by taking advantage of Business Central's filtering and SIFT capabilities. There is no doubt that the existing library can be used as a foundation for many of the special reports that customers require to match their own specific business management needs.

The fact is that Business Central's standard reports are basic. To obtain more complex or more sophisticated reports, we must use features that are part of the product, such as analysis views, or feed processed data for external reporting tools, such as Excel. Through the creative use of these features, many different types of complex report logic may be implemented.

We'll create our report layouts in this chapter with Microsoft Excel. Later in *Chapter 6, Introduction to AL*, we will also gain practice in designing layouts with Microsoft Word. We'll examine the data flow of a standard report and the concept of reports, which will be used for processing only (with no printed or displayed output).

What is a report?

A **report** is a vehicle for organizing, processing, and displaying data in a format that's suitable for outputting to the user. Reports may be displayed onscreen in **Preview** mode, output to a file in Word, Excel, or PDF format (or, when appropriately designed, output in HTML, CSV, or XML format), emailed to a user (or other consumers of this information), or printed to hard-copy—the old-fashioned way. All of the report screenshots in this book were taken from **Preview** mode reports.

Once generated, the data contents of a report are static. When a Business Central report is output in **Preview** mode, the report can have interactive capabilities. Those capabilities only affect the presentation of the data; they do not change the actual data that's included in the report dataset. **Report Definition Language Client-Side** (RDLC) interactive capabilities include dynamic sorting, visible/hidden options, and detail/summary expand/collapse functions. Excel and Word offer editing and changes to aspects unrelated to the core data passed in the file, such as form letter text. All of the specifications for the data selection criteria for a report must be done at the beginning of the report run before the report view is generated. Business Central also allows dynamic functionality in preview mode so that you can drill down into the underlying data, drill through to a page, and even drill through into another report.

In Business Central, report objects can be classified as processing only, such as report 795 **Adjust Cost - Item Entries**, by setting the correct report property, that is, by setting the `ProcessingOnly` property to `true`. A **processing-only report** will not display data to the user—it will simply process table data. Report objects are convenient to use for processing because the report's automatic **read-process-write** loop and the built-in request page reduce coding that would otherwise be required. A report can add, change, or delete data in tables, regardless of whether the report is processing only or a typical report that generates output for viewing.

In general, reports are associated with one or more tables. A report can be created without being externally associated with any table, but that is an exception. Even if a report is associated with a particular table, it can freely access and display data from other referenced tables.

Five Business Central report designers

Any Business Central report design project uses at least two report development tools. The first is the report dataset and code (in AL) file, which is part of the Visual Studio Code development environment. The second is the developer's choice of Visual Studio, SQL Report Builder, Microsoft Excel, or Microsoft Word. There is a free version of Visual Studio, the Community edition, which is available at `https://msdn.microsoft.com/en-us/visual-studio-community-vs.aspx`.

For our work, we will use a combination of Visual Studio Code and Microsoft Excel.

The option of using Microsoft Excel is aimed at the goal of allowing customers to be more self-sufficient in handling quick, simple changes in format while requiring less technical expertise.

> **Note**
>
> The report development process for a Business Central report begins with a data definition in Visual Studio Code. All the data structure, working data elements, data flow, and AL logic are defined there. We must start in Visual Studio Code to create or modify report objects. Once all of the elements of the dataset definition and request page are in place, the development work proceeds to SQL Report Builder, Visual Studio, Word, or Excel, where the display layout work is done, including any desired dynamic options.

When an RDLC report layout is defined in the **Rendering** section and is created, SQL Report Builder builds a definition of the report layout in the XML-structured RDLC. Excel will generate an XLSX workbook with a data table on a sheet labeled *Data*, which contains the dataset definition. If Word is used to build a Business Central report layout, the result is a custom XML part that is used to map the data into a report at runtime.

Business Central allows us to create reports of many types with different *look and feel* attributes. The consistency of the report's look and feel does not have the same level of design importance as it has for pages. Patterns may have been developed that relate to reports, so before starting a new format of report, it is best to check if there is an applicable pattern in existing reports.

Good design practice dictates that enhancements should integrate seamlessly, both in process and appearance, unless there is an overwhelming justification for being different. There are still many opportunities for reporting creativity. The tools that are available within Business Central to access and manipulate data for reports are very powerful. Of course, there is always the option to output report results to other processing and presentation tools, such as PDF or third-party products utilizing XML output.

Business Central report types

The standard Business Central application uses only a few of the possible report styles, most of which are in a relatively basic format. The following are the types of reports that are included in Business Central:

- **Analytical**: There are two types of analytical reporting in Business Central, both of which are configured by users and not developed:

  - **Financial analytics**: This configures row and column definitions that report from ledger transactions, such as sales, purchases, transfers, and inventory adjustments. These are configured in the **Analysis Report** and **Analysis by Dimension** areas of the finance module.

  - The **data analysis mode** enables you to analyze data directly from any list page, without having to run a report or switch to another application, such as Excel. It provides an interactive and versatile way to calculate, summarize, and examine data. Instead of running reports using different options and filters, you can add multiple tabs that represent different tasks or views on the data. More information can be found about the configuration and layout of the **data analysis mode** at `https://learn.microsoft.com/en-us/dynamics365/business-central/analysis-mode`.

- **List**: This is a formatted list of data. A standard list is the **Inventory - List** report (report 701):

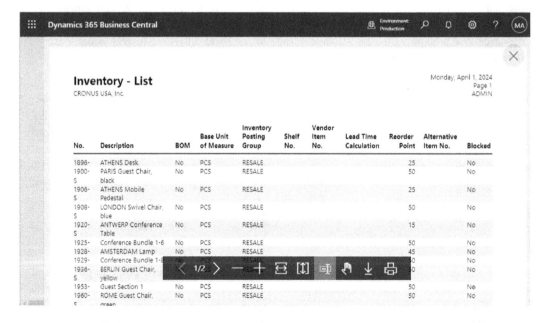

Figure 5.1 – The List report

- **Document**: This is formatted similarly to a pre-printed form, where a page (or several pages) contains a header, detail, and footer section with dynamic content. Examples of document reports include `Standard Sales - Invoice` (captioned as **Sales – Invoice**), **Picking List** (even though it's called a list, it's a document report), and `Standard Purchase - Order` (**Purchase – Order**):

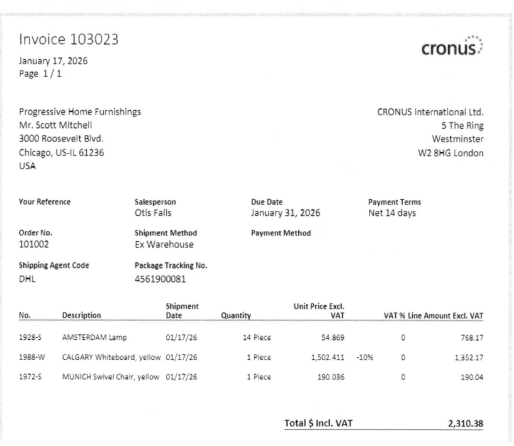

Figure 5.2 – Document report

List and document report types are defined based on their layouts. The following three report types are defined based on their usage rather than their layouts, and are as follows:

- **Transaction**: This provides a list of ledger entries for a particular master table. For example, a transaction list of Item ledger entries for all the items matching particular criteria, or a list of general ledger entries for some specific accounts:

G/L Register

CRONUS International Ltd.

Posting Date	Document Type	Document No.	G/L Account No.	Name	Description	VAT
Register No.: 1						
08/28/24	Payment	201	5420	Vendors, Foreign	Graphic Design Institute	
08/28/24	Payment	201	2920	Bank, LCY	Check for Vendor 30000	
08/28/24	Payment	202	5410	Vendors, Domestic	Wide World Importers	
08/28/24	Payment	202	2920	Bank, LCY	Check for Vendor 40000	
08/28/24	Payment	203	5420	Vendors, Foreign	Fabrikam, Inc.	
08/28/24	Payment	203	2920	Bank, LCY	Check for Vendor 10000	
Register No.: 1						

Figure 5.3 – Transaction report

- **Test:** These reports are printed from journal and document pages prior to posting the transactions. Test reports are used to pre-validate data before it's posted. The following screenshot is a test report invoked from the **Test Report...** action on the **General Journals** page:

General Journal - Test

CRONUS International Ltd.

Thursday, August 29, 2024
Page 1 / 1
ADMIN

Journal Template Name: GENERAL
Journal Batch: DAILY

Gen. Journal Line: Journal Template Name: GENERAL, Journal Batch Name: DAILY

Posting Date	Document Type	Document No.	Account Type	Account No.	Name	Description	Gen. Posting Type	Gen. Bus. Posting Group	Gen. Prod. Posting Group	Amount	Bal. Account No.	Balance (LCY)
01/18/24	Payment	BANK1	Bank Account	SAVINGS	World Wide Bank	Transfer, January 2024				-1,780.49	CHECKING	0.00
01/18/24	Payment	BANK2	Bank Account	SAVINGS	World Wide Bank	Transfer of funds for				-2,670.73	CHECKING	0.00
01/18/24	Payment	DEPOSIT3	Bank Account	SAVINGS	World Wide Bank	Deposit 3, 2024				-3,560.98	CHECKING	0.00
01/18/24	Payment	DEPOSIT4	Bank Account	SAVINGS	World Wide Bank	Deposit 4, 2024				-3,560.98	CHECKING	0.00
								Total (LCY)		-11,573.18		0.00

Reconciliation

No.	Name	Net Change in Jnl.	Balance after Posting
2920	Bank, LCY	11,573.18	8,512.26
2940	Giro Account	-11,573.18	-11,573.18

Figure 5.4 – Test report (the intention of this image is to show the layout; text readability is not essential)

- **Posting:** These reports are printed as an audit trail as part of a post and print process. Posting report printing is controlled by the user's choice of either a **Post** option or a **Post and Print** option. The posting portions of both options work the same. **Post and Print** runs a report that is selected in the application's setup (in the applicable **Templates** page in columns that are hidden by default). This type of posting audit trail report, which is often needed by accountants, can be regenerated completely and accurately at any time.

Item Register - Value													8/29/2024
CRONUS International Ltd.													Page 1
													ADMIN

Item Register:

Posting Date	Entry Type	Item No.	Description	Invoiced Quantity	Unit Amount	Amount	Cost per Unit	Cost Amount (Actual)	Cost Amount (Expected)	Item Ledger Entry Type	Entry No.	Item Ledger Entry No.
Register No.	**1**											
5/13/2024	Direct Cost	2000-S	SYDNEY Swivel Chair, green	-3	-123.30	369.90	96.10	-288.30	0.00	Sale	1	1
	Direct Cost Revaluation	-288.30			Purchase Sale	369.90		-288.30				
				Total		369.90		-288.30	0.00			
Register No.	**2**											
4/22/2024	Direct Cost	1920-S	ANTWERP Conference Table	-8	-420.40	3,363.20	328.00	-2,624.00	0.00	Sale	2	2
	Direct Cost Revaluation	-2,624.00			Purchase Sale	3,363.20		-2,624.00				
				Total		3,363.20		-2,624.00	0.00			
Register No.	**3**											
5/1/2024	Direct Cost	1968-S	MEXICO Swivel Chair, black	-10	-123.30	1,233.00	96.10	-961.00	0.00	Sale	3	3
5/1/2024	Direct Cost	1928-S	AMSTERDAM Lamp	-7	-35.60	249.20	27.80	-194.60	0.00	Sale	4	4
	Direct Cost Revaluation	-1,155.60			Purchase Sale	1,482.20		-1,155.60				
				Total		1,482.20		-1,155.60	0.00			

Figure 5.5 – Posting register report (the intention of this image is
to show the layout; text readability is not essential)

The different types of reports are also relevant for report naming, as we will learn in the following section.

Report naming

Simple reports are often named the same as the table with which they are primarily associated, plus a word or two describing the basic purpose of the report. Common key report purpose names include the words "Journal," "Register," "List," "Test," and "Statistics." Some examples include **General Journal - Test**, **G/L Register**, and **Customer - Order Detail**.

When there are conflicts between naming based on the associated tables and naming based on the use of the data, the usage context should take precedence in naming reports, just as it does with pages. One absolute requirement for names is that they must be unique; no duplicate names are allowed for a single object type. Remember, the **caption** (what is searched on in the **Tell Me** prompt) is not the same as the **name** (the internal name of the report object). The report name and caption are each a different report property.

Report components – overview

What we generally refer to as the report or report object that's created with SQL Report Builder or Visual Studio Report Designer is technically referred to as an **RDLC report**. (From here on out, we will focus on the SQL Report Builder tool. The tools are somewhat different, but the end results are basically the same.) An **RDLC report** includes information that describes the logic to be followed when processing the data (the data model), the dataset structure that is generated by Visual Studio Code, and the output layout that's designed with SQL Report Builder. RDLC reports are stored in the

Business Central database. Word report XML layouts and Excel XLSX layout files are also stored in the Business Central database. Business Central allows there to be multiple formats for a single report. We will use the term "report" when we are referring to the output, the description, or the object.

Reports share some attributes with pages, including aspects of the data layout, features of various controls, some of the triggers, and even some of the properties. Where those parallels exist, we should take advantage of those parallels. Where there is consistency in the Business Central toolset, it is easier to learn and use.

Report structure

The overall structure of a Business Central report object consists of the following elements:

- Report properties
- Report triggers
- Request page:
  - Request page properties
  - Request page triggers
  - Request page controls:
    - Request page control triggers
- DataItems:
  - DataItem properties
  - DataItem triggers
  - Data columns:
    - Data column properties
- RDLC layout:
  - RDLC controls:
    - RDLC control properties
- Excel layout
  - Excel layout with Data sheet

- Word layout:

  - Word layout template

  - Word controls:

    - Word control properties

Report layouts contain the data structure Business Central will process through in order, the data to be passed to the layout application (SQL, Word, or Excel), and the triggers where the data is processed before, during, and after the data is queried from the database.

Report data overview

Report components, consisting of the report itself, the request page, and the DataItems define the data flow and overall processing of the data through their respective properties and triggers. Another set of components, Data Columns and working storage, are defined as being subordinate to the DataItems (or request page). These are all designed and defined in Visual Studio Code.

> **Note**
>
> **Data Columns** are defined in this book as the fields that are contained in the DataItem (application tables). **Working storage** (also called working data or variables) fields are defined in this book as the data elements defined within a report (or other object) for use in that object. The contents of working storage data elements aren't permanently stored in the database. All of these are collectively referred to in the Microsoft documentation as columns.

These components define the data elements that are made available to Visual Studio as a dataset, which will be used in the layout and delivery of results to the user. In addition, labels (text literals) for display can be defined separately from any DataItem, but are also included in the dataset that's passed to Visual Studio. If the report is to be used in a multi-language environment, the CaptionML label or Caption in addition to the translation file (**XLIFF**) must be properly defined to support the alternate languages.

> **Note**
>
> Report Builder cannot access any data elements that are not defined within the report object in AL. Each data element that's passed in the dataset, whether it's a Data Field or working data, must be associated with a DataItem (except for labels).

The report **request page** displays when a report is invoked. Its purpose is to allow users to enter information to control the report. Control information that's entered through a request page may include filters, control dates, other parameters, and specifications, as well as formatting or processing options to use for this report run. The request page appears once at the beginning of a report, at runtime.

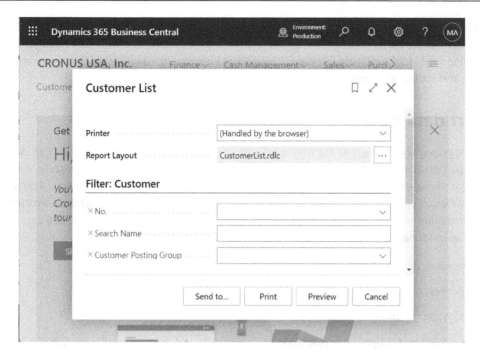

Figure 5.6 – Sample request page as shown for Customer List (report 101)

Now that the report has asked how the report is to query and/or process the data, we move on to the actual execution and output of the report.

Report layout overview

The report dataset is designed in Visual Studio and then made available to the various layout toolsets, including RDLC (SQL Report Builder or Visual Studio), Microsoft Word, and Microsoft Excel. Each toolset manages the header, body, and footer through controls specific to each application. RDLC and Word layouts use tables/tablix controls and header and footer sections, while Excel uses grouping functions or pivot tables.

The font, field positioning, and graphics are all defined as part of the report layout. The same is true for pagination control, headings and footers, some totaling, column-width control, color, and many other display details.

Most notably with RDLC layouts, if the display target changes dramatically, for example, from a desktop workstation display to a browser on a phone, the appearance of the report layout will change dramatically as well. One of the advantages of the Business Central reporting layout toolset is to support the required flexibility. Because we must expect significant variability in our user's output devices (desktop video, browser, tablet, phone), we should design and test accordingly.

Report layouts can be customized for existing reports within the Business Central client without the use of Visual Studio Code. The main limitation is that the layout must work with the existing dataset definition installed in the existing extension. The **Report Layouts** page lists all the reports and layouts available, and actions for exporting, replacing, and setting default layouts.

Report data flow

One of the principal advantages of the Business Central report is its built-in data flow structure. At the beginning of any report, we will define the DataItems (the tables) that the report will process. We can create a processing-only report that has no DataItems (if no looping through database data is required), but that situation often calls for a code unit to be used. In a report, Business Central automatically creates a data flow process for each DataItem or table reference. This automatically created data flow provides specific triggers and processing events for each DataItem, as follows:

- Preceding the DataItem
- After reading each record of the DataItem
- Following the end of the DataItem

The underlying "black-box" report logic (the part we can't see or affect) automatically loops through the named tables, reading and processing one record at a time. Therefore, any time we need a process that steps through a set of data one record at a time, it is often easier to use a processing-only report than using a procedure in another object type.

The reference to a database table in a report is referred to as a **DataItem**. The report data flow structure allows us to nest DataItems to create a hierarchical grandparent, parent, and child structure. If `DataItem2` is nested within `DataItem1`, and related to `DataItem1`, then for each record in `DataItem1`, all of the related records in `DataItem2` will be processed.

The following example uses tables from our WDTU system. The design is for a report to list all the scheduled instances of a `Radio Show Playlist` DataItem grouped by `Radio Show`, which in turn is grouped by `Radio Show Type`. Thus, `Radio Show Type` is the primary table (`DataItem1`). For each `Radio Show Type`, we want to list all the radio shows of that type (`DataItem2`). For each `Radio Show`, we want to list all the scheduled instances of that show that have been recorded in `Playlist Header` (`DataItem3`).

Just to gain a better understanding of the example, let's temporarily create a report that we can delete again at the end of this section. Open Visual Studio Code and add a new file named `Demo.report.al`. At the top of the file, type `treport` and select the report snippet. Tabbing through the snippet, type in the report ID, `50103`, and then the name, which is Demo. Keep `UsageCategory` of `ReportsAndAnalysis` and `ApplicationArea` of `All`. The next tab will jump to the first DataItem source table name. Type in `"Radio Show Type"` and rename `DataItemName` as `DataItem1` without spaces. For our example, we have renamed the DataItems to better illustrate report data flow. The normal behavior would be for `Name` in the left parameter of DataItem to default to the table name (for example, the name for Radio Show would be "Radio Show" by default). This default DataItem name would only need to be changed if the same table appeared twice within the DataItem list. If there were a second instance of Radio Show, for example, we could simply give it the name RadioShow2, but it would be much better to give it a name describing its purpose in context.

For each record in the parent DataItem, the indented DataItem will be fully processed, depending on the filters and the defined relationships between the superior and indented tables. In other words, the visible indentation is only part of the necessary parent-child definition.

For our example, we will enter a third table, Playlist Header, and our example name, DataItem3.

```
7      dataset
8      {
           0 references
9          dataitem(DataItem1; "Radio Show Type")
10         {
               0 references
11             dataitem(DataItem2; "Radio Show")
12             {
                   0 references
13                 dataitem(DataItem3; "Playlist Header")
14                 {
15                 }
16             }
17         }
18     }
```

Figure 5.7 – Indented DataItems indicating intended looping relationships

The following diagram shows the data flow for the preceding DataItem structure. The chart boxes are intended to show the nesting that results from the indentation of the DataItems in the preceding screenshot. The Radio Show DataItem is indented under the Radio Show Type DataItem. This means that for every processed Radio Show Type record, all of the selected Radio Show records will be processed. The same logic applies to the Playlist Header records and the Radio Show records, that is, for each Radio Show record processed, all selected Playlist Header records are processed:

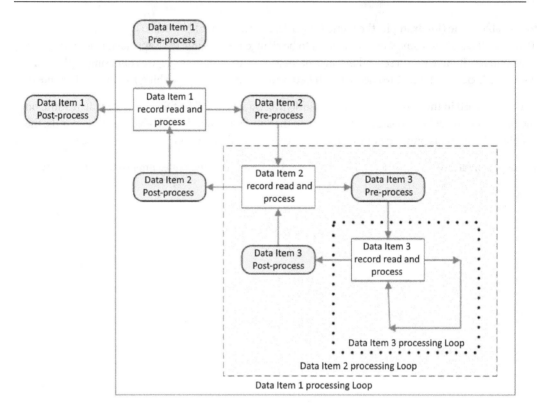

Figure 5.8 – Illustration of DataItem nesting and process loop control

As we can see, the full range of processing for `DataItem2` occurs for each `DataItem1` record. In turn, the full range of processing for `DataItem3` occurs for each `DataItem2` record.

In Business Central, report processing occurs in two separate steps: the first is tied primarily to what has been designed in AL, and the second is tied to what has been designed in a report layout designer (Visual Studio, SQL Report Builder, Microsoft Excel, or Microsoft Word). The data processing that's represented in the preceding diagram all occurs in the first step, yielding a complete dataset that contains all the data that is to be rendered for output.

Report components – detail

Earlier, we reviewed a list of the components of a report object. Now, we'll review detailed information about each of those components. Our goal here is to understand how the pieces of the report puzzle fit together.

Report properties

A subset of Business Central's report properties is shown in the following screenshot. Some of these properties have essentially the same purpose as similarly named properties in pages and other objects:

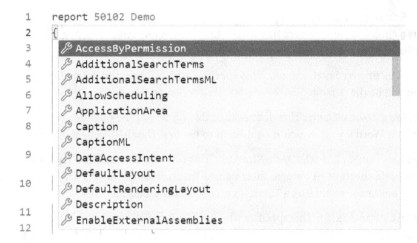

```
1    report 50102 Demo
2    {
3        AccessByPermission
4        AdditionalSearchTerms
5        AdditionalSearchTermsML
6        AllowScheduling
7        ApplicationArea
8        Caption
         CaptionML
9        DataAccessIntent
         DefaultLayout
10       DefaultRenderingLayout
         Description
11       EnableExternalAssemblies
12
```

Figure 5.9 – Subset of properties for the report object

The properties in the preceding screenshot are defined as follows:

- Caption or CaptionML contains the defined caption for different languages, including English.

- Description: This is for internal documentation.

- UseRequestPage: This can either be true or false, and controls whether or not the report will begin with a request page so that user parameters can be entered.

- ProcessingOnly: This is set to true when the report object is being used only to process data and no reporting output is to be generated. If this property is set to true, then that overrides any other property selections that would apply in a report-generating situation.

- ShowPrintStatus: If this property is set to true (which is the default value) and the ProcessingOnly property is set to false, then a **Report Progress** window, including a **Cancel** button, is displayed. When ProcessingOnly is set to true, if we want a **Report Progress** window, we must create our own dialog box.

- TransactionType: This can be in one of four basic options: Browse, Report, Snapshot, UpdateNoLocks, and Update. These control the record-locking behavior that will be applied in this report. The default is UpdateNoLocks. This property is generally only used by advanced developers.

- **Permissions**: This provides a report-specific setting of permissions, which are the rights to access data tables, subdivided into `Read`, `Insert`, `Modify`, and `Delete`. This allows the developer to define report and processing permissions that override the user-by-user permissions security setup.

- `PaperSourceFirstPage`, `PaperSourceDefaultPage`, and `PaperSourceLastPage` give us a choice of paper source tray for the first, last, or any remaining page. This is meant for pre-printed forms, and if this property is not set, then it is ignored.

- `DefaultRenderingLayout`: This specifies which rendering defined in the **Rendering** section will be the default.

- `WordMergeDataItem`: This defines the table on which the outside processing loop will occur for a Word layout, which is equivalent to the first DataItem's effect on an RDLC layout.

- `ExcelLayoutMultipleDataSheets`: This sets whether an Excel layout will render to multiple data sheets or in a single sheet named `Data`. Multiple sheets will be named `Data_DataItemName`, where `DataItemName` is the `dataitem` name used in the report design.

- `PdfFontEmbedding`: This specifies whether the font will be embedded in generated PDF files from the report. If not defined, it will depend on the fonts available on the service tier.

Report triggers

The following screenshot shows the report triggers, all of which are available in a report:

```
1     report 50102 "Demo"
2     {
3         trigger OnInitReport()
4         begin
5         end;
6
7         trigger OnPreReport()
8         begin
9         end;
10
11        trigger OnPostReport()
12        begin
13        end;
14
```

Figure 5.10 – Report-level triggers where AL code is executed

Descriptions for the report triggers are as follows:

- `OnInitReport()`: This executes once when the report is opened, but before the request page is run.

- `OnPreReport()`: This executes once after the request page completes. All the DataItem processing follows this trigger.

- `OnPostReport()`: This trigger executes once at the end of all other report processing if the report completes normally. If the report terminates with an error, this trigger does not execute. All of the DataItem processing precedes this trigger.

Request page properties

The request page properties are a subset of page properties, which are covered in detail in *Chapter 4, Pages – The Interactive Interface*.

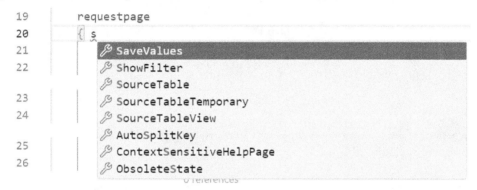

Figure 5.11 – Subset of request page properties

Usually, most of these properties are not changed, simply because the extra capability is not needed. An exception is the `SaveValues` property, which, when set to `true`, causes entered values to be retained and redisplayed when the page is invoked another time.

Request page triggers

Request pages have a full complement of triggers, as they are essentially a page object attached to a report object. This allows complex interaction with the user as well as pre-report processing logic.

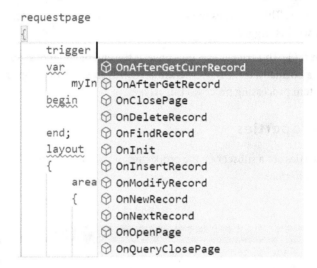

Figure 5.12 – Request page triggers

However, because of their comparatively simplistic nature, request pages seldom need to take advantage of these trigger capabilities.

Dataset analysis

Business Central has the option to run a report but not utilize any layout tool. This allows the developer or advanced user to analyze the dataset generated by the DataItem and column definitions. This allows for ad hoc analysis of the data and diagnosis of any issues. To export a report dataset to an Excel workbook, open the report in the client, then on the request page, click **Send To....** At the bottom of the **Send To…** options is **Microsoft Excel Document (data only)**:

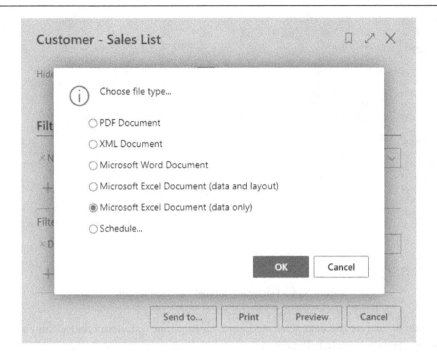

Figure 5.13 – Microsoft Excel Document (data only) for report data analysis

The Excel workbook consists of two worksheets: `Data` and `CaptionData`. `CaptionData` is where the fixed value field caption and labels reside. The `Data` sheet contains all of the nested DataItems and column data flattened out into a table. The column names are the headers, and any parent DataItem column data is repeated for each child DataItem column set. You will see this behavior repeated in **Reports**, **Queries**, and **XMLports** in text format, each having flattened datasets exported.

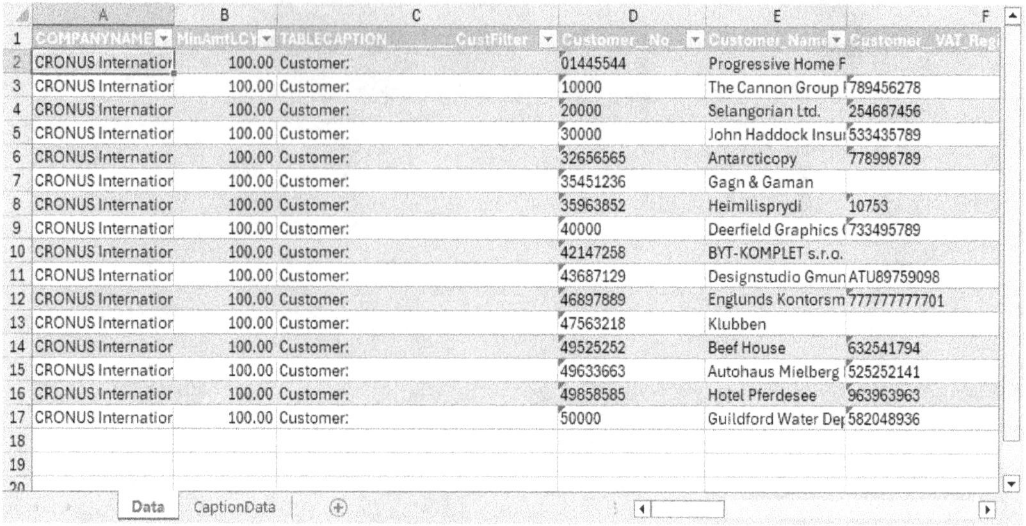

	A	B	C	D	E	F
1	COMPANYNAME	MinAmtLCY	TABLECAPTION CustFilter	Customer_No	Customer_Name	Customer_VAT_Regi
2	CRONUS Internatior	100.00	Customer:	01445544	Progressive Home F	
3	CRONUS Internatior	100.00	Customer:	10000	The Cannon Group I	789456278
4	CRONUS Internatior	100.00	Customer:	20000	Selangorian Ltd.	254687456
5	CRONUS Internatior	100.00	Customer:	30000	John Haddock Insu	533435789
6	CRONUS Internatior	100.00	Customer:	32656565	Antarcticopy	778998789
7	CRONUS Internatior	100.00	Customer:	35451236	Gagn & Gaman	
8	CRONUS Internatior	100.00	Customer:	35963852	Heimilisprydi	10753
9	CRONUS Internatior	100.00	Customer:	40000	Deerfield Graphics (	733495789
10	CRONUS Internatior	100.00	Customer:	42147258	BYT-KOMPLET s.r.o.	
11	CRONUS Internatior	100.00	Customer:	43687129	Designstudio Gmun	ATU89759098
12	CRONUS Internatior	100.00	Customer:	46897889	Englunds Kontorsm	777777777701
13	CRONUS Internatior	100.00	Customer:	47563218	Klubben	
14	CRONUS Internatior	100.00	Customer:	49525252	Beef House	632541794
15	CRONUS Internatior	100.00	Customer:	49633663	Autohaus Mielberg I	525252141
16	CRONUS Internatior	100.00	Customer:	49858585	Hotel Pferdesee	963963963
17	CRONUS Internatior	100.00	Customer:	50000	Guildford Water De	582048936
18						
19						
20						

Figure 5.14 – Flattened dataset from the report

This allows you to analyze the data generated, making sure that DataItem relationships and filters are outputting the data expected. The data is regenerated with each run of the report. A method to analyze would be to copy the data to another workbook and compare and contrast different runs of the report. There are limits to the Excel sheet contents; it is not possible to export more than 1,048,576 rows or 16,384 columns. Regardless, this is a very effective way to view the dataset without a layout getting in the way and causing confusion.

Rendering layout

Rendering layouts is the second most important design feature of a report object. First is the DataItem. As discussed earlier, layouts can be designed in multiple rendering applications, such as SQL Reporting using RDLC, Microsoft Word, or Microsoft Excel. There is no limitation to the number or type of layouts available, as it may be desirable to have multiple layouts of the same type based on design requirements. If the layout file does not exist prior to the building of the extension in Visual Studio Code, it will be generated and appear in the explorer view on the left pane. The generated layout files contain the dataset from the report and are updated every time the extension package is built.

There are two parts to the rendering definition required for reports: the definition of the layouts in the `rendering` section and the `DefaultRenderingLayout` property of the report.

```al
DefaultRenderingLayout = ExcelLayout;

rendering
{
    1 reference
    layout(ExcelLayout)
    {
        Type = Excel;
        LayoutFile = './ShowsByTypeExcel.xlsx';
        Caption = 'Excel Layout';
        Summary = 'Shows by Type Excel';
    }
    0 references
    layout(WordLayout)
    {
        Type = Word;
        LayoutFile = './ShowByTypeWord.docx';
        Caption = 'Word Layout';
        Summary = 'Shows by Type Word';
    }
    0 references
    layout(RDLCLayout)
    {
        Type = RDLC;
        LayoutFile = './ShowsByTypeRDLC.rdlc';
        Caption = 'RDLC Layout';
        Summary = 'Shows by Type RDLC';
    }
}
```

Figure 5.15 – DefaultRenderingLayout and rendering definitions

Note that the `DefaultRenderingLayout` property goes at the top of the report AL and the actual `rendering` section goes at the bottom of the report after the request page.

DataItem properties

The DataItem controls what and how the information is passed to the layout and/or processed in the looping mechanisms. Some of them are listed in the following screenshot:

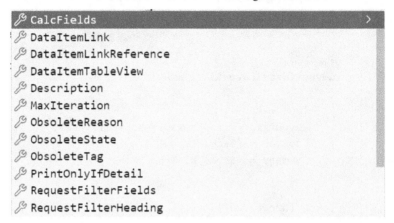

Figure 5.16 – DataItem properties

Here are the definitions of the properties that are used most often:

- `DataItemTableView`: This is the definition of the fixed limits to be applied to the DataItem (the key, ascending or descending sequence, and what filters to apply to this field).

> **Note**
>
> If we don't define a key in `DataItemTableView`, then the users can choose a key to control the data sequence during processing. If we do define a key in the DataItem properties, and, in the `RequestFilterFields` property, we do not specify any filter field names to be displayed, this DataItem will not have a FastTab displayed as part of the request page. This will stop the user from filtering this DataItem unless we provide the capability in the AL code.

- `DataItemLinkReference`: This names the parent DataItem to which this one is linked.
- `DataItemLink`: This identifies the field-to-field linkage between this DataItem and its parent DataItem. That linkage acts as a filter because only the records in this table that have a value that matches the linked field in the parent DataItem will be processed. If no field linkage filter is defined, all the records in the child table will be processed for each record that's processed in its parent table.

- `RequestFilterFields`: This property allows us to choose certain fields to be named in the report request page to make it easier for the user to access them as filter fields. So long as the report request page is activated for a DataItem, the user can choose any available field in the table to filter, regardless of what is specified here.

- `CalcFields`: This names the FlowFields that are to be calculated for each record that's processed. Because FlowFields do not contain data, they have to be calculated to be used. When a FlowField is displayed on a page, Business Central automatically does the calculation. When a FlowField is to be used in a report, we must instigate the calculation. This can either be done here in this property or explicitly within the AL code.

- `MaxIteration`: This can be used to limit the number of iterations the report will make through this DataItem. For example, we would set this to 7 to make the virtual date table process one week's data.

- `PrintOnlyIfDetail`: This should only be used if this DataItem has a child DataItem, that is, one indented/nested below it. If `PrintOnlyIfDetail` is `true`, then controls associated with this DataItem will only print when data is processed for the child DataItem.

- `UseTemporary`: This specifies that a temporary table is supplying the dataset to populate the columns for this DataItem.

After the DataItem properties, the last remaining report component to review are DataItem triggers.

DataItem triggers

Each DataItem has the following triggers available:

Figure 5.17 – DataItems have three triggers available

The DataItem triggers are where most of the flow logic is placed for a report. Developer-defined procedures may be freely added but, generally, they will be called from within the following three triggers:

- `OnPreDataItem()`: This is the logical place for any preprocessing to take place that can't be handled in report or DataItem properties or in the two report preprocessing triggers.

- `OnAfterGetRecord()`: This is the data *read and process* loop. The code that›s placed here has full access to the data of each record, one record at a time. This trigger is repetitively processed until the logical end of the table is reached for this DataItem. This is where we would typically access data in related tables by code. This trigger is represented on our report data flow diagram (*Figure 5.8*) as any one of the boxes labeled **Data Item processing Loop**.

- `OnPostDataItem()`: This executes after all the records in this DataItem are processed unless the report is terminated by means of a manual user cancelation, by execution of an AL `Break` or `Quit` method, or by an error.

We'll now close this section on report components and exercise our knowledge in the following section.

Creating a report in Business Central

Because our Business Central report layouts in this chapter will all be developed in Microsoft Excel, our familiarity with Visual Studio Code will only get us part way to having Business Central report development expertise. We've covered most of the basics of the Visual Studio Code part of Business Central report development. Now, we need to dig into the Microsoft Excel part. If you are already a Microsoft Excel expert, you won't need to spend much time on this part of the book. If you know little or nothing about the Microsoft Excel layout tools, you will need to experiment and practice.

Learn by experimentation

One of the most important learning tools available is experimentation. Report development is one area where experimentation will be extremely valuable. We need to know which report layouts, control settings, and field formats work well for our needs and which do not. The best way to find out is by experimentation.

Create a variety of test reports, beginning with the very simple, and make them progressively more complex. Document what you learn as you make discoveries. You will end up with your own personal report development documentation. Once we've created a number of simple reports from scratch, we should modify test copies of some of the standard reports that are part of the Business Central system.

Some reports will be relatively easy to understand, and others that are very complex will be difficult to understand. The more we test, the better we will be able to determine which standard Business Central report designs can be borrowed for our work, and where we are better off starting from scratch. Of course, we should always check to see if there is a pattern that is applicable to the situation that we are working on.

Report building – phase 1

Our goal is to create `report 50101 "Shows By Type"` for our WDTU data, which will give us a list of all the scheduled radio show instances that have been organized within `Radio Show` by `Radio Show Type`. For the layout part, we will use Excel.

We will begin with adding a new file named `ShowsByType.report.al` and using the `treport` snippet. Tabbing through the file, we will first adjust the report ID to `50101` and the name to `Shows By Type`. The snippet has provided us with one `dataitem` and `column` control each, which we can now delete. A better way to add DataItems is to simply use IntelliSense. Type the letter D, and the snippet for `dataitem` will appear. Hit *Tab*, type a reference name, and then the target table name (in this case, `Radio Show Type`, then `Radio Show`, and then `Playlist Header`).

The basic dataset will look as follows:

```
8        dataset
9        {
10           dataitem(DataItem1; "Radio Show Type")  {
11               dataitem(DataItem2; "Radio Show")       {
12                   dataitem(DataItem3; "Playlist Header")
13                   {
14                   }
15               }
16           }
17       }
```

Figure 5.18 – Indented data items indicating the intended parent/child relationship

In the `rendering` control, we will specify the Excel layout as follows:

```
layout(ExcelLayout)
{
    Type = Excel;
    LayoutFile = './ShowsByTypeExcel.xlsx';
    Caption = 'Excel Layout';
    Summary = 'Shows by Type Excel';
}
```

Then, we will declare its layout name as the default `rendering` layout in the report properties:

```
DefaultRenderingLayout = ExcelLayout;
```

Before we go any further, let's make sure we've got some test data in our tables. To enter data, we can use the pages we built earlier. The specifics of our test data aren't critical. We simply need a reasonable distribution of data so that our report test will be meaningful. The following three screenshots provide an example minimal set of data. The first one is a copy from *Chapter 2*, *Figure 2.20*, where we already had entered some **Radio Show Types**:

Radio Show Types
+ New
Edit List
Delete
Code ↑
Description
CALL-IN
Talk and Listener Interview
MUSIC
Music and Misc
NEWS
In-depth Stories
ROCK
70-ies and 80-ies Rock
TALK
Mostly Talk

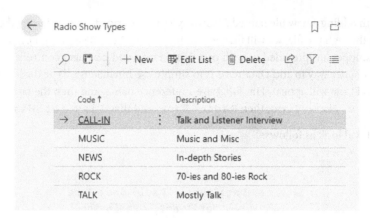

Figure 5.19 – The Radio Show Type sample data

Radio Show List could be populated like this:

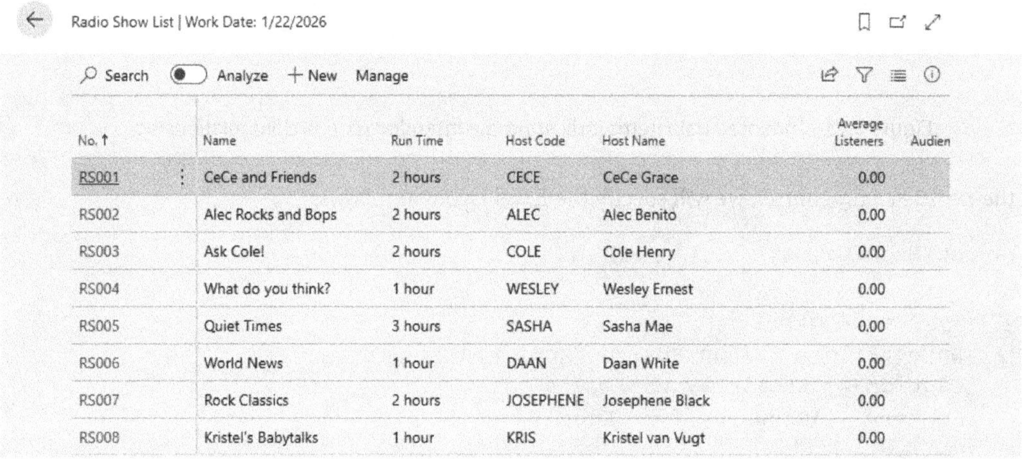

Radio Show List | Work Date: 1/22/2026
Search
Analyze
+ New
Manage
No. ↑
Name
Run Time
Host Code
Host Name
Average Listeners
Audien
RS001 CeCe and Friends 2 hours CECE CeCe Grace 0.00
RS002 Alec Rocks and Bops 2 hours ALEC Alec Benito 0.00
RS003 Ask Cole! 2 hours COLE Cole Henry 0.00
RS004 What do you think? 1 hour WESLEY Wesley Ernest 0.00
RS005 Quiet Times 3 hours SASHA Sasha Mae 0.00
RS006 World News 1 hour DAAN Daan White 0.00
RS007 Rock Classics 2 hours JOSEPHENE Josephene Black 0.00
RS008 Kristel's Babytalks 1 hour KRIS Kristel van Vugt 0.00

Figure 5.20 – The Radio Show sample data

As the third step, we enter the following rows into **Playlist Document List**:

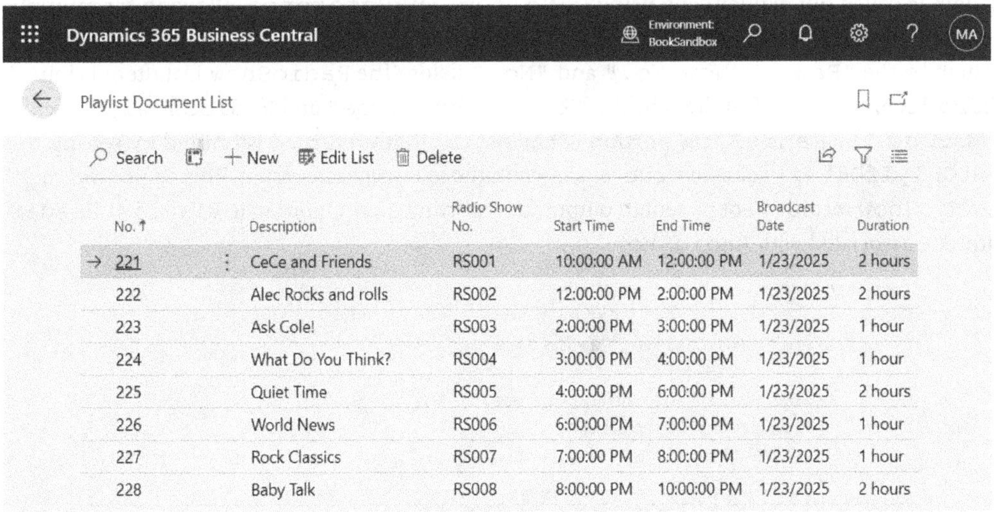

Figure 5.21 – The Playlist Document List sample data

Since the Visual Studio Code part of our report design is relatively simple, we can do it as part of our phase 1 effort. It's simple because we aren't building any processing logic, and we don't have any complex relationships to address. We just want to create a nice, neat, nested list of data.

The next step is to define the data fields we want to be available for processing and in the layout:

```
1   report 50101 "Shows By Type"
2   {
3       DefaultRenderingLayout = ExcelLayout;
4       Caption = 'Shows by Type';
5       UsageCategory = ReportsAndAnalysis;
6
7       dataset
8       {
9           dataitem(RadioShowType; "Radio Show Type")
10          {
11              column(Code_RadioShowType; Code) { }
12              column(Type; Description) { }
13              dataitem(RadioShow; "Radio Show")
14              {
15                  column(No_RadioShow; "No.") { }
16                  column(Title; Name) { }
17                  column(Hours; "Run Time" / 86400000) { }
18                  dataitem(PlaylistHeader; "Playlist Header")
19                  {
20                      column(PostingDate_PlaylistHeader; "Broadcast Date") { }
21                      column(StartTime_PlaylistHeader; "Start Time") { }
```

Figure 5.22 – Nested DataItems with columns for data

Each of the subordinate nested DataItems must be properly linked to its parent DataItem. The parent DataItem is called out explicitly by using `DataItemLinkReference`, allowing for multiple child DataItems at the same level. The `PlaylistHeader` DataItem is joined to the `RadioShow` DataItem by the `"Radio Show No."` and `"No."` fields. The `RadioShow` DataItem is joined to the `RadioShowType` DataItem by the `"Radio Show Type"` and `RadioShowType` fields, that is, `Code`. The `RadioShow` portion of the dataset that's returned is limited by setting the `PrintOnlyIfDetail` value to `true`, as shown in the following screenshot. This choice will cause the `RadioShow` record to not be sent to output for reporting if no subordinate `PlaylistHeader` records are associated with `RadioShow`:

```
dataset
{
    dataitem(RadioShowType; "Radio Show Type")
    {
        column(Code_RadioShowType; Code) { }
        column(Type; Description) { }
        dataitem(RadioShow; "Radio Show")
        {
            DataItemLinkReference = RadioShowType;
            DataItemLink = "Radio Show Type" = field(Code);
            DataItemTableView = sorting("Radio Show Type");
            PrintOnlyIfDetail = true;
            column(No_RadioShow; "No.") { }
            column(Title; Name) { }
            column(Hours; "Run Time" / 86400000) { }
            dataitem(PlaylistHeader; "Playlist Header")
            {
                DataItemLinkReference = RadioShow;
                DataItemLink = "Radio Show No." = field("No.");
                DataItemTableView = sorting("No.");
                column(PostingDate_PlaylistHeader; "Broadcast Date") { }
                column(StartTime_PlaylistHeader; "Start Time") { }
            }
        }
    }
}
```

Figure 5.23 – Subordinate DataItems linked with DataItemLink

In *Figure 5.22* and *Figure 5.23*, there is an additional feature that should be explained. Column data sent to a layout does not necessarily need to be directly related to table data but can be variables or calculations. Note the calculation in the `Hours` column. In order for the data to be displayed in an *hour:minute* format in Excel, the data must be converted from the Business Central standard of milliseconds to a 24-hour fraction. The numerical factoring is 86,400,000.

The other data that we can pass to Microsoft Excel are the labels. Labels will be used later as captions in the report and are enabled for multi-language support. Let's create a title label and column headings that we will hand over the fence to the layout. Go to the end of the .al file and type *L* or use *Ctrl +* the spacebar:

```
61      labels
62      {
63          ReportTitle = 'Show Schedule by Type';
64          ShowTitle = 'Title';
65          ShowTypeTitle = 'Type';
66          HourTitle = 'Hours';
67      }
```

Figure 5.24 – Labels show as Captions in generated Excel Workbook

Now that we have our AL dataset definition completed, we should save and publish our work before doing anything else.

```
report 50101 "Shows By Type"
{
    DefaultRenderingLayout = ExcelLayout;
    Caption = 'Shows by Type';
    UsageCategory = ReportsAndAnalysis;
    ApplicationArea = All;

    dataset
    {
```

Figure 5.25 – Don't forget UsageCategory so it is searchable!

Then, before we begin our layout work, it's a good idea to check that we don't have some hidden error that will get in our way later. The easiest way to do that is just to run what we have now. What we expect to see is a basic Shows by Type request page display, allowing us to run a report with an Excel layout defined.

Report building – phase 2

As we mentioned earlier, there are several tools we can use for Business Central report layout development. The specific screen appearance depends somewhat on which tool is being used.

To begin our report development work in Microsoft Excel, we must compile and build the app. Then, we need to navigate to the generated Excel document and use the right mouse button to select **Open Externally** in order to start editing in Microsoft Excel. We will see the following screen:

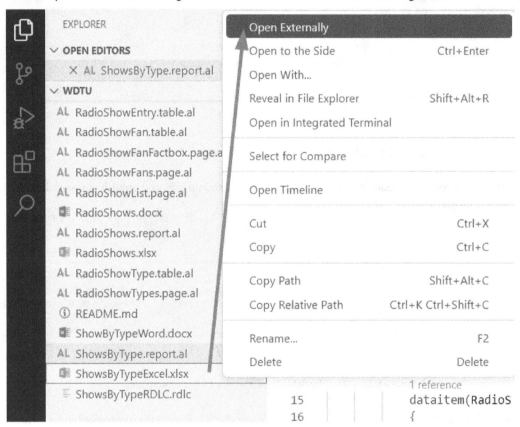

Figure 5.26 – Open the generated Excel file directly from VS Code

The Excel workbook will have four sheets: Data, TranslationData, CaptionData, and Aggregated Metadata. Aggregated Metadata will not show when the Excel sheet is generated from Business Central by a user. The two tabs we will focus on are the Data and CaptionData tabs.

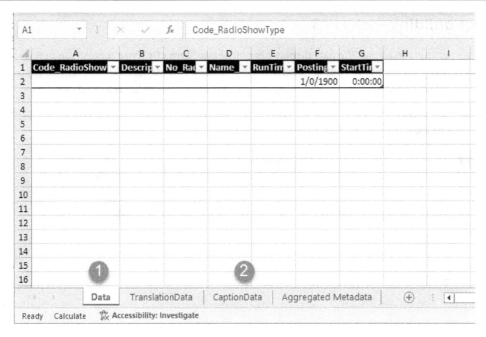

Figure 5.27 – The Data and CaptionData tabs generated by Visual Studio

Click the plus symbol at the bottom of the screen to the right of the auto-generated sheets to create Sheet1, and rename it Shows by Type FILTER. First, we are going to add the report title by referencing the label defined in the AL code. This label is in the CaptionData tab. The order of the labels in Excel will be the same as defined in the dataset; we know ReportTitle is going to reside in the first cell under the Value heading. In cell A2, use the FILTER function to limit the Value column on a predetermined Caption. Note that since there is no data available yet in this template, the field will be empty after entering the formula.

Figure 5.28 – Use of FILTER with sheet and column names is preferred

This isn't especially impressive, but it's not bad if this is your first try at creating a Business Central report. In general, it is better to reference the sheet name and XML column heading rather than referencing exact cells, the exception being a caption that is repeated in the Data tab. The FILTER function is also useful to return multiple rows of data.

We could experiment with various properties of the heading fields, choosing different fonts, bolding, colors, and so on. As we only have a small number of simple fields to display (and could recreate our report if we have to do so), this is a good time to learn more about some of the report appearance capabilities that Microsoft Excel provides.

Report building – phase 3

Finally, we are ready to lay out the data display portion of our **Shows by Type** report. The first step of this phase is to decide how to lay out the data in the report. The two methods we can choose from are using the pivot and suggested chart, and using the `FILTER` function to list repeated data.

Open the `Data` sheet. In the Excel actions, select the **Insert** ribbon and select **PivotTable** | **From Table/Range**.

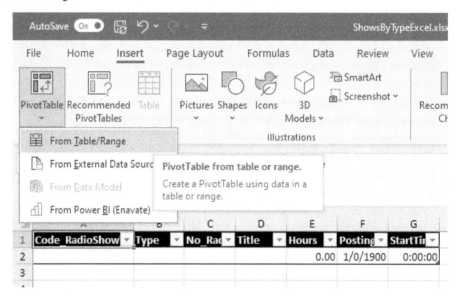

Figure 5.29 – Create PivotTable

In the **PivotTable from table or range** screen, leave **Table/Range** on `Data` and **New Worksheet**:

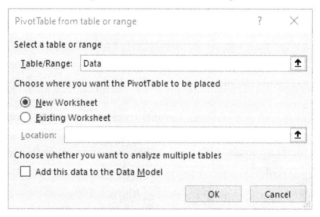

Figure 5.30 – PivotTable from table or range screen

This will create Sheet2 (renaming it Shows by Type PIVOT) with the **PivotTable Fields** selection screen showing. Select Type, Title, and Hours. Type and Title should go in **Axis (Categories)** or **Axis (Rows)**, depending on the Microsoft Excel version, and Hours should appear as Sum of Hours in **Values**. The table will have the titles grouped by show type, with the hours subtotaled and grand totaled. Next, we will add a pie chart. To do this, click the **Recommended Charts** icon in the **Insert** ribbon and select the pie chart.

Both the pivot table and the chart will be interactively linked such that you can show or hide titles or types and they will update on the fly.

Your tab should now resemble the one on the following screenshot:

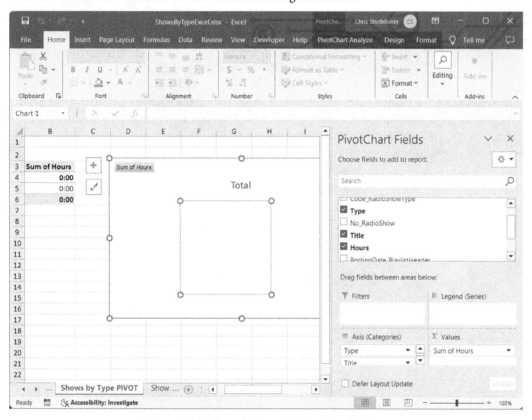

Figure 5.31 – Sheet by Type PIVOT with selections

Add a new tab/worksheet and rename it Shows by Type FILTER. This sheet will have the following elements: the report title caption, table column captions, and repeating rows of data. The FILTER function in Microsoft Excel displays all the values in an array in a repeating table. The report title and table column captions will only return single values, whereas the data array will return as many rows as are returned in the Data sheet.

The FILTER function in Excel filters an array based on a true/false statement:

```
=FILTER(array,include,[if_empty])
```

Argument	Description
array (required)	The array or range to filter
include (required)	A Boolean statement based on an array with the same dimensions as the first parameter
if_empty	The value of the return if all values in the included array are empty or nothing

Table 5.1 – Excel FILTER function arguments

For the report title, we use the exact same function as we did on the Shows by Type PIVOT sheet. Don't forget to bold the title cell using the standard Excel font formatting. For the table column captions, we will use the same filter but with the Caption filter to match each column. Feel free to format the table headings to make the column headings stand out.

```
=FILTER(CaptionData[Value],CaptionData[Caption] = "ShowTypeTitle","")
```

Figure 5.32 – Repeater table column caption

For the repeater portion, we will use the FILTER function. The generated list will show the values from the Data tab as long as the primary dataset column (Code_RadioShowType) is not blank. Otherwise, it will display a blank cell.

```
=FILTER(Data[Type],Data[Code_RadioShowType]<>"","")
```

	A	B	C	D	E	F	G	H
1								
2								
3								
4	]<>"","")	#CALC!	#CALC!					
5								

Figure 5.33 – Repeater row FILTER statement

To make the Hours column more readable, format the cells likely to be populated (B4 to B6 in the Shows by Type PIVOT sheet and below C3 in the Shows by Type FILTER sheet) with the h:mm time format.

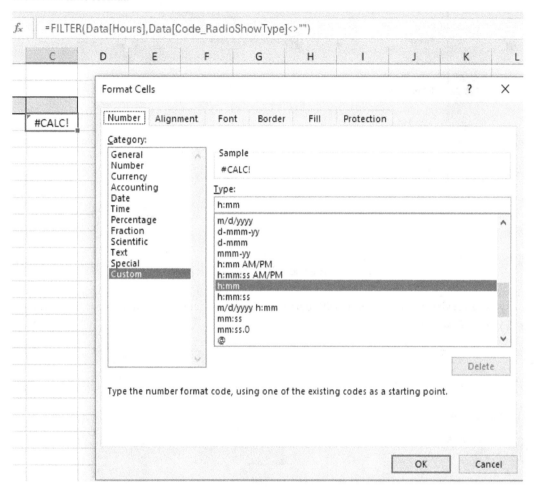

Figure 5.34 – Format the Hours data in Excel to be easier to read

Save the Excel template and then build and publish the extension to Business Central. Search for the report using Shows by Type and run it.

On the request page, click **Download** and save the generated report locally.

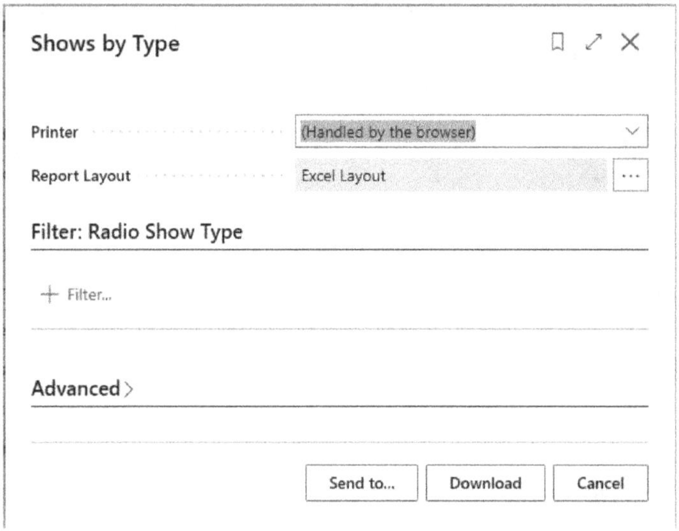

Figure 5.35– The Shows by Type request page

Now, you can review your two sheets with data from Business Central. The first one is the Shows by Type PIVOT sheet:

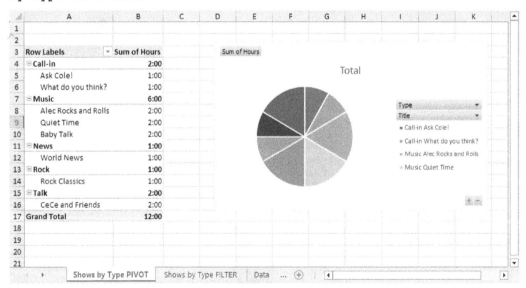

Figure 5.36 – The Shows by Type PIVOT sheet

In general, for analytical reports with subtotals and totals, pivot tables and related charts are most likely the method of choice. For more list or table-driven reports based on repeater or static elements, use FILTER or other reference functions to the data and caption sheets, as we did in the Shows by Type FILTER sheet:

	A	B	C	D	E	F	G	H	I	J	K	L
1	Show Schedule by Type											
2												
3	Type	Title	Hours									
4	Call-in	Ask Cole!	1:00									
5	Call-in	What do you think?	1:00									
6	Music	Alec Rocks and Rolls	2:00									
7	Music	Quiet Time	2:00									
8	Music	Baby Talk	2:00									
9	News	World News	1:00									
10	Rock	Rock Classics	1:00									
11	Talk	CeCe and Friends	2:00									
12												
13												
14												
15												
16												
17												
18												
19												
20												
21												

Shows by Type PIVOT | Shows by Type FILTER | Data | ... ⊕

Figure 5.37 – The Shows by Type FILTER sheet

Depending on what we want to achieve, it may be preferable to not create a new report from scratch but to extend an existing one from Business Central. The decision depends on some factors that the next section will cover.

Extending an existing report with SQL Report Builder or Microsoft Office

The decision to extend an existing report in Business Central or create a custom report is dependent on several factors:

- Are you just looking to just create a different layout (RDLC, Word, or Excel)? *Extend the report.*
- Are you only going to add columns or DataItems without radically altering the report flow? *Extend the report.*
- Is there new or additional logic, triggers, or processing required not related to events available? *Create a copy in the custom object range.*

In most cases where anything more than the most basic changes, it is best practice to make the necessary modifications to a copy of the original. Not only is this safer because it eliminate the possibility of creating problems with the original version, but it will make upgrades easier. On the other hand, as our application is updated we must also remember to manually copy any interim improvements or bug fixes from the original report.

A vast majority of Business Central report layouts can be modified by a developer using SQL Report Builder because most standard reports have been developed with **RDLC layouts**. Over thirty standard reports also have **Word layouts** available in the initial distribution of Business Central. These include reports 1304 "Standard Sales - Quote", 1305 "Standard Sales - Order Conf.", 1306 "Standard Sales - Invoice", and 1307 "Standard Sales - Credit Memo". Less than 10 reports have **Excel layouts**, but they include aged accounts, trial balance, and customer/vendor top trends reports ranging from ID 4402 to 4409.

> **Note**
>
> As the Excel reports have been published with the **Dynamics BC Excel Reports** extension, we cannot find them in the AL Explorer in Visual Studio Code. In environments where this extension has been installed, we can find them and export their layout on the **Report Layouts** client page.

It is likely that future releases of Business Central will have additional report layouts available both in Word and Excel format. In the meantime, if we want other reports, whether they be standard or custom, to have Word or Excel layout options available, we will have to create them ourselves. The primary advantage of having Word or Excel layout options for reports is to allow for the modification of the layouts by a trained user or developer. As the modifications must still conform to good (and correct) report layout practices, appropriate training, careful work, and considerable common sense are needed to make such modifications, even though the tool is Microsoft Office.

Request page

A **request page** is a page that is executed at the beginning of a report. Its presence or absence is under the developer's control. A request page looks similar to what's shown in the following screenshot, which is based on one of the standard system reports, the **Customer – Order Detail** report, report 108:

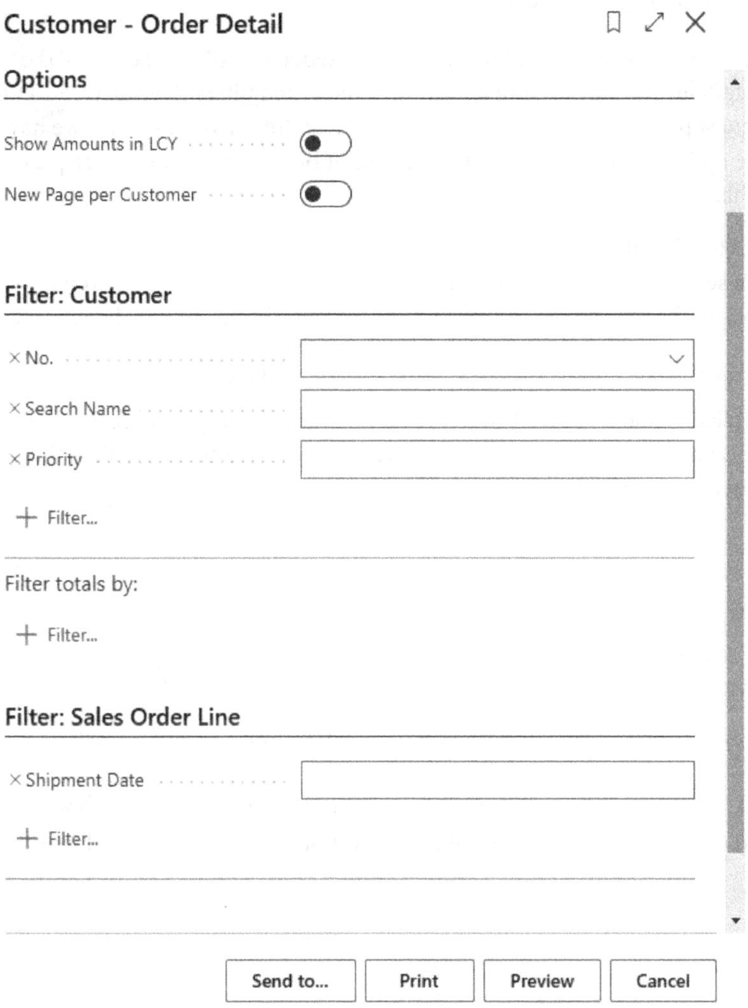

Customer - Order Detail

Options

Show Amounts in LCY · · · · · · · · · ⬤

New Page per Customer · · · · · · · · ⬤

Filter: Customer

× No. · ⌄

× Search Name · · · · · · · · · · · ·

× Priority · · · · · · · · · · · · · · · · · ·

\+ Filter…

Filter totals by:

\+ Filter…

Filter: Sales Order Line

× Shipment Date · · · · · · · · · · · ·

\+ Filter…

Send to…   Print   Preview   Cancel

Figure 5.38 – Request page for a report object

There are three FastTabs on this page. The **Options** FastTab exists because the software developer wanted to allow some additional user options for this report. The **Filter: Customer** and **Filter: Sales Order Line** FastTabs are tied to the data tables associated with this report. These FastTabs allow the user to define both data filters and flow filters to control report processing.

Adding a request page option

Because in our report we have defined the default sort sequences (DataItemTableView), except for the first DataItem, and we have not defined any requested filters (RequestFilterFields), the default request page for our report has only one DataItem FastTab. Since we have not defined any processing options that would require user input before the report is generated, we have no **Options** FastTab.

Our goal now is to allow the user to optionally input text that will be printed at the top of the report. This could be a secondary report heading, instructions on interpreting the report, or some other communications to the report reader. To add this capability, perform the following steps:

1. Open Report 50101 "Shows by Type" in Visual Studio Code.

2. Add a global variable named UserComment with a data type of Text. We will not define the Length field, as shown in the following screenshot; this will allow the user to enter a comment of any length:

```
66
67        var
68            UserComment: Text;
69
70    }                        I
```

Figure 5.39 – Global variables defined below the Layout section

3. Add this variable as a data column. column must be a subordinate of the DataItem. We do not need a caption defined as we will use the variable name for this field in the report layout.

```
1   report 50101 "Shows By Type"
2   {
3       DefaultRenderingLayout = ExcelLayout;
4       Caption = 'Shows by Type';
5       UsageCategory = ReportsAndAnalysis;
6
7       dataset
8       {
9           dataitem(RadioShowType; "Radio Show Type")
10          {
11              column(UserComment; UserComment) { }
12              column(Code_RadioShowType; Code) { }
13              column(Type; Description) { }
```

Figure 5.40 – column is of a variable, not a table field

4.   Add the request page to the report, between the dataset and rendering sections.

```
35    requestpage
36    {
37        layout
38        {
39            area(Content)
40            {
41                group(Options)
42                {
43                    field(UserComment; UserComment)
44                    {
45                        ApplicationArea = All;
46                        Caption = 'User Comment';
47                    }
48                }
```

Figure 5.41 – Building the request page definition

5.   Save and compile the report by running this Visual Studio Code command: `AL: Package`.

6.   Access Microsoft Excel through **Open Externally**.

7.   On both the `PIVOT` and `FILTER` sheets, just below the report title, select the cell.

8.   Enter the following function into the cell: `=Data[@UserComment]`.

9.   Save the Excel workbook and exit Microsoft Excel. Then, publish the project.

10. Run `Shows by Type`.

To test the updated request page, we need to run the report in the client.

Running the report

There are several ways to run reports during development. The most obvious way is to build and publish the extension to Business Central and use the **Tell Me** feature. There are additional methods without using **Tell Me**, which are useful if you have not or cannot set the `UsageCategory` and `ApplicationArea` properties to make an object searchable. Regardless of the method the report is called, it is still required that the code is published to the environment. The most basic is to use the URL. The syntax for running an object is as follows: `https://businesscentral.dynamics.com/<environment name>]/?[company=<companyname>]&[page|query|report|table=<ID>]`.

An example to run our report would be `https://businesscentral.dynamics.com/Sandbox/?company=CRONUS%20International%20Ltd.&report=50101`.

You can also run an object directly from the Visual Studio Code project using AL Explorer. Select the object you want to view and click **Run**:

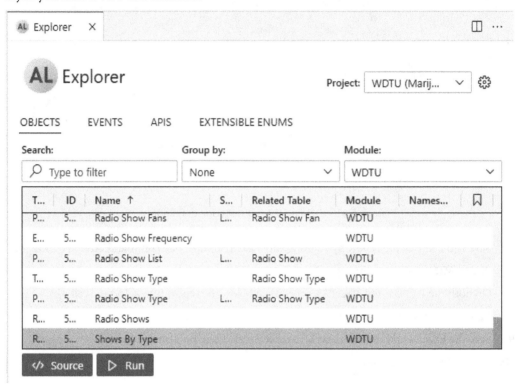

Figure 5.42 – AL Explorer will execute the direct URL to an object

Within the client itself, you can use **Tell Me** to navigate to the **Report Layout** page. From this list, it is possible to use the **Run Report** action. If during development it is desired to immediately review a table, page, report, or query object, it is possible to use the launch.json file. There are two properties that must be used in conjunction with each other: startupObjectType and startupObjectId.

No matter which of the previous methods are utilized, the request page will display the new option to enter a comment.

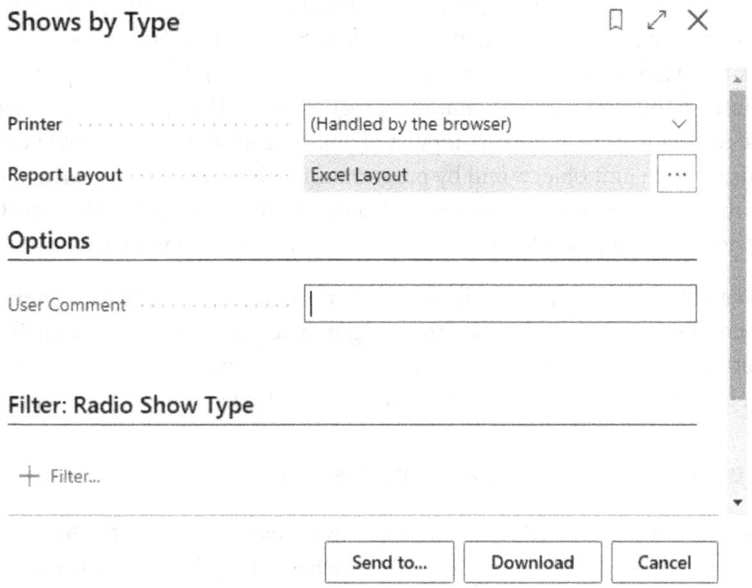

Figure 5.43 – The Shows by Type request page with User Comment

The report heading then shows the comment in whatever font, color, or other display attribute the developer has defined:

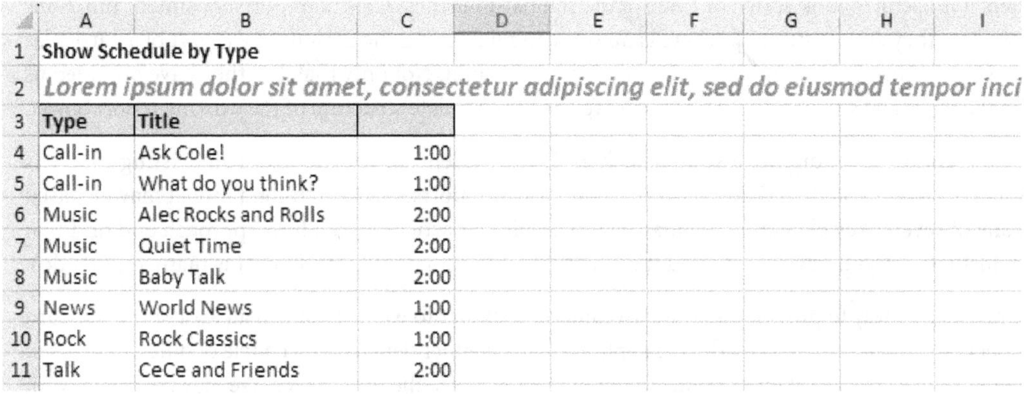

	A	B	C
1	Show Schedule by Type		
2	*Lorem ipsum dolor sit amet, consectetur adipiscing elit, sed do eiusmod tempor inci*		
3	Type	Title	
4	Call-in	Ask Cole!	1:00
5	Call-in	What do you think?	1:00
6	Music	Alec Rocks and Rolls	2:00
7	Music	Quiet Time	2:00
8	Music	Baby Talk	2:00
9	News	World News	1:00
10	Rock	Rock Classics	1:00
11	Talk	CeCe and Friends	2:00

Figure 5.44 – The comment variable is passed in the dataset

Because we didn't specify a maximum length on our `UserComment` field, we can type in as much information as we want. Try it out; type in an entire paragraph for a test.

Processing-only reports

One of the report properties we reviewed earlier was `ProcessingOnly`. If that property is set to `true`, then the report object will not output a dataset for displaying or printing—it will simply process the data we program it to process. The beauty of this capability is that we can use the built-in processing loop of the Business Central report object, along with its sorting and filtering capabilities, to create a variety of data-updating routines with minimal programming. The use of report objects also gives us access to the request page to allow user input and guidance for the run. We could create the same functionality using code unit objects and by programming all of the loops, filtering, user interface request pages, and so on, ourselves. However, with a processing-only report, Business Central gives us a lot of help and makes it possible to create some powerful routines with minimal effort.

At the beginning of the run of a processing-only report, there is very little user interface variation compared to a normal printing report. The processing-only request page looks much like it would for a printing report, except that the **Print** and **Preview** options are not available. Everything else looks the same. Of course, we have a big difference of no visible output at the end of processing.

Creative report plagiarism and patterns

In the same fashion as we discussed regarding pages in *Chapter 4, Pages – The Interactive Interface*, when we want to create a new report of a type that we haven't made recently (or at all), it's a good idea to find another report that is similar in an important way and study it. We should also check if there is a Business Central pattern defined for an applicable category of report. At the minimum, in both of these investigations, we will learn how the developers of Business Central solved a data flow, totaling, or filtering challenge. In the best case, we will find a model that we can follow closely, respectfully plagiarizing (copying) a working solution, thus saving ourselves much time and effort.

Often, it is useful to look at two or three of the standard Business Central reports for similar functions to see how they are constructed. There is no sense in reinventing the design for a report of a particular type when someone else has already invented a version of it. Not only that, but they have provided us with the plans and given us the AL code, as well as the complete structure of the existing report object.

When it comes to modifying a system such as Business Central, copying from an existing source is a very effective research and design tool. In the case of reports, our search for a model may be based on any of several key elements. We may be looking for a particular data flow approach and find that the Business Central developers used the `Integer` table for some DataItems (as many reports do).

We may need a way to provide some creative filtering, similar to what is done in an area of the standard product. We might want to provide users options to print either detailed or a couple of different levels of totaling, with a layout that looks good, no matter which choice the user makes. We may be dealing with all three of these design needs in the same report. In such a case, it is likely that we are using multiple Business Central reports as our models: one for this feature, another for that feature, and so forth.

If we have a complicated, application-specific report to create, we may not be able to directly model our report on a model that already exists. However, often, we can still find ideas in standard reports that we can apply to our new design. We will almost always be better off using a model rather than inventing a totally new approach.

If our design concept is too big a leap from what was done previously, we should consider what we might change in our design so that we can build on the strengths of AL and existing Business Central routines. Creating entirely new approaches may be very satisfying (when it works) but, too often, the extra costs exceed the incremental benefits.

Reports extract data using a looping mechanism in order to extract data from multiple tables. Each loop, related `dataitem`, and even record variable usage would consist of a separate SQL statement sent to the database. This is not always the most efficient method, and Business Central offers an option that is much closer to using Transact SQL statements: the `query` object.

Queries

Reports have always been available in Business Central as a data retrieval tool. Reports are used to process and/or manipulate the data through the `Insert`, `Modify`, or `Delete` procedures, with the option of presenting the data in a formatted, printable format. The `query` object was created with performance in mind. Instead of multiple calls to SQL to retrieve multiple datasets, which would then be manipulated in AL, queries allow us to utilize familiar Business Central tools to create advanced **T-SQL** queries.

A Business Central developer can utilize the `query` object as a source of data both in Business Central and externally. Some of the external uses of Business Central queries are as follows:

- A web service source for OData or as a REST API endpoint. Queries of the API type are used to generate web service endpoints and this type of query cannot be used to display data in the user interface. A query of the API type can be used to join data from different data sources. The data can only be viewed.

- Feeding data as `.xml` or `.csv` files to external reporting tools, such as Excel, SharePoint, and SSRS.

  Internally, Business Central queries can be used as follows:

  - Allowing users to analyze data from a query using the **data analysis mode**. For more information, see `https://learn.microsoft.com/en-us/dynamics365/business-central/analysis-mode`.

  - Retrieving aggregated values or only distinct records (SQL `SELECT DISTINCT`) from a record set. See `https://learn.microsoft.com/en-us/dynamics365/business-central/dev-itpro/developer/devenv-query-totals-grouping` for further guidance.

- As providers of data to which **Cues** (displayed in Role Centers) are bound. A Cue can be based on a FlowField or Normal field. If you use a Normal field, you'll typically add the logic that calculates the Cue data to an AL trigger or method. Unlike a FlowField, where data is extracted from tables, a Normal field enables you to extract data from other objects such as queries.

- As a dataset variable in AL to be accessed by other object types (reports, pages, code units, and so on). See `https://learn.microsoft.com/en-us/dynamics365/business-central/dev-itpro/developer/devenv-query-using-instead-record-variables` for guidance on using the Read method to consume data from a query.

Query objects are more limited than SQL-stored procedures. Queries are more similar to a SQL view. Some compromises in the design of query functionality were made for better performance. Data manipulation is not supported in queries. Variables, subqueries, and dynamic elements, such as building a query based on selective criteria, are not allowed within the query object. Queries are not extensible.

One of the features that allow Business Central to generate advanced T-SQL statements is the use of **SQL joins**. These include the following join methods for two tables, A and B:

- **Inner**: This query compares each row of table A with each row of table B to find all the pairs of rows that satisfy the join criteria.

- **Full outer**: This join does not require each record in the two joined tables to have a matching record so that all records from both A and B will appear at least once.

- **Left outer join**: In this join, every record from A will appear at least once, even if matching B is not found.

- **Right outer join**: In this join, every record from B will appear at least once, even if matching A is not found.

- **Cross join**: This join returns the Cartesian product of the sets of rows from A and B. The Cartesian product is a set made up of rows that includes the columns of each row in A, along with the columns of each row in B for a number of rows; in other words, it includes the columns of the rows in A, plus those in B.

Note

The **union join**, which joins all records from A and B without the join criteria, is not available at this time.

Building a simple query

Sometimes, it is necessary to quickly retrieve detailed information from one or more ledgers that may contain hundreds of thousands to many millions of records. The query object is the perfect tool for such data selection as it is totally scalable and can retrieve selected fields from multiple tables at once. The following example (using Cronus data) will show the aggregated quantity per bin of lot-tracked items in stock. This query can be presented to a user by means of either a report or a page:

1. We will define the logic we need to follow and the data that's required to support that logic, and then we will develop the query. It is necessary to know what inventory is in stock, which also contains a lot number. This is accomplished using the Item Ledger Entry table.

2. However, the Item Ledger Entry record does not contain any bin information. This information is stored in the Warehouse Ledger Entry table.

3. The Location Code, Item No., and Lot No. columns are used to match the Item Ledger Entry and Warehouse Ledger Entry records to make sure that the correct items are selected.

4. To determine which bins are designated as pick bins, the Bin Type records that are marked as Pick are equal to true need to be matched with the bins in Warehouse Ledger Entry.

5. Lastly, Quantity on each Warehouse Entry needs to be summed per Location Code, Zone Code, Bin Code, Item No., and Lot No. to show the amount that's available in each bin.

Now that we have defined the necessary logic and data sources, we can create the desired query object, as follows:

1. In Visual Studio Code, we create a new .al file called query 50100 "Lot Avail. by Bin". We use the snippet tquery and select normal query (not API).

2. Now, we define the primary DataItem. The first DataItem is for the Item Ledger Entry table. We can use IntelliSense to find the correct table.

3. After defining the first DataItem, we will add columns. column is a field from the DataItem table that will be output as an available field from the query dataset. The other Type option is Filter, which allows us to use the source column as a filter and does not output column in the dataset. Use IntelliSense to add the Item No. and Lot No. fields under Item Ledger Entry, as shown in the following screenshot:

```
AL LotAvailablebyBin.query.al  ✕

Radio Show > AL LotAvailablebyBin.query.al > ⚡ Query 50100 "Lot Avail. by Bin"
  1    query 50100 "Lot Avail. by Bin"
  2    {
  3        QueryType = Normal;
  4
  5        elements
  6        {
  7            dataitem(Item_Ledger_Entry; "Item Ledger Entry")
  8            {
  9                column(Item_No; "Item No.") { }
 10                column(Lot_No; "Lot No.") { }
 11            }
 12        }
```

Figure 5.45 – Query after starting with snippet

4. The next DataItem we need is for the `Warehouse Entry` table. We must join it to the `Item Ledger Entry` by filling in the `DataItemLink` property. Link the `Location Code`, `Item No.`, and `Lot No.` fields between the two tables.

```
  7            dataitem(Item_Ledger_Entry; "Item Ledger Entry")
  8            {
  9                column(Item_No; "Item No.") { }
 10                column(Lot_No; "Lot No.") { }
 11                dataitem(Warehouse_Entry; "Warehouse Entry")
 12                {
 13                    DataItemLink = "Location Code" = Item_Ledger_Entry."Location Code",
 14                                   "Item No." = Item_Ledger_Entry."Item No.",
 15                                   "Lot No." = Item_Ledger_Entry."Lot No.";
 16                }
```

Figure 5.46 – Link Warehouse Entry (child) to Item Ledger Entry (parent)

The following steps will define the rest of the DataItems, columns, and filters for this query:

1. Select `Entry No.`, `Location Code`, `Zone Code`, `Bin Code`, and `Quantity` as columns under the `Warehouse_Entry` DataItem.

2. Add a `Bin` table as the next DataItem.

3. Set the DataItem link between `Bin` and `Warehouse_Entry` as the `Bin` table Code field linked to the `Bin Code` field for the `Warehouse Entry` table.

4. Add the `Bin Type` table as the last DataItem for this query. Create a DataItem link between the `Bin Type` table's Code field and the `Bin` table's `Bin Type Code` field.

5. Set the DataItem filter as `Pick = const(true)` to only show the quantities for bins that are enabled for picking.

6. For the dataset that's returned by the query, we will only want the total quantity per combination of the `Location`, `Zone`, `Bin`, `Item`, and `Lot number`. For the column where `Quantity` is in the `Warehouse_Entry` DataItem, set the `Method` property to `Sum`.

```
7         dataitem(Item_Ledger_Entry; "Item Ledger Entry")
8         {
9             column(Item_No; "Item No.") { }
10            column(Lot_No; "Lot No.") { }
11            dataitem(Warehouse_Entry; "Warehouse Entry")
12            {
13                DataItemLink = "Location Code" = Item_Ledger_Entry."Location Code",
14                               "Item No." = Item_Ledger_Entry."Item No.",
15                               "Lot No." = Item_Ledger_Entry."Lot No.";
16                column(Entry_No_; "Entry No.") { }
17                column(Location_Code; "Location Code") { }
18                column(Zone_Code; "Zone Code") { }
19                column(Bin_Code; "Bin Code") { }
20                column(Sum_Quantity; Quantity) { Method = Sum; }
21                dataitem(Bin; Bin)
22                {
23                    DataItemLink = Code = Warehouse_Entry."Bin Code";
24                    dataitem(Bin_Type; "Bin Type")
25                    {
26                        DataItemLink = Code = Bin."Bin Type Code";
27                        DataItemTableFilter = Pick = const(true);
28                    }
29                }
30            }
```

Figure 5.47 – Query with additional DataItems

This query can be utilized internally in Business Central as an indirect data source in a page or a report object. Although the `SourceTable` in pages and DataItems reports can only be database tables, we can define a query as a variable, and then use the query dataset result to populate a temporary `SourceTable`. In a page, we set the `SourceTableTemporary` property to `true` and then load the table via the AL code located in the `OnOpenPage` trigger.

In our example, we use the `Warehouse Entry` table to define our temporary table because it contains all the fields in the query dataset. In the page properties, we set `SourceTableTemporary` to `true` (if we neglect to mark this table as temporary, we are quite likely to corrupt the live data in the `Warehouse Entry` table). In the `OnOpenPage` trigger, the query object (`LotAvail`) is filtered and opened. As long as the query object has a dataset line available for output, the query column values can be placed in the temporary record variable and are available for display. Because this code is located in the `OnOpenPage` trigger, the temporary table is empty when this code begins execution. If the code were to be invoked from another trigger, the `Rec.DeleteAll()` statement would be needed at the beginning to clear any previously loaded data from the table.

```al
AL LotAvailbyBin.page.al  ●
Radio Show > AL LotAvailbyBin.page.al > ...
    1    page 50141 "Lot Avail. by Bin"
    5        PageType = List;
    6        SourceTable = "Warehouse Entry";
    7        SourceTableTemporary = true;
    8        UsageCategory = Lists;
    9        layout {
   10            area(content) {
   11                repeater(General) {
   12                    field("Item No."; Rec."Item No.") { ApplicationArea = All; }
   13                    field("Location Code"; Rec."Location Code") { ApplicationArea = All; }
   14                    field("Bin Code"; Rec."Bin Code") { ApplicationArea = All; }
   15                    field("Lot No."; Rec."Lot No.") { ApplicationArea = All; }
   16                    field(Quantity; Rec.Quantity) { ApplicationArea = All; }
   17        } } }
   18        trigger OnOpenPage()
   19        var
   20            LotAvail: Query "Lot Avail. by Bin";
   21        begin
   22            LotAvail.SetFilter(Entry_No_, '<>0');
   23            LotAvail.Open();
   24            while LotAvail.Read() do begin
   25                Rec.Init();
   26                Rec."Entry No." := LotAvail.Entry_No_;
   27                Rec."Item No." := LotAvail.Item_No;
   28                Rec."Location Code" := LotAvail.Location_Code;
   29                Rec."Bin Code" := LotAvail.Bin_Code;
   30                Rec."Lot No." := LotAvail.Lot_No;
   31                Rec.Quantity := LotAvail.Sum_Quantity;
   32                Rec.Insert(false);
   33            end;
   34        end;
   35    }
```

Figure 5.48 – The LotAvailbyBin.page example

When we run the page, all temporary records inserted in the `OnOpenPage` trigger will be displayed, as shown in the following screenshot:

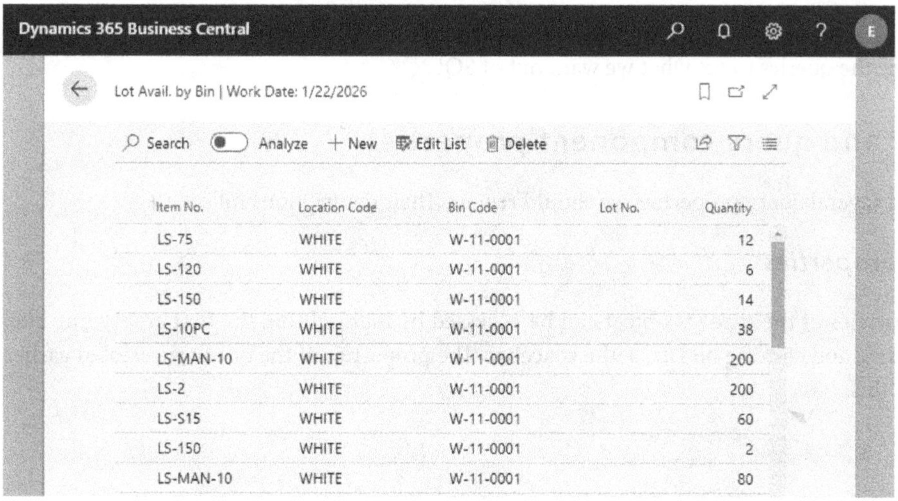

Figure 5.49 – The Lot Avail. by Bin page

When a query is used to supply data to a report, the Temporary property is defined to control stepping through the query results. Before the report read loop begins, the query is filtered and invoked so that it begins processing. As long as the query object continues to deliver records, the Temporary DataItem will continue looping. At the end of the query output, the report will proceed to its OnPostDataItem trigger processing, just as though it had completed processing a normal table rather than a query-created dataset. This approach is a faster alternative to a design that would use several FlowFields, particularly if those FlowFields were only used in one or two periodic reports.

Queries are not limited to temporary data displayed on a page or report; they can be displayed directly through a page action. This allows the user to easily slice and dice the data presented by the query.

```al
AL ItemListExtension.pageext.al ●

AL ItemListExtension.pageext.al > ...
  1    pageextension 50100 "Item List Extension" extends "Item List"
  2    {
  3        actions
  4        {
  5            addafter("Inventory - List")
  6            {
  7                action("Lot Avail. by Bin")
  8                {
  9                    ApplicationArea = All;
 10                    Caption = 'Lot Avail. by Bin';
 11                    RunObject = query "Lot Avail. by Bin";
 12                }
 13            }
 14        }
 15    }
```

Figure 5.50 – Show query in client for Analysis View reporting

As you can see, queries can be utilized in many different ways to present data; let's get into how we can define the queries to get what we want out of SQL.

Query and query component properties

There are several query properties we should review. Their descriptions follow.

Query properties

The properties of the `query` object can be accessed by highlighting the first empty line after the object name and clicking on *Ctrl* + the spacebar. The properties of the query we created earlier will look like this:

Figure 5.51 – A few of the properties of the query object

We'll review three of these properties:

- `OrderBy`: This provides the capability to define a sort, data column by column, and ascending or descending, giving the same result as if a key had been defined for the query result, but without the requirement for a key.

- `TopNumberOfRows`: This allows for the specification of the number of data rows that will be presented by the query. Skipping this property or setting it to 0 shows all rows. Specifying a limit can make the query complete much faster. This property can also be set dynamically from the AL code.

- `ReadState`: This controls the state (committed or not) of data that is included and the type of lock that is placed on the data read.

DataItem properties

A query line can be one of three types: `dataitem`, `column`, and `filter`. Each has its own property set:

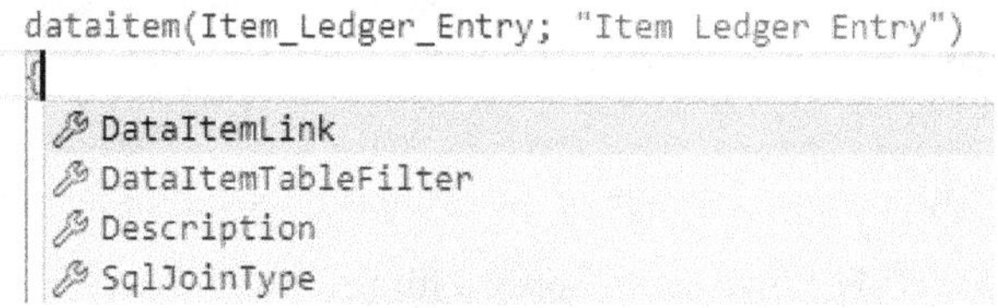

Figure 5.52 – Query DataItem properties

For DataItems, we'll review a selected subset of these properties:

- `SqlJoinType`: This property allows the specification of one of five different SQL join types (inner, left outer, right outer, full outer, or cross join). In our example, we could set `SqlJoinType` to `InnerJoin` on the `Warehouse_Entry` DataItem to limit the results to only the shared `Item` and `Warehouse_Entry` records. Look for the `SqlJoinType` property in `https://learn.microsoft.com/en-us/dynamics365/business-central/dev-itpro/developer/devenv-query-links-joins`.

- `DataItemTableFilter`: This provides the ability to define filters that will be applied to the DataItem.

- Column properties.

The following screenshot is a `column` property screen showing the `Item No.` column for our simple query:

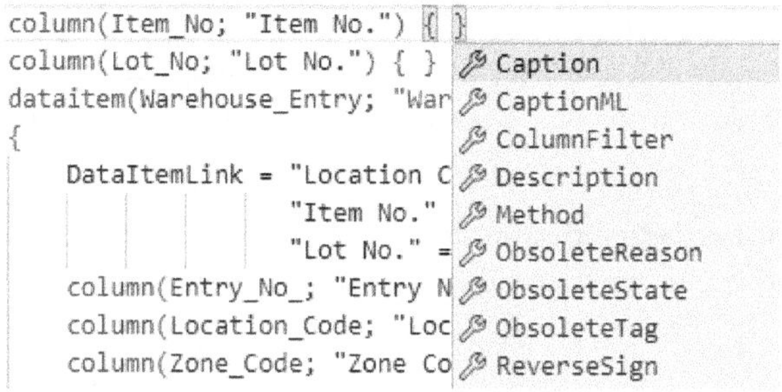

Figure 5.53 – Query column properties

The properties shown in the preceding screenshot are as follows:

- `Method`: Can be `Sum`, `Count`, `Average`, `Min`, `Max`, `Day`, `Month`, or `Year`. The result in the column will be based on the appropriate computation. Check the following for more information: https://learn.microsoft.com/en-us/dynamics365/business-central/dev-itpro/developer/devenv-query-totals-grouping.

- `ReverseSign`: This reverses the sign of the column value for numeric data.

- `ColumnFilter`: This allows us to apply a filter to limit the rows in the query result. Filtering here is similar to, but more complicated than, the filtering rules that apply to `DataItemTableFilter`. Static `ColumnFilters` can be dynamically overridden and can also be combined with `DataItemTableFilters`. Check the following for more information: https://learn.microsoft.com/en-us/dynamics365/business-central/dev-itpro/developer/devenv-query-filters.

Summary

In this chapter, we focused on the structural and layout aspects of Business Central report objects. We studied the primary structural components, data, and format, along with the request page. We also experimented with some of the tools and modestly expanded our WDTU application.

You should be comfortable with creating a report object that not only creates output with Excel but also adds business logic and customizes input requests to the user. Report objects are the most powerful and versatile object type in Business Central as they accept input, process data, and show output in a variety of formats. The looping mechanisms are built to make data extraction and processing from SQL fast and efficient for developers.

Reports are not the only data extraction object in Business Central, as queries are designed for complex data extraction and analytics. They not only have a user interface that allows for "slicing and dicing" but can be made available to external software through web services with no additional development required.

In the next chapter, we will begin exploring the key tools that pull the pieces of the Visual Studio Code developer experience and the AL programming language together.

Questions

1. The following are defined in the AL Report object (choose three):

   - DataItems
   - Field display editing

- Request page
- Data processing/updating

ANSWER: DataItems, request page, data processing/updating

2. Reports can be set to a `ProcessingOnly` status dynamically by AL code. True or false?

ANSWER: False

3. Reports are fixed displays of data that are extracted from the system and designed only for hardcopy output. True or false?

ANSWER: False

4. Business Central report data flow includes a structure that makes "child" DataItems fully processed for each record that's processed in the "parent" DataItem. What is the visible indication that this structure exists in a report (choose one)?

- Nesting
- Indentation
- Linking

ANSWER: Nesting

5. Queries can be used to directly feed SQL Report Builder. True or false?

ANSWER: True

6. Which of the following SQL joins are NOT available in Query objects?

- `InnerJoin`
- `LeftOuterJoin`
- `Union`
- `CrossJoin`

ANSWER: `Union`

7. A report that only does processing and generates no printed output can be defined. True or false?

ANSWER: True

8. Which of the following are properties of queries (choose two)?

- `TopNumberOfRows`
- `FormatAs`

- `OrderBy`

- `FilterReq`

ANSWER: `TopNumberOfRows`, `OrderBy`

9. Business Central has several report designers. Reports can be created using any one of these by itself. True or false?

    ANSWER: False

10. Business Central queries can directly generate OData, XML, and CSV files. True or false?

    ANSWER: True

11. Which of the following are Business Central Report Types (choose three)?

    - List

    - Document

    - Invoice

    - Posting

    ANSWER: List, Document, Posting

12. Queries cannot have multiple DataItems on the same indentation level. True or false?

    ANSWER: False

13. Report formatting in Word and Excel has all the capabilities of report formatting in SQL Reporting Designer. True or false?

    ANSWER: False

14. Business Central reports can be run for testing directly from Visual Studio Code with *Alt + R*. True or false?

    ANSWER: False

15. It is recommended to always use column letter and row number references in Excel reports. True or false?

    ANSWER: False

16. Queries are used to support what items (choose two)?

    - XMLport importing

    - Analysis mode

- Cues

- Data sorting

 ANSWER: Analysis mode, Cues

17. Most reports can be initially created using the Report Wizard. True or false?

    ANSWER: False. There is no Report Wizard.

18. Interactive capabilities that are available after an RDLC report is displayed include what (choose two)?

    - Font definition

    - Data Show/Hide

    - Sorting by columns

    - Data filtering

     ANSWER: Data Show/Hide, Data filtering

19. DataItem parent-child relationships that are defined in Visual Studio Code must also be considered in SQL Report Builder in order to have data displayed properly in a parent-child format. True or false?

    ANSWER: false. The dataset is flattened before rendering

20. Users can create report layouts based on an existing dataset and put them into production without having access to Visual Studio Code. True or false?

    ANSWER: True

6

Introduction to AL

"Programs must be written for people to read, and only incidentally for machines to execute."

– Harold Abelson and Julie Sussman

"The details are not the details. They make the design."

– Charles Eames

So far, we have reviewed the basic objects of Business Central, such as tables, pages, enums, queries, and reports. For each of these except enums, we reviewed triggers in various areas, the purpose of which is to be containers for AL code. When triggers are fired (invoked), the AL code within is executed.

In this chapter, you'll start learning the AL programming language, though you should already know about many of the things we will cover from your experience programming in other languages. The basic AL syntax and method definitions can be found in Microsoft Docs for Microsoft Dynamics 365 Business Central.

As with most programming languages, we have considerable flexibility to define our own model for our code structure. However, when we are writing new code to extend the standard application, it's always a good idea to utilize the model and follow the structure that exists in the standard code.

The goal of this chapter is to help us be comfortable in AL. We'll focus on the tools and processes that we will use the most often. We will also review concepts that we can apply to more complex tasks down the road. In this chapter, we will cover the following topics:

- Understanding Visual Studio Code
- AL syntax, naming conventions, variable operators, and frequently used AL methods
- Creating custom procedures
- Simple coding modifications including creating a Word layout for reports

Understanding Visual Studio Code

With a few exceptions, all of the development for Business Central applications takes place within Visual Studio Code. Exceptions include the use of Microsoft Excel or Word (or SQL Server Report Builder) for reporting, as we saw in *Chapter 5*, *Queries and Reports*, plus the work we may do in the JavaScript language to create compatible add-ins. While it is possible, development using a text editor is only appropriate for special cases, such as making modifications to existing objects, which is done by an advanced developer.

As an **Integrated Development Environment** (**IDE**), Visual Studio Code provides us with a rich set of tools for our AL development work. While Visual Studio Code is not as fully featured as Microsoft's Visual Studio, it is intended to be a cross-platform, modern development toolkit that can be extended to your needs. Most importantly, Visual Studio Code is the most popular IDE (according to a recent Stack Overflow survey) and chances are you are already familiar with it.

Explorer

All Business Central object development work starts from within Visual Studio Code in the **EXPLORER**. After opening a project folder or workspace file, you should be able to see the following screen:

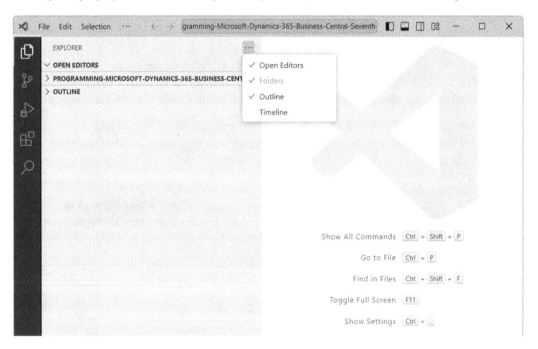

Figure 6.1 – EXPLORER and command overview in VS Code

The type of object that we'll be working on is chosen by the object definition, which we can view by clicking on one of the files in the menus, as shown in the following screenshot:

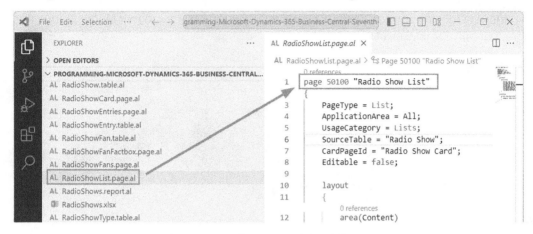

Figure 6.2 – Looking up an object definition

It is considered a best practice to apply logical naming to our files so that we can see which object name and type is used without having to open each individual file. That way, we can easily find and open every object by selecting **Go | Go to File...** or using the *Ctrl + P* keyboard shortcut for Windows and ⌘ + *P* for macOS.

Starting a new object

When we select **New Text File** from the **File** menu (as shown in the following screenshot), or **New File...** from the context menu after right-clicking on the empty space below the last file or on a folder, we get a blank file to create a new object.

Figure 6.3 – Selecting New Text File in VS Code

The fastest way to define a skeleton object is to use snippets. To enable the snippets, we must first save our new file using the `.al` file extension.

This forces us to think about file naming before defining the object, but we can always rename the file after the object's declaration is done.

To start using snippets after saving the file, we simply type the letter t and wait for IntelliSense to show the list of available snippets:

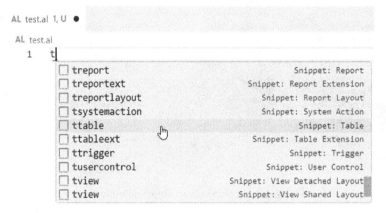

Figure 6.4 – Selecting a snippet using IntelliSense

Once we select a snippet, the cursor automatically takes us to the first variable we have to populate. We can use the *Tab* key to move through the fields one by one:

```
AL test.al 7, U ●

AL test.al > ⁇ Table 0 id
        0 references
    1    table id MyTable
    2    {
    3        DataClassification = ToBeClassified;
    4
    5        fields
    6        {
            1 reference
    7            field(1;MyField; Integer)
    8            {
    9                DataClassification = ToBeClassified;
   10
   11            }
   12    }
```

Figure 6.5 – Highlighted snippet variables

Keyboard shortcuts

In many places within Visual Studio Code, there are standard keyboard shortcuts available. This book will further concentrate on the Windows version only. Some of these keyboard shortcuts are as follows:

- *Ctrl + N* to create a new empty text file
- *Ctrl + O* to open any existing file
- *Ctrl + P* to go to a file, line, or symbol within the current project
- *Ctrl + spacebar* to access AL IntelliSense, which shows us what we can do for the object that we are working on
- *F5* to publish the project with debugging
- *Ctrl + F5* to publish the project without debugging
- *Ctrl + Shift + B* to do an on-the-fly build (very useful for error checking as we go). This corresponds to the **AL: Package** VS Code command *Ctrl + /* (sometimes *Ctrl + #*, depending on your system language) to toggle line comments
- *Ctrl + Shift + K* to delete a line
- *Ctrl + X*, *Ctrl + C*, and *Ctrl + V* in normal Windows mode for deletion (or cut), copy, and paste, respectively

We can cut, copy, and paste AL code—even procedures—relatively freely within an object, from object to object, or to a text-friendly tool (for example, Word or Excel) much as if we were using a text editor. The source and target objects don't need to be of the same type.

The easiest way to copy a complete object is to create a new version. You can do this as follows: open the object to copy, assign a new object number and object name (no duplicate object names are allowed), then click on **File | Save As...**, or press *Ctrl + Shift + S*.

> Tip
> **Help | Keyboard Shortcut Reference** displays a condensed PDF version suitable for printing. There is a separate version per platform (Windows, macOS, Linux).

AL programming

Many of the things that we do during development in Visual Studio Code might not be called programming by some people as they don't involve writing AL code statements. However, so long as these activities contribute to the definition of the object and affect the processing that occurs, we'll include them in our broad definition of AL programming.

These activities include setting properties at the object and DataItem levels, creating request pages in reports, defining controls and their properties, defining report data structures and their properties, creating source expressions, defining procedures, and, of course, writing AL statements in all of the places where we can put AL. We will primarily focus on programming as it relates to tables, reports, and code units.

We will touch on programming for pages and XMLports. In the case of reports, AL statements can only reside in the components that are developed within the report object.

Business Central objects are generally consistent in structure. Most have some properties and triggers. Pages and reports have controls, though their choice is specific to the individual object type. Reports have a built-in DataItem looping logic. XMLports also have DataItem looping logic, but those are structured differently from reports; for example, reports can have multiple DataItems at 0 level and XMLports can only have one node at 0 level.

All of the object types that we are considering, except the enum object type, can contain AL code in one or more places. All of these can contain procedure definitions that can be called either internally or externally (if not marked as local or internal). Remember, good design practice says that any procedures designed as a library, or reusable procedures that are called from a variety of objects, should be placed in a code unit or, in some circumstances, in the primary table.

> **Note**
>
> Don't forget that our fundamental coding work should focus on tables and procedure libraries as much as possible, as these are the foundation of the Business Central system.

To gain a first overview of the AL language, we will start with some naming conventions, then talk about variables, and finally learn about methods and procedures in general.

AL naming conventions

In the previous chapters, we discussed naming conventions for tables, pages, and reports. In general, the naming guidelines for Business Central objects and AL encourage consistency, common sense, and readability. Use meaningful names. These make the system more intuitive to the users and more self-documenting.

When we name variables, we must try to keep the names as self-documenting as possible. We should differentiate between similar, but different, variable meanings, such as Cost (cost from the vendor) and Amount (selling price to the customer). Embedded spaces, periods, or other special characters should be avoided (even though we find some violations of this in the base product). If we want to use special characters for the benefit of the user, we should put them in the caption, not in the name. If possible, we should stick to letters and numbers in our variable names. We should always avoid Hungarian naming styles (see https://en.wikipedia.org/wiki/Hungarian_notation); keep names simple and descriptive.

There are a number of reasons to keep variable names simple. Other software products that we may interface with may have limitations on variable names. Some special characters have special meanings to other software or in another human language. In Business Central, symbols such as ? and * are wildcards and must be avoided in variable names. The $ symbol has a special meaning in other software. SQL Server adds its own special characters to table and field names in Business Central, and the resultant combinations can get quite confusing (not just to us, but to the software). The same can be said for the names that are constructed by the internal RDLC generator, which replaces spaces and periods with underscores.

When we are defining multiple instances of a table, we should either differentiate clearly by name (for example, `Item` and `NewItem`) or by a descriptive suffix (for example, `Item`, `ItemForVariant`, and `ItemForLocation`). In the very common situation where a name is a compound combination of words, begin each abbreviated word with a capital letter (for example, `NewCustBalDue`).

> **Tip**
>
> Common abbreviations in AL code are listed at `https://alguidelines.dev/docs/bestpractices/suggested-abbreviations/`.

Avoid creating variable names that are common words that might be reserved words (for example, `Page`, `Column`, `Number`, and `Integer`), even though Visual Studio Code will not warn us that we have used a reserved word.

Do not start variables with a prefix, `x`, which is used in some automatically created variables, such as `xRec`. We should make sure that we can clearly differentiate between working storage variable names and the field names originating in tables. Sometimes, Visual Studio Code will allow us to have a global name, local name, and/or record variable name, all with the same literal name. If we do this, we are practically guaranteeing a variable misidentification bug where the compiler uses a different variable than what we intended to reference.

When defining a temporary table, preface the name logically, for example, with `Temp`. In general, use meaningful names that help in identifying the type and purpose of the item being named. When naming a new procedure, we should be reasonably descriptive.

In short, be careful, be consistent, be clear, and use common sense.

> **Tip**
>
> Additional **code analyzers** can assist us prevent such ambiguities. For more information, refer to the Microsoft docs *The code analysis tool* article (`https://learn.microsoft.com/en-us/dynamics365/business-central/dev-itpro/developer/devenv-using-code-analysis-tool`).

Variables

As we've gone through examples showing various aspects of Visual Studio Code and AL, we've seen and referred to variables in a number of situations. Some of the following are obvious, but for clarity's sake, we'll summarize them here.

In *Chapter 3*, *Data Types and Fields*, we reviewed various data types for variables that are defined within objects (referred to in *Chapter 3* as **working storage** data). Working storage consists of all of the variables that are defined for use within an object, but whose contents disappear when the object closes. Working storage data types, as discussed in *Chapter 3*, are those that can be defined as either AL global, protected, or local variables.

Global variables

Global variables are defined on the `var` section of most objects in AL. There can be multiple `var` sections within one object. That way, we can create regions of code with their own global variables. Still, we should define as few global variables as possible.

In extensions without translation files, **text constants** are mostly defined as global variables. The primary purpose of text constants is to allow for easier translation of messages from one language to another. By putting all message text in one place in each object, a standardized process can be defined for language translation. Since all Microsoft extensions use translation files instead, we won't find any sample code for text constants in Microsoft objects. Instead, **labels** are used. For the translation process using translation files, it is irrelevant whether all labels are put in one place or not.

The following screenshot highlights the global variable section in the Microsoft `Format Document` code unit:

```
18    codeunit 368 "Format Document"
19    {
20
21        trigger OnRun()
22        begin
23        end;
24
25        var
26            GLSetup: Record "General Ledger Setup";
27            AutoFormat: Codeunit "Auto Format";
28
29            PurchaserTxt: Label 'Purchaser';
30            SalespersonTxt: Label 'Salesperson';
31            TotalTxt: Label 'Total %1', Comment = '%1 = Currency Code';
32            TotalInclVATTxt: Label 'Total %1 Incl. VAT', Comment = '%1 = Currency Code';
33            TotalExclVATTxt: Label 'Total %1 Excl. VAT', Comment = '%1 = Currency Code';
34            COPYTxt: Label 'COPY', Comment = 'COPY';
35
36        procedure GetRecordFiltersWithCaptions(RecVariant: Variant) Filters: Text
--
```

Figure 6.6 – Global variables section with labels

Within the global variables section, we identify the first two variables pointing to other standard AL objects, and six labels, some with a comment explaining the placeholders.

Local variables

Local identifiers only exist if they're defined within the range of a procedure or trigger. This is true regardless of whether the trigger is a developer-defined procedure, one of the default system triggers, or a standard application-supplied procedure.

Procedure-local identifiers are declared in the definition of the procedure using the `var` keyword, as can be seen in the following screenshot:

```
procedure InsertShowType(TypeCode: Code[10]; Descr: Text)
var
    RadioShowType: Record "Radio Show Type";
begin
    RadioShowType.Code := TypeCode;
    RadioShowType.Description := Descr;
    RadioShowType.Insert();
end;
```

Figure 6.7 – Local variables

Protected variables

Whereas global variables are accessible from all procedures and controls within our object, they are not reachable for apps extending our object. To share variables with other extensions, we must declare variables within a `protected var` section instead of declaring a global `var` section. AL objects can contain both `var` and `protected var` sections at the same time, as can be seen in the following screenshot taken from the `Cash Flow Worksheet` page object:

```
var
    SuggestWkshLines: Report "Suggest Worksheet Lines";
    CashFlowManagement: Codeunit "Cash Flow Management";
    CFName: Text[100];
    CFAccName: Text[100];
    SourceNumEnabled: Boolean;
    IsSaaSExcelAddinEnabled: Boolean;

protected var
    ShortcutDimCode: array[8] of Code[20];
```

Figure 6.8 – Protected variables

> **Note**
>
> Keep protected variables in mind when developing pages with global variables used as control sources or assigned to control properties.

Special working storage variables

Some working storage variables have additional attributes to be considered. We will learn about temporary tables, arrays, and system-defined variables.

Temporary tables

Temporary tables were discussed in *Chapter 2, Tables*. Let's take a quick look at how one is defined. Defining a temporary table begins just like any other variable definition of the `Record` data type. To make it temporary, we add the `temporary` keyword after the table name, as shown in the following screenshot:

```
procedure InsertShowType(TypeCode: Code[10]; Descr: Text)
var
    RadioShowType: Record "Radio Show Type" temporary;
begin
    RadioShowType.Code := TypeCode;
    RadioShowType.Description := Descr;
    RadioShowType.Insert();
end;
```

Figure 6.9 – Declaring a temporary record variable

We can use a temporary table as though it were a permanent table, with some specific differences:

- The table only contains the data we add to it during this instance of the object in which it resides.

- We cannot change any aspect of the definition of the table, except by changing or extending the permanent table.

- Processing for a temporary table is done wholly in the client system, in a user-specific instance of the business logic. It is, therefore, inherently a single user.

- A properly utilized temporary table reduces network traffic and eliminates any locking issues for that table. It is often much faster than processing the same data in a permanent database-resident table because both data transmission and physical storage I/O are significantly reduced.

> **Note**
>
> In some cases, it's a good idea to copy the database table data into a temporary table for repetitive processing within an object. This can give us a significant speed advantage for a particular task by updating data in the temporary table, then copying it back out to the database table at the end of processing.
>
> When using temporary tables, we need to be very careful that references from the AL code in the temporary table, such as data validations, don't inappropriately modify permanent data elsewhere in the database. We must also remember that, if we forget to properly mark the table as temporary, we will likely corrupt production data with our processing.

Arrays

Arrays of up to 10 dimensions containing up to a total of 1,000,000 elements in a single variable can be created in a Business Central object. Defining an array is done simply by setting the `array` keyword of a variable. An example is shown in the following screenshot, which defines a record array of 3 rows, with 99 elements in each row:

```
procedure InsertShowType(TypeCode: Code[10]; Descr: Text)
var
    RadioShowType: array[3, 99] of Record "Radio Show Type";
begin
    RadioShowType[1, 1].Code := TypeCode;
    RadioShowType[1, 1].Description := Descr;
    RadioShowType[1, 1].Insert();
end;
```

Figure 6.10 – Array definition

The comma separates the dimensions of the array. The numbers indicate the maximum number of elements of each of the dimensions. An array variable such as `TotalCountArray` is referred to in AL as follows:

- The 15th entry in the first row is `TotalCountArray[1,15]`
- The last entry in the last row is `TotalCountArray[3,99]`

> **Caution**
>
> In contrast to most other programming languages, AL arrays are 1-based instead of 0-based. This means the first element is 1, not 0.

An array of a complex data type, such as a `Record`, may behave differently than a single instance of the data type, especially when passed as a parameter to a procedure. As in all cases, we must make sure that the code is thoroughly tested so that we aren't surprised by unexpected results.

> **Tip**
>
> The Microsoft docs *Array methods* article (https://learn.microsoft.com/en-us/dynamics365/business-central/dev-itpro/developer/methods/devenv-array-methods) provides extra information about arrays of temporary records.

System-defined variables

Business Central also provides us with some variables automatically, such as Rec, xRec, CurrPage, CurrReport, and CurrXMLport. Which variables are provided is dependent on the object that we are operating on. Descriptions of some of these can be found in the Microsoft docs *System-defined variables* article (https://learn.microsoft.com/en-us/dynamics365/business-central/dev-itpro/developer/devenv-system-defined-variables).

In later versions of Business Central, all these different system-defined variables will be replaced with a single this keyword that you may already know from object-oriented languages. However, both the old and new keywords will co-exist for a while.

Initialization

When an object is initiated, the variables in that object are automatically initialized. Booleans are set to false. Numeric variables are set to 0. Text and code data types are set to the empty string. Dates are set to 0D (the undefined date) and times are set to 0T (the undefined time). The individual components of complex variables are appropriately initialized. The system also automatically initializes all system-defined variables.

Of course, once the object is active, through our code and property settings, we can do whatever additional initialization we wish. If we wish to initialize variables at intermediate points during processing, we can use any of several approaches. First, we will reset a Record variable (for example, the RadioShowType record defined in the preceding example) with the Reset method, then initialize it with the Init method in statements in the form, as follows:

```
TempRadioShowLedger.Reset();
TempRadioShowLedger.Init();
```

The Reset method makes sure that all of the previously set filters on this table are cleared. The Init method makes sure that all of the fields, except those in the primary key, are set either to their InitValue property value or to their data type default value. The primary key fields must be explicitly set by the AL code.

For all types of data, including complex data types, we can initialize fields with the Clear or ClearAll method in a statement in the following form:

```
Clear(TotalArray[1,1]);
Clear(TotalArray);
```

```
Clear(Rec."Shipment Code");
Clear(RadioShowType);
```

The first example would clear a single element of the array—the first element in the first row. Since this variable is an `Integer` data type, the element would be set to `Integer` zero when cleared. The second example would clear the entire array. In the third example, a table field defined as a `Code` data type would simply be set to an empty string. In the fourth example, we remove all filters from the `RadioShowType` record variable and restore all its fields to their initial value, including the primary key.

Methods and procedures

A procedure, method, or function is a defined set of logic that performs a specific task.

Like many other programming languages, AL includes a set of methods that are available to us to perform a wide variety of different tasks. The underlying logic for AL methods is hidden and not modifiable.

On the other hand, the Business Central standard application provides us with reusable procedures written in AL, also referred to as standard procedures, and gives us the possibility to write custom procedures.

> **Note**
> Whereas this book distinguishes between methods (AL language components written in C# language) and procedures (any procedure written in AL language), the Microsoft docs refer to both as methods.

Methods

As stated in the previous section, methods are supplied as part of the AL programming language. Some simple examples of non-modifiable procedures are as follows:

- `Date2DMY`: Supply a date to this method and, depending on a calling parameter, it will return the integer value of the day, month, or year of that date

- `StrPos`: Supply a string variable and a string constant to this method and it will return the position of the first instance of that constant within the variable, or a zero if the constant is not present in the string that's contained in the variable

- `Get`: Supply a value and a table to this method and it will read the record in the table with a primary key value equal to the supplied value if a matching record exists

- `Insert`: This method will add a record to a table

- `Message`: Supply a string and optional variables and this method will display a message to the operator

Such methods are the heart of AL code. On the whole, they are designed around the essential purpose of a Business Central system—business and financial applications data processing. These methods are not modifiable; they operate according to their predefined rules. For development purposes, they act as basic language components.

Standard procedures

In addition to the prewritten AL language component methods, there are a large number of prewritten application component procedures, also referred to as standard procedures. The difference between the two types is that the code implementing the latter is visible and modifiable through cloning, though we should be extremely cautious about making such clones.

An example of an application component procedure might be one to handle the task of processing a customer's shipping address to eliminate empty lines and standardize the layout based on user-defined setup parameters. Such a procedure would logically be placed in a code unit and hence made available to any routine that needs this capability.

In fact, this procedure exists. It is called `SalesHeaderShipTo` and is located in the `Format Address` code unit. We can explore the following code units for some procedures we might find useful to use or that we can borrow logic from. This is not an all-inclusive list, as there are many procedures in other code units that we may find useful in a future development project, either to be used directly or as templates to design our own, similar procedure. Many library code units have the words `Management` or `Mgt` in their name, but as you can see there are exceptions:

Object number	Name
356	DateComprMgt
358	DateFilter-Calc
365	Format Address
1483	XmlWriter
8901	Email

Table 6.1 – Some library code units

The prewritten application procedures, generally, have been provided to address the needs of the Business Central developers working at Microsoft. However, we can use them too. Our challenge will be to find out whether they exist and to understand how they work. There is very little documentation of these application component procedures. If we highlight the procedure reference in the in-line code, or click somewhere into it and then right-click it or press *F12*, we are given the **Go to Definition** option. This allows us to easily find the procedure's code and review it.

One significant aspect of these application procedures is the fact that they are written in AL, and their construction is totally exposed. In theory, they can be cloned, though this is not advisable. If we decide to change one of these procedures, we should choose published events.

> **Tip**
>
> If no events exist, or if existing events lack parameters that we need, we can create **event requests** for free by creating an issue in the Microsoft ALAppExtensions repository (`https://github.com/microsoft/ALAppExtensions`).

Custom procedures

We can also create our own custom procedures to meet any need. The most common reason to create a new procedure is to provide a single, standardized instance of logic to perform a specific task. When we need to use the same logic in more than one place, we should consider creating a callable procedure.

We should also create a new procedure when we're modifying standard Business Central processes through events. Our procedure then becomes an **event subscriber**.

> **Tip**
>
> More information about event subscribers can be found in the Microsoft docs, in the *Subscribing to events* article (`https://learn.microsoft.com/en-us/dynamics365/business-central/dev-itpro/developer/devenv-subscribing-to-events`).

If a new procedure is going to be used in several objects, it should be housed in our library code unit (we may choose to have multiple library code units for the purpose of clarity or project management). If a new procedure is only for use in a single object, then it can be resident in that object. This latter option also has the advantage of allowing the new procedure direct access to the global variables within the object being modified.

Procedures can be created as local, internal, or global. Internal means that the app declaring the procedure treats it as if it was global, whereas other apps do not have access to it. The Microsoft docs provide more procedure options in the *Working with AL methods* article (`https://learn.microsoft.com/en-us/dynamics365/business-central/dev-itpro/developer/devenv-al-methods`).

Creating a procedure

Let's take a quick look at how a procedure can be created. We'll use the small date formula app we created in *Chapter 3, Data Types and Table Fields*, and add a new code unit, `codeunit 50141`. We will call it `Date Formula Mgt`.

We will create our new codeunit by simply clicking on **New Text File** in the **File** menu, then choosing **File | Save As...**, and entering `DateFormulaMgt.codeunit.al`. We will select the code unit snippet (`tcodeunit`) and populate the variables. The result should look like the following screenshot:

```al
AL DateFormulaMgt.codeunit.al  X

AL DateFormulaMgt.codeunit.al > ...
        0 references
    1   codeunit 50141 "Date Formula Mgt."
    2   {
            0 references
    3       trigger OnRun()
    4       begin
    5
    6       end;
    7
    8       var
                0 references
    9           myInt: Integer;
   10   }
```

Figure 6.11 – Creating the DateFormulaMgt. codeunit

Next, we can delete the `trigger` code and the `var` section, including the `myInt` variable. Now comes the important part—designing and coding our new procedure. When we had the procedure operating as a local procedure inside the table where it was called, we didn't worry about passing data back and forth. We simply used the data fields that were already present in the table and treated them as global variables, which they were. Now that our procedure will be external to the object that it was called from, we have to pass data values back and forth. Here's the basic calling structure of our procedure:

```
Output := procedure(InputParameter1, InputParameter2)
```

In other words, we need to feed two values into our new callable procedure and accept a **return value** on completion of the procedure being processed.

The result of the function should be similar to the following:

```al
procedure CalculateNewDate(InputDateFormula: DateFormula;
ReferenceDate: Date): Date
begin
    exit(CalcDate(InputDateFormula, ReferenceDate));
end;
```

Press *Ctrl + Shift + B* to check whether we have a clean build, or check the **PROBLEMS** section in Visual Studio Code. If we get an error, we must do the traditional programmer thing: find it, fix it, and rebuild it. Repeat this until we experience no errors.

Finally, we will return `table 50140 Date Formula` to our test to complete the changes that are necessary so that we can use the external procedure rather than the internal procedure. We have two obvious choices for doing this. One is to replace the internal formula in our existing internal procedure with a call to our external procedure. This approach results in fewer object changes.

The other choice is to replace each of our internal procedure calls with a call to the external procedure. This approach may be more efficient at runtime because, when we need the external procedure, we will invoke it in one step rather than two. We will walk through the first option here and then you should try the second option on your own.

Which option is the best? It depends on our criteria. Such a decision comes down to a matter of identifying the best criteria on which to judge the design options, then applying those criteria. Remember, whenever feasible, simple is good.

For the first approach (calling our new code unit resident procedure), we must add our new `codeunit 50141 Date Formula Mgt` variable to the `Date Formula` table. After opening the table object, navigate to the procedure and add a new line between the procedure declaration and the `begin` keyword. Add the local variable, as shown in the following screenshot (it's good practice to define variables as local unless global access is required):

```
local procedure CalculateNewDate()
var
    DateFormulaMgt: Codeunit "Date Formula Mgt.";
begin
    "Result Date" := CalcDate("Date Formula", "Reference Date");
end;
```

Figure 6.12 – Adding a local variable to CalculateNewDate

The two lines of code that called the internal procedure, `CalculateNewDate`, must be changed to call the external procedure. The syntax for that call is as follows:

```
Global/LocalVariable := Global/LocalObjectName.
ProcedureName(Parameter1,Parameter2,...)
```

Based on that, the new line of code should be as follows:

```
"Result Date" := DateFormulaMgt.CalculateNewDate("Date Formula",
"Reference Date");
```

If all has gone well, we should be able to build our application. When that step works successfully, we can run the page and experiment with different reference dates and date formulas, just like we did back in *Chapter 3*. We should get the same results for the same entries that we saw before.

When you try out the other approach of replacing each of the calls to the internal procedure by directly calling the external procedure, you will want to do the following:

- Either define the `Date Formula Mgt.` code unit as a global variable or as a local variable for each of the triggers where you are calling the external procedure

- Delete the now-unused local `CalculateNewDate` procedure

We should now have a better understanding of the basics of constructing both internal and external procedures and some of the optional design features that are available to us for building procedures.

Let's now learn about the AL syntax to apply inside procedures.

AL syntax

AL syntax is relatively simple and straightforward. The basic structure of most AL statements is essentially similar to what you learned with other programming languages. AL is modeled on Pascal and tends to use many of the same reserved words and syntax practices as Pascal.

Assignment and punctuation

Assignment is represented with a colon followed by an equal sign, the combination being treated as a single symbol. The evaluated value of the expression, to the right of the assignment symbol, is assigned to the variable on the left-hand side, as shown in the following line of code:

```
Customer."Phone No." := '312-555-1212';
```

All statements are terminated with a semicolon. Multiple statements can be placed on a single program line, but that makes the code hard for others to read.

Fully qualified data fields are prefaced with the name of the record variable that they are a part of (see the preceding code line as an example wherein the record variable is named `Customer`). The same structure applies to fully qualified procedure references; the procedure name is prefaced with the variable name of the object that they are defined in.

Single quotes are used to surround string literals (see the phone number string in the preceding line of code).

Double quotes are used to surround an identifier (for example, a variable or a table field name) that contains any character other than numerals or upper and lowercase letters. For example, the `Phone No.` field name in the preceding line of code is constructed as `"Phone No."` because it contains a space and a period. Other examples would be `"Post Code"` (contains a space), `"E-Mail"` (contains a dash), and `"No."` (contains a period).

> **Tip**
>
> Double quotes are also used to surround identifiers consisting of a single word only, but conflicting with AL-reserved words, such as this being constructed as `this`.

Parentheses are used much the same as in other languages—to indicate sets of expressions that will be interpreted according to their parenthetical groupings. The expressions are interpreted in sequence, first by the innermost parenthetical group, then the next level, and so forth. The *(A / (B + (C * (D + E))))* expression would be evaluated as follows:

Sum *(D + E)* into `Result1`.

Multiply `Result1` by *C*, yielding `Result2`.

Add `Result2` to *B*, yielding `Result3`.

Divide *A* by `Result3`.

Brackets ([ ]) are used to indicate the presence of subscripts for indexing array variables. A text string can be treated as an array of characters, and we can use subscripts with the string name to access individual character positions within the string, but not beyond the terminating character of the string. For example, `Address[1]` represents the leftmost character in the `Address` text variable contents.

Brackets are also used for `in` (in range) expressions, as shown in the following code snippet:

```
Boolean := SearchValue in [SearchTarget1, SearchTarget2];
```

In this line, `SearchValue`, `SearchTarget1`, and `SearchTarget2` are text variables.

Statements can be continued on multiple lines without any special punctuation; however, we can't split a variable or literal across two lines. The following example shows two instances that are interpreted in exactly the same manner by the compiler:

```
Customer."Phone No." := '312' + '-' + '555' + '-' + '1212';
Customer."Phone No." := '312' +
    '-' + '555' +
    '-' + '1212';
```

Expressions

Expressions in AL are made up of four elements—constants, variables, operators, and procedures. We could include a fifth element, expressions, because an expression may include a subordinate expression within it. As we become more experienced in coding AL, we will find that the capability of nesting expressions can be both a blessing and a curse, depending on the specific use and readability of the result.

We can create complex statements that will conditionally perform important control actions and operate in much the same way that a person would think about a task. We can also create complex statements that are very difficult for a person to understand. These are tough to debug and sometimes almost impossible to deal with in a modification.

One of our responsibilities is to be able to know the difference so that we can write code that makes sense in operation but is also easy to read and understand.

According to the Microsoft docs (https://learn.microsoft.com/en-us/dynamics365/business-central/dev-itpro/developer/devenv-al-simple-statements#assignment-statements), an AL expression is a value that you assign to a variable. It can be a constant, another variable, or a procedure return value, or it can consist of multiple elements of AL expressions linked with operators. The following are two code statements that accomplish the same result in slightly different ways. They each assign a literal string to a text data field. In the first one, the right-hand side is a literal data value. In the second, the right-hand side of the : = assignment symbol is an expression:

```
Customer."Phone No." := '312-555-1212';
Customer."Phone No." := '312' + '-' + '555' + '-' + '1212';
```

Operators

Now, we'll review AL operators grouped by category. Depending on the data types we are using with a particular operator, we may need to know the type conversion rules by defining the allowed combinations of operator and data types for an expression. The Microsoft docs provide good information on type conversion rules in the *AL variables* article (https://learn.microsoft.com/en-us/dynamics365/business-central/dev-itpro/developer/devenv-al-variables#assignment-and-type-conversion). The *AL operators* article can be found at https://learn.microsoft.com/en-us/dynamics365/business-central/dev-itpro/developer/devenv-al-operators.

Before we review the operators that can be categorized, let's discuss some operators that don't fit well into any of the categories. The Microsoft docs refer to them as **general operators**. These include the following:

.	Member of
: =	Assignment; assigns the value on the right side of the operator to the variable on the left side
( )	Grouping of elements
[ ]	Indexing
: :	Scope

..	Range
@	Case-insensitive

Table 6.2 - General operators

Explanations regarding the use of the operator symbols in the preceding list are as follows:

- The symbol represented by a single dot or period doesn't have a given name in the Business Central documentation, so we'll call it the **member symbol** or **dot operator** (as it is referred to in the MSDN Visual Basic Developer documentation). It indicates that a field is a member of a table (`TableName.FieldName`), a control is a member of a page (`PageName.ControlName`) or report (`ReportName.ControlName`), or a procedure is a member of an object (`ObjectName.ProcedureName`).

- Parentheses (`( )`) and brackets (`[ ]`) can be considered operators based on the effect their use has on the results of an expression. We discussed their use in the context of parenthetical grouping and indexing using brackets, as well as with the `in` expression earlier. Parentheses are also used to enclose the parameters in a procedure call, as shown in the following code snippet: `ObjectName.ProcedureName(Param1, Param2, Param3);`.

- The **scope operator** is a two-character sequence consisting of two colons in a row (`::`). The scope operator is used to allow AL code to refer to a specific option or enum value using the text descriptive value rather than the integer value that is actually stored in the database. For example, in our AL database table, `Radio Show`, we have an option field defined, called `Frequency`, with `Hourly`, `Daily`, `Weekly`, and `Monthly` option string values. Those values will be stored as integers 0, 1, 2, or 3, but we can use the strings to refer to them in code, which makes our code more self-documenting. The scope operator allows us to refer to `Frequency::Hourly` (rather than 0) and `Frequency::Monthly` (rather than 3). In a similar fashion, we can refer to objects in the `[Object Type::"Object Name"]` format to be translated into the object number, as shown in the following code snippet: `Page.Run(Page::"Bin List");` is equivalent to `Page.Run(7303);`.

- The **range operator** is a two-character sequence, "`..`", with two dots in a row. This operator is very widely used in Business Central, not only in AL code (including `case` statements and `in` expressions) but also in filters that are entered by users. The English lowercase alphabet can be represented by the *a..z* range, the set of single digit numbers by the `-9..9` range (that is, minus nine dot nine), and all of the entries starting with the lowercase *a* letter by `a..a*`. Don't underestimate the power of the range operator.

Arithmetic operators and procedures

The arithmetic operators include the following set of operators:

Arithmetic Operators		
Symbol	**Action**	**Data Types**
+	Addition	Numeric, Date, Time, Text and Code (concatenation),
-	Subtraction	Numeric, Date, Time
*	Multiplication	Numeric
/	Division	Numeric
DIV	Integer Division (provides only the integer portion of the quotient of a division calculation)	Numeric
MOD	Modulus (provides only the integer remainder of a division calculation)	Numeric

Figure 6.13 – Arithmetic operators

As we can see in the **Data Types** column, these operators can be used on various data types. Numeric types include `Integer`, `Decimal`, `Boolean`, and `Character`. `Text` and `Code` are both string data.

Sample statements using `div` and `mod` are shown in the following code, where `BigNumber` is an integer containing `200`:

```
DivIntegerValue := BigNumber div 60;
```

The contents of `DivIntegerValue`, after executing the preceding statement, will be `3`:

```
ModIntegerValue := BigNumber mod 60;
```

The contents of `ModIntegerValue`, after executing the preceding statement, will be `20`.

The syntax for these `div` and `mod` statements is as follows:

```
IntegerQuotient := IntegerDividend div IntegerDivisor;
IntegerModulus := IntegerDividend mod IntegerDivisor;
```

Boolean operators

`Boolean` operators only operate on expressions that can be evaluated as `Boolean`. These are shown in the following table:

Boolean Operators	
Symbol	Evaluation
NOT	Logical NOT
AND	Logical AND
OR	Logical OR
XOR	Exclusive Logical OR

Figure 6.14 – Boolean operators

The result of an expression based on a `Boolean` operator will also be `Boolean`.

Relational operators

The relational operators are listed in the following screenshot. Each of these is used in an expression of the following format:

```
Expression RelationalOperator Expression
```

An example is **(Variable1 + 97) > ((Variable2 * 14.5) / 57.332)**. The following operators can be used:

Relational Operators	
Symbol	Evaluation
<	Less than
>	Greater than
<=	Less than or Equal to
>=	Greater than or Equal to
=	Equal to
<>	Not equal to
IN	IN Valueset

Figure 6.15 – Relational operators

We will spend a little extra time on the **in operator** because this can be very handy and is not documented elsewhere. The **Valueset** term in the **Evaluation** column for `in` refers to a list of defined values. It would be reasonable to define **Valueset** as a container of a defined set of individual values, expressions, or other value sets. Some examples of `in` are as follows:

```
GLEntry."Posting Date" in [0D, WorkDate()]

Description[I + 2] in ['0'..'9']
```

```
Rec."Gen. Posting Type" in [Rec."Gen. Posting Type"::Purchase,
Rec."Gen. Posting Type"::Sale]


SearchString in ['','=><']


No[i] in ['5'..'9']


Rec."FA Posting Date" in [20240101D..20141231D]
```

Here is another example of what the `in` operator, as used in an expression, might look like:

```
TestString in ['a'..'d','j','q','l'..'p'];
```

If the value of `TestString` were a or m, then this expression would evaluate to `true`. If the value of `TestString` were z, then this expression would evaluate to `false`. Note that the data type of the search value must be the same as the data type of **Valueset**.

Precedence of operators

When expressions are evaluated by the AL compiler, the parsing routines use a predefined precedence hierarchy to determine which operators to evaluate first, what to evaluate second, and so forth. This precedence hierarchy is provided in the *AL Operators – Operator hierarchy* section in the Microsoft docs (`https://learn.microsoft.com/en-us/dynamics365/business-central/dev-itpro/developer/devenv-al-operators`), but for convenience, the information is repeated here:

1. `.` (fields in records), `[]` (indexing), `()` (parentheses), `::` (scope), `@` (case-insensitive)
2. `not`, `-` (unary), `+` (unary)
3. `*`, `/`, `div`, `mod`, `and`, `xor`
4. `+`, `-`, `or`
5. `>`, `>=`, `<`, `<=`, `=`, `<>`, `in`
6. `..` (range)

For complex expressions, we should always freely use parentheses to make sure that the expressions are evaluated the way we intend them to be.

Frequently used AL methods

It's time to learn about more of the standard methods that are provided by the AL programming language. We will focus on two main groups of methods: `Dialog` and `Record`.

Dialog methods

The purpose of `Dialog` methods is to allow communication (that is, dialog) between the system and the user. In addition, the `Dialog` methods can be useful for quick and simple testing/debugging. To make it easier for us to proceed with our next level of AL development work, we'll take time now to learn about these four dialog methods. None of these methods will operate if the AL code is running on the Business Central processes, such as the job queue, API, or web services, as they have no GUI available. They simply ignore `Dialog` methods.

In each of these methods, data values can be inserted through the use of a substitution string. The substitution string is the `%` (percent sign) character, followed by numbers `1` through `10`, located within a message text string. This could look like the following code snippet:

```
Message('A message + a data element to display = $%1', OrderAmount);
```

If the `OrderAmount` value was `100.53`, the output from the preceding code would be as follows:

```
A message + a data element to display = $100.53
```

We can have up to ten substitution strings in one dialog method. The use of substitution strings and their associated display values is optional. We can use any of the dialog methods to simply display a completely predefined text message with nothing that is variable. The use of text constant or label for the message is recommended as it makes maintenance and multi-language enabling easier.

We will focus on the following short list of frequently used `Dialog` methods: `Message`, `Error`, `Confirm`, and `StrMenu`.

Message method

`Message` is easy to use for the display of transient data and can be placed almost anywhere in our AL code. All it requires of the user is acknowledgement that the message has been read. The disadvantage of messages is that they are not displayed until either the object completes its run or pauses for some other external action. Plus, if we inadvertently create a situation that generates hundreds or thousands of messages, there is no graceful way to terminate their display once they are displaying.

It's common to use `Message` as the elementary trace tool. We can program the display of messages to only occur under particular circumstances and use them to view either the flow of processing (by outputting simple identifying codes from different points in our logic) or to view the contents of particular data elements through multiple processing cycles.

> **Note**
>
> To display information to the user without interrupting them in their work, **notifications** can be used. Notifications are different than messages as they do not require immediate action from the user. You can learn more about notifications via the following Microsoft docs article: `https://learn.microsoft.com/en-us/dynamics365/business-central/dev-itpro/developer/devenv-notifications-developing`.

Message has a `Message(String [, Value1, Value2, ...])` syntax, where there are as many `ValueX` entries as there are `%X` substitution strings.

Here is a sample debugging message:

```
Message('Loop %1, Item No. %2', LoopCounter, Rec."Item No.");
```

The display would look as follows (when the `LoopCounter` was 14 and the `Item No.` was BX0925):

Figure 6.16 – Message method in the client

> **Note**
>
> When `Message` is used for debugging, make sure that all messages are removed before releasing the object to production.

Error method

When an `Error` method is invoked, the execution of the current process terminates, the message is immediately displayed, and the database returns to the status it had following the last (implicit or explicit) `Commit` method as though the process that was calling the `Error` method had not run at all. The `Commit` method is used to manually commit a transaction to the database during a code process rather than naturally at the end.

> **Note**
>
> We can use the `Error` method in combination with the `Message` method to assist in repetitive testing. `Message` methods can be placed in code to show what is happening with an `Error` method that's been placed just prior to where the process would normally complete. Since the `Error` method rolls back all database changes, this technique allows us to run through multiple tests against the same data without any time-consuming backup and restoration of our test data. The enhanced testing procedure that's built into Business Central can accomplish the same things in a much more sophisticated fashion, but sometimes there's room for a temporary, simple approach.

An `Error` method call is formatted almost exactly like a `Message` call. `Error` has the `Error(String[, Value1, Value2, ...])` syntax, where there are as many `ValueX` entries as there are `%X` substitution strings. If the preceding `Message` call was an `Error` procedure instead, the code line would be as follows:

```
Error('Loop %1, Item No. %2', LoopCounter, Rec."Item No.");
```

The display would look as follows:

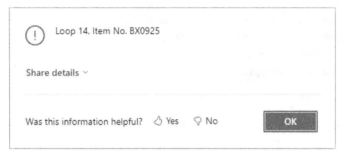

Figure 6.17 – Error method in the client

The **Share details** button automatically enables users to copy and share the error message text and the AL call stack for troubleshooting purposes.

Even in the best of circumstances, it is difficult for a system to communicate clearly with users. Sometimes, our tools, in their effort to be flexible, make it too easy for developers to take the easy way out and communicate poorly or not at all. For example, an error statement of the `Error('')` form will terminate the run and roll back all data processing without even displaying a message at all. An important part of our job, as developers, is to ensure that our systems communicate clearly and completely.

Confirm method

A third dialog method is the Confirm method. A Confirm method call causes processing to stop until the user responds to the dialog. In Confirm, we will include a question in our text because the method provides **Yes** and **No** button options. The application logic can then be conditioned on the user's response.

> **Note**
>
> We can also use Confirm as a simple debugging tool to control the path the processing will take. Display the status of data or processing flow and then allow the operator to make a choice (**Yes** or **No**) that will influence what happens next. Execution of a Confirm method will also cause any pending Message method output values to be displayed before the Confirm method displays. Combined with Message and Error, the creative use of Confirm can add to our elementary debugging/diagnostic toolkit.

Confirm has the following syntax:

```
BooleanValue := Confirm(String [, Default] [, Value1] , Value2 ...])
```

When we do not specify a value for Default, the system will choose false (which displays as **No**). We should almost always choose the Default option as it will do no damage if accepted inadvertently by an inattentive user. The default choice is false, which is often the safest choice (but true may be specified by the programmer). There are as many ValueX entries as there are %X substitution strings.

If we just code OK := Confirm(String), the default choice will be false.

A Confirm method call with similar content to the preceding examples might look like the following sample for the code and the display:

```
Answer := Confirm('Loop %1, Item No. %2\OK to continue?', true,
LoopCounter, Rec."Item No.");
```

The output screen is shown in the following screenshot:

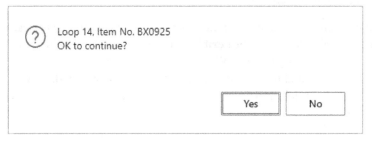

Figure 6.18 – Confirmation method in the client

In typical usage, the Confirm method is part of, or is referred to by, a conditional statement that uses the Boolean value that's returned by the Confirm method.

An additional feature for on-screen dialogs is the use of the **backslash** (\) that's embedded in the text. This forces a new line in the displayed message. This works throughout Business Central screen display methods.

> **Tip**
>
> To display a backslash on-screen, we must use it as a value for the substitution string (ValueX).

StrMenu method

A fourth dialog method is the StrMenu method. A StrMenu method call also causes processing to pause while the user responds to the dialog. The advantage of the StrMenu method is its ability to provide several choices, rather than just two (**Yes** or **No**). A common use is to provide an option menu in response to the user calling a page action.

StrMenu has the following syntax:

```
OptionNumber := StrMenu(OptionMembers[, DefaultNumber][, Instruction])
```

OptionMembers is a comma-separated string. Each substring in OptionMembers specifies an option on the menu. The string can be a label that is enabled for multilanguage functionality. OptionNumber will contain the user's selection entry, and DefaultNumber is an integer representing which option will be selected by default when the menu displays. If we do not provide a DefaultNumber value, the first option that's listed will be used as the default. Instruction is an optional text string that will display the preceding list of options. If the user responds with **Cancel** or presses the *Esc* key, the value that's returned by the method is 0.

The use of the StrMenu method eliminates the need to use a page object when asking the user to select from a limited set of options. It can also be utilized from within a report or code unit when calling a page would restrict processing choices.

If we phrase our Instruction as a question rather than simply an explanation, then we can use StrMenu as a multiple-choice inquiry to the user:

```
OptionNo := StrMenu('Blue,Plaid,Yellow,Hot Pink,Orange,Unknown', 6,
'Which of these is not like the others?');
```

The output screen is shown in the following screenshot:

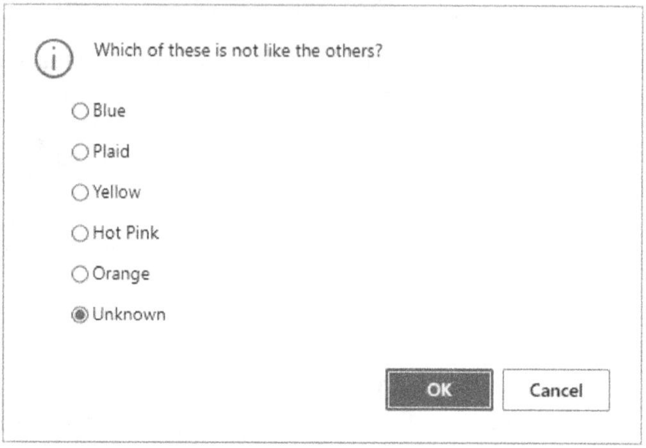

Figure 6.19 – StrMenu method in the client

Setting the default to 6 caused the sixth option (**Unknown**) to be the active selection when the menu is displayed.

That's it for now about dialog methods. Let's switch to another type of method: record methods.

Record methods

Now, we will review some of the methods that we commonly use in record processing: `SetCurrentKey`, `SetRange`, `SetFilter`, `Get`, and `Find*`, where `Find*` represents a subgroup of related methods whose names all begin with "Find".

> **Important**
>
> While all the mentioned AL record methods serve the purpose of building a SQL `select` command, only the `Get` und `Find*` methods will actually send it to the SQL server.
>
> On executing `Find*` code lines, previous `SetCurrentKey`, `SetRange`, and `SetFilter` methods are evaluated for the SQL `select` statement.

SetCurrentKey method

The syntax for `SetCurrentKey` is as follows:

```
[BooleanValue :=] Record.SetCurrentKey(FieldName1[, FieldName2,
FieldName3, ...])
```

Since Business Central is based on the SQL Server database, `SetCurrentKey` simply determines the order in which the data will be presented for processing. The actual choice of the index to be used for the query is made by the SQL Server Query Analyzer. For this reason, it is very important that the data and resources available to the SQL Server Query Analyzer are well maintained. This includes making sure that efficient index options have been defined. Even though SQL Server picks the actual index, the developer's choice of the appropriate `SetCurrentKey` parameter can have a major effect on performance.

> **Note**
>
> The fields that are used in the `SetCurrentKey` command do not have to match a key in the table definition. You can also use `FlowFields` as fields for `SetCurrentKey` but expect slower performance when doing this.

SetRange method

The `SetRange` method provides the ability to set a simple range filter on a `Record` field. The `SetRange` syntax is as follows:

```
Record.SetRange(FieldName [,From-Value] [,To-Value]);
```

Prior to applying its range filter, the `SetRange` method removes any filters that were previously set for the defined field (filtering procedures are defined in more detail in the next chapter). If `SetRange` is executed with only one value, that one value will act as both the `From` and `To` values. If `SetRange` is executed without any `From` or `To` values, it will clear the filters on the field. This is a common use of `SetRange`. Some examples of the `SetRange` method in code are as follows:

- Clear the filters on `Item."No."`:

```
Item.SetRange("No.");
```

- Filter to get only items with `No.` from `1300` through `1400`:

```
Item.SetRange("No.", '1300', '1400');
```

- Alternatively, you can use the variable values from `LowVal` through `HiVal`:

```
Item.SetRange("No.", LowVal, HiVal);
```

> **Note**
>
> To be effective in a record, `SetRange` must be directly or indirectly followed by a `Find*` method on the same record variable. To be effective in a query, `SetRange` must be called before the `Open`, `SaveAsXml`, and `SaveAsCsv` methods.

`SetFilter` is similar to, but much more flexible than, the `SetRange` method because it supports the application of any of the supported Business Central filter expressions to table fields. The `SetFilter` syntax is as follows:

```
Record.SetFilter(FieldName, FilterExpression [, Value1, Value2, ...]);
```

The `FilterExpression` consists of a string (text or code) in standard Business Central filter format, including any of the operators (<, >, *, &, |, and =) in any legal combination. Replacement fields (%1, %2, ..., %) are used to represent the values that will be inserted into `FilterExpression` by the compiler to create an operating filter that's formatted as though it were entered from the keyboard. Just like `SetRange`, prior to applying its filter, the `SetFilter` method clears any filters that were previously set for the defined field, as in the following example:

- Filter to get only items with `No.` from `1300` through `1400`:

  ```
  Item.SetFilter("No.", '%1..%2', '1300', '1400');
  ```

- Alternatively, you can do this with any of the variable values of `LowVal`, `MedVal`, or `HiVal`:

  ```
  Item.SetFilter("No.", '%1|%2|%3', LowVal, MedVal, HiVal);
  ```

> **Note**
>
> Just like `SetRange`, to be effective in a record, `SetFilter` must be directly or indirectly followed by a `Find*` method on the same record variable. To be effective in a query, `SetFilter` must be called before the `Open`, `SaveAsXml`, and `SaveAsCsv` methods.

Get method

`Get` is the basic data retrieval procedure in AL. `Get` retrieves a single record based only on the primary key. It has the following syntax:

```
[BooleanValue :=] Record.Get([KeyFieldValue1] [, KeyFieldValue2,
KeyFieldValue3 ,...]);
```

The parameter for the `Get` method is the primary key value (or all of the values, if the primary key consists of more than one field).

Assigning the `Get` procedure result to `BooleanValue` is optional. If the `Get` procedure is not successful (no record found) and the statement is not part of an `if` statement, the process will terminate with a runtime error. Typically, therefore, the `Get` method is encased in an if statement, which is structured like so:

```
if Customer.Get(SomeCustNo) then ...
```

> **Note**
>
> Get data retrieval is not constrained by filters, except for **security filters** (see *Using Security Filters* in the Microsoft docs at `https://learn.microsoft.com/en-us/dynamics365/ business-central/dev-itpro/security/security-filters`), or keys. If there is a matching record in the table, Get will retrieve it.

Find methods

The Find* family of methods is the general-purpose data retrieval method in AL. It is much more flexible than Get, and therefore widely used. Get has the advantage of being faster as it operates only on unfiltered direct access through the primary key, looking for a single uniquely keyed entry. There are two forms of Find* methods in AL: one is a remnant from a previous database structure and the other is designed specifically to work efficiently with SQL Server. Both are supported, and we will find both in standard code.

The older version of the Find method has the following syntax:

```
[BooleanValue :=] Record.Find([Which]);
```

The newer SQL Server-specific members of the Find* method family (FindFirst, FindLast, and FindSet) have slightly different syntax, as we will see shortly. We can explore the different Which parameter values in *Record.Find([Text]) Method*, which can be found in the Microsoft docs at `https://learn.microsoft.com/en-us/dynamics365/business-central/ dev-itpro/developer/methods-auto/record/record-find-method`.

Just like the Get method, assigning the Find* method result to a Boolean value is optional. However, in almost all cases, Find* is embedded in a condition that controls subsequent processing appropriately. Either way, it is important to structure our code to handle the instance where Find* is not successful.

Find* differs from Get in several important ways, some of which are as follows:

- Find* operates under the limits of whatever filters are applied to the subject field.
- Find* (except FindFirst and FindLast) presents the data in the sequence of the key that is currently selected by default or by AL code.
- When Find* is used, the index that's used for the data reading is controlled by the SQL Server Query Analyzer.
- Find* does not calculate FlowFields unless the SetAutoCalcFields method was used earlier.
- Different variations of the Find* method are designed specifically for use in different situations. This allows coding to be optimized for better SQL Server performance. All of the Find* methods are described further in the Microsoft docs, in the *AL Database Methods and Performance on SQL Server* article, at `https://learn.microsoft.com/en-us/ dynamics365/business-central/dev-itpro/administration/optimize- sql-al-database-methods-and-performance-on-server`.

The forms of `Find*` are as follows:

- `Find('-')`: This finds the first record in a table that satisfies the defined filter and current key.

- `FindFirst`: This finds the first record in a table that satisfies the defined filter and key choice. Conceptually, it is equivalent to `Find('-')` for a single record read but better for SQL Server when a filter or range is applied.

- `Find('+')`: This finds the last record in a table that satisfies the defined filter and defined key choice. Often, this is not an efficient option for SQL Server because it causes it to read a set of records when, many times, only a single record is needed. The exception is when a table is to be processed in reverse order. Then, it is appropriate to use `Find('+')` with SQL Server.

- `FindLast`: This finds the last record in a table that satisfies the defined filter and current key. It is conceptually equivalent to `Find('+')` but, often, much better for SQL Server as it reads a single record, not a set of records.

- `FindSet`: This is the most efficient way to read a set of records from SQL Server for sequential processing within a specified filter and range. In on-premises environments, `FindSet` allows you to define the standard size of the read record cache as a setup parameter but, normally and in the cloud, it defaults to reading 50 records (table rows) for the first server call. The syntax includes an optional `true/false` parameter, as follows:

    ```
    [BooleanValue :=] FindSet([ForUpdate]);
    ```

    The `ForUpdate` parameter controls whether or not the read is in preparation for an update.

For all `Find*` methods, the results always respect the applied filters.

The `Find('-')` and `FindSet` methods are often used as the first step of reading a set of data, such as reading all of the sales invoices for a single customer. In such a case, the `Next` method is used to trigger all subsequent data reads after the sequence is initiated with `Find('-')` or `FindSet`.

> **Note**
>
> Generally, `FindSet` should be used rather than `Find('-')`; however, `FindSet` only works to read forward, not in reverse. `Find('-')` is also preferred if we expect the loop to end early due to an error. We should use `FindFirst` or `FindLast` if only the first or last record in the specified range is of interest.

One form of the typical AL database read loop is as follows:

```
MyData.SetCurrentKey(...);

MyData.SetRange(MyField, SomeValue);if MyData.FindSet() then
    repeat
      // Processing logic here
    until MyData.Next() = 0;
```

We will discuss the `repeat-until` control structure in more detail in the next chapter. Essentially, it does what it says; *repeat the following logic until the defined condition is true*. For the `Find*-Next` read loop, the `Next` method provides both the definition of how the `read` loop will advance through the table and when the loop is to exit.

When `DataTable.Next()` = 0, there are no more records to be read. We have reached the end of the available data, based on the filters and other conditions that apply to our reading process.

The specific syntax of the `Next` method is `DataTable.Next([Step])`. `DataTable` is the name of the table being read. `Step` defines the number of records Business Central will move forward (or backward) per read. The default `Step` is 1, meaning that Business Central moves ahead one record at a time, reading every record. A `Step` of 0 results in staying on the current record. If the `Step` is set to 2, Business Central will move ahead two records at a time and the process will only be presented with every other record.

`Step` can also be negative, in which case Business Central moves backward through the table. This would allow us to execute a `Find('+')` procedure for the end of the table, then a `Next(-1)` method to read backward through the data. This is very useful if, for example, we need to read a table sorted ascending by date and want to access the most recent entries first.

Conditional statements

Conditional statements are the heart of process flow structure and control.

The begin-end compound statement

In AL, there are instances where the syntax only allows the use of a single statement. However, a design may require the execution of several code statements.

AL provides at least two ways to address this need. One method is to have the single statement call a procedure that contains multiple statements.

However, inline coding is often more efficient to run and understand. So, AL provides a syntax structure to define a compound statement or block of code. A compound statement containing any number of statements can be used in place of a single code statement.

A compound statement is enclosed by the reserved `begin` and `end` words. The compound statement structure looks like this:

```
begin
    <Statement-1>;
    <Statement-2>;
    . .
    <Statement-n>;
end
```

Upon saving an AL file in VS Code, the AL code contained within a `begin-end` block will be automatically indented by four characters, as shown in the preceding pseudocode snippet, to make it obvious that it is a block of code.

if-then-else statement

`if` is the basic conditional statement of most programming languages. It operates in AL in much the same way as it does in other languages. The basic structure is as follows: `if` a conditional expression is true, `then` execute `Statement-1`, or (if the condition is not `true`) execute `Statement-2`. The `else` portion is optional. The syntax is as follows:

```
if <Condition> then <Statement-1>[ else <Statement-2>];
```

Note that the statements within an `if` statement do not have terminating semicolons unless they are contained in a `begin-end` framework. `if` statements can be nested so that conditionals are dependent on the evaluation of other conditionals. Obviously, you need to be careful with such constructs, because it is easy to end up with convoluted code structures that are difficult to debug and difficult for the developers following us to understand. In the next chapter, we will review the `case` statement that can make some complicated conditionals much easier to format and understand.

As we work with AL code, we will see that, often, `<Condition>` is really an expression built around a standard AL method. This approach is frequently used when the standard AL method returns a Boolean. Some examples are as follows:

- `if Customer.FindSet then... else...`
- `if Confirm('OK to update?', true) then... else...`
- `if TempData.Insert() then... else...`

Indenting code

Since we have just discussed the `begin-end` compound statements and the `if` conditional statements, which also are compound (that is, containing multiple expressions), this seems like a good time to discuss indenting code.

In AL, the standard practice for indenting subordinate, contained, or continued lines is relatively simple. Always indent such lines by four characters, except where there are left and right parentheses to be aligned. Usually, the AL formatter indents code automatically for us upon saving, or upon pressing *Shift + Alt + K*, but there might be some cases in which the auto-formatting does not work as expected.

> **Note**
>
> To indent a block of code by four characters at a time with the Business Central AL code editor, select them and use the *Tab* key. To remove the indentation of four characters at a time, select the code and press *Shift + Tab*.

In the following examples, the parentheses are not required in all of the instances, but they don't cause any problems. A part of the AL programming community finds the additional parentheses easier to read.

Some examples are as follows:

```
if (A <> B) then
    A := A + Count1
else
    B := B + Count2;
```

Here's another:

```
if (A <> B) then
    A := A + Count1;
```

Check out this example as well:

```
if (A <> B) then begin
    A := A + Count1;
    B := A + Count2;
    if C > (A * B) then
        C := A * B;
end else
    B := B + Count2;
```

Throughout the last sections, we already gained a lot of knowledge about AL programming – let's put that theory into practice with some hands-on coding!

Some simple coding modifications

Now, we'll add some AL code to objects we've created for our WDTU application. We will add validation code to a table field, add code and a request page to a report, and finally, test the completed report.

Adding field validation to a table

In *Chapter 4, Pages – The Interactive Interface*, we created the 50110 "Radio Show Fan" table. We've decided that we want to be able to use this list for promotional activities, such as having drawings for concert tickets. Of course, we want to send the tickets to the winners at their mailing addresses. We didn't originally include these fields in our table design, so we must add them now.

To keep our design consistent with the standard product, we will model these address fields after the equivalent ones in the 18 - Customer table. Our updated table will look as follows:

```al
table 50110 "Radio Show Fan"
{
    fields
    {
        field(1; "No."; Code[20]) { }
        field(2; "Radio Show No."; Code[20]) { }
        field(3; Name; Text[100]) { }
        field(4; "E-Mail"; Text[80]) { }
        field(5; "Last Contacted"; Date) { }
        field(6; Address; Text[100]) { }
        field(7; "Address 2"; Text[50]) { }
        field(8; City; Text[30]) { }
        field(9; "Country/Region Code"; Code[10]) { }
        field(10; County; Text[30]) { }
        field(11; "Post Code"; Code[20]) { }
```

Figure 6.20 – Updated Radio Show Fan table

Part of modeling our 50110 "Radio Show Fan" table fields on those in the 18 - Customer table is faithfully copying the applicable properties and triggers. For example, the TableRelation property for the Post Code field in the Customer table looks as follows:

```al
TableRelation =
if ("Country/Region Code" = const('')) "Post Code" else
if ("Country/Region Code" = filter(<> '')) "Post Code" where("Country/
Region Code" = field("Country/Region Code"));
```

We should not overlook the ValidateTableRelation property:

```al
ValidateTableRelation = false;
```

The OnValidate trigger, on the other hand, contains the following line of code, which we also should include for the Post Code field in our Radio Show Fan table:

```al
PostCode.ValidatePostCode(City, "Post Code", County, "Country/Region
Code", (CurrFieldNo <> 0) and GuiAllowed);
```

> **Note**
>
> The standard code also contains events, which are procedures whose names begin with On, such as OnBeforeValidatePostCode, and variables attached to them (typically IsHandled). Let's ignore both for now and look for the remaining application code only.

When a Radio Show Fan record is added with a postcode or the Post Code field is changed, we would like to update the appropriate address information. We will see that Post Code is a reference to the record, that is, the Post Code table. To learn as much as we can about how this procedure works, how we should call it, and what information is available from the Post Code table (table 225), we will look at the Post Code table field list.

First, here's the field list in the 225 "Post Code" table:

- field(1; "Code"; Code[20])

- field(2; City; Text[30])

- field(3; "Search City"; Code[30])

- field(4; "Country/Region Code"; Code[10])

- field(5; County; Text[30])

- field(30; "Time Zone"; Text[180])

Here's the signature for the ValidatePostCode procedure declared in the Post Code table:

```
procedure ValidatePostCode(var CityTxt: Text[30]; var PostCode:
Code[20]; var CountyTxt: Text[30]; var CountryCode: Code[10];
UseDialog: Boolean)
```

By doing some analysis of what we have dissected, we can see that the ValidatePostCode procedure call uses five calling parameters. There is no return value. The procedure avoids the need to return a value by passing four of the parameters *by reference* (not *by value*), as we can tell by the var keyword on the parameters.

We conclude that we can just copy the code from the Customer table OnValidate trigger into the equivalent trigger in our Radio Show Fan table. This will give us the Post Code maintenance we want. The result looks as follows (the CurrFieldNo variable is a system-defined variable left over from previous versions and has been retained for compatibility reasons):

```
field(11; "Post Code"; Code[20])
{
    TableRelation = if ("Country/Region Code" = const('')) "Post Code"
    else if ("Country/Region Code" = filter(<> '')) "Post Code"
    where("Country/Region Code" = field("Country/Region Code"));
    ValidateTableRelation = false;

    0 references
    trigger OnValidate()
    var
        PostCode: Record "Post Code";
    begin
        PostCode.ValidatePostCode(City, "Post Code", County, "Country/Region Code",
            (CurrFieldNo <> 0) and GuiAllowed);
    end;
}
```

Figure 6.21 – Finalized Post Code field in the Radio Show Fan table

As the last coding task, we will add the new address fields to the Radio Show Fans page object, and finally publish our new code. We can now test our work by running the **Radio Show Fans** page on the client. All we need to do is move to the **Post Code** field, click on it, and choose an entry from the displayed list of codes. The result should be the population of the **Post Code** field, the **Country/Region Code** field, and the **City** field. If we fill in the new data fields for some Radio Show Fan records, our **Radio Show Fans** page should look as follows:

No. ↑	Name	E-Mail	Last Contacted	Address	Post Code	City	Country/R... Code
AG	Andrew Good	agood@libertystuff.com	31.01.2024	Somewhere	DE-40593	Dusseldorf	DE
MS	Maryann Smith	smith925@tigerfire.com	31.01.2024	Elsewhere	AU-2000	Sydney, NSW	AU

Figure 6.22 – Populated Radio Show Fans page

We've accomplished our goal. The way we've done it may seem disappointing. It didn't feel like we really designed a solution or wrote any code. What we did was find where in Business Central the same problem had already been solved, figure out how that solution worked, and clone it into our object, then we were done.

Each time we start this approach, we should look at the defined patterns (https://alguidelines. dev/docs) to see whether any patterns fit our situation. The benefit of starting with a pattern is that the general structural definition is defined for how this procedure should be done within Business Central. Whether you find a matching pattern or not, the next step is to find and study applicable AL code within Business Central.

Obviously, this approach doesn't work every time. However, every time it does work, it is a small triumph of efficiency. This helps us keep the structure of our solution consistent with the standard product and allows us to reuse existing code constructs and minimize the debugging effort and chances of production problems.

After having added field validation to a table, we now continue our simple coding modifications journey by adding code to a report.

Adding code to a report

Most reports require some embedded logic to process user-selected options, calculate values, or access data in related tables. To illustrate some possibilities, we will extend our WDTU application to add a new report with a Word layout. To support promotions giving away posters, concert tickets, and so on, we must further enhance the `Radio Show Fan` table and create a new report to generate mailing information from it.

Our first step is hence to create `report 50102 "Fan Promotion List"` by using the `treport` snippet, and to populate it for a default Word layout. Our next step is to add a `dataset`. We should define the data fields we want to include for mailings (including a global variable of `CountryName` that we will populate later), as shown in the following screenshot:

```
1    report 50102 "Fan Promotion List"
2    {
3        UsageCategory = ReportsAndAnalysis;
4        ApplicationArea = All;
5        DefaultRenderingLayout = FanPromotionList;
6
7        dataset
8        {
9            dataitem(RadioShowFan; "Radio Show Fan")
10           {
11               column(Name; Name) { }
12               column(Address; Address) { }
13               column(Address_2; "Address 2") { }
14               column(City; City) { }
15               column(Post_Code; "Post Code") { }
16               column(Country_Region_Code; "Country/Region Code") { }
17               column(CountryName; CountryName) { }
18           }
19       }
20
21   >   rendering...
29
30       var
31           CountryName: Text;
32   }
```

Figure 6.23 – Dataset in the Fan Promotion List report

Next, we will begin the design of the report layout in Word instead of Excel.

Laying out the new report heading

If we run the **AL: Package** Visual Studio Code command for our application, a Microsoft Word file will be created (or updated, if it had been created earlier), which we can open externally, just as we learned in *Chapter 5* using Excel layouts.

We will add a report header by simply creating it with a default style, as shown in the following screenshot:

Figure 6.24 – Formatting the Fan Promotion List report header

Saving and testing

At this point, it's time to save and test what we've done so far. Exit Microsoft Word. Save the report layout changes. Build and publish your application and run the report using **Tell me**.

This first test is very simple (assuming it works). The report request page will appear in the web client. Click on **Preview & Close** to see the report display on-screen. The layout shown in the preceding screenshot will result in the following report page (or something similar):

Figure 6.25 – Fan Promotion List preview

Lookup-related table data

Once we have a successful test of the report (heading only), we'll move on to laying out the body of the report. As we think through the data, we will want to include a mailing address, such as name, address, second address, city, country name, and postcode, and realize that our table data includes country code, not country name. So, we will look up the country name from the Country/Region table (table 9). Let's take care of that now.

Each time we read a `RadioShowFan` record, we'll look up the country name for that fan and store it in `CountryName`, inside the `OnAfterGetRecord` trigger:

```
17                      column(CountryName; CountryName) { }
18

                        0 references
19                      trigger OnAfterGetRecord()
20                      var
21                          CountryRegion: Record "Country/Region";
22                      begin
23                          CountryRegion.Get("Country/Region Code");
24                          CountryName := CountryRegion.Name;
25                      end;
26              }
27          }
28
29      rendering
```

Figure 6.26 – Populating the CountryName global variable

On the next report run, the populated `CountryName` value will be passed to Microsoft Word.

While what we've done will probably work most of the time, how could it be made better? For one thing, shouldn't we handle the situation where there is no `Country/Region Code` in the fan record? Do we really need to move the country name to a variable instead of simply reporting it directly from the `Country/Region` record?

Both of these issues could be handled better. Look up the `Record.Get` method in the Microsoft docs to see what should be done in terms of error handling. Additionally, after we work through the report as we're doing here, we can enhance it by eliminating the use of the `CountryName` global variable. For now, let's just move on and complete an initial version of our report by creating the rest of our report layout in Microsoft Word.

Laying out the new report body

Open the Word file, and make sure the **Developer** tab is visible.

> **Note**
>
> To design reports with Microsoft Word, the Word **Developer** tab needs to be exposed. If it is not visible, go to **File** | **Options** | **Customize Ribbon** and then select **Developer**. Inside the **Developer** tab, we will utilize the **XML Mapping Pane**.

Inside the Word body, add a new table control. The table should contain five columns and two rows. In the top row, we will type captions.

Open the **XML Mapping Pane**, and switch its **Custom XML Part** control to the one beginning with **urn:microsoft-dynamics-nav/reports**:

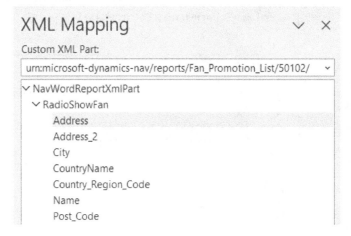

Figure 6.27 – Word XML Mapping for the Fan Promotion List report

We will select the second row of the table control. Within the **XML Mapping** on the right, we will right-click on the **RadioShowFan** data item name and use **Insert Content Control | Repeating**. We will add the data fields from the **XML Mapping** into each of the data row text boxes (the bottom row) by placing the cursor in the target cell, then right-click the source field and select **Insert Content Control**. For visual appeal, we will add a style to the table. The resulting Word body should resemble the following figure:

Fan Promotion List

Name	Address	City	Post Code	Country Name
Name	Address	City	Post_Code	CountryName

Figure 6.28 – Laying out the Fan Promotion List in Word

Saving and testing

After we lay out, save, exit, and publish, it's time to do another test run of our report in process. If we simply preview it without doing any filtering, we should see all of our test data address information (complete with country name), as shown in the following screenshot:

Fan Promotion List

Name	Address	City	Post Code	Country Name
Andrew Good	Somewhere	Dusseldorf	DE-40593	Germany
Maryann Smith	Elsewhere	Sydney, NSW	AU-2000	Australia

Figure 6.29 – Previewing the Fan Promotion List

> **Tip**
>
> If the report preview does not display any records, just the caption row, try deleting the table and redesigning it from scratch.

Handling user-entered report options

Part of our report design includes allowing the user to choose fans based on some simple demographic data, such as age and gender. We'll need to add two more fields to our Radio Show Fan table definition, one for Gender and the other for Birth Date, from which we can calculate the fan's age, as shown in the following code snippet:

```
field(12; Gender; Option) {
    OptionMembers = " ",Male,Female,Nonbinary; }
field(13; "Birth Date"; Date) { }
```

We'll also need to add the two new fields to the Radio Show Fans page object, run it, and complete our sample records on the **Radio Show Fans** page.

> **Note**
>
> This back-and-forth process of updating one object, then a different one, then yet another is typical of the Business Central development process much of the time. Exceptions are those cases when either the task is so simple we think of everything the first time through, or when we create a completely documented, full-featured design before any development starts (but nobody thinks of everything, there are always changes; our challenge is to keep the changes under control).
>
> An advantage to the more flexible approach we are following is that it allows us to view (and share with others) intermediate versions of the application as it is developed. Design issues can be addressed as they come up, and overlooked features can be considered midstream. Two downsides are the very real possibility of scope creep (the project growing uncontrollably) and poorly organized code. Scope creep can be controlled by good project management. If the first pass-through results in poorly organized code, then thoughtful refactoring is appropriate, cleaning up the code while retaining the design.

For the user to choose which Fan demographics will be used to filter the Fan data for a particular promotion, we will have to create a request page for entry of the desired criteria. This, in turn, requires the definition of a set of global variables in our report object to support the request page data entry fields and as working variables for the age calculation and Fan selection. We've decided that if Fan fits any of the individual criteria, we will include them. This makes our logic simpler. Our final global variable list in report 50102 Fan Promotion List looks as follows:

```
var
    CountryName: Text;
    Age12orLess: Boolean;
    Age13to18: Boolean;
    Age19to34: Boolean;
    Age35to50: Boolean;
    AgeOver50: Boolean;
    Male: Boolean;
    Female: Boolean;
    Nonbinary: Boolean;
    SelectThisFan: Boolean;
    FanAge: Integer;
```

Defining the request page

Now, let's define the request page. Between the dataset and rendering areas, add a requestpage area and make the entries necessary to describe the page's contents, as shown in the following screenshot:

```
requestpage
{
    layout
    {
        area(content)
        {
            group(Options)
            {
                field(Age12orLess; Age12orLess) { Caption = 'Age 12 or less'; }
                field(Age13to18; Age13to18) { Caption = 'Age 13 to 18'; }
                field(Age19to34; Age19to34) { Caption = 'Age 19 to 34'; }
                field(Age35to50; Age35to50) { Caption = 'Age 34 to 50'; }
                field(AgeOver50; AgeOver50) { Caption = 'Age over 50'; }
                field(Male; Male) { Caption = 'Male'; }
                field(Female; Female) { Caption = 'Female'; }
                field(Nonbinary; Nonbinary) { Caption = 'Nonbinary'; }
```

Figure 6.30 – Fan Promotion List request page code

Finishing the processing code

Next, we will create the AL code to calculate a fan's age (in years) based on their birth date and the current work date. The logic is simple—subtract the birthdate from the WorkDate. This gives a number of days. So, we will divide by 365 (not worrying about leap years) and round down to integer years (if someone is 25 years, 10 months, and 2 days old, we will just consider them 25). In the following code, we did the division as though the result were a decimal field.

> **Note**
>
> However, because our math is done in integers, we could have used the simpler `FanAge :=` `(WorkDate() - "Birth Date") div 365;` expression.

Finally, we'll write the code to check each `Fan` record data against our selection criteria, determining whether we want to include that fan in our output data (`SelectThisFan` set to `true`). This code will select each fan who fits any of the checked criteria; there is no combination logic here.

The following is our commented `OnAfterGetRecord` trigger code for `report 50102 Fan Promotion List`:

```
trigger OnAfterGetRecord()
var
    CountryRegion: Record "Country/Region";
begin
    // Look up the Country Name using the Country/Region Code
    CountryRegion.Get("Country/Region Code");
    CountryName := CountryRegion.Name;

    // Calculate the fan's age
    FanAge := Round(((WorkDate() - "Birth Date") / 365), 1.0, '<');

    // Select Fans to receive promotional material
    SelectThisFan := false;
    if Age12OrLess and (FanAge <= 12) then
        SelectThisFan := true;
    if Age13to18 and (FanAge > 12) and (FanAge < 19) then
        SelectThisFan := true;
    if Age19to34 and (FanAge > 18) and (FanAge < 35) then
        SelectThisFan := true;
    if Age35to50 and (FanAge > 34) and (FanAge < 51) then
        SelectThisFan := true;
    if AgeOver50 and (FanAge > 50) then
        SelectThisFan := true;
    if Male and (Gender = Gender::Male) then
        SelectThisFan := true;
    if Female and (Gender = Gender::Female) then
        SelectThisFan := true;
    if Nonbinary and (Gender = Gender::Nonbinary) then
        SelectThisFan := true;

    // If this Fan not selected, skip this Fan record on report
    if not SelectThisFan then
        CurrReport.Skip();
end;
```

Figure 6.31 – Completed OnAfterGetRecord

After this version of the report is successfully tested, enhance it. Make the report support choosing any of the options (as it is now) or, at the user option, choose a combination of age range plus gender. Hint: add additional checkboxes to allow the user to control which set of logic will be applied.

> **Note**
> We should also change the code to use `case` statements (rather than `if` statements). We will cover `case` statements in *Chapter 7*.

Testing the completed report

After we save and compile our report, we'll run it again. Now, we will get an expanded request option page. After this, we check-marked some of the selection criteria, as shown in the following screenshot:

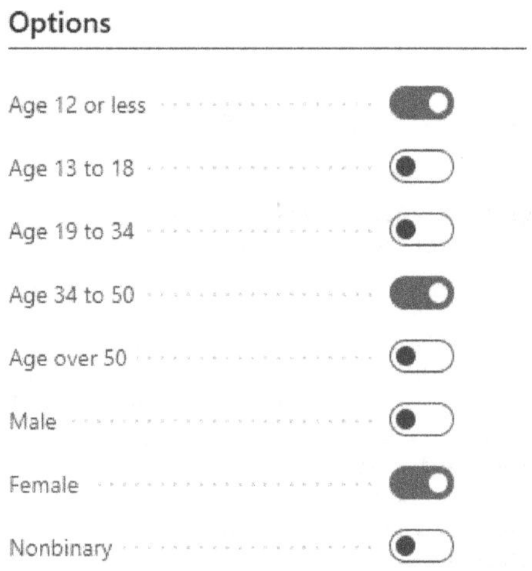

Options

Age 12 or less · · · · · · · · · · · · · · · ⬤

Age 13 to 18 · · · · · · · · · · · · · · · ⬤

Age 19 to 34 · · · · · · · · · · · · · · · ⬤

Age 34 to 50 · · · · · · · · · · · · · · · ⬤

Age over 50 · · · · · · · · · · · · · · · ⬤

Male · · · · · · · · · · · · · · · · · · ⬤

Female · · · · · · · · · · · · · · · · ⬤

Nonbinary · · · · · · · · · · · · · · · ⬤

Figure 6.32 – Fan Promotion List request page options

Now, let's preview our report. Using the sample data we previously entered, our report output shows only records complying with at least one of the selected request page options.

At this point, we have a report that runs and is useful. It can be enhanced to support more complex selection criteria. As usual, there are a number of different ways to accomplish essentially the same result. Some of those paths would be significantly different for the developer, but nearly invisible to the user. Some might not even matter to the next developer who has to work on this report. What is important at this point is that the result works reliably, provides the desired output, operates with reasonable speed, and does not cost too much to create or maintain. If all of these goals are met, most of the other differences are usually not very important.

Summary

In this chapter, we covered Visual Studio Code navigation. We covered a number of AL language areas, including methods and procedures and how they may be used, variables of various types (both development and system), basic AL syntax, expressions, and operators. Some of the essential AL methods that we covered include user dialogs, SetRange filtering, Get, variations of Find, and begin-end for code structures, plus if-then for basic process flow control. Finally, we got some hands-on experience by adding validation code to a table and creating a new report that included embedded AL code, a request page, and a Word layout.

In the next chapter, we will expand our exploration and practice using AL. We will learn about additional AL methods, flow control structures, input/output methods, and filtering.

Questions

1. All Business Central objects can contain AL code—true or false?

   Answer: True

2. Which object type has to be designed partly outside of Visual Studio Code? Choose one:

   - Page
   - XmlPort
   - Table
   - Report

   Answer: Report

3. All AL Assignment statements are represented with a colon followed by an equals sign —true or false?

   Answer: True

4. One setting defines how parameters are passed to procedures, that is, whether a parameter is passed by reference or by value. Choose that one setting identity:

   - Include
   - Object
   - var
   - val

   Answer: var

5. What is the difference between the scope operator and the range operator?

    Answer: The scope operator (two colons together) is used to refer to a specific option or enum value. The range operator (two dots) is to represent all the data including and in between two values.

6. The AL code cannot be inserted into the RDLC generated by the Visual Studio Report Designer (or the SQL Server Report Builder)—true or false?

    Answer: True

7. Object numbers and names are so flexible that we can (and should) choose our own approach to numbering and naming—true or false?

    Answer: False

8. begin-end is always required in if statements—true or false?

    Answer: False

9. All business central development work starts from visual studio code—true or false?

    Answer: True

10. Filter wildcards include which three of the following?

    - ?
    - ::
    - *
    - ^
    - @

    Answer: ?, *, @

11. Choice of the proper version of the Find statement can make a significant difference in processing speed—true or false?

    Answer: True

12. When an Error statement is executed, the user is given the choice to terminate processing, cause a rollback, or ignore the error and continue processing—true or false?

    Answer: False; the error cannot be ignored

7

Intermediate AL

"You need to "listen deeply"—listen past what people say they want to hear to what they need."

– Jon Meads

"People's behavior makes sense if you think about it in terms of their goals, needs, and motives."

– Thomas Mann

In the previous chapter, you learned enough AL to create a basic operational set of code. In this chapter, you will learn about more AL methods and pick up a few more good habits along the way. If you are getting started as a professional Business Central developer, the built-in AL methods represent a significant portion of the knowledge that you will need on a day-to-day basis. If you are a manager or consultant needing to know what Business Central can do for your business or your customer, an understanding of these methods will help you too.

Our goal is to competently manage **Create, Read, Update, Delete** (**CRUD**) operations, create moderately complex program logic structures, and understand data filtering and sorting as handled in Business Central and AL. Since the methods and features in AL are designed for business and financial applications, we can do a surprising amount of ERP work in Business Central with a relatively small number of language constructs.

Keep in mind that anything discussed in this chapter relates only indirectly to those portions of Business Central objects that contain no AL, for example, Microsoft **SQL Server Report Builder** (**SSRB**) and Microsoft Excel or Word report layouts.

This chapter's goals are to accomplish the following:

- Learn about a variety of useful (and widely used) AL methods

- Better understand filtering

- Apply what you've learned to expand your WDTU application using some of the AL development tools

- Learn how the multi-language system for Business Central works

- Get to know the debugger in Visual Studio Code

Let's begin our journey with the very first group of AL methods – validation methods.

Validation methods

AL includes a number of utility methods that are designed to facilitate data validation or initialization. Some of these methods are as follows:

- `TestField`

- `FieldError`

- `Init`

- `Validate`

We will discuss these methods more in the following sections.

TestField method

The `TestField` method is widely used in standard Business Central code. With `TestField`, we can test a table field value and generate an error message in a single statement if the test fails. The syntax is as follows:

```
Record.TestField(Field[, Value]);
```

If `Value` is specified and the field does not equal that value, the process terminates with an error condition, and an error message is issued.

If no `Value` is specified, the field contents are checked for values of zero or blank. If the field is zero or blank, then an error message is issued.

The advantage of `TestField` is ease of use and consistency in code and in the message displayed. The disadvantage is that the error message is not as informative as a careful developer would provide, and users find this message too technical.

The following snippet of the `TestField` method usage is from `Table 36 - Sales Header`, the `TestStatusOpen()` procedure. This code checks to make sure that the `Sales Header field` `Status` is equal to the `Open` enum value before allowing the value of the `Sell-to Customer` `No.` field to be entered:

```
TestField(Status, Status::Open);
```

An example of the client error message that is generated when attempting to change the customer on a sales order when `Status` is not equal to the `Open` enum value is as follows:

Status must be equal to 'Open' in Sales Header: Document Type=Order, No.=101001. Current value is 'Released'.

FieldError method

Another method, which is very similar to the `TestField` method, is `FieldError`. However, where `TestField` performs a test and terminates with either an error or an `OK` result, `FieldError` presumes that the test was already performed and the field failed the test. `FieldError` is designed to display an error message and then terminate the process. This approach is followed in much of the standard Business Central logic, especially in the **posting codeunits** (for example, the `12 Gen.` `Jnl.-Post Line`, `80 Sales-Post`, and `90 Purch.-Post` codeunits). The syntax is as follows:

```
Record.FieldError(FieldName[, MsgText]);
```

To make our own `MsgText` multilingual, we can define a text constant or label variable. Then, we can reference the variable in code as in the following snippet added to the `End Time` field of the `Playlist Header` table object:

```
trigger OnValidate()
var
    MustBeGreaterErr: Label 'must be greater than Start Time';
begin
    if "End Time" <= "Start Time" then
        FieldError("End Time", MustBeGreaterErr);
end;
```

> **Important**
> The first word of our individual `FieldError` texts must not be capitalized. Since the error message begins with the name of the field, we will need to be careful that our individual text is structured to make the resulting error message easy to read.

The result is an error message from `FieldError`, as shown in the following screenshot. Be aware that the highlighted parts were added automatically:

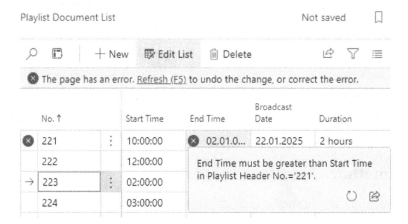

Figure 7.1 – FieldError with a customized message text

An error message that simply identifies the data field, but does not reference a message text, is as follows, with the record key information displayed:

End Time must not be 10:00:00 in Playlist Header No.='221'.

If we don't include our own message text, the default message comes in two flavors. The first instance is the case where the referenced field is not empty. Then, the error message presumes that the error is due to a wrong value, as mentioned previously. In this case, where the referenced data field is empty, the error message logic presumes that the field should not be empty:

You must specify End Time in Playlist Header No.='221'.

Init method

The `Init` method initializes a record in preparation for its use, typically in the course of building a record entry to insert in a table. The syntax is as follows:

```
Record.Init();
```

All the data fields in the record are initialized as follows:

- Fields that have an `InitValue` property defined are initialized to the specified value.
- Fields that do not have a defined `InitValue` are initialized to the default value for their data type.
- Primary key fields and timestamps are not automatically initialized. If they contain values, those will remain. If new values are desired, they must be assigned in code.

> **Tip**
> To initialize the primary key fields as well, use `Clear(Record);` instead.

Validate method

The syntax of the `Validate` method is as follows:

```
Record.Validate(Field[, Value]);
```

`Validate` will fire the `OnValidate` trigger of `Record.Field`. If we have specified a `Value`, it is assigned to the field, and the field validations are invoked.

If we don't specify a `Value`, then the field validations are invoked using the field value that already exists in the field. This function allows us to easily centralize our code design around the table—one of Business Central's strengths.

For example, if we were to code and change `Item."Base Unit of Measure"` from one unit of measure to another, the code should make sure that the change is valid. We should get an error if the new unit of measure has any quantity other than 1, because the quantity being equal to 1 is a requirement of the `Base Unit of Measure` field. Making the unit of measure change with a simple assignment statement would not catch a quantity value error.

The following are two forms of using `Validate` that give the same end result.

Form 1 is as follows:

```
Item.Validate("Base Unit of Measure", 'BOX');
```

Form 2 is as follows:

```
Item."Base Unit of Measure" := 'BOX';
Item.Validate("Base Unit of Measure");
```

Making sure the data entered is correct and basic error handling is very important. We have covered different ways this can be done with properties and simple AL commands.

Business Central is a date-driven application. Accounting processes, historical auditing, forecasting, and reporting all depend on the date (and sometimes time) values of data entered into the system. There are a multitude of different methods available to help manage this.

Date and time methods

Business Central provides many date and time methods. In the following sections, we will cover several of those that are more commonly used, especially in the context of accounting date-sensitive activity:

- `Today`, `Time`, and `CurrentDateTime` methods

- `WorkDate` method

- `Date2DMY`, `Date2DWY`, `DMY2Date`, `DWY2Date`, and `CalcDate` methods

Today, Time, and CurrentDateTime methods

`Today` retrieves the current system date. `Time` retrieves the current system time, as set in the operating system. Both `Today` and `Time` are influenced by the time zone client setting.

`CurrentDateTime` retrieves the current date and time in the `DateTime` format, which is stored in **UTC international time** (formerly referenced as **Greenwich Mean Time (GMT)**) and then displayed in local time. The syntax for each of these is as follows:

```
DateField := Today;
TimeField := Time;
DateTimeField := CurrentDateTime;
```

These are often used for date- and time-stamping transactions or for filling in default values in fields of the appropriate data type. For data-entry purposes, the current system date can be entered by simply typing the letter `T` in the date-entry field (this is not a case-sensitive entry, but the letter varies per client language). Business Central will automatically convert that entry into the current system date.

The undefined date in Business Central is represented by the earliest valid `DateTime` in SQL Server, which is `January 1, 1753 00:00:00:000`. The undefined date in AL is represented as `0D` (zero *D*, as in days), with subsequent dates handled through December 31, 9999. A date outside this range will result in a runtime error.

The Microsoft Dynamics Business Central undefined time (`0T`) is represented by the same value as an undefined date (`0D`) is represented.

If a two-digit year is entered or stored as a date and has a value of `50` to `99`, it is assumed to be in the 1900s. If the two-digit date is in the range of `00` to `49`, then it is treated as a 2000s date.

WorkDate method

Many standard Business Central routines default dates to the **work date** rather than to the system date. When a user logs into the system, the work date is initially set equal to the system date. However, at any time, the operator can set the work date to any date by accessing the application bar, clicking on **My Settings**, and then entering the new work date. For data entry purposes, the current work date can be entered by the operator by simply typing the letter `w` or `W` (depending on the current client language) into the date entry field. Business Central will automatically convert that entry into the current work date.

The syntax to access the current work date value from within AL code is as follows:

```
DateField := WorkDate();
```

The syntax to set the WorkDate to a new date while within AL code is as follows:

```
WorkDate(NewDate);
```

Date2DMY method

Date2DMY allows us to extract the sections of a date (day of the month, month, and year) from a Date field. The syntax is as follows:

```
IntegerVariable := Date2DMY(DateField, ExtractionChoice);
```

IntegerVariable and DateField are just as their names imply. The ExtractionChoice parameter allows us to choose which value (day, month, or year) will be assigned to the IntegerVariable field. The following table provides the Date2DMY extraction choices:

Date2DMY extraction choice	Integer value result
1	Two-digit day (1–31)
2	Two-digit month (1–12)
3	Four-digit year

Table 7.1 – Day to Day Month Year parameter results

Date2DWY method

Date2DWY allows us to extract the sections of a date (day of the week, week of the year, and year) from a DateField in exactly the same fashion as Date2DMY. The ExtractionChoice parameter allows us to choose which value (day, week, or year) will be assigned to IntegerVariable, as shown in the following table:

Date2DWY extraction choice	Integer value result
1	Two-digit day (1–7 for Monday to Sunday)
2	Two-digit week (1–53)
3	Four-digit year

Table 7.2 - Date to Day Week Year parameter results

DMY2Date and DWY2Date methods

DMY2Date allows us to create a date from integer values (or defaults) representing the day of the month, the month of the year, and the four-digit year. If an optional parameter (MonthValue or YearValue) is not specified, the corresponding value from the system date is used. The syntax is as follows:

```
DateVariable := DMY2Date(DayValue[, MonthValue][, YearValue]);
```

The only way to have the method use work date values for month and year is to extract those values and then use them explicitly. An example is as follows:

```
DateVariable := DMY2Date(22, Date2MDY(WorkDate(), 2),
Date2MDY(WorkDate(), 3));
```

This example also illustrates how expressions can be built up of nested expressions and methods. We have WorkDate within Date2MDY within DMY2Date.

DWY2Date operates similarly to DMY2Date, allowing us to create a date from integer values representing the day of the week (from 1 to 7, representing Monday to Sunday), and the week of the year (from 1 to 53), followed by the four-digit year. The syntax is as follows:

```
DateVariable := DWY2Date(DayValue[, WeekValue][, YearValue]);
```

An interesting result can occur for week 53 because it can span two years. By default, such a week is assigned to the year in which it has four or more days. In that case, the year of the result will vary, depending on the day of the week in the parameters (in other words, the year of the result may be one year greater than the year specified in the parameters). This is a perfect example of why thorough testing of our code is always appropriate.

CalcDate method

CalcDate allows us to calculate a date value that's been assigned to a date data type variable. The syntax for CalcDate is as follows:

```
DateVariable := CalcDate(DateExpression[, BaseDateValue]);
```

The calculation is based on DateExpression that's been applied to a base date (reference date). If we don't specify BaseDateValue, the current system date is used as the default date. We can specify BaseDateValue either in the form of a Date variable or as a date constant.

There are a number of ways in which we can build a DateExpression. The rules for the DateExpression are similar to the rules for DateFormula, which are described in *Chapter 3, Data Types and Table Fields*.

If there is a CW, CM, CP, CQ, or CY (current week, current month, current period, current quarter, or current year in client language, respectively) parameter in an expression, then the result will be evaluated based on the `BaseDateValue`. If we have more than one of these in our expression, the results are unpredictable. Any such expression should be thoroughly tested before being released to users.

If `DateExpression` is stored in a `DateFormula` variable, then the `DateExpression` will be language-independent. Also, if we create our own `DateExpression` in the form of a string constant within our inline AL code, surrounding the constant with < > delimiters as part of the string will make the constant language independent. Otherwise, the `DateExpression` constant will be language-dependent.

Regardless of how we have constructed our `DateExpression`, it is important to test it carefully and thoroughly before moving on. Incorrect syntax will result in a runtime error. One easy way to test it is by using a report whose sole task is to evaluate our expression and display the result. If we want to try different base dates, we can use the request page, accept the `BaseDateValue` as input, then calculate and display the `DateVariable` in the `OnValidate` trigger.

Some sample `CalcDate` expression evaluations are as follows:

- (`'<CM>'`, `20240310D`) will yield `03/31/2024`, that is, the last day of the current month for the date 3/10/2024

- (`'<-WD2>'`, `20240316D`) will yield `03/12/2024`, that is, the `WeekDay` #2 (the prior Tuesday) before the date 3/16/2024 (a Saturday)

- (`'<CM+1D>'`, `BaseDate`), where `BaseDate` equals `03/10/24`, will yield `04/01/2024`, that is, the last day of the month of the base date plus one day (the first day of the month following the base date)

Data manipulation can include changing data types, making data fit a requirement, or just for the presentation to the user. Let's go over some of the commonly utilized conversion and formatting methods in AL.

Data conversion and formatting methods

Some data-type conversions are handled in the normal process flow by AL without any particular attention on the part of the developer, such as code to text and character to text. Some data-type conversions can only be handled through AL methods. Formatting is included because it can also include a data type conversion. Rounding does not do a data type conversion, but it does result in a change in format (the number of decimal places). Let's review the following methods:

- `Round` method
- `Format` method
- `Evaluate` method

Round method

The Round method allows us to control the rounding precision for a decimal expression. The syntax for the Round function is as follows:

```
DecimalResult := Round(Number[, Precision][, Direction]);
```

Here, Number is rounded, Precision spells out the number of digits of decimal precision, and Direction indicates whether to round up, down, or to the nearest number. Some examples of Precision values are shown in the following table:

Precision value	Rounding effect
100	To a multiple of 100
1	To an integer format
0.01	To two decimal places (the US default)
0.0001	To four decimal places

Table 7.3 - Examples of Precision values

If no Precision value is specified, the rounding default is controlled by a value set in **General Ledger Setup** in the **Amount Rounding Precision (LCY)** field on the **General** tab. If no value is specified, rounding will default to two decimal places. If the precision value is, for example, 0.04 rather than 0.01, the rounding will be done to multiples of four at the number of decimal places specified.

The options available for the Direction value are shown in the following table:

Direction value (a text value)	Rounding effect
'='	Round to the nearest (mathematically correct and the default)
'>'	Round up
'<'	Round down

Table 7.4 - Examples of Direction values

Consider the following statement:

```
DecimalValue := Round(1234.56789, 0.001, '<');
```

This would result in a DecimalValue containing 1234.567. Let's check out the following statements:

```
DecimalValue := Round(1234.56789, 0.001, '=');
DecimalValue := Round(1234.56789, 0.001, '>');
```

These both result in a DecimalValue containing 1234.568.

Format method

The Format method allows you to convert an expression of any simple data type (for example, integer, decimal, date, option, time, or Boolean) into a formatted string. The syntax is as follows:

```
String := Format(ExpressionToFormat [, OutputLength]
[, FormatString or FormatNumber]);
```

The formatted output of the ExpressionToFormat will be assigned to the output of String. The optional parameters control the conversion according to a complex set of rules. Whenever possible, we should always apply Format in its simplest form. The best way to determine the likely results of a Format expression is to test it through a range of the values to be formatted. We should make sure that we include the extremes of the range of possible values in our testing.

The optional OutputLength parameter can be zero (the default), a positive integer, or a negative integer. The typical OutputLength value is either zero, in which case the defined format is fully applied, or it is a value designed to control the maximum character length and padding of the formatted string result.

The last optional parameter has two mutually exclusive sets of choices. One set, represented by a FormatNumber integer, allows the choice of a particular predefined (standard) format, of which there are up to nine choices depending on the ExpressionToFormat. Use of the optional number 9 parameter will convert AL format data types into XML standard data types, as for the following decimal:

```
XMLText := Format('1002.534', 0, 9);
```

The other set of choices allows us to build our own **format expression**.

> **Note**
>
> The Microsoft docs article *Formatting values, dates, and time* (https://learn.microsoft.com/en-us/dynamics365/business-central/dev-itpro/developer/devenv-format-property) provides a description of the available **format numbers** and tools from which we can build our own format expression.

An erroneous Format function will result in a runtime error that will terminate the execution of the process. Thus, to avoid production crashes, it is very important that we thoroughly test any code where Format is used.

Evaluate method

The `Evaluate` method is essentially the reverse of the `Format` function, allowing for the conversion of a string value into the defined data type. The syntax of the `Evaluate` function is as follows:

```
[BooleanVariable := ] Evaluate(ResultVariable,
 StringToBeConverted[, FormatNumber]);
```

The handling of a runtime error can be done by specifying `BooleanVariable` or including `Evaluate` in an expression to deal with an error, such as an `if` statement. The `ResultVariable` data type will determine what data conversion the `Evaluate` function will attempt. The format of the data in `StringToBeConverted` must be compatible with the `ResultVariable` data type; otherwise, a runtime error will occur. Any simple data type is supported.

The optional parameter, `FormatNumber`, only supports values `9` and `10`. The use of the number `9` will convert Business Central format data types into XML standard data types. This deals with the fact that several equivalent XML data types are represented differently at the base system level. Number `10` is used to convert data from a bookmark.

One of, if not the most important features of Business Central is the FlowField. Instant calculations based on simple query definitions prevent dependence on "bucket" totals that can easily be outdated or cause errors with business logic processing. Let's delve into this key feature.

FlowField and SumIndexField methods

In *Chapter 3*, *Data Types and Table Fields*, we discussed SumIndexFields and FlowFields in the context of table, field, and key definition. To recap briefly, `SumIndexFields` are defined where the table keys are defined. They allow for the very rapid calculation of values in filtered data. In most ERP and accounting software systems, the calculation of group totals, periodic totals, and so on requires time-consuming processing of all the data to be totaled.

The **SumIndexField Technology** (**SIFT**) allows a Business Central system to respond almost instantly with totals in any area where the `SumIndexField` was defined and is maintained. In fact, the use of SIFT totals combined with Business Central's retention of detailed data supports totally flexible ad hoc queries of the *"What were our sales for red widgets between the dates of November 15th through December 24th?"* form. The answer is returned almost instantly! SumIndexFields are the basis of FlowFields that have a `Sum` or `Average` method; such a FlowField must refer to a data element that is defined as a SumIndexField.

When we access a record that has a `SumIndexField` defined, there is no visible evidence of the data sum that `SumIndexField` represents. When we access a record that contains FlowFields, the FlowFields are empty virtual data elements until they are calculated. When a FlowField is displayed on a page or report, it is automatically calculated by Business Central; the developer doesn't need to do so. However, in any other scenario, the developer is responsible for calculating FlowFields using the `CalcFields` method.

> **Note**
>
> Including FlowFields in a list page display is almost always a bad idea because each FlowField instance must be calculated as it is displayed. Applicable methods include `CalcFields`, `CalcSums`, and `SetAutoCalcFields`. FlowFields are one of the key areas where Business Central systems are subject to significant processing bottlenecks. Even with the improved design, it is still critical that the table keys used for the `SumIndexField` definition are designed with efficient processing in mind. Sometimes, as part of a **performance tuning** effort, it's necessary to revise existing keys or add new keys to improve FlowField performance.

In addition to being careful about the SIFT-key structure design, it is also important not to define any `SumIndexFields` that are not necessary. Each additional `SumIndexField` adds additional processing requirements and thus adds to the processing load of the system.

> **Tip**
>
> To continue reading about performance factors to consider, refer to the *SIFT and Performance* article in the Microsoft docs at `https://learn.microsoft.com/en-us/dynamics365/business-central/dev-itpro/developer/devenv-sift-performance`.

CalcFields method

The syntax for `CalcFields` is as follows:

```
[BooleanVariable := ] Record.CalcFields(FlowField1[, FlowField2,...]);
```

Executing the `CalcFields` method will cause all the specified FlowFields to be calculated. Specification of the `BooleanVariable` allows us to handle any runtime error that may occur. Any runtime errors for `CalcFields` usually result from a coding error or a change in a table key structure.

The FlowField calculation takes into account the filters (including FlowFilters) that are currently applied to the record (we need to be careful not to overlook this). After the `CalcFields` execution, the included FlowFields can be used similarly to any other data fields. The `CalcFields` must be executed for each cycle through the subject table.

Whenever the contents of a `Blob` field are to be used, `CalcFields` is used to load the contents of the `Blob` field from the database into memory.

When the following conditions are true, `CalcFields` uses dynamically maintained SIFT data:

- The Business Central key contains the fields that are used in the filters that were defined for the FlowField

- The `SumIndexFields` on the operative key contains the fields that are provided as parameters for the calculation

- The `MaintainSiftIndex` property on the key is set to `true`; this is the default setting

If any of these conditions are not true and `CalcFields` is invoked, we will not get a runtime error, but SQL Server will calculate the requested totals the hard way – by reading all the necessary records. This could be very slow and inefficient, and should not be used for frequently processed routines or large datasets. On the other hand, if the table does not contain a lot of data or the SIFT data will not be used very often, it may be better to have the `MaintainSiftIndex` property set to `false`.

SetAutoCalcFields method

The syntax for `SetAutoCalcFields` is as follows:

```
[BooleanVariable := ] Record.SetAutoCalcFields([FlowField1,
FlowField2, ...]);
```

When `SetAutoCalcFields` for a table is inserted in code in front of record retrieval, the specified FlowFields are automatically calculated as the record is read. This is more efficient than performing `CalcFields` on the FlowFields after the record has been read.

If we want to end the automatic FlowField calculation to a record, call the method without any parameters:

```
[BooleanVariable := ] Record.SetAutoCalcFields();
```

An automatic FlowField calculation equivalent to `SetAutoCalcFields` is automatically set for the system record variables, `Rec` and `xRec`, on pages.

CalcSums method

The `CalcSums` method is conceptually similar to `CalcFields` for the calculation of sums only. However, `CalcFields` operates on FlowFields and `CalcSums` operates directly on the record. The syntax for `CalcSums` is as follows:

```
[ BooleanVariable := ] Record.CalcSums(Field1 [, Field2 ,...]);
```

Before executing the `CalcSums` method, we also need to specify any filters that we want to apply to the `Record` from which the sums are to be calculated. The `Fields` calculations take into account the filters that are currently applied to the record.

Executing the `CalcSums` function will cause the specified `Fields` totals to be calculated. Specification of the `BooleanVariable` allows us to handle any runtime error that may occur. Runtime errors for `CalcSums` usually result from a coding error or a change in a table key structure. If possible, `CalcSums` uses the defined SIFT. Otherwise, SQL Server creates totals on the fly.

Before the execution of `CalcSums`, `Fields` contained only the data from the individual record that was read. After the execution of `CalcSums`, the included `Fields` contain the totals that were calculated by the `CalcSums` method (these totals are only in memory, not in the database). These totals can then be used the same as data in any field; however, if we want to access the individual record's original data for that field, we must either save a copy of the record before executing the `CalcSums` or we must reread the record. The `CalcSums` must be executed for each read cycle through the subject table.

Comparing CalcFields and CalcSums

In the `Sales Header` table, there are FlowFields defined for `Amount` and `"Amount Including VAT"`. These FlowFields are all based on sums of entries in the `Sales Line` table. The `CalcFormula` for `Amount` is as follows:

```
sum("Sales Line".Amount where("Document Type" = field("Document
Type"), "Document No." = field("No.")));
```

> **Note**
>
> `CalcSums` can be used on any integer, big integer, or decimal field with any filter on any table, but for larger datasets, creating a key with a `SumIndexField` is recommended.

To calculate a `TotalOrderAmount` value while referencing the `SalesHeader` record, the code can be as simple as this:

```
SalesHeader.CalcFields(Amount);
TotalOrderAmount := SalesHeader.Amount;
```

To use `CalcSums` to calculate the same value from code directly referencing the `SalesLine` record, the required code is similar to the following (assuming a `SalesHeader` record has already been read):

```
SalesLine.SetRange("Document Type", SalesHeader."Document
Type");
SalesLine.SetRange("Document No.", SalesHeader."No.");
SalesLine.CalcSums(Amount);
TotalOrderAmount := SalesLine.Amount;
```

Looping in code is required when more than a single instance is necessary, such as records, or an array. Let's go through the repetitive statements in AL that we as developers use over and over.

AL control statements

Control statements execute the decision-making and resultant logic branches in executable code. The `if-then-else` **conditional statement**, as discussed in *Chapter 6, Introduction to AL*, is also a member of control statements.

Here, we will discuss the following repetitive statements, conditional statements, and flow control methods:

- `repeat-until`
- `while-do`
- `for-to` and `for-downto`
- `case-else`
- `Quit`, `Break`, `exit`, and `Skip`

> **Tip**
>
> For more possibilities (`foreach`), programming conventions, and examples, visit the *AL control statements* page in the Microsoft docs at `https://learn.microsoft.com/en-us/dynamics365/business-central/dev-itpro/developer/devenv-al-control-statements`.

repeat-until

`repeat-until` allows us to create a repetitive code loop, which **repeats** a block of code **until** a specific conditional expression evaluates to `true`. In that sense, `repeat-until` defines a block of code, operating somewhat like the `begin-end` compound statement structure that we covered in *Chapter 6, Introduction to AL*. `repeat` tells the system to keep reprocessing the block of code, while the `until` serves as the exit doorman, checking whether the conditions for ending the processing are true. Since the exit condition is not evaluated until the end of the loop, a `repeat-until` structure will always process at least once through the contained code.

`repeat-until` is very important in Business Central because it is often part of the data input cycle, along with the `Find-Next` structure, which will be covered shortly.

Here is an example of the `repeat-until` structure to process and sum data in the 10-element `CustSales` array:

```
LoopCount := 0;
Repeat
    LoopCount := LoopCount + 1;
    TotCustSales := TotCustSales + CustSales[LoopCount];
until LoopCount = 10;
```

while-do

A `while-do` control structure allows us to create a repetitive code loop that will **do** (execute) a block of code **while** a specific conditional expression evaluates to `true`. `while-do` is different from `repeat-until`, both because it may need a `begin-end` structure to define the block of code to be executed repetitively (`repeat-until` does not), and because it has different timings for the evaluation of the exit condition.

The syntax of the `while-do` control structure is as follows:

```
while <Condition> do <Statement>;
```

The `Condition` can be any Boolean expression that evaluates to `true` or `false`. The `Statement` can be simple or the most complex compound `begin-end` statement. Most `while-do` loops will be based on a `begin-end` block of code. The `Condition` will be evaluated at the beginning of the loop. When it evaluates to `false`, the loop will terminate. Thus, a `while-do` loop can be exited without processing.

A `while-do` structure to process data in the 10-element `CustSales` array is as follows:

```
LoopCount := 0;
while LoopCount < 10 do begin
    LoopCount := LoopCount + 1;
    TotCustSales := TotCustSales + CustSales[LoopCount];
end;
```

In Business Central, `repeat-until` is much more frequently used than `while-do`.

for-to or for-downto

The syntax for `for-to` and `for-downto` control statements are as follows:

```
for <Control Variable> := <Start Number> to <End Number> do
<Statement>;
for <Control Variable> := <Start Number> downto <End Number> do
<Statement>;
```

A `for` control structure is used when we wish to execute a block of code a specific number of times.

The `Control Variable` is an integer variable. `Start Number` is the beginning count for the `for` loop and `End Number` is the final count for the loop. If we wrote the `for LoopCount := 5 to 7 do [block of code]` statement, then `[block of code]` would be executed three times.

`for-to` increments the `Control Variable`. `for-downto` decrements the `Control Variable`.

> **Tip**
>
> We must be careful not to manipulate the `Control Variable` in the middle of our loop. Doing so will likely yield unpredictable results.

case-else statement

The `case-else` statement is a conditional expression, which is very similar to `if-then-else`, except that it allows more than two choices of outcomes for the evaluation of the controlling expression, and it stops checking other choices after a matching one has been found. The syntax of the `case-else` statement is as follows:

```
case <ExpressionToBeEvaluated> of
  <Value Set 1>: <Action Statement 1>;
  <Value Set 2>: <Action Statement 2>;
  <Value Set 3>: <Action Statement 3>;
  . . .
  . . .
  <Value Set n>: <Action Statement n>;
  [else <Action Statement n + 1>;
end;
```

The `ExpressionToBeEvaluated` must not be a record. The data type of the `Value Set` must be able to be automatically converted into the data type of the `ExpressionToBeEvaluated`. Each `Value Set` must be an expression, a set of values, or a range of values. The following example illustrates a typical instance of a `case-else` statement:

```
case Customer."Salesperson Code" of
    '2', '5', '9':
        Customer."Territory Code" := 'EAST';
    '16'..'20':
        Customer."Territory Code" := 'WEST';
    'N':
        Customer."Territory Code" := 'NORTH';
    '27'..'38':
        Customer."Territory Code" := 'SOUTH';
    else
        Customer."Territory Code" := 'FOREIGN';
    end;
```

In the preceding code example, we can see several alternatives for the `Value Set`. The first line (EAST) `Value Set` contains a list of values. If `"Salesperson Code"` is equal to `'2'`, `'5'`, or `'9'`, the EAST value will be assigned to `Customer."Territory Code"`. The second line, (WEST) `Value Set`, is a range of any value from `'16'` through `'20'`. The third line, (NORTH)

Value Set, is just a single value ('N'). If we look through the standard Business Central code, we will see that a single value is the most frequently used case structure in Business Central. In the fourth line of our example (SOUTH), the Value Set is again a range ('27'..'38'). If nothing in any Value Set matches ExpressionToBeEvaluated, the else clause will be executed, which sets Customer."TerritoryCode" to 'FOREIGN'.

An example of an if-then-else statement equivalent to the preceding case-else statement is as follows:

```
if Customer."Salesperson Code" in ['2', '5', '9'] then
    Customer."Territory Code" := 'EAST'
else
    if Customer."Salesperson Code" in ['16' .. '20'] then
        Customer."Territory Code" := 'WEST'
    else
        if Customer."Salesperson Code" = 'N' then
            Customer."Territory Code" := 'NORTH'
        else
            if Customer."Salesperson Code" in ['27' .. '38'] then
                Customer."Territory Code" := 'SOUTH'
            else
                Customer."Territory Code" := 'FOREIGN';
```

The following is a slightly less intuitive example of the case-else statement. In this instance, ExpressionToBeEvaluated is simply true and the Value Set statements are all conditional expressions. The first line containing a Value Set expression that evaluates to true will be the line whose Action Statement is executed:

```
case true of
    AvailableQty >= DemandQty:
        NeededQty := 0;
    AvailableQty < 0:
        NeededQty := DemandQty;
    else
        NeededQty := DemandQty - AvailableQty;
end;
```

Flow control methods

This group of AL methods also controls process flow. Each method acts to interrupt flow in different places and with different results. To get a full appreciation for how these functions are used, we should review them in code in Business Central.

Quit method

The Quit method is the ultimate processing interrupt for report or XMLport objects. When Quit is executed, processing immediately terminates, preventing even the OnPost<Object> triggers from being called. No database changes are committed. Quit is often used in reports to terminate processing when the report logic determines that no useful output will be generated by further processing.

The syntax of the Quit method is as follows:

```
CurrReport.Quit();
currXMLport.Quit();
```

Break method

Break can only be used in DataItem triggers in reports and XMLports. There, the Break method terminates the DataItem in which it occurs. It can be used to terminate the sequence of processing one DataItem segment of a report while allowing subsequent DataItem processing to continue.

The Break syntax is as follows:

```
CurrReport.Break();
currXMLport.Break();
```

exit statement

exit is used to end the processing within an AL trigger or a procedure, regardless of whether it is executed within a loop.

Called from a trigger or procedure that does not have a return value defined, exit is used without returning a value:

```
exit;
```

The syntax for exit inside procedures or triggers with a return value defined is as follows:

```
exit(ReturnValue);
```

The ReturnValue must be of the same data type as the return value defined by the calling procedure. It can be a constant, another procedure, or an expression returning a value. Using plain exit; inside procedures with a return value is allowed – however, the procedure will then return either the data type's initial value (if the procedure's return variable is unnamed) or the value that was assigned to the named return variable before exit was called.

We cannot write exit(); – as soon as brackets are used, a value must be passed.

Skip method

When executed, the `Skip` method will skip the remainder of the processing in the current record cycle of the current report or XmlPort trigger. Unlike `Break`, it does not terminate the DataItem processing completely. It can be used only in the `OnAfterGetRecord` trigger of a report or XMLport object. In reports, when the results of processing in the `OnAfterGetRecord` trigger are determined not to be useful for output, the `Skip` method is used to terminate that single iteration of the trigger without interfering with any subsequent processing.

The `Skip` syntax can be either of the following:

```
CurrReport.Skip();
currXMLport.Skip();
```

We've talked about exiting, ending, or skipping a procedure or trigger. Now we can move on to how to access and navigate reading from the data tables in Business Central. The looping mechanisms mentioned previously will come into play here in a big way.

CRUD record methods

CRUD (Create, Read, Update, and Delete) methods form the basis of interacting with the Microsoft SQL server. In the previous chapter, you learned about the basics of the `Find*` methods, which represent the "Read" part in CRUD. You learned about `FindSet` and `Find('-')` to read from the beginning of a selected set of records, as well as `Find('+')` to begin reading at the far end of the selected set of records.

Now we will review additional CRUD methods that are generally used in typical production code. While we are designing code that uses the `Modify` and `Delete` record methods, we need to consider possible interactions with other users on the system. There might be someone else modifying and deleting records in the same table that our application is updating.

We may want to utilize the `Record.ReadIsolation` method to gain total control of the data briefly while updating it, referred to as **locking**. We can find more information in the *Record instance isolation level* article in the Microsoft docs (`https://learn.microsoft.com/en-us/dynamics365/business-central/dev-itpro/developer/devenv-read-isolation`). The SQL Server database supports **record level locking**. There are a number of factors that we should consider when coding data locking in our processes.

Next method

The `Next` method is often used with `Find` or `FindSet` to step through the records of a table. The syntax defined for the `Next` method is as follows:

```
IntegerValue := Record.Next(ReadStepSize)
```

The full assignment statement format is rarely used to set an `IntegerValue`. In addition, there is no documentation for the usage of a non-zero `IntegerValue`. When `IntegerValue` goes to zero, it means a `Next` record was not found.

If the `ReadStepSize` value is negative, the table will be read in reverse; if `ReadStepSize` is positive (the default), the table will be read forward. The size of the value in `ReadStepSize` controls which records should be read. For example, if `ReadStepSize` is 2 or -2, then every second record will be read. If `ReadStepSize` is 10 or -10, then every tenth record will be read. The default value is 1, in which case every record will be read and the read direction will be forward.

In a typical data-read loop, the first read is a `Find` or `FindSet` method, followed by a `repeat-until` loop. The exit condition is the `until Record.Next() = 0;` expression. The full AL syntax for this typical loop looks as follows:

```
if Customer.FindSet() then
    repeat
        <Block of AL logic>
    until Customer.Next() = 0;
```

Insert method

The purpose of the `Insert` method is to add a new record to a table. The syntax for the `Insert` method is as follows:

```
[BooleanValue :=] Record.Insert([RunTriggerBoolean]);
```

If `BooleanValue` is not used and the `Insert` function fails (for example, if the insertion would result in a duplicate primary key), the process will terminate with an error. We should almost always handle a detected error in code using the `BooleanValue` and supplying our own error-handling logic, rather than allow a default termination.

By default, Business Central automatically buffers inserts in order to send them to Microsoft SQL Server at one time. By using **bulk inserts**, the number of server calls is reduced, thereby improving performance. However, we must be aware of bulk insert constraints, as documented at https://learn.microsoft.com/en-us/dynamics365/business-central/dev-itpro/administration/optimize-sql-bulk-inserts.

Caution

In case of unhandled insert errors, bulk inserts cause the debugger to stop at other code lines than on the `Insert` method.

The RunTriggerBoolean value controls whether or not the table's OnInsert trigger fires when the Insert occurs. The default value is false. Using the default value, we run the risk of not performing error checking that the table's designer assumed would be run when a new record was added.

> **Note**
>
> When we are reading a record set, and we also need to insert records into that same table, the Insert should be done to a separate instance of the table. We can use another variable for that second instance. If we Insert into the same table we are reading, we run the risk of reading the new records as part of our processing (likely a very confusing action). We also run the risk of changing the sequence of our processing unexpectedly due to the introduction of new records into our dataset. While the database access methods are continually improved by Microsoft and this warning may be overcautious, it is better to be safe than sorry.

Modify method

The purpose of the Modify method is to modify (update) existing data records. The syntax for Modify is as follows:

```
[BooleanValue :=] Record.Modify([RunTriggerBoolean ]);
```

If BooleanValue is not used and Modify fails, for example, if another process changes the record after it was read by this process, then the process will terminate with an error statement. The code should either handle a detected error or gracefully terminate the process. The RunTriggerBoolean value controls whether the table's OnModify trigger fires when this Modify occurs. The default value is false, which would not perform any OnModify processing.

> **Note**
>
> Modify cannot be used to cause a change in a primary key field. In that case, the Rename method must be used.

System-based checking can be performed to make sure that a Modify is done using the current version of the data record. This is done by making sure that another process hasn't modified and committed the record after it was read by this process. Our logic should refresh the record using the Get method, then change any values, and then call the Modify method.

Rec and xRec

In the table and page objects, the system automatically provides us with the system record variables, Rec and xRec. As both variables point to the current base table, they have the same fields. Until a record has been updated by Modify, Rec represents the current record data in process and xRec represents the record data before it was modified. By comparing field values in Rec and xRec, we can determine whether changes have been made to the record in the current process cycle.

Delete method

The purpose of the Delete function is to delete an existing data record. The syntax for Delete is as follows:

```
[BooleanValue :=] Record.Delete([RunTriggerBoolean]);
```

If Delete fails and the BooleanValue option is not used, the process will terminate with an error statement. Our code should handle any detected error or terminate the process gracefully, as appropriate.

The RunTriggerBoolean value is true or false, and it controls whether the table's OnDelete trigger fires when this Delete occurs. The default value is false. If we let the default false prevail, we run the risk of not performing error checking that the table's designer assumed would be run when a record was deleted.

In Business Central, there is a check to make sure that a Delete is using the current version of the record and to make sure that another process hasn't modified and committed the record after it was read by this process. An error will occur if the version being deleted is obsolete. To prevent this, a table lock would have to occur prior to the Find method, as Business Central does in many of the posting processes.

ModifyAll method

ModifyAll is the high-volume version of the Modify method. If we have a group of records in which we wish to modify one field in all of these records to the same new value, we should use ModifyAll. It is controlled by the filters that are applied at the time of invoking. The other choice for doing a mass modification would be a Find-Next loop in which we modify each record, one at a time. The advantage of ModifyAll is that it allows the developer and the system to optimize code for the volume update. Any system optimization will be a function of the SQL statements are generated by the AL compiler.

The syntax for ModifyAll is as follows:

```
Record.ModifyAll(FieldToBeModified, NewValue
[, RunTriggerBoolean]);
```

The RunTriggerBoolean value, a true or false entry, controls whether the table's OnModify trigger fires when this Modify occurs. The default value is false. In a typical situation, a filter or series of filters would be applied to a table, followed by the ModifyAll function. A simple example where we will reassign all Territory Code for a particular Salesperson to NORTH is as follows:

```
Customer.Reset();
Customer.SetRange("Salesperson Code", 'DAS');
Customer.ModifyAll("Territory Code", 'NORTH', true);
```

> **Note**
>
> While ModifyAll supports the table's OnModify trigger, it does not call the field's OnValidate trigger.
>
> During ModifyAll execution, all global variables of the record variable will be initialized to their default value.

DeleteAll method

DeleteAll is the high-volume version of the Delete method. If we have a group of records that we wish to delete, we should use DeleteAll. The other choice would be a Find-Next loop, in which we delete each record, one at a time. The advantage of DeleteAll is that it allows the developer and the system to optimize code for volume deletion. Any system optimization will be a function of what SQL statements are generated by the AL compiler.

The syntax for DeleteAll is as follows:

```
Record.DeleteAll([, RunTriggerBoolean]);
```

The RunTriggerBoolean value, a true or false entry, controls whether the table's OnDelete trigger fires when this Delete occurs. The default value is false. If the RunTriggerBoolean value is true, then the OnDelete trigger will fire for each record that's deleted. In that case, there is little to no speed advantage for DeleteAll versus the use of a FindSet-Delete-Next loop.

In a typical situation, a filter or series of filters would be applied to a table, followed by the DeleteAll method, similar to the preceding example. Like ModifyAll, DeleteAll respects the filters that are set and does not do any referential integrity error checking.

CRUD is the basis for any database-based application, but Business Central offers much more than that. There are many ways that Business Central allows the developer to locate the correct records and limit the dataset returned to just what is needed, in as efficient a way as possible.

Filtering methods

Few other systems have filtering implemented as comprehensively as Business Central, nor do they have it tied so neatly to the detailed retention of historical data. The result of Business Central's features is that even the most basic implementation of Business Central includes very powerful data analysis capabilities that are available to the end user.

As developers, we should appreciate the fact that we cannot anticipate every need of any user, let alone anticipate all the needs of all users. We know we should give the users as much freedom as possible to allow them to selectively extract and review data from their system. Wherever feasible, users should be given the opportunity to apply their own filters so that they can determine the optimum selection of data for their particular situation. On the other hand, freedom, here as everywhere, is a double-edged sword. With the freedom to decide just how to segment our data comes the responsibility of figuring out what constitutes a good segmentation to address the problem at hand.

As experienced application software designers and developers, we presumably have considerable insight into good ways to analyze and present the data. On that basis, it may be appropriate for us to provide some predefined selections. In some cases, constraints of the data structure only allow a limited set of options to make sense. In such a case, we should provide specific access to data (through pages, queries, and/or reports). However, we should allow more sophisticated users to access and manipulate the data flexibly on their own.

When applying filters using any of these options, be very conscious of the table key that will be activated when the filter takes effect. In a table containing a lot of data, filtering on a field that is not very high in the currently active key (in other words, not near the beginning of the key field sequence) may result in poor (or even very poor) response time for the users. In the same context, in a system suffering from a poor response time during processing, we should first investigate the relationships of active keys to applied filters, as well as how the keys are maintained. This may require SQL Server expertise, in addition to Business Central expertise.

The `SetCurrentKey`, `SetFilter`, and `SetRange` methods are important in the context of data filtering. These were reviewed in *Chapter 6, Introduction to AL*, so we won't review them again here.

CopyFilter and CopyFilters methods

These methods allow you to copy the filter of a single field or all the filters on a record (table) and apply those filters to another record.

For single fields, the `CopyFilter` syntax is as follows:

```
FromRecord.CopyFilter(FromField, ToRecord.ToField);
```

The `From` and `To` fields must be of the same data type. The `From` and `To` records do not have to point to the same table.

For copying all filters, `CopyFilters` is used as follows:

```
ToRecord.CopyFilters(FromRecord)
```

`ToRecord` and `FromRecord` must be different instances of the same table.

> **Note**
> The `CopyFilter` field-based method begins with the `FromRecord` variable, while the `CopyFilters` record-based method begins with the `ToRecord` variable.

GetFilter and GetFilters methods

These methods allow us to retrieve the filter on a single field or all the filters on a record (table) and assign the result to a text variable. Their syntax is as follows:

```
ResultString := FilteredRecord.GetFilter(FilteredField);
ResultString := FilteredRecord.GetFilters();
```

Similar functions exist for query objects. Those syntaxes are as follows:

```
ResultString := FilteredQuery.GetFilter(FilteredColumn);
ResultString := FilteredQuery.GetFilters();
```

The text contents of the `ResultString` will contain an identifier for each filtered field and the currently applied value of the filter. `GetFilters` is often used to retrieve the filters on a table and print them as part of a report heading. The `ResultString` for `GetFilters` on a `Customer` table will look similar to the following:

```
No.: 10000..99999, Balance: >0
```

FilterGroup method

The `FilterGroup` method can change or retrieve the filter group that is applied to a table or a query data item. A filter group contains a set of filters that were previously applied to the table or query by the `SetFilter` or `SetRange` methods, or as object properties. The `FilterGroup` syntax is as follows:

```
[CurrentGroupInteger ] :=Record.FilterGroup([NewGroupInteger]);
```

Using just the `Record.FilterGroup([NewFilterGroupInteger])` portion sets the active **filter group**.

All the currently defined filter groups are active and apply in combination (in other words, they are logically ANDed, resulting in a logical intersection of the sets). The only way to eliminate the effect of a filter group is to remove the filters in a group.

The default filter group for Business Central is 0 (zero). Users have access to the filters in this filter group. Other filter groups, numbered up through 7, have assigned Business Central uses. We should not redefine the use of any of these filter groups but use higher numbers for any custom filter groups in our code.

> **Note**
> Check out the Microsoft docs for *Record.FilterGroup([Integer]) Method* for more information (https://learn.microsoft.com/en-us/dynamics365/business-central/dev-itpro/developer/methods-auto/record/record-filtergroup-method).

One use of a filter group is to assign a filter that the user cannot see is operative and cannot change. Our code could change the filter group, set a special filter, and then return the active filter group to its original state. The following lines of code are an example of this:

```
Rec.FilterGroup(10);
Rec.SetRange("Salesperson Code", 'MIKE');
Rec.FilterGroup(0);
```

This could be used to apply special application-specific permissions to a particular system function, such as filtering out access to customers by salespeople so that each salesperson can only examine data for their own customers.

Mark method

A mark on a record is an indicator that disappears when the current session ends and is only visible to the process that is setting the mark. The Mark method sets the mark. The syntax is as follows:

```
[BooleanValue := ] Record.Mark([SetMarkBoolean]);
```

If the optional BooleanValue and assignment operator (:=) are present, the Mark method will give us the current Mark status (true or false) of the record. If the optional SetMarkBoolean parameter is present, the record will be marked (or unmarked) according to that value (true or false). The default value for SetMarkBoolean is false.

> **Note**
> Marks should be used carefully, and only when a simpler solution is not readily available. Marking records can cause significant performance problems on large datasets.

ClearMarks method

`ClearMarks` clears all the marks from the specified record, that is, from the particular instance of the table in this instance of the object. The syntax is as follows:

```
Record.ClearMarks();
```

MarkedOnly method

`MarkedOnly` is a special filtering function that can apply a mark-based filter.

The syntax for `MarkedOnly` is as follows:

```
[BooleanValue := ] Record.MarkedOnly([SeeMarkedRecordsOnlyBoolean]);
```

If the optional `BooleanValue` parameter is defined, it will be assigned a `true` or `false` value to tell us whether the special `MarkedOnly` filter is active. Omitting the `BooleanValue` parameter, `MarkedOnly` will set the special filter depending on the value of `SeeMarkedRecordsOnlyBoolean`. If that value is `true`, it will filter to show only marked records; if that value is `false`, it will remove the marked filter and show all records. The default value for `SeeMarkedRecordsOnlyBoolean` is `false`.

Although it may not seem logical, there is no option to see only the unmarked records. A possible method would be to set a boolean field value and filter on that instead.

Reset method

This method allows us to reset, that is, clear all filters in all filter groups that are currently applied to a record. `Reset` also sets the current key back to the primary key and the current filter group back to `0`. It removes any marks and clears all internal variables (not fields) in the current instance of the record. The syntax is `FilteredRecord.Reset();`.

So far, we have focused on business logic used within an object, a trigger, or a procedure. What about calling a different object or procedure? We will discuss this in the following section, *Inter-object communication*, namely data sharing, passing procedure parameters, and executing objects.

Inter-object communication

There are several ways to communicate between objects during Business Central processing. We will review some of the more commonly used ways in the following sections.

Communicating through data

The most widely used and simplest communication method is through data tables. For example, the `No. Series` table in the Business Foundation app is the central control for all document numbers.

Each object that assigns numbers to a document (for example, order, invoice, shipment, and so on) uses the 310 "No. Series" or 308 "No. Series - Batch" codeunits to access the No. Series table for the next number to use. It then updates the No. Series table so that the next object needing to assign a number to the same type of document will have the updated information.

Communicating through procedure parameters

When an object calls a procedure in another object, information is generally passed through the calling and return parameters. The calling and return parameter specifications are defined when the procedure is developed. The generic syntax for a procedure call is as follows:

```
[ReturnValue := ] ProcedureName([Parameter1, Parameter2, ...])
```

The rules for including or omitting the various optional fields are specific to the local variables that are defined for each individual procedure. As developers, when we design the procedure, we define the rules and thereby determine just how communications with the procedure will be handled. It is obviously important to define complete and consistent parameter-passing rules prior to beginning a development project.

Communication via object calls

Sometimes, we need to create an object that calls other objects. We may simply want to allow the user to be able to run a series of processes and reports but only enter the controlling parameters once. Our user interface object will be responsible for invoking the subordinate objects after having communicated the setup and filter parameters.

An important set of standard methods has been designed for various modes and circumstances of invoking other objects. Examples of these methods are SetTableView, SetRecord, and GetRecord on pages (there are others as well). There are also instances where we will need to build our own data-passing procedure.

To properly manage these relatively complex processes, we need to be familiar with the various versions of the Run and RunModal methods. We will also need to understand the meaning and effect of a single instance or multiple instances of an object. Briefly, the key differences between invoking a page or report object from within another object through Run versus RunModal are as follows:

- Run will clear the instance of the invoked object every time the run completes, which means that all of the internal variables are initialized. This clearing behavior does not apply to a codeunit object; the state will be maintained across multiple calls to Run.

- RunModal does not clear the instance of the invoked object, so internal global variables are not reinitialized each time the object is called. The object can be reinitialized using Clear(Object).

- `RunModal` does not allow any other object to be active in the same user session while it is running, whereas `Run` allows another object instance to run in parallel with the object instance initiated by `Run`.

Covering these topics in more detail is too advanced for this book, but once you have mastered the material covered here, you should study the information in the Microsoft docs section that relates to this topic. There is also pattern documentation on this topic, which is defined at `https://alguidelines.dev/docs/navpatterns/patterns/posting-routine-select-behavior/`. Though it was written for C/AL code, it still applies.

That was a lot of material to cover. Let's do some exercises to put all the knowledge we have gained into practice!

Enhancing the WDTU application

Now that we have some new tools to work with, let's enhance our WDTU application. This time, our goal is to implement functionality to allow the program manager to plan the playlist schedules for radio shows. The process, from the user's point of view, will essentially be as follows:

1. Call up the **Playlist Document** page that displays the header, details, and FactBox workspaces.
2. Enter `Playlist Header` using the `Radio Show` table data.
3. Enter `Playlist Line` using the `Resource` table for DJ data; the `Radio Show` table data for news, weather, or sports shows; and the `Item` table data for music, **Public Service Announcements** (**PSAs**), and advertisements.
4. The FactBox will display the required program-element fields from `Radio Show/Playlist Header`. These will include news (yes or no), weather (yes or no), sports (yes or no), and the number of required PSAs and advertisements.
5. The FactBox will also track each of the five possible required elements.

Since this development effort is an exercise to learn more about developing Business Central applications, we have some specific Business Central AL components we want to use so that we can learn more about them. Among those are the following:

- Create a `case` statement as well as a multipart `if` statement for contrast
- Add code to the `OnValidate` trigger of fields in a table
- Implement a lookup into a related table to access needed data
- Cause FlowFields to be processed for display
- Implement a FactBox to display `Radio Show` requirements for news, sports, weather, PSAs, and advertisements
- Create a new procedure, passing a parameter in and getting results passed back

As with any application enhancement, there will be a number of auxiliary tasks we'll have to accomplish to get the job done. These include adding some new fields to one or more tables. Not surprisingly, adding new data fields often leads to adding the new fields to one or more pages for maintenance or display. We'll have to create some test data in order to test our modifications. It's not unusual in the course of an enhancement to also find that other changes are needed to support the new functionality.

Modifying table fields

Since we want the Business Central tables to be the core of the design and to host as much of the processing as makes sense, we will start our enhancement work with table modifications.

The first table modification is to add the data fields to the `Playlist Header` table, as shown in the following code snippet, to support the definition and tracking of various program segment requirements. In the `Radio Show` table, each show has requirements defined for a specific number of PSAs and advertisements, as well as for the presence of news, sports, and weather spots. The `Playlist Header` table needs this requirement information stored, along with the associated PSA and advertisement counts for this show instance. We will obtain the news, sports, and weather line counts by means of a procedure call.

We can copy fields 12 to 19 from the `Radio Show` table into the `Playlist Header` table, remove their `InitValue`, renumber fields 12 to 11, and manually add `Count` fields 10 and 12 as follows:

```
field(10; "PSA Count"; Integer) { }
field(11; "PSAs Required"; Boolean) { }
field(12; "Ads Count"; Integer) { }
field(13; "Ads Required"; Boolean) { }
field(14; "News Required"; Boolean) { }
field(15; "News Duration"; Duration) { }
field(16; "Sports Required"; Boolean) { }
field(17; "Sports Duration"; Duration) { }
field(18; "Weather Required"; Boolean) { }
field(19; "Weather Duration"; Duration) { }
```

Since `Playlist Line` includes an Enum field that identifies the PSA and advertisement records, we will use a FlowField to calculate the counts for each of those line types. We will construct the FlowField definition for the `PSA Count` field as follows:

```
field(10; "PSA Count"; Integer)
{
    FieldClass = FlowField;
    CalcFormula = count("Playlist Line" where ("Document No." =
    field("No."), Type = const(Item), "Data Format" = const(PSA)));
    Editable = false;
}
```

The Ads Count FlowField will look very similar:

```
field(12; "Ads Count"; Integer)
{
    FieldClass = FlowField;
    CalcFormula = count("Playlist Line" where ("Document
    No." = field("No."), Type = const(Item), "Data Format" =
    const(Advertisement)));
    Editable = false;
}
```

The only additional change we want to make to the Playlist Line table is to ensure that the Duration field is not editable. We do this so that the Start Time and End Time entries define Duration rather than the other way around. Making the Duration field non-editable is done by simply setting the field's Editable property to false:

```
field(8; Duration; Duration)
{
    Editable = false;
}
```

Creating the Playlist document page

In *Chapter 2, Tables*, we created the editable Playlist Document List page (page 50103). We are now going to create the corresponding PlaylistDocument.page.al document page. The easiest way to do so is to create a new empty text file and use the tpage snippet (with the **Page** subtype). After setting the ID to 50104 and the name to "Playlist Document", we change the PageType property to Document, and set SourceTable to "Playlist Header". As the list page shall remain the only page to be found by **Tell me**, we additionally specify None as the UsageCategory for the document page. We now copy all fields from the list's repeater control into the document's group control (that we rename to Playlist). As the last step, we delete any existing actions or var areas.

Next, we'd like to call the new document page from the list page, simply by adding the CardPageId = "Playlist Document"; property to the list page. As we want users to enter or modify playlist data on the new document page only, we prevent changes on the list page by setting the Editable = false; property.

We need validation logic for both our Playlist tables, that is, Header and Line. We will start with Playlist Header validation.

Playlist Header validation

The `Playlist Header` data fields are as follows (note that FlowField definitions and table relations will not be shown in detail):

- `No.`: This is the ID number for this instance of a radio show; its contents are user-defined

- `Radio Show No.`: This is selected from the `Radio Show` table (set `TableRelation`)

- `Description`: This is displayed by means of a lookup FlowField from the `Radio Show` table

- `Broadcast Date`: This is the show's scheduled broadcast date; it also serves as the posting date for any data analysis filtering

- `Start Time`: This is the show's scheduled broadcast start time

- `End Time`: This is the show's scheduled broadcast end time

- `Duration`: This is the show's broadcast length, displayed by means of a lookup FlowField from the `Radio Show` table

- `PSAs Required` and `Ads Required`: These show whether PSAs and advertisements are required for broadcast during the show; they are copied from the `Radio Show` table

- `News Required`, `Sports Required`, and `Weather Required`: These check whether each of these program segments is required during the show; they are copied from the `Radio Show` table

> **Tip**
>
> If we've already published fields as normal fields, then turned them into FlowFields and tried to publish them again, we will receive a **Removing fields is not allowed** error in Visual Studio Code. To circumvent this, update the `launch.json schemaUpdateMode` setting to `ForceSync` and publish again. Note that any data previously stored in the field is now lost. After publishing, delete the setting, or set it to the default (`Synchronize`) to prevent accidental table schema changes.

When the user chooses the `Radio Show` to be scheduled, we want the five different feature requirements fields in the `Playlist Header` to be filled in by AL logic using the following validation code:

```
field(2; "Radio Show No."; Code[20])
{
    TableRelation = "Radio Show"."No.";
    trigger OnValidate()
    var
        RadioShow: Record "Radio Show";
    begin
```

```
        if RadioShow.Get("Radio Show No.") then begin
            "PSAs Required" := RadioShow."PSAs Required";
            "Ads Required" := RadioShow."Ads Required";
            "News Required" := RadioShow."News Required";
            "Sports Required" := RadioShow."Sports Required";
            "Weather Required" := RadioShow."Weather Required";
        end else begin
            "PSAs Required" := false;
            "Ads Required" := false;
            "News Required" := false;
            "Sports Required" := false;
            "Weather Required" := false;
        end;
    end;
}
```

Even though the Radio Show No. was entered in the data field, our validation code needs to read the Radio Show record (here, defined as the local RadioShow variable). Once we have read the Radio Show record, we can assign all five show feature requirements fields from the Radio Show record into the Playlist Header record.

Then, because two fields in the Playlist Header record are lookup FlowFields, we need to update the Playlist Document page after the entry of the Radio Show No.. The update is done through a CurrPage.Update() command, as shown in the following snippet:

```
field("Radio Show No."; Rec."Radio Show No.")
{
    trigger OnValidate()
    begin
        CurrPage.Update();
    end;
}
```

> **Tip**
>
> An alternative approach to the page update is adding validation code to the Radio Show No. table field that will calculate the Description and Duration FlowFields using the CalcFields method.

Returning to the Playlist Header table, the next validation we need is to calculate the End Time as soon as the Start Time is entered. The calculation is simple: add the length (the Run Time field) of the show to the Start Time. We have defined the Duration field in the Playlist Header to be a lookup reference (FlowField) to the source field in the Radio Show record. As a result, to calculate with that field, we would need to use a `CalcFields` method first. Instead, we'll obtain the show length from the `Radio Show` record:

```
field(6; "Start Time"; Time)
{
    trigger OnValidate()
    var
        RadioShow: Record "Radio Show";
    begin
        RadioShow.Get("Radio Show No.");
        "End Time" := "Start Time" + RadioShow."Run Time";
    end;
}
```

Now we can see that we have one of those situations that we sometimes encounter when developing a modification. It might have been better to have the `Duration` field of `Playlist Header` be a normal data field rather than a FlowField. If this is the only place where we will use `Duration` from `Playlist Header` for calculation or assignment, then the current design is fine. Otherwise, perhaps we should change the `Duration` field to a `Normal` field and assign `Run Time` from `RadioShow` to it at the same time the several requirements fields are assigned. At this point, though, for the purposes of our WDTU scenario, we will stick with what we have already created.

Creating the Playlist subpage

Another necessary part of a document page is the subpage. Our subpage can be created using the `tpage` snippet (the **Page of type List** subtype) based on the `Playlist Line` table, and define it as `page 50109 "Playlist Subpage"`. Remember to set the `PageType` to `ListPart`, and the `UsageCategory` to `None`. We can also remove any placeholders for FactBoxes or actions. The result will be as follows:

```
page 50109 "Playlist Subpage"
{
    PageType = ListPart;
    ApplicationArea = All;
    UsageCategory = None;
    SourceTable = "Playlist Line";

    layout
    {
        area(Content)
        {
            repeater(GroupName)
            {
                field(Type; Rec.Type) { }
```

```
                    field("No."; Rec."No.") { }
                    field("Data Format"; Rec."Data Format") { }
                    field(Description; Rec.Description) { }
                    field(Duration; Rec.Duration) { }
                    field("Start Time"; Rec."Start Time") { }
                    field("End Time"; Rec."End Time") { }
                }
            }
        }
    }
```

To make the document work the way we are used to having Business Central document pages work, we will need to set some properties for this new page:

```
AutoSplitKey = true;
DelayedInsert = true;
```

We have set the DelayedInsert and AutoSplitKey properties to true. These settings will allow the Playlist Line to not be saved until the primary key fields are all entered (DelayedInsert), and will support the easy insertion of new entries between two existing lines (AutoSplitKey).

Finally, we will need to connect our new Playlist Subpage page to the Playlist Document page to give us a basic and complete document page. All we need to do to accomplish that is add a new part section to the Playlist Document page, on the same level as the group controls:

```
part(Lines; "Playlist Subpage")
{
    SubPageLink = "Document No." = field("No.");
    SubPageView = sorting("Document No.", "Line No.");
}
```

Now that the Playlist subpage has been created, let's return to the underlying table, Playlist Line, and add the missing validation code there.

Playlist Line validations

The Playlist Line data fields are as follows:

- Document No.: This is the automatically assigned SubPageLink to the No. field in the parent Playlist Header record, as per Playlist Document page part properties

- Line No.: This is an automatically assigned number (based on page properties that we have already set), and the rightmost field in the Playlist Line primary key

- Type: This is a user-selected Option that defines whether this entry is a Resource, such as an announcer; a Show, such as a news show; or an Item, such as a recording to play on the air

- No.: This is the ID number of the selected entry in its parent Type table
- Data Format: This is information from the Item table for a show or recording
- Description: This is assigned from the parent table, but can be edited by the user
- Duration, Start Time and End Time: Assigned from the Item table, this is information about a show or recording that indicates the length and its position within the schedule of this Radio Show

The source of contents of the No., Data Format, Description, and time-related fields of the record depend on the Type field. If the Type field is Resource, the fields are filled in from the Resource table; for Item, from the Item table; and for Show, from the Radio Show table.

To support this, our OnValidate trigger in the No. field looks at the Type entry and uses a case statement to choose which set of actions to take.

First, we will build the basic case statement, as shown in the following code snippet, and compile it. That way, we can ensure that we've got all the components of the structure in place and only need to fill in the logic for each of the option choices:

```
trigger OnValidate()
begin
    case Type of
        Type::Resource:
            begin
            end;
        Type::Item:
            begin
            end;
        Type::Show:
            begin
            end;
    end;
end;
```

Next, we must add a variable for each of the tables from which we will pull the Resource, Item, and Show data. The use of IntelliSense makes it much easier to find the correct field names for each of the variables we want to select to assign to the Playlist Line record fields:

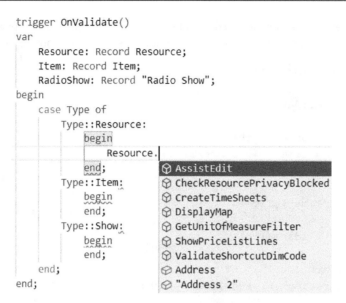

Figure 7.2 – Using IntelliSense to add code

When we are all done constructing the case statement, it should look like this:

```
case Type of
    Type::Resource:
        begin
            Resource.Get("No.");
            Description := Resource.Name;
        end;
    Type::Item:
        begin
            Item.Get("No.");
            Description := Item.Description;
            "Data Format" := Item."Data Format";
            Duration := Item.Duration;
        end;
    Type::Show:
        begin
            RadioShow.Get("No.");
            Description := RadioShow.Name;
        end;
end;
```

The last set of OnValidate code we need to add is to calculate the End Time from the supplied Start Time and Duration (or Start Time from End Time and Duration):

```
field(9; "Start Time"; Time)
{
    trigger OnValidate()
    begin
        if Duration <> 0 then
            "End Time" := "Start Time" + Duration;
    end;
}
field(10; "End Time"; Time)
{
    trigger OnValidate()
    begin
        if "Start Time" <> 0T then
            Duration := "End Time" - "Start Time";
    end;
}
```

Obviously, the design could be expanded to have the Duration value be user-editable, along with an appropriate change in the AL logic. After our initial work on the Playlist functionality is completed, making that change would be a good exercise for you. The addition of the "housekeeping" commands to clear out fields that are not used by the assigned record Type, such as clearing the Data Format field for a RadioShow record, would also be a good exercise.

Creating a procedure for our FactBox

For this application, we want our FactBox to display information relating to the specific radio show we are scheduling. The information to be displayed includes the five show segment requirements and the status of fulfillment (counts) of those requirements. The requirements come from the Playlist Header fields: PSAs, advertisements, news, sports, and weather are required. The counts come from summing up data in the Playlist Line records for a show. We can use the Playlist Header field's PSA Count and Ads Count for those two counts. These counts can be obtained through the FlowField property definitions we defined earlier for these two fields.

For the other three counts, news, weather, and sports, we must read through the Playlist Line and sum up each of the counts. To accomplish that, we'll create a procedure that we can call from the FactBox page. Since our new procedure is local to the Playlist Header and Playlist Line tables, we will define the procedure in the Playlist Header (table 50102).

The logic of our counting process is described in the following pseudocode:

1. Filter the `Playlist Line` table for `Radio Show` we are scheduling and for segment entries that represent shows.

2. Look up the `Radio Show` record for each of those records.

3. In the `Radio Show` record, use the `Radio Show Type` field to determine which `Playlist Line` counter should be incremented.

Based on this logic, we must have local variables defined for the two tables: `Playlist Line`, and `Radio Show`.

Translating our pseudocode into executable AL, our procedure looks as follows:

```
procedure GetNewsWeatherSportsCount(Category: Option
,News,Weather,Sports) Count: Integer
var
  PlaylistLine: Record "Playlist Line";
  RadioShow: Record "Radio Show";
begin
  PlaylistLine.SetRange("Document No.", "No.");
  PlaylistLine.SetRange(Type, PlaylistLine.Type::Show);
  if PlaylistLine.FindSet() then
    repeat
      RadioShow.Get(PlaylistLine."No.");
      case Category of
        Category::News:
          if RadioShow."Radio Show Type" = 'NEWS' then
            Count += 1;
        Category::Weather:
          if RadioShow."Radio Show Type" = 'WEATHER' then
            Count += 1;
        Category::Sports:
          if RadioShow."Radio Show Type" = 'SPORTS' then
            Count += 1;
      end;
    until PlaylistLine.Next = 0;
end;
```

In the process of writing this code, we noticed another design flaw. We defined the type of Radio Show with code that allows users to enter their choice of text strings. We just wrote code that depends on the contents of that text string being specific values. A better design would be to have the critical field be an Option or Enum data type in the Radio Show Type table so that we can depend on the choices being members of a predefined set. We will continue with our example with the design as is, but you should consider how to improve it. Making that improvement will be excellent practice.

Creating a FactBox page

All the hard work is now done. We just have to define a FactBox page and add it to the Playlist page. First, we create a new file and save it as PlaylistFactbox.page.al. We can create a FactBox page using the tpage snippet (with the **Page** subtype) to define page 50112 "Playlist Factbox". Then, we will set the page properties as follows:

```
PageType = CardPart;
ApplicationArea = All;
UsageCategory = None;
SourceTable = "Playlist Header";
```

Our FactBox will contain the fields from the Playlist Header that relate to two of the five required show segments, that is, the PSA Count and Ads Count fields. We will also add all fields ending with Required. We will delete the field group and place the fields directly in the Content area:

```
layout
{
    area(Content)
    {
        field("PSAs Required"; Rec."PSAs Required") { }
        field("PSA Count"; Rec."PSA Count") { }
        field("Ads Required"; Rec."Ads Required") { }
        field("Ads Count"; Rec."Ads Count") { }
        field("News Required"; Rec."News Required") { }
        field(NewsCount; Rec.GetNewsWeatherSportsCount(1)) { }
        field("Weather Required"; Rec."Weather Required") { }
        field(WeatherCount; Rec.GetNewsWeatherSportsCount(2)) { }
        field("Sports Required"; Rec."Sports Required") { }
        field(SportsCount; Rec.GetNewsWeatherSportsCount(3)) { }
    }
}
```

At this point, we will need to add the logic to take advantage of the `GetNewsWeatherSportsCount` procedure that we created earlier. This procedure is designed to return the count of the segment type that's identified in the calling parameter. Since a page field source can be an expression, we can simply add the procedure calls to new page fields with an appropriate name defined. We will intersperse the new `Count` fields for a consistent appearance on the page:

```
field("News Required"; Rec."News Required") { }
field("News Count"; Rec.GetNewsWeatherSportsCount(1)) { }
field("Weather Required"; Rec."Weather Required") { }
field("Weather Count"; Rec.GetNewsWeatherSportsCount(2)) { }
field("Sports Required"; Rec."Sports Required") { }
field("Sports Count"; Rec.GetNewsWeatherSportsCount(3)) { }
```

> **Tip**
>
> `Option` and `Enum` variables can be referenced by the ordinal or named value. In this example, we are passing the ordinal value. To pass the option value as a name (`Category::Sports`) instead of an integer (3), we need to add a new global variable and pass that for the parameter value. If the procedure used an `Enum` parameter instead, we could have passed the value by name even without a global variable (`Enum::EnumName::Sports`).

We finish the FactBox development by deleting the `actions` and `var` sections previously inserted by the snippet.

One final development step is required. We must connect the new FactBox Card Part to the `Playlist Document` page. All that is required in `Playlist Document` is to define the `FactBoxes` area beneath the `Content` area, and to add our FactBox as an element in that area:

```
area(FactBoxes)
{
    part(Factbox; "Playlist Factbox")
    {
        SubPageLink = "No." = field("No.");
    }
}
```

Multiple FactBoxes can be part of a primary page. If we look at page 21, **Customer Card**, we will see a `FactBoxes` area with more than ten FactBoxes, of which two are system parts. Most of them, however, are not visible by default.

The end result of our development effort is shown in the following screenshot when we run page `50104`, **Playlist Document**, with some sample test data, which we entered by running the various tables:

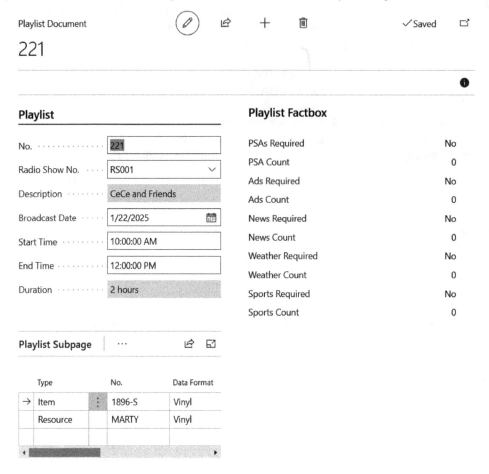

Figure 7.3 – Running the Playlist Document page

Having a page with lines and key information available all on the same screen is wonderful, but what if you can't understand any of the text? Next, we will explain the different methods available to AL developers to implement multiple languages within the application and extensions.

Multi-language system

The Business Central system is designed as a multi-language system, meaning it can interface with users in many languages. The base product is distributed with American English as the primary language, but each local version comes with one or more other languages ready for use. Additional languages can be installed as apps from the **Microsoft AppSource**. Users can switch their individual application language at any time on the **My Settings** page. The change is immediate, once they've been automatically signed out and in again, and it will be applied on all devices.

Since the system can display interfaces in several different languages, Business Central is particularly suitable for firms operating from a central system serving users in multiple countries. Business Central is used by businesses all over the world, operating in dozens of different languages. It is important to note that, when the application language is changed, it has no effect on the data in the database. The data is not multi-language unless we provide that functionality by means of our own enhancements or data structure.

The translations for the user interface are provided directly in AL.

Translations in AL

When developing in AL, there are two methods of providing translations:

1. Adding all translations (including English) directly as an *ML named property to a field, group, and so on, such as `CaptionML = ENU = 'Name', ESP = 'Nombre';`, is the first method. The languages are provided as the standard Windows three-letter language ID. For texts in messages, errors, and so on, the `TextConst` data type is used. The programmer provides all translations in time of defining corresponding properties. If no translation for the current client language is found, the name will be displayed in the UI. Direct translation is the usual way of translating **Per Tenant Extensions** (**PTEs**) for customers.

2. Providing all translations in a separate **translation file** (`*.xlf` file, also referred to as **XLIFF file**) per target language, such as `*.de-DE.xlf` for the German language, is the second method. The programmer provides the English version only in properties without the *ML ending, for example, `Caption = 'Name';`, or using the `Label` data type for message and error texts. During compilation, all translatable texts are automatically gathered in one `*.g.xlf` file. The file can be passed to external translators or a translation memory. The translated version of the file is then put back into code. If no translation was provided for the current client language, then the original (English) language will be displayed. This method is mandatory for developing apps for Microsoft AppSource, but it may also be used for other applications.

We cannot mix these methods within one extension; either we choose the direct approach in all files, or we work with translation files. When working with translation files, any direct translations will be ignored.

To learn more about enabling and managing translation files, visit *Working with translation files* in the Microsoft docs (`https://learn.microsoft.com/en-us/dynamics365/business-central/dev-itpro/developer/devenv-work-with-translation-files`).

> **Note**
>
> Our WDTU application provides (almost) no translations. In the client, it will be displayed in English, no matter which client language is chosen. This was decided to keep the code snippets in this book short and easy to read.

When developing real-life extensions, we should always stick to the following pattern (reduced to those elements that we have used for WDTU already):

- Define `Caption` or `CaptionML` in every object definition (except API pages and API queries), but also for every table field and enum value

- Define `Caption` or `CaptionML` for every page action, field group, or action group, as well as for all page fields that do not use a `SourceTable` field as their source

- Use the `Label` or `TextConst` data type for all messages, errors, and confirmation dialogs

- Whenever an `OptionMember` is defined, an `OptionCaption` or `OptionCaptionML` should also be provided

- In general, check and use the properties offered by IntelliSense

Applying these rules to the WDTU app and testing the translations in the client is a great practice!

In *Chapter 6, Introduction to AL*, we learned to use AL **dialog methods** (`Message`, `Error`, and `Confirm`) to not only communicate between the system and user but also for quick and simple testing or debugging. For more complex debugging scenarios, we will use the debugger in Visual Studio Code as our primary tool.

Debugging in AL

Debugging is the process of finding and correcting errors and performance bottlenecks by observing variables, SQL statistics, and data while running code. Business Central uses the debugger from Visual Studio Code, controlled by specific settings in the `launch.json` file. The launch configurations that we use for publishing our code are also valid for debugging.

The symbols in our `.alpackages` folder must match those in the environment we intend to debug in. If they do not, we must either publish our changes first or download the symbols from the environment.

> **Note**
>
> Full documentation of the debugging capabilities can be found in the *Debugging in AL* Microsoft docs article (https://learn.microsoft.com/en-us/dynamics365/business-central/dev-itpro/developer/devenv-debugging).

Before we activate the debugger for the first time, we must decide when exactly the code execution should be stopped. Without any **breakpoints**, the code runs without interruption when the debugger is active.

Breakpoints

The basic concept in debugging is the breakpoint, which is a mark that we set on a line of code. When the program flow reaches the breakpoint, the debugger stops execution until we instruct it to continue. We set (and remove) a breakpoint by placing the cursor somewhere on the target code line, and then pressing *F9*, or by calling it via **Run | Toggle Breakpoint**. Active breakpoints are represented in code by a solid circle to the left of the line number. An example is shown in the following code screenshot:

```
79        begin
● 80          PlaylistLine.SetRange("Document No.", "No.");
81          PlaylistLine.SetRange(Type, PlaylistLine.Type::Show);
```

Figure 7.4 – Active debugger breakpoint

> **Note**
>
> Breakpoints work on AL statements inside procedures and triggers only. Even with breakpoints set, the debugger neither breaks on properties nor definitions of any kind (fields, groups, etc.), nor on lines containing keywords only (`begin`, `end`, `repeat`, etc.).

In addition to breakpoint toggles, we can use the following `launch.json` settings to gain control over debugger breaks:

- `breakOnError` defaults to `None`, but it can be set to `All` and `ExcludeTry`, the latter being the preferred alternative in most cases. When it is not set to `None`, the debugger will automatically break at the next error.

- `breakOnRecordWrite` defaults to `None`, but it can be set to `All` and `ExcludeTemporary`. When it is not set to `None`, the debugger will automatically break on record changes. On `ExcludeTemporary`, the debugger ignores changes to temporary records.

Having at least one breakpoint, `breakOnError`, or `breakOnRecordWrite` set, we can now run the debugger.

Running the AL debugger

In Visual Studio Code, we can call any of the main debug commands using the **Command Palette** (*F1*), or using direct shortcuts:

- `AL: Debug without publishing` (*Ctrl + Shift + F5*)
- `AL: Publish with debugging` (*F5*)

This will launch a debugging session in a new browser window. Now, we will have to watch both the browser and Visual Studio Code.

> **Important**
>
> Debugging may be used in development or test environments only. For debugging production environments, we will cover the alternative (**snapshot debugging**) very soon.

To let the debugger stop the breakpoint that we have set in *Figure 7.4*, we first open the **Playlist Document List** in the web client, and then double-click one of the lines. In Visual Studio Code, the moveable **debug toolbar** at the top now indicates that we are in debugging mode, but we also should note the **debug sidebar** on the left, as well as the currently hit breakpoint in line **80**:

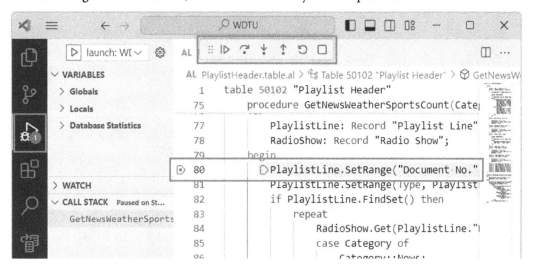

Figure 7.5 – Debugger stopping at a breakpoint

In the debug sidebar, we can now inspect **variables** and **database statistics**. Variables can be put into the **WATCH** section, either by typing them in manually or simply by choosing **Add to Watch**:

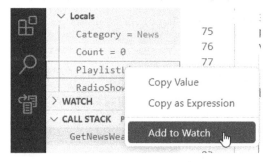

Figure 7.6 – Add to Watch

The **CALL STACK** view lists previous and clickable lines of code that were run until the current one was reached.

Using the debug toolbar actions, we can now jump to the next breakpoint (**Continue**, *F5*), to the next code line (**Step Over**, *F10*), into the currently called procedure (**Step Into**, *F11*), or to the next code line outside the current procedure or trigger (**Step Out**, *Shift + F11*).

> **Note**
>
> Don't forget to close the debugging session (**Stop**, *Shift + F5*), especially if you decide to publish code changes.

In the following sections, we will review further troubleshooting tools based on the debugger.

Attach and debug next

When we don't want to publish and invoke functionality to debug it, we can instead attach a session to a specified server and await a process to trigger the breakpoint we've set. Then debugging starts when the code that the breakpoint is set on is hit. We can also attach to a specific ongoing session, and we can debug on behalf of another user.

For more details and some configuration examples, refer to the Microsoft docs at `https://learn.microsoft.com/en-us/dynamics365/business-central/dev-itpro/developer/devenv-attach-debug-next`.

When we don't want to publish and invoke functionality to debug it, we can instead attach a session to a specified server, and await a process to trigger the breakpoint we've set. Then debugging starts when the code that the breakpoint is set on is hit. We can also attach to a specific ongoing session, and we can debug on behalf of another user.

Before invoking the attach functionality, we first need to create a new attach configuration in the `launch.json` file by setting `"request": "attach",`. The `breakOnNext` setting specifies the next client to break on when the debugging session starts. The available options are `WebServiceClient`, `WebClient`, and `Background`. The optional `sessionId` and `userId` properties allow attaching to an ongoing session and also debugging on behalf of another user.

After having set at least one breakpoint in our code, we can start an attach session by pressing *F5*.

For more details and some configuration examples, refer to the Microsoft docs at `https://learn.microsoft.com/en-us/dynamics365/business-central/dev-itpro/developer/devenv-attach-debug-next`.

Snapshot debugging and performance profiling

With snapshot debugging, we can record AL code that runs on the server, and when it has completed, we can debug the recorded snapshot in Visual Studio Code. Snapshot debugging lets us inspect code execution and variables in the production environment on a cloud service for a specified user session.

Detailed information on how to initialize a snapshot debugging session is documented at `https://learn.microsoft.com/en-us/dynamics365/business-central/dev-itpro/developer/devenv-snapshot-debugging`.

The **perfomance profiling** capabilities (also referred to as the **AL profiler**) allow us to collect data about performance and analyze this data with the goal of optimizing a certain area in the code or a certain process.

To learn more about the profiling capabilities, visit the Microsoft Docs *AL Profiler* article at `https://learn.microsoft.com/en-us/dynamics365/business-central/dev-itpro/developer/devenv-al-profiler-overview`.

Troubleshoot directly from the web client

We can open a new Visual Studio Code session directly from the web client for a specific customer production or sandbox environment. This enables performing troubleshooting, such as debugging, inspecting variables, setting breakpoints, and viewing source code. Depending on the context, Visual Studio Code opens to allow inspecting objects and source, and allows attaching to debug or snapshot debug and profile the current web client session.

From the Business Central web client, we can open Visual Studio Code in the following ways:

- Open a page from **Page Inspector**
- Troubleshoot the current session from within **Help and Support**

For more details, refer to the *Troubleshoot in Visual Studio Code directly from the web client* Microsoft Docs article (`https://learn.microsoft.com/en-us/dynamics365/business-central/dev-itpro/developer/devenv-troubleshoot-vscode-webclient`).

Summary

In this chapter, we covered a number of practical tools and topics regarding AL coding and development. We started by reviewing AL methods and then we dived into a long list of methods and statements that we will need on a frequent basis.

We covered a variety of selected data-centric methods, including some for computation and validation, some for data conversion, and others for date handling. Next, we reviewed methods that affect the flow of logic and the flow of data, including FlowFields, control statements, CRUD, and filtering. Then, we put a number of these to work in an enhancement for our WDTU application. Finally, we gained knowledge about the multilanguage system that Business Central provides, and about debugging in AL.

In the next chapter, we will move on from focusing on data from within the application and change the focus to outside Business Central. How can external systems read, write, or modify Business Central data? How do we get information from a system unrelated to the Microsoft Azure architecture? How do we not only exchange data, but validate, process, and manage it as well? Business Central offers many different toolsets to open that two-way communication through its **Application Programming Interfaces (APIs)**. We will learn about all of this in the next chapter.

Questions

1. Which three of the following are valid date-related Business Central functions?

    - `Date2DWY`

    - `CalcDate`

    - `DMY2Date`

    - `Date2Num`

    ANSWER: `Date2DWY`, `CalcDate`, `DMY2Date`

2. `Reset` is used to clear the current sort key setting from a record. True or false?

    ANSWER: False

3. The `Init` method is used to reset all the values in a record to the data type default or the `InitValue` property value. True or false?

    ANSWER: True

4. The `Format` method cannot convert which of the following data types to a string:

    - `Blob`

    - `DateTime`

    - `Decimal`

    - `Boolean`

    ANSWER: `Blob`

5. Which functions can be used to cause FlowFields to be calculated? Choose two:

    - `CalcSums`

    - `CalcFields`

    - `SetAutoCalcFields`

    - `SumFlowField`

    ANSWER: `CalcFields`, `SetAutoCalcFields`

6. Which of the following functions should be used within a report's `OnAfterGetRecord` trigger to end processing just for a single iteration of the trigger? Choose one:

    - `exit`

    - `Break`

    - `Quit`

    - `Skip`

    ANSWER: `Skip`

7. The `WorkDate` value can be set to a different value from the system date. True or false?

    ANSWER: True

8. Only one FactBox is allowed on a page. True or false?

    ANSWER: False

9. Braces { } are used as a special form of a repeating `case` statement. True or false?

    ANSWER: False

10. Which of the following is not a valid AL flow control combination? Choose one:

    - `repeat-until`

    - `do-until`

    - `case-else`

    - `if-then`

    ANSWER: `do-until`

11. The `repeat-until` looping structure is most often used to control data reading processes. True or false?

    ANSWER: True

12. Which of the following formats of `Modify` will cause the table›s `OnModify` trigger to fire? Choose one:

- `Modify`

- `Modify(true)`

- `Modify(Run)`

- `Modify(Ready)`

ANSWER: `Modify(true)`

13. A `case` statement structure should never be used in place of a nested `if` statement structure. True or false?

ANSWER: False

14. The `TestField` function can be used to assign new values to a variable. True or false?

ANSWER: False

15. The `OnValidate` trigger can be used to assign new values to a variable. True or false?

ANSWER: True

16. If `MaintainSiftIndex` is set to `false` and `CalcFields` is invoked, the process will terminate with an error. True or false?

ANSWER: False

17. `SetRange` is used to filter a single value or a sequential set for a single field. True or false?

ANSWER: True

18. It is not possible to directly debug a production cloud environment, alternative methods such as Snapshot Debugging are required. True or false?

Answer: True

19. How do you debug without invoking a process manually? Set the `"request"` in the `launch.json` file to which of the following:

- `"debug next"`

- `"attach"`

- `"session id"`

- None of the above

Answer: `"attach"`

20. When working with translation files, any direct translations will be ignored. True or false?

Answer: True

21. Switching languages for users in Business Central requires a web client restart. True or false?

Answer: False

Extensibility beyond AL

"It is far better to adapt the technology to the user than to force the user to adapt to the technology."

– Larry Marine

"Design must reflect the practical and aesthetic in business but above all good design must primarily serve people."

– Thomas J. Watson, Sr.

Business Central is extremely flexible and suitable for addressing many types of problems, so there are a lot of choices for advanced Business Central topics. First, we will discuss the different types of web services or **Application Programming Interfaces** (**APIs**) that are available in Business Central for external applications to interface with. These include **Simple Object Access Protocol** (**SOAP**), **Open Data Protocol** (**OData**), and **RESTful** web services. Each has its own benefits and use case scenarios and we will discuss them all. In addition to offering passive APIs, we will discuss calling and utilizing RESTful APIs from within AL. As well as discussing calling and parsing the response, we will discuss authentication methods including OAuth2.

The topics we will cover in this chapter include the following:

- SOAP using Pages and XMLports objects
- OData using Pages and Query objects
- API type Page and Query objects
- Using RESTful APIs external to Business Central
- Basic data flow through Business Central

Business Central web services (SOAP/OData)

SOAP is a lightweight XML protocol utilizing HTTP and was first implemented in the late 1990s. Pages and codeunits (with XMLports as procedure parameters) can be used to read, write, or delete data using HTTP calls.

OData is a Microsoft-only RESTful service that differs from other REST-based APIs in that the format is predefined. OData services can be exposed using Page or Query objects. Pages exposed can read, write, or delete data, while Queries are read-only.

OData is used in other Microsoft products and technologies, including the following:

- Microsoft Excel implements OData for its Power Query feature
- Microsoft Power BI can read data from OData services
- Microsoft SharePoint can expose its list-oriented data with OData

Authentication

Currently, the only method to access a Business Central web service or API is through Azure-based authentication, or OAuth using Microsoft Entra ID. The Microsoft authentication server issues security tokens to grant access after the user signs in. Within the authentication server, a resource owner is defined that grants or denies access to the Business Central server. This is done by registering Business Central as a trusted app in Microsoft Entra ID. Once the token is granted, packets of information are transferred securely between the user/service logging in and Business Central. Learn more about OAuth and Business Central at `https://learn.microsoft.com/en-us/dynamics365/ business-central/dev-itpro/webservices/authenticate-web-services- using-oauth`.

SOAP page

Page objects can be exposed as a SOAP XML API through the **Web Services** setup page. By checking **Published**, the **Uniform Resource Locator** (**URL**) will be displayed and will have the format of `https:// api.businesscentral.dynamics.com/v2.0/<tenantId>/<EnvironmentName>/ WS/<CompanyName>/Page/<WebServiceName>`.

> **Note**
>
> At the time of the publication of this book, Business Central page objects exposed as a SOAP XML API are set to be deprecated in version 26. It is recommended to convert existing or create new page-based APIs to OData or RESTful type objects. More information can be found here: `https://learn.microsoft.com/en-us/dynamics365/business- central/dev-itpro/upgrade/deprecated-features-platform#changes- in-2025-release-wave-1-version-260`.

Pages have the following operations available:

- `Create`: Insert a single record
- `CreateMultiple`: Insert a set of records
- `Delete`: Delete a single record
- `Delete_part`: Delete the subpage of a page result
- `GetRecIdFromKey`: Obtain a record ID from a key retrieved from a page result
- `IsUpdated`: Check whether an object has been updated since the key was retrieved
- `Read`: Read a single record
- `ReadByRecId`: Read a record identified by record ID; can use `GetRecIdFromKey` to obtain the record ID
- `ReadMultiple`: Read a set of records
- `Update`: Update a single record
- `UpdateMultiple`: Update a set of records

Page objects published as a SOAP web service in Business Central are automatically converted into an XML format and can communicate (read and write) in the format defined. There is no need for additional development to convert to a web service.

SOAP codeunits

Codeunits are the most flexible object that can be exposed as a SOAP web service. Each procedure will be exposed as an operation. Procedures can have both simple data types as parameters and a complex data type of XMLport. XMLports are objects that are used to map file content for import or export. The file types can be XML, fixed text, or variable (delimited) text. When used as a parameter of a procedure in a codeunit exposed as a SOAP web service, they must be in the XML data format. This allows for data not related to a Business Central page or table to be sent or received and processed inside the XMLport. XMLport is an object type that is used for the import/export of data. We will discuss components, properties, and triggers next.

XMLports

eXtensible Markup Language (**XML**) is a structured text format developed to describe data to be shared by dissimilar systems. XML has become a standard for communications between systems. To make handling XML-formatted data simpler and more error-resistant, Business Central provides XMLport, a data import/export object. In addition to processing XML-formatted data, XMLports can also handle a wide variety of other text file formats, including CSV files, generic flat files, and so on. XML-formatted data is text-based, with each piece of information structured in one of two basic formats: elements or attributes. An element is the overall logical unit of information, while an attribute is a property of an element. They are formatted as follows:

- `<Tag>elementvalue</Tag>` (an **element** format)

- `<Tag AttribName="attribute datavalue">` (an **attribute** format)

> **Note**
>
> Elements can be nested but must not overlap. Element and attribute names are case-sensitive. Names cannot start with a number, punctuation character, or the letters xml (upper or lowercase), and cannot contain spaces. An attribute value must always be enclosed in single or double quotation marks. Some references suggest that elements should be used for data and attributes for metadata. Complex data structures are built of combinations of these two formats.

For example, let's consider the following code:

```
<Table Name='Sample XML format'>
    <Record>
        <DataItem1>12345</DataItem1>
        <DataItem2>23456</DataItem2>
    </Record>
    <Record>
        <DataItem1>987</DataItem1>
    </Record>
    <Record>
        <DataItem1>22233</DataItem1>
        <DataItem2>7766</DataItem2>
    </Record>
</Table>
```

In this instance, we have a set of data identified as `Table` with an attribute of `Name` equal to `'SampleXMLformat'`, which contains three `Record` instances, with each `Record` instance containing data in one or two fields named `DataItem1` and `DataItem2`. The data is in a clearly structured text format, so it can be read and processed by any system prepared to read this particular XML format. If the field tags are well designed, the data is easily interpretable by humans, as well. The key to a successful exchange of data using XML is the sharing and common interpretation of the format between the transmitter and recipient.

XML is a standard format in the sense that the data structure options are clearly defined. It is very flexible in the sense that the identifying tag names (in < > brackets) and the related data structures are totally open-ended in how they can be defined and processed. The specific structure and the labels are whatever the communicating parties decide they should be. The rules of XML only determine how the basic syntax should operate.

XML data structures can be as simple as a flat file consisting of a set of identically formatted records or as complex as a sales order structure with headers containing a variety of data items, combined with associated detail lines containing their own assortments of data items. An XML data structure can be as complicated as the application requires.

XML standards are maintained by the **World Wide Web Consortium** (**W3C**), whose website is at www.w3.org. There are many other useful websites for basic XML information.

XMLport components

Although, in theory, XMLports can operate in both an import and an export mode, in practice, individual XMLport objects tend to be dedicated to either import or export. This allows the internal logic to be simpler. XMLports utilize a process of looping through and processing data, similar to that of report objects.

The components of XMLports are as follows:

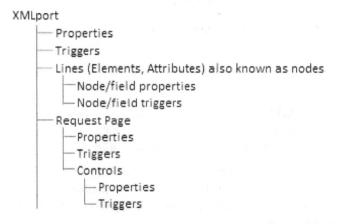

Figure 8.1 – XMLport object component outline

Let's take a look at the properties first.

XMLport properties

XMLport properties are shown in the following screenshot of the properties of the XMLport object, 9170:

```
1   xmlport 9170 "Profile Import/Export"
2   {
3       Caption = 'Profile Import/Export';
4       Encoding = UTF8;
5       FormatEvaluate = Xml;
6
7       schema
8       {
9           textelement(Profiles)
```

Figure 8.2 – XMLport object properties

Descriptions of the individual properties are as follows:

- Caption: This is the name that is displayed for the XMLport; it defaults to the contents of the Name property.

- Direction: This defines whether this XMLport can only import, export, or both; the default is <Both>.

- DefaultFieldsValidation: This defines the default value (True or False) for the FieldValidate property for individual XMLport data fields. The default for this field is True, which will set the default for individual field FieldValidate properties to True.

- Encoding (or TextEncoding): This defines the character encoding option to be used – UTF-8 (ASCII-compatible), UTF-16 (not ASCII-compatible), or ISO-8859-2 (for certain European languages written in Latin characters). UTF-16 is the default. This is inserted into the heading of the XML document.

- The TextEncoding option is only available if the Format property is FixedText or VariabeText. In this case, a character coding option of MSDOS is available and is the default.

- XMLVersionNo: This defines to which version of XML the document conforms, Version1.0 or 1.1. The default is Version1.0. This is inserted into the heading of the XML document.

- UseDefaultNamespace and DefaultNamespace: These properties are provided to support compatibility with other systems that require the XML document to be in a specific namespace, such as the use of a web service as a reference within Visual Studio. UseDefaultNamespace defaults to False. A default namespace in the form of **URN** (short for **Uniform Resource Name**, or, in this case, a **namespace identifier**), concluding with the object number of the XMLport, is supplied for the DefaultNamespace property. This property is only active if the Format property is Xml.

- Namespaces: This property takes you to a new screen where you can set up multiple namespaces for the XMLport, including a prefix.

- InlineSchema: This property defaults to false. An inline schema allows the XML schema document (an XSD) to be embedded within the XML document. This can be used by setting the property to true when exporting an XML document, which will add the schema to that exported document. This property is only active if the Format property is Xml.

- Format: This property has the options of Xml, VariableText, or FixedText. It defaults to Xml. This property controls the import/export data format that the XMLport will process. Choosing Xml means that the processing will only deal with a properly formatted XML file. Choosing VariableText means that the processing will only deal with a file formatted with delimiters set up as defined in the FieldDelimiter, FieldSeparator, RecordSeparator, and TableSeparator properties, such as CSV files. Choosing FixedText means that each individual element and attribute must have its Width property set to a value greater than 0 (zero), and the data to be processed must be formatted accordingly. If enabled, these four fields can also be changed programmatically from within AL code.

- FieldDelimiter: This applies to Variable Text format external files only. It defaults to a double quote (< " >), the standard for text files commonly called *comma-delimited* files. This property supplies the string that will be used as the starting delimiter for each data field in the text file. If this is Import, then the XMLport will look for this string, and then use the string following as data until the next FieldDelimiter string is found, terminating the data string. If this is Export, the XMLport will insert this string at the beginning and end of each data field contents string.

- FieldSeparator: This applies to VariableText format external files only. It defaults to a comma (< , >), the standard for text files commonly called *comma-delimited* files. This property supplies the string that will be used as the delimiter between each data field in the text file (looked for on Import or inserted on Export). For the tab delimiter, use <TAB>.

- RecordSeparator: This applies to VariableText or FixedText format external files only. This defines the string that will be used as the delimiter at the end of each data record in the text file. If this is Import, the XMLport will look for this string to mark the end of each data record. If this is Export, the XMLport will append this string at the end of each data record output. The default is <<NewLine>>, which represents any combination of **CR** (short for **carriage return** –ASCII value 13) and LF (short for **line feed** –ASCII value 10) characters.

- TableSeparator: This applies to VariableText or FixedText format external files only. This defines the string that will be used as the delimiter at the end of each DataItem – for example, each text file. The default is <<NewLine><NewLine>>.

- UseRequestPage: This determines whether a request page should be displayed to allow the user choice of sort sequence, entry of filters, and other requested control information. The options are True or False. The default is True. An XMLport request page only has the **OK** and **Cancel** options.

- `Permissions`: This property provides report-specific settings of permissions, which are rights to access data, subdivided into `Read`, `Insert`, `Modify`, and `Delete`. This allows the developer to define permissions that override the user-by-user permissions security setup.

XMLport triggers

XMLport has a very limited set of triggers, which are as follows:

- `OnInitXmlPort()` is executed once when the XMLport is loaded before the table views and filters have been set.

- `OnPreXmlPort()` is executed once after the table views and filters have been set. Those can be reset here.

- `OnPostXmlPort()` is executed once after all the data is processed, if the XMLport completes normally.

The XMLport schema

The schema defines the mapping of the data into or from Business Central. Each node in the schema defines the element, attributes, and properties. The nodes can be a text, table, or field. Text is a variable and can be expressed as an element or an attribute in the XML output. A table element is not exported directly but indicates a looping node. The node can be nested to form parent/child relationships. A field element or attribute is related to the parent table element and is per table record loop, just like in a report dataset definition.

> **Note**
>
> In an XML schema, there must be a single `<root>` node; it must be the first node, and it must be of the `textelement` type.

Node as text

The `textelement` and `textattribute` nodes define a value not mapped directly to a database field or when a value does not need to be sent, only the node. The text node name is also the variable name of the `Text` type, which can be referred to and assigned in the XMLport AL code within the triggers. The node has the following format:

```
textelement(VariableName) {}
```

A description of the text-specific properties is as follows:

- `TextType`: This defines the Business Central data type as `Text` or `BigText`. `Text` is the default.

- `VariableName`: This contains the name of the global variable, which can be referenced by AL code.

Node as table

The `tableelement` is a looping mechanism that iterates for each record in the table specified. The node has the following format:

```
tableelement(VariableName; SourceTable) {}
```

The properties of the table element include the following:

- `SourceTable`: This defines the Business Central table being referenced.

- `VariableName`: This defines the name to be used in AL code for the Business Central table. It is the functional equivalent of the definition of a global variable.

- `SourceTableView`: This enables the developer to define a view by choosing a key and sorting order or by applying filters on the table.

- `ReqFilterHeading`: These fields allow for the definition of the name of the request page filter definition tab that applies to this table.

- `CalcFields`: This lists the FlowFields in the table that are to be calculated automatically.

- `ReqFilterFields`: This lists the fields that will initially be displayed on the request page filter definition tab.

- `LinkTable`: This allows for the linking of a field in a higher-level item to a key field in a lower-level item. If, for example, we were exporting all of the purchase orders for a vendor, we might link `Buy-From Vendor No.` in `Purchase Header` to `No.` in a vendor record. `LinkTable`, in this case, would be `Vendor` and `LinkField` would be `No.`; therefore, `LinkTable` and `LinkFields` work together. The use of `LinkTable` and `LinkFields` operates the same as applying a filter on the higher-level table data so that only records relating to the defined lower-level table and field are processed. See the *Microsoft docs* for more details.

- `LinkTableForceInsert`: This can be set to force insertion of the linked table data and execution of the related `OnAfterInitRecord()` trigger. This property is tied to the `LinkTable` and `LinkFields` properties. It also applies to `Import`.

- `LinkFields`: This defines the fields involved in a table + **Field** linkage.

- `UseTemporary`: This defaults to `false`. If this property is set to `true`, it allows for the creation of a **temporary table** in working storage. Data imported into this table can then be evaluated, edited, and manipulated, before being written out to the database. This temporary table has the same capabilities and limitations as a temporary table defined as a global variable.

- `AutoSave`: If set to `true` (the default), an imported record will automatically be saved to the table. Either `AutoUpdate` or `AutoReplace` must also be set to `Yes`.

- `AutoUpdate`: If a record exists in the table with a matching primary key, all the data fields are initialized, and then all the data from the incoming record is copied into the table record.

- `AutoReplace`: If a record exists in the table with a matching primary key, the populated data fields in the incoming record are copied into the table record; all the other fields in the target record are left undisturbed. This provides a means to update a table by importing records with a limited number of data fields filled in.

The `Width`, `NamespacePrefix`, `MinOccurs`, and `MaxOccurs` properties are discussed later in this chapter.

Node as field

The `fieldelement` and `fieldattribute` controls are fields from a record in the `tableelement` specified above it in the schema. The node has the following format:

```
fieldelement(VariableName; SourceField) {}
```

A description of the field-specific properties is as follows:

- `SourceField`: This defines the data field being referenced. It can be a field in any defined table.

- `VariableName`: This defines the name to be used in AL code for the Business Central field. It is the functional equivalent of the definition of a global variable.

- `FieldValidate`: This only applies to `Import`. If this property is `true`, then whenever the field is imported into the database, the `OnValidate()` trigger of the field will be executed.

- `AutoCalcField`: This applies to `Export` and `FlowField` data fields only. If this property is set to `true`, the field will be calculated before it is retrieved from the database. Otherwise, `FlowField` will export as an empty field.

The details of the `Width`, `NamespacePrefix`, `MinOccurs`, and `MaxOccurs` properties will be discussed in the next section.

Element or attribute

An element node can appear many times, but an attribute node can appear only once.

Node element properties

The element-specific properties are as follows:

- `Width`: When the XMLport `Format` property is `FixedText`, then this field is used to define the fixed width of this element's field.

- `MinOccurs`: This defines the minimum number of times this data item can occur in the XML document. This property can be `Zero` or `Once` (the default).

- `MaxOccurs`: This defines the maximum number of times this data item can occur in the XML document. This property can be `Once` or `Unbounded`. `Unbounded` (the default) means any number of times.

- `NamespacePrefix`: When an XMLport has multiple namespaces, this property allows you to select a specific one.

Node attribute properties

The attribute-specific property is `Occurrence`: this is either `Required` (the default) or `Optional`, depending on the text file being imported.

XMLport node triggers

There are different XMLport triggers, depending on whether the node is `Table`, `Text`, or `Field`.

Node as Table

The triggers for having the node as `Table` are as follows:

- `OnAfterInsertRecord()`, for `Import` only: This trigger is typically used when the data is being imported into temporary tables. This is where we would put the AL code to build and insert records for the permanent database tables.

- `OnBeforeModifyRecord()`, for `Import` only: When `AutoSave` is `true`, this is used to update the imported data before saving it.

- `OnAfterModifyRecord()`, for `Import` only: When `AutoSave` is `false`, this is used to update the data after updating.

- `OnPreXMLItem()`, for `Export` only: This trigger is typically used for setting filters and initializing before finding and processing the first database record.

- `OnAfterGetRecord()`, for `Export` only: This trigger allows for access to the data after the record is retrieved from the Business Central database. This trigger is typically used to allow manipulation of the table fields being exported.

- `OnAfterInitRecord()`, for `Import` only: This trigger is typically used to check whether a record should be processed further or to manipulate the data.

- `OnBeforeInsertRecord()`, for `Import` only: This is another place where we can manipulate data before it is inserted into the target table. This trigger is executed after the `OnAfterInitRecord()` trigger.

Node as text or field

The triggers for having the node as Text or Field (either element or attribute) are as follows:

- OnBeforePassVariable(), for Export only: This trigger is typically used for manipulation of the text variable
- OnAfterAssignVariable(), for Import only: This trigger gives us access to the imported value in a text format

SOAP XMLport through WDTU codeunit

For more complicated scenarios not offered by presenting page objects as web services, you can utilize XMLports as parameters in a codeunit function. We will create a simple example to retrieve a customer number and export the customer address.

First, create xmlport 50100 "WDTU Export Customer Address". To enable use in a web service, you must enable the following properties:

```
Format = Xml;
UseDefaultNamespace = true;
DefaultNamespace = 'urn:microsoft-dynamics-nav/xmlports/x50000';
```

This property specifies the default namespace for both import and export. A default namespace is a namespace that does not include a prefix. The default prefix is applied to all the elements that do not include a prefix and is unique for different XMLports. For example, the following string specifies a namespace: urn:microsoft-dynamics-nav/xmlports/x50100, where 50100 is the ID of the XMLport. There can only be one default namespace, so if you specify the default namespace in the Namespaces property, you must set the DefaultNamespace property to false.

```
xmlport 50100 "WDTU Export Customer Address"
{
    Caption = 'Export Address';
    Format = Xml;
    UseDefaultNamespace = true;
    DefaultNamespace = 'urn:microsoft-dynamics-nav/xmlports/x50100';
```

Figure 8.3 – Object properties for Xmlport to be used in SOAP web service codeunit

The Xmlport will give two elements, the first being the customer name, and the second will be the formatted address as determined by the country/region and/or the General Ledger Setup values using the Format Address codeunit. In order to preserve the line breaks in the address, we will append carriage return (Cr)/line feed (Lf) characters (Char values 13 and 10, respectively). The Format Address codeunit contains a function to populate and compress the CustAddr text array based on the customer record passed.

```
var
    FormatAddr: Codeunit "Format Address";
    CustAddr: array[8] of Text[50];
    Cr: Char;
    Lf: Char;
```

Figure 8.4 – Variables to be used in the XmlPort

The Xmlport has a schema structure of the root as a text element, the looping table element, and the two text elements, CustName and FullAddress. Each of the repeating text elements contains an OnBeforePassVariable trigger that will populate the text element value. The text value for FullAddress will be populated in a for loop utilizing the += string concatenation.

```
8     schema
9     {
10        textelement(RootNodeName)
11        {
12            tableelement(Cust; Customer)
13            {
14                textelement(CustName)
15                {
16                    trigger OnBeforePassVariable()
17                    begin
18                        CustName := Cust.Name;
19                    end;
20                }
21                textelement(FullAddress)
22                {
23                    trigger OnBeforePassVariable()
24                    var
25                        i: Integer;
26                    begin
27                        Cr := 13;
28                        Lf := 10;
29                        FormatAddr.Customer(CustAddr, Cust);
30                        for i := 1 to 8 do begin
31                            if CustAddr[i] <> '' then
32                                FullAddress += CustAddr[i] + Format(Cr) + Format(Lf);
33                        end;
34                    end;
35                }
36            }
37        }
38    }
```

Figure 8.5 – Overview of the AL for the XmlPort

Next, we will create codeunit 50100 "WDTU SOAP Web Services" with an empty OnRun trigger. The single function will have two parameters; the first is the primary key value of the customer in question and the second is a complex variable of the "WDTU Export Customer Address" Xmlport. The Xmlport variable is set as a var as it can be used as import or export, though in our example it is used as export only.

```
47      procedure FilterCustRec(pCustNo: Code[20])
48      begin
49          Cust.SetRange("No.", pCustNo);
50      end;
```

Figure 8.6 – Function to filter XMLport record

A single-line procedure in the XMLport is used to pass the customer number, as shown in the preceding figure. Call this procedure prior to running the Export function of the XMLport.

```
1   codeunit 50100 "WDTU SOAP Web Services"
2   {
        0 references
3       trigger OnRun()
4       begin
5       end;
6
        0 references | 0% Coverage
7       procedure ExportCustAddress(pCustNo: Code[20];
8               var ExportAddress: XmlPort "WDTU Export Customer Address")
9       begin
10          ExportAddress.FilterCustRec(pCustNo);
11          ExportAddress.Export();
12      end;
13
14  }
```

Figure 8.7 – SOAP codeunit to export customer address

Now we have our code in place, we need to expose the codeunit object as a web service.

Publishing a web service

Publishing a web service is one of the easiest things we will ever do in Business Central. However, as stated earlier, this doesn't mean that we will be able to simply publish existing objects without creating versions specifically tailored for use with web services. However, for the moment, let's just go through the basic publishing process.

The first column allows us to specify whether the object is a page, codeunit, or query. This is followed by **Object ID**, and then **Service Name**. Finally, the **Published** flag must be checked:

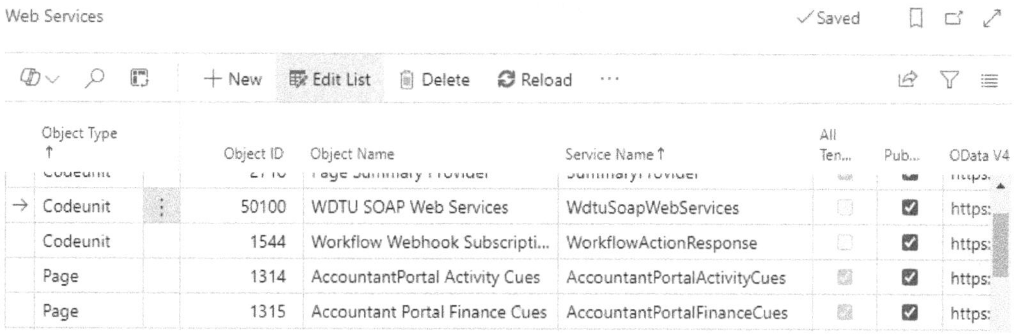

Figure 8.8 – The Web Services page

For our example, click **New**, then select **Codeunit** as **Object Type** and enter in the **Object ID** value of 50100. Enter a web URL-friendly name such as WdtuSoapWebServices (with no spaces) and make sure the **Published** column is checked. As you can see, at this point, the web services for that object are published.

Executing web services externally

Now that the web service is published and available to an authorized login, it can be utilized by an outside application. The **Web Services Description Language** (**WSDL**) is passed to the caller as a definition of the parameters expected in the body of the request and the values returned in the response. The following figure shows how the WSDL displays the parameters of the pCustNo simple data type and the complex data type of the Xmlport and its full definition.

```
<Envelope xmlns="http://schemas.xmlsoap.org/soap/envelope/">
    <Body>
        <ExportCustAddress xmlns="urn:microsoft-dynamics-schemas/codeunit/WdtuSoapWebServices">
            <pCustNo>10000</pCustNo>
            <exportAddress>
                <Cust xmlns="urn:microsoft-dynamics-nav/xmlports/x50000">
                    <CustName>[string]</CustName>
                    <FullAddress>[string]</FullAddress>
                </Cust>
            </exportAddress>
        </ExportCustAddress>
    </Body>
</Envelope>
```

Figure 8.9 – SOAP web service pass parameter content

When the web service is called from an external source, such as the Postman API tool, the result of the POST call is shown here:

```
<Soap:Envelope xmlns:Soap="http://schemas.xmlsoap.org/soap/envelope/">
    <Soap:Body>
        <ExportCustAddress_Result xmlns="urn:microsoft-dynamics-schemas/codeunit/WdtuSoapWebServices">
            <exportAddress>
                <Cust xmlns="urn:microsoft-dynamics-nav/xmlports/x50000">
                    <CustName>The Cannon Group PLC</CustName>
                    <FullAddress>The Cannon Group PLC
Mr. Andy Teal
192 Market Square
Birmingham, B27 4KT
Great Britain
</FullAddress>
                </Cust>
            </exportAddress>
        </ExportCustAddress_Result>
    </Soap:Body>
</Soap:Envelope>
```

Figure 8.10 – Returned XML of the web service call

XMLports are extremely versatile and are not limited to just XML. Even though SOAP will be deprecated as an API protocol in Business Central in the future, banks, governments, and other institutions communicate data in XML format as well as formatted text flat files, all of which can be imported, processed, and exported using the XMLport object.

RESTful calls

Both OData and Business Central API pages utilize RESTful methods to perform CRUD operations in a web service. The following HTTP methods are used to interact with an API:

- GET: Request to retrieve information only.

- POST: Used to create new entities only. To create both parent and child entities at the same time, the API must support **deep insert**.

- PATCH: Used to update an existing entity and requires the unique ID (GUID) to be passed as part of the request.

- DELETE: Used to delete an existing item and requires the unique ID (GUID) to be passed as part of the request.

The OData and API type pages have different rules and requirements for the general methods, which we will discuss next.

OData page

When you expose a page as an **OData** web service, you can query that data to return a service metadata (**EDMX**) document, an AtomPub document, or a **JavaScript Object Notation (JSON)** document. You can also write back to the database if the exposed page is writable. Page-based web services offer built-in optimistic concurrency management. Each operation calls in a page-based web service and is managed as a single transaction. It is important to remember that pages have code executed that only works in a user interface and not as a web service. Please make sure that any **Graphical User Interface (GUI)** methods will be surrounded by an `if..then` statement testing for `GuiAllowed`.

The format for calling an OData web service EDMX document is `https://api.businesscentral.dynamics.com/v2.0/<tenantId>/<environmentName>/ODataV4/Company('<UrlSafeCompanyName')/<webService>/$metadata`.

The format for calling an OData web service JSON document is `https://api.businesscentral.dynamics.com/v2.0/<tenantId>/<environmentName>/ODataV4/Company('<UrlSafeCompanyName')/<webService>?$format=json`.

If an editable page is exposed as a web service, the data in the underlying table can be accessed and modified by an OData call. Business Central supports the following **OData operations** for modifying data:

Call	Table and Page Triggers
POST	`OnInsert()` and `OnNewRecord()`
PATCH	`OnModify()`
DELETE	`OnDelete()`

Table 8.1 – OData operations for editing data

All calls fail if the user does not have the relevant permissions, and if the relevant property on the page, `InsertAllowed`, `ModifyAllowed`, or `DeleteAllowed`, is set to `No`.

You can use an OData web service in applications where you want users to be able to modify Business Central data outside the Business Central web client. For example, you can show fields from the `Customer` table on a mobile device or in a browser so that a user can create, update, or delete customers in the Business Central database.

PATCH operations require the "If-Match" header to be set, either with a retrieved **Entity Tag (ETag)** or with `*`. An ETag is used to identify the record updated in the PATCH command. **Deep insert** (inserting or updating related nested records in the request) is not supported on pages exposed as ODataV4 web services. Although ODataV4 web services with deep insert might work in some cases, it's not recommended. Business Central doesn't support deep patching. Multiple requests will need to be issued when patching nested entities.

OData filters

When you expose a Business Central query as an OData web service, you can query that data to return a service metadata (EDMX) document or an AtomPub document. The following table lists the possibilities that we have:

Expression	Example	AL Equivalent
Select a range of values	`$filter=Entry_No gt 610 and Entry_No lt 615`	..
And	`$filter=Country_Region_Code eq 'US' and Payment_Terms_Code eq '30 DAYS'`	&
Or	`$filter= Country_Region_Code eq 'ES' or Country_Region_Code eq 'US'`	|
Less than	`$filter=Entry_No lt 610`	<
Greater than	`$filter= Entry_No gt 610`	>
Greater than or equal to	`$filter=Entry_No ge 610`	>=
Less than or equal to	`$filter=Entry_No le 610`	<=
Different from (not equal)	`$filter=VAT_Bus_Posting_Group ne 'EXPORT'`	<>
Ends with	`$filter=endswith(VAT_Bus_Posting_Group,'DEM'`	*
Starts with	`$filter=startswith(Name, 'A')`	*
Contains	`$filter=contains(Name, 'avi')`	
Index of	`$filter=indexof(Location_Code, 'WHITE') eq 0`	
Replace	`$filter=replace(City, 'Chicago', 'Madison') eq 'ROCKNROLL'`	
Substring	`$filter=substring(Location_Code, 5) eq 'ROCK'`	
To lower	`$filter=tolower(Location_Code) eq 'rock n roll'`	
To upper	`$filter=toupper(FText) eq 'NIGHT SHIFT'`	
Trim	`$filter=trim(FCode) eq 'TALK'`	

Expression	Example	AL Equivalent
Concatenate	`$filter=concat(concat(FText, ', '), FCode) eq 'SOME, thing'`	
Round	`$filter=round(FDecimal) eq 1`	
Floor	`$filter=floor(FDecimal) eq 0`	
Ceiling	`$filter=ceiling(FDecimal) eq 1`	

Table 8.2 – OData filter examples

OData has functionality that integrates very well into Microsoft platforms such as Office and SharePoint but is not used much elsewhere. For more simplistic, more flexible output, Business Central includes JSON RESTful integration points using object types marked as API.

API objects in AL

AL in Business Central gives you the ability to create two types of objects dedicated to the RESTful API if the built-in pages are not sufficient to interchange data with external systems. If you need to read and write data, use a page of the API type. If you need to read data, possibly from multiple tables, use a query of the API type:

- **API page**: Supports read-write transactions. Cannot be extended. Exposes data from a single table.
- **API query**: Read-only operations. Cannot be extended. Can expose calculated data from multiple tables.

API pages have a set of required properties that must be filled in, as listed in the following table:

`APIPublisher`	Sets the publisher of the API endpoint the page is exposed in. `APIPublisher` contains the first part of the URL for the endpoint.
`APIGroup`	Sets the group of the API endpoint the page is exposed in.
`APIVersion`	Sets the version(s) of the API endpoint the page is exposed in, in the format of *vX.Y*. If `APIVersion` isn't specified, the default value is beta. It can be specified as one version, or a list of versions if the API is supported through multiple versions.
`EntityName`	Sets the singular entity name with which the page is exposed in the API endpoint.

EntitySetName	Sets the plural entity name with which the page is exposed in the API endpoint.
ODataKeyFields	Specifies the fields that determine the primary key of the record.

Table 8.3 – Required properties for API pages

> **Tip**
>
> You can use the snippet tpage – **Page of type API** to list the required properties automatically.

It is strongly recommended to specify a single field of the GUID type (such as the SystemId field) in the ODataKeyFields API page property. Otherwise, some external integrations, such as those in the Power Architecture, will not work well with the API. It is also recommended to include all the fields used in TableRelations and SubPageLinks in the API page to make the relationship understandable to the developer who wants to use it.

When you publish the API page in your extension, the URL format is as follows:

```
https://api.businesscentral.dynamics.
com/v2.0/<tenantid>/<environment name>/
api/<APIPublisher>/<APIGroup>/<APIVersion>/
companies(<companyid>)/<api entityset name>(<api entity GUID>)
```

Let's go through the URL components. The base of the URL will never change; this is https://api.businesscentral.dynamics.com/v2.0/.

The next portion is optional, depending on how you are authenticating. If your user authenticates to more than one tenant hosted by Microsoft, then you need to specify the <tenantid> in the form of a GUID. If your user only authenticates to a single tenant, then it is not necessary to include it. The environment name is also optional, but only if the API is being accessed in the production environment. Any sandbox environments will need to be specified by name. The <APIPublisher>, <APIGroup>, and <APIVersion> values come from the six required API page properties defined previously.

Up to this point in the URL, we have environment-wide settings that are not data-specific yet. First in the variable values is the <companyid> (a GUID), which can be retrieved through an initial call to the companies API service, as shown here in Postman:

```
1   {
2       "@odata.context": "https://api.businesscentral.dynamics.com/v2.0/
            16297619-dab1-43fa-bb74-a28582f37ea2/Sandbox/api/v2.0/$metadata#companies",
3       "value": [
4           {
5               "id": "f196cdfe-b238-ef11-8e61-6045bdfb9316",
6               "systemVersion": "24.3.21374.21517",
7               "timestamp": 3833,
8               "name": "CRONUS International Ltd.",
9               "displayName": "",
10              "businessProfileId": "",
11              "systemCreatedAt": "2024-07-02T20:38:11.213Z",
12              "systemCreatedBy": "00000000-0000-0000-0000-000000000001",
13              "systemModifiedAt": "2024-07-02T20:38:11.213Z",
14              "systemModifiedBy": "00000000-0000-0000-0000-000000000001"
15          },
16          {
```

Figure 8.11 – Company API response in Postman API tool

The `<companyid>` value is fixed and will not change, so the calling system can safely store that information rather than having to call Business Central every time. This unique GUID value is assigned at the creation of the company in the initial setup processing of the application and is used to uniquely identify the company within API calls.

The last two elements are in relation to the actual API page itself. The URL has the option to either list all the records in the database for the source table or list a single record specified by `<api entity GUID>`. These results can be filtered by any field exposed by adding to the calling URL using the GET method.

API pages for WDTU playlist

Creating an API page is very similar to a normal page with several key differences. The first is there are additional fields required, namely, GUID references in the table structure. Secondly, you do not need different page types to show multiple or single instances (List versus Card), as both are available depending on the URL parameters.

Because entities are referenced in APIs by their unique identifiers (GUIDs), we need to add the linkage GUID to the playlist line table. Open `table 50103 "Playlist Line"` and add a `PlaylistId` GUID field. This field will link the lines to the header by the header `SystemId` field:

```
58          field(10; "End Time"; Time)
59          {
60              trigger OnValidate()
61              begin
62                  if "Start Time" <> 0T then
63                      Duration := "End Time" - "Start Time";
64              end;
65          }
66          field(11; PlaylistId; Guid) { }
67      }
```

Figure 8.12 – New PlaylistID field in the Playlist Line table

Now, we can start creating the API pages themselves. Add a new file and name it `APIPlaylistSubpage.page.al`. Start the file with the `tpage` snippet of the `API` type.

tpage

tpage	Page
tpage	Page of type API
tpage	Page of type List
tpage	Page of type PromptDialog

Figure 8.13 – The tpage snippet for "Page of type API"

When defining the properties, follow the naming convention using **camelCase** for the `APIPublisher`, `APIGroup`, `EntityName`, and `EntitySetName` values. Any alphanumeric value is allowed. Also, make sure the version code is either in `vX.Y` format or `beta` only. It is a good idea to set the `DelayedInsert` property to `true` to allow for **deep insert** (header and lines all at the same time) from the external source.

```al
1    page 50113 "API Playlist Subpage"
2    {
3        APIGroup = 'radio';
4        APIPublisher = 'wdtu';
5        APIVersion = 'v1.0';
6        ApplicationArea = All;
7        Caption = 'apiPlaylistSubpage';
8        DelayedInsert = true;
9        EntityName = 'playlistLine';
10       EntitySetName = 'playlistLines';
11       PageType = API;
12       SourceTable = "Playlist Line";
13
14       layout
15       {
16           area(Content)
17           {
18               repeater(PlaylistLine)
19               {
20                   field(systemId; Rec.SystemId) { }
21                   field(dataFormat; Rec."Data Format") { }
22                   field(type; Rec."Type") { }
23                   field(itemNo; Rec."No.") { }
24                   field(description; Rec.Description) { }
25                   field(publisherCode; Rec."Publisher Code") { }
26                   field(startTime; Rec."Start Time") { }
27                   field(endTime; Rec."End Time") { }
28                   field(lineDuration; Rec."Duration") { }
29                   field(systemModifiedAt; Rec.SystemModifiedAt) { }
30               }
31           }
32       }
33   }
```

Figure 8.14 – The Playlist Line subpage

If you wanted the page to be read-only, the following properties could be added with `true` or `false` values: `InsertAllowed`, `ModifiedAllowed`, and `DeleteAllowed`.

Note that the field names are also in **camelCase**, as this is the standard for JSON metadata. In the retrieval and update operations (GET and PATCH, respectively) of the API, it is necessary to have the GUID. It is necessary to show the ID with each record, both header and lines. In addition, it is best practice to also show the `SystemModifiedAt` field for potential filtering by the API caller.

The Playlist page will consist of two parts, similar to the document page: the fields belonging to the Playlist Header table, and the part showing the lines of the Playlist subpage. Create a new file and save it as APIPlaylist.page.al. Use the tpage snippet for the API again and add a new OdataKeyFields property with a value of SystemId:

```
1    page 50112 "API WDTU Playlist"
2    {
3        PageType = API;
4        APIPublisher = 'wdtu';
5        APIGroup = 'radio';
6        APIVersion = 'v1.0';
7        EntityName = 'playlist';
8        EntitySetName = 'playlists';
9        SourceTable = "Playlist Header";
10       DelayedInsert = true;
11       ODataKeyFields = SystemId;
12
13       layout
14       {
15           area(Content)
16           {
17               repeater(Playlist)
18               {
19                   field(id; Rec.SystemId) { }
20                   field(playlistNo; Rec."No.") { }
21                   field(radioShowNo; Rec."Radio Show No.") { }
22                   field(description; Rec.Description) { }
23                   field(broadcastDate; Rec."Broadcast Date") { }
24                   field(startTime; Rec."Start Time") { }
25                   field(endTime; Rec."End Time") { }
26                   field(showDuration; Rec.Duration) { }
27                   field(lastModifiedDateTime; Rec.SystemModifiedAt) { }
28                   part(Lines; "API Playlist Subpage")
29                   {
30                       EntityName = 'playlistLine';
31                       EntitySetName = 'playlistLines';
32                       SubPageLink = PlaylistId = field(SystemId);
33                   }
34               }
35           }
36       }
37   }
```

Figure 8.15 – API WDTU Playlist page

For the repeater grouping, add the fields to be entered by the user as well as the two key fields: No. and SystemId. Below the repeater control, add a part control for the subpage. Each subpage needs to have EntityName and EntitySetName included, as well as the SubPageLink property. In this case, SubPageLink is the SystemId field from Playlist Header and PlaylistId from the Playlist Line tables.

The link is not between the line's Document No. and the header No. fields. Because this is an API type page, the link is between the header SystemId and the new line field, PlaylistId. In order to query the API for the header and the lines, it is necessary to add an additional parameter to the URL:

```
https://api.businesscentral.dynamics.com/
v2.0/<tenant>/<environment>/api/wdtu/radio/v1.0/companies(<company
GUID>)/playlists?$expand=playlistLines
```

Now, the nested subpage data will be displayed with the playlist header information:

```
1    {
2        "@odata.context": "https://api.businesscentral.dynamics.com/v2.0/16297619-dab1-43fa-bb74-a28582f37ea2/
         Sandbox/api/wdtu/radio/v1.0/$metadata#companies(f196cdfe-b238-ef11-8e51-6045bdfb9315)/playlists",
3        "value": [
4            {
5                "@odata.etag": "W/\"JzE6OzkyNzc0NjMxNzQ3MjU5Njg4MjExOzAwOyc=\"",
6                "id": "26031da4-3f49-ef11-bfe3-000d3ae9ce93",
7                "playlistNo": "221",
8                "radioShowNo": "RS001",
9                "description": "CeCe and Friends",
10               "broadcastDate": "2024-07-23",
11               "startTime": "10:00:00",
12               "endTime": "12:00:00",
13               "showDuration": "P0DT2H0M0.0S",
14               "lastModifiedDateTime": "2024-07-23T22:05:16.737Z",
15               "playlistLines": [
16                   {
17                       "@odata.etag": "W/\"JzE6OzUyMTQyNjQyNDQzMDU20TAxMjQxOzAwOyc=\"",
18                       "documentNo": "221",
19                       "lineNo": 0,
20                       "systemId": "b2de6bdf-ca49-ef11-bfe3-000d3ae9ce93",
21                       "dataFormat": "Vinyl",
22                       "type": "Item",
23                       "itemNo": "1000",
```

Figure 8.16 – Postman GET result from the Playlist API page and subpage

Specialized page objects can be created to use as interfaces for external systems in Business Central. It is not possible to extend APIs, but it is not difficult to create new APIs because you already know how to create page objects in Business Central. With a few new properties, and some additional rules to know and understand, it is possible to extend Business Central beyond the application to external systems such as Microsoft Power Automate, Power Applications, Azure Functions, and any REST API-capable application. With those systems, you can read, write, or update any entity exposed in the API pages you wish.

API query for WDTU listenership

In addition to using page objects to retrieve data from Business Central, it is possible to create query objects with an additional property, QueryType, set to API. Like pages, there are the same five required object properties (APIPublisher, APIGroup, APIVersion, EntityName, and

EntitySetName). Why use a query rather than a page? Like the app version of the query, it is optimized for quick extraction of data based on multiple data tables. Unlike the standard query object, the API type allows for seamless data transfer and integration with external applications and reporting solutions.

WDTU has various dashboards and KPIs using external reporting solutions. It is required to get viewership information based on ledgers quickly and easily to update the external data reporting solutions. Create a new file and start a new tquery snippet of the Query of type API type.

Figure 8.17 – New tquery snippet

Populate the key properties of APIPublisher and APIGroup with the same values as the other APIs. For EntityName and EntitySetName, set the values to programListener and programListeners, respectively.

For the first dataitem, choose Listenership Entry as the source and the *camelCase* listernshipEntry as the name. Unlike the pages, it is not necessary to define SystemId as the key nor to display the system-created GUID. The query now looks as follows:

```
 1    query 50101 "API Listenership"
 2    {
 3        APIGroup = 'radio';
 4        APIPublisher = 'wdtu';
 5        APIVersion = 'v1.0';
 6        EntityName = 'programListener';
 7        EntitySetName = 'programListeners';
 8        QueryType = API;
 9
10        elements
11        {
12            dataitem(listenershipEntry; "Listenership Entry")
13            {
14                column(radioShowNo; "Radio Show No.") { }
15                column(showDate; "Date") { }
16                column(audienceShare; "Audience Share") { }
17                column(ageDemographic; "Age Demographic") { }
18                column(listenerCount; "Listener Count") { }
19                filter(dateFilter; Date) { }
20                dataitem(radioShow; "Radio Show")
21                {
22                    DataItemLink = "No." = listenershipEntry."Radio Show No.";
23                    SqlJoinType = InnerJoin;
24                    column(Name; Name) { }
25                    column(Host_Name; "Host Name") { }
26                }
27            }
28        }
29    }
```

Figure 8.18 – Program Listener API query object

So far, we have talked about the ways to extend AL objects into API interfaces to exchange data from Business Central to external applications. These are all passive interfaces, depending on external queries to Business Central.

Consuming external API

But what if your AL extension needs to query an external API? Business Central AL in Visual Studio Code has several valuable tools to develop, test, and deploy code to call and consume external RESTful APIs. To test authentication, calls, and responses in Visual Studio Code, you can download the **REST Client** extension and create `.http` files:

`https://marketplace.visualstudio.com/items?itemName=humao.rest-client.`

> **Be prepared!**
> The following example includes not only what we have learned up to this point but also some additional techniques and system methods for which you may need to look online. The solution presented here should be seen as motivation for continued self-learning!

WDTU Tidal integration

In our WDTU example, we will utilize the free Tidal streaming service API in order to find and download high-quality cover art for the music entered into the `Item` table. To learn more information on how to sign up for free, go to `https://developer.tidal.com/`. After creating a developer login (instructions at `https://developer.tidal.com/documentation/api-sdk/api-sdk-quick-start`), you will be provided with a Client ID and Client Secret. These will be used to authenticate via OAuth bearer tokens into the service. The Tidal API documentation states that to find a specific album, the barcode in EAN-13 or UPC-A format must be submitted in the GET request. To get that information, it needs to be stored in a new custom field in our `Item` table extension. Add a `Barcode` field of the `Text` type with a length of `30` characters as the `50105` field:

```
1   tableextension 50100 Item extends Item
2   {
3       fields
4       {
5           field(50100; "Publisher Code"; Code[10]) { TableRelation = Publisher.Code; }
6           field(50101; "ACSAP ID"; Integer) { }
7           field(50102; Duration; Duration) { }
8           field(50103; "Data Format"; Enum "Playlist Data Format") { }
9           field(50104; "MP3 Location"; Text[250]) { }
10          field(50105; Barcode; Text[30]) { }
11      }
12  }       Natalie Karolak, 4 months ago • Added chapter 02.
```

Figure 8.19 – Barcode field added to the Item table extension

In order to allow data entry, expose the field to the `Item Card` page extension. Use the `addafter` element to put the field right after the `GTIN` field in the **Item Card General** FastTab:

```
1    pageextension 50101 "Item Card Extension" extends "Item Card"
2    {
3        layout
4        {
5            addafter(GTIN)
6            {
7                field(Barcode; Rec.Barcode)
8                {
9                    ApplicationArea = All;
10               }
11           }
12       }
```

Figure 8.20 – Adding Barcode to Item Card

In Business Central, add an item to the catalog with the following information:

Field	Value
No.	COPCD029
Description	Deathline Int'l - Arashi Syndrom
Base Unit of Measure	Each
Barcode	703513002928

Table 8.4 – Item specifics

WDTU API codeunit

In order to create our API, we will create `codeunit 50101 "WDTU Tidal API Mgmt"` with the following procedures outlined:

```
local procedure GetAccessToken(URL: Text; ClientId: Text; ClientSecret:
Text) AccessToken: Text
```

This procedure will receive the authorization URL, the Client ID, and the Client Secret provided by the Tidal API and return the token in a text variable. In a normal business, these values would be stored in the database so it is easier to update and can be made to have multiple values if multiple APIs are to be utilized. In our example, these values will be hardcoded in the codeunit as `Label` variables. First, we will set the content of the request, which will consist of the information necessary for Tidal to authenticate and respond with the access key token. Those URL values will be `grant_type`, scope, client_id, and client_secret. The content format is fixed and only the values are variable so we can set this as a global variable. So far, our global variables consist of the following labels:

```
var
    lblContent: Label 'grant_type=%1&scope=%2&client_id=%3&client_secret=%4';
    lblGrantType: Label 'client_credentials';
    lblScope: Label 'https://auth.tidal.com/v1/oauth2/token';
    lblClientId: Label '5avqWnb4dNe9TQWf';
    lblClientSecret: Label 'UQat7j0F7Db9sBs4p9zNlru2sor0f9qEf5MlhVEIAlU=';
    lblOAuthURL: Label 'https://auth.tidal.com/v1/oauth2/token';
```

Figure 8.21 – Global variables

The GetAccessToken procedure needs local variables, the **HTTP objects** (HttpRequestMessage, HttpResponseMessage, HttpClient, HttpContent, and HttpHeaders) to make the call, as well as the **JSON objects** (JsonObject, JsonToken, and JsonValue) to parse the response. We need some text variables to manage our content and pass the JSON response from the HTTP object to the JSON object:

```
var
    HttpResponseMessage: HttpResponseMessage;
    HttpRequestMessage: HttpRequestMessage;
    HttpClient: HttpClient;
    HttpContent: HttpContent;
    HttpHeaders: HttpHeaders;
    JsonObject: JsonObject;
    JsonToken: JsonToken;
    JsonValue: JsonValue;
    ContentText: Text;
    ResponseText: Text;
```

Figure 8.22 – Local variables

We can assign the content to the request message, set HttpHeader Content-Type to application/x-www-form-urlencoded, set the URL to the same URL as the scope, and the method to POST. Using the HttpClient object, send the request and pass a HttpResponseMessage object variable to hold the response (in JSON format):

```
//set content body
ContentText := StrSubstNo(lblContent, lblGrantType, lblScope, lblClientId, lblClientSecret);
HttpContent.WriteFrom(ContentText);

// Retrieve the content headers associated with the content, assign form content type
HttpContent.GetHeaders(HttpHeaders);
HttpHeaders.Clear();
HttpHeaders.Add('Content-Type', 'application/x-www-form-urlencoded');

// Assign content to Request Message Content, set method to POST
HttpRequestMessage.Content := HttpContent;
HttpRequestMessage.SetRequestUri(URL);
HttpRequestMessage.Method := 'POST';

//Send the message and get the response
HttpClient.Send(HttpRequestMessage, HttpResponseMessage);
```

Figure 8.23 – Building the message and sending

Once `HttpResponseMessage` is returned, some handling of potential errors should be included, and then we need to move the response object content to a text variable so it can be read by a JSON object. Now that `JsonObject` has the JSON response content, it is easy to parse the part of the message we want, which is the `access_token` element and the associated value.

```
// Retrieve the access token
JsonObject.Get('access_token', JsonToken);
JsonValue := JsonToken.AsValue();
JsonToken.WriteTo(AccessToken);
AccessToken := DelChr(AccessToken, '<>', '"');
```

Figure 8.24 – Reading and retrieving the token

The `AccessToken` text variable defined as the return value will exit and pass the authorization back to the calling procedure. In our case, it will be `procedure GetTidalApiArtwork(Barcode: Text[30]; ItemNo: Code[20])`.

This procedure will be the core of the codeunit by making the actual artwork API query, handling the response, and sending the information to the item card for upload. The goal of this procedure is to get the value of the first URL in the response from the GET call. Here is a portion of the JSON response, most importantly, the image URL information:

```
{
    "data": [
        {
            "attributes": {
                "title": "Arashi Syndrom",
                "barcodeId": "703513002928",
                "numberOfVolumes": 1,
                "numberOfItems": 11,
                "duration": "PT43M34S",
                "explicit": false,
                "releaseDate": "1997-06-03",
                "copyright": "COP International",
                "popularity": 1.0,
                "availability": [
                    "STREAM",
                    "DJ"
                ],
                "mediaTags": [
                    "LOSSLESS"
                ],
                "imageLinks": [
                    {
                        "href": "https://resources.tidal.com/images/0ed55204/ecb6/4ad1/9be9/844aa49e1f60/1080x1080.jpg",
                        "meta": {
                            "width": 1080,
                            "height": 1080
                        }
```

Figure 8.25 – Image URL return message from Tidal

This procedure will follow a very similar flow of creating the content, defining the headers, adding the authorization, and the URL with query values of the HTTP objects. The URL does pass two required parameters: `barcodeId` and `countryCode`. In our example, we are hardcoding the URL and parameters except for `barcodeId`, which will come from the item record. Instead of using the JSON objects to parse through the message, we will use the `JSON Buffer` table in Business Central. This table allows us to read the JSON message as one would any Business Central table using `SetRange`, `SetFilter`, `FindFirst`, `FindLast`, and so on.

```
var
    HttpClient: HttpClient;
    HttpHeaders: HttpHeaders;
    HttpResponseMessage: HttpResponseMessage;
    HttpRequestMessage: HttpRequestMessage;
    HttpContent: HttpContent;
    Response: Text;
    JsonBuffer: Record "JSON Buffer" temporary;
    lblURL: Label 'https://openapi.tidal.com/v2/albums?countryCode=US&include=artists&filter%5BbarcodeId%5D=%1';
```

Figure 8.26 – Local variables to the GetTidalApiArtwork procedure

Tidal API requires a unique content type, which is `application/vnd.tidal.v1+JSON`. Before setting this in `HttpHeader`, it is necessary to clear any default values that may exist when the header object is instantiated:

```
// Retrieve the content headers associated with the content
HttpContent.GetHeaders(HttpHeaders);

//To prevent error message about multiple content-type attributes
if HttpHeaders.Contains('Content-Type') then
    HttpHeaders.Remove('Content-Type');

//Tidal specific content type
HttpHeaders.Add('Content-Type', 'application/vnd.tidal.v1+json');
HttpRequestMessage.Content := HttpContent;
HttpRequestMessage.GetHeaders(HttpHeaders);
```

Figure 8.27 – Tidal API content type

The other header value that needs to be set is `Authorization`. This is where the OAuth bearer token is passed to the API. The `GetAccessToken` procedure is nested inside the `HttpHeader` assignment. Like `Content-Type`, the attribute needs to be cleared to prevent multiple values from being assigned (default and custom).

```
HttpRequestMessage.GetHeaders(HttpHeaders);

//To prevent error message for multiple authorization attributes
if HttpHeaders.Contains('Authorization') then
    HttpHeaders.Remove('Authorization');

//Call the GetAccessToken function to get access_token from Tidal
HttpHeaders.Add('Authorization', StrSubstNo('Bearer %1',
                GetAccessToken(lblOAuthURL, lblClientId, lblClientSecret)));
```

Figure 8.28 – OAuth token assigned to the Authorization header

With the `HttpHeader` values assigned, we can build the URL dynamically with the `Barcode` parameter passed into the procedure. Because we are querying the Tidal API, the method used is set to `GET`. The request message is sent, and a response is received. Determine whether the message is successful before executing any code attempting to read the JSON:

```
//Send URL with Barcode value from Item
HttpRequestMessage.SetRequestUri(StrSubstNo(lblUrl, Barcode));
HttpRequestMessage.Method := 'GET';
if HttpClient.Send(HttpRequestMessage, HttpResponseMessage) then begin
    HttpResponseMessage.Content.ReadAs(Response);
```

Figure 8.29 – Building the query URL and sending the GET request

If the JSON object set is used, then there are multiple looping iterations that would have to occur to get to the URL we are looking for in the response JSON. With the Business Central JSON Buffer table, we can find what we are looking for in just a few lines of code:

```
//Populate Json Buffer table with response for easy data retrieval
JsonBuffer.ReadFromText(Response);
JsonBuffer.SetRange(Path, 'data[0].attributes.imageLinks[0].href');
//After getting the 1080x1080.jpg image url, load it into the item Picture Blob field
if JsonBuffer.FindLast() then
    ImportItemPictureFromURL(JsonBuffer.Value, ItemNo);
```

Figure 8.30 – Using the JSON Buffer table to get the first URL value

The URL can then be passed to our last procedure in the ImportItemPictureFromURL codeunit, which will have brought the album cover into the Picture Blob field on the Item record:

```
procedure ImportItemPictureFromURL(ImageURL: Text; ItemNo: Code[20])
var
    Item: Record Item;
    HttpClient: HttpClient;
    HttpResponseMessage: HttpResponseMessage;
    InStr: InStream;
begin
    If not HttpClient.Get(ImageURL, HttpResponseMessage) then
        Error('URL is not a valid image: %1', ImageURL);
    HttpResponseMessage.Content.ReadAs(InStr);
    if Item.Get(ItemNo) then begin
        Clear(Item.Picture);
        Item.Picture.ImportStream(InStr, 'Album cover for ' + Format(Item."No."));
        Item.Modify(true);
    end;
end;
```

Figure 8.31 – Import picture procedure

HttpClient is used to just get the Item.Picture value and return the binary information in HttpResponse. InStream is a generic streaming object that can read to a binary Blob type field. The Item field called Picture has a method that reads from the InStream object into the field.

Adding the new WDTU action

In order to put our Tidal API into action, add an Action to the **Item Card** extension page and promote it:

```
actions
{
    addafter(CopyItem)
    {
        action(FetchAlbumCover)
        {
            Caption = 'Get Tidal Artwork';
            Image = Download;
            ApplicationArea = All;

            trigger OnAction()
            var
                WdtuTidalAPI: Codeunit "WDTU Tidal API Mgmt";
            begin
                WdtuTidalAPI.GetTidalApiArtwork(Rec.Barcode, Rec."No.");
            end;
        }
    }
    addafter(CopyItem_Promoted)
    {
        actionref(FetchAlbumCover_Promoted; FetchAlbumCover) { }
    }
}
```

Figure 8.32 – Action to execute API call for album art

APIs are an extremely powerful toolset in Business Central, allowing both passive and active data exchange between external software. This not only opens Business Central to data interfaces between disparate systems but also implements access to defined business logic as well. Extensions are not limited in scope to the software itself, but you can utilize any software with an API that can communicate with XML, OData, JSON, or even text files.

This book has covered the application structure and business logic language but has not gone into great detail about the application process flow. This more than anything else will guide any extensions built for the Business Central ERP.

Business Central process flow

Primary data, such as sales orders, purchase orders, production orders, and financial transactions, flow through the Business Central system, as follows:

1. **Initial setup**: This is where the essential master data, reference data, and control and setup data is entered. Most of this preparation is done when the system (or a new application) is prepared for production use.

2. **Transaction entry**: Transactions are entered into documents and then transferred as part of a posting sequence into a `Journal` table, or data may be entered directly into a `Journal` table. Data is preliminarily validated as it is entered, with master and auxiliary data tables being referenced as appropriate. The entry can be through manual keying, an automated transaction generation process, or an import function that brings in transaction data from another system.

3. **Testing**: This step provides for additional data validation processing of a set of one or more transactions, often in batches, prior to submitting it to `Posting`.

4. **Post**: This step posts a `Journal` batch that includes completing transaction data validation, adding entries to one or more `Ledger` tables, and perhaps also updating a `Register` table and document history.

The following diagram provides a simplified picture of the flow of application data through a Business Central system:

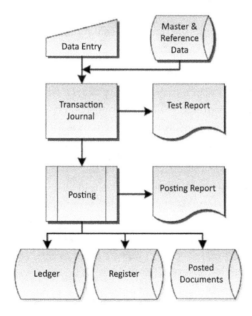

Figure 8.33 – Application data flow in Business Central

As you can see, many of the transaction types include additional reporting, multiple ledgers to update, and even auxiliary processing. However, this represents the basic data flow in Business Central whenever a `Journal` table and a `Ledger` table are involved.

When we enhance an existing Business Central functional area, such as Jobs or Service Management, we may need to enhance related process flow elements by extending tables with new fields to journals, ledgers, posted documents, and so on.

When we create a new functional area, we will likely want to replicate the standard Business Central process flow in some form for the new application's data. For example, for our WDTU application, we will handle the entry of playlists in the same fashion as Journal is entered. A day's playlists would be similar to a Journal batch in another application. After a day's shows have been broadcast, the completed playlist will be posted into the Radio Show ledger as a permanent record of the broadcasts.

Utilizing the flow shown in *Figure 8.33*, the flow of data setup and preparation, transaction data entry and testing and posting will be described in detail.

Initial setup and data preparation

Data must be maintained as new master data becomes available or when various system operating parameters and other elements change. The standard approach for Business Central data entry allows records to be entered that have just enough information to define the primary key fields, but not necessarily enough to support processing. This allows for a great deal of flexibility in the timing and responsibility for entry and completeness of new data. This approach applies to both setup data entry and ongoing production transaction data entry.

For example, a salesperson might initialize a new customer entry with a name, address, and phone number, just entering the data to which they have easy access. At this point, there is not enough information recorded to process orders for this new customer. At a later time, someone in the accounting department can set up posting groups, payment terms, and other control data that should not be controlled by the sales department. With this additional data, the new customer record is ready for production use.

The Business Central data entry approach allows the system to be updated on an incremental basis as the data arrives, providing an operational flexibility many systems lack. This works well because data often comes into an organization on a piecemeal basis. The other side of this flexibility is the added responsibility for users to ensure that partially updated information is completed in a timely fashion. For a user organization that can't manage this, it may be necessary to create special procedures that enforce the necessary discipline.

Transaction entry

Transactions are entered into a Journal table. Data is preliminarily validated as it is entered; master and auxiliary data tables are referenced as appropriate. Data validation is one of the more powerful existing features in Business Central, such as FlowFields. Validations are based on the evaluation of the individual transaction data, plus the related master records and associated reference tables – for example, lookups being satisfied, application or system setup parameter constraints being met, and so on.

Testing and posting the Journal batch

Any additional validations that are needed to ensure the integrity and completeness of the transaction data prior to being posted are done either in pre-post routines or directly in the posting processes. The actual posting of a `Journal` batch occurs after the transaction data is completely validated.

Depending on the specific application, when `Journal` transactions don't pass muster during this final validation stage, either the individual transaction is bypassed while acceptable transactions are posted, or the entire `Journal` batch is rejected until the identified problem is resolved.

The posting process adds entries to one or more ledgers, and sometimes to a document history table. When a `Journal Line` is posted to a ledger, it becomes part of the permanent accounting record. Most data cannot be changed or deleted once it resides in a ledger (an example exception would be the due date on a payable).

Register tables may also be updated during posting, recording the ID number ranges of ledger entries posted, when they are posted, and in what batches. This adds to the transparency of the Business Central application system for audits and analysis.

In general, Business Central follows the standard accounting practice of requiring ledger revisions to be made by posting reversing entries, rather than by deletion of problem entries. The overall result is that Business Central is a very auditable system, a key requirement for a variety of government, legal, and certification requirements for information systems.

Summary

In this chapter, we reviewed some of the more advanced Business Central tools and techniques. By now, you should have a strong admiration for the power and flexibility of Business Central. Many of these subject areas will require more study and hands-on practice. We spent a lot of time on API construction because that opens Business Central to the power of the Azure architecture. By now, you should almost be ready to begin your own development project.

That said, there is always more to learn, and Packt books are here to help. There are additional books the authors of this book would like to recommend:

- *Mastering Microsoft Dynamics 365 Business Central: The complete guide for designing and integrating advanced Business Central solutions* by Stefano Demiliani and Duilio Tacconi will go deeper into the extensibility of Microsoft Business Central with GitHub, the Azure Power Platform, and the AL language itself

- An important aspect of any development project is to test prior to deployment, and for repeated, though (and most importantly) automated testing, read *Automated Testing in Microsoft Dynamics 365 Business Central: Efficiently automate test cases for faster development cycles with less time needed for manual testing* by Luc van Vugt

Questions

1. API is used for proprietary data formats with Microsoft software. True or false?

   Answer: False

2. Which data formats can Business Central APIs work with?

   A. JSON

   B. XML

   C. OData

   D. Fixed or Delimited Text

   E. All of the above

   Answer: E

3. Users cannot delete or modify database data through web services. True or false?

   Answer: False

4. Which objects can be used as a web service endpoint?

   A. Codeunit

   B. XMLport

   C. Query

   D. Page

   E. All of the above

   Answer: E

5. In Business Central, the main data flow is from transaction journals to ledger entries through a posting routine. Multi-language capability in Business Central requires external software. True or false?

   Answer: False

6. It is possible to preview the result of a posting. True or false?

   Answer: True

7. Any software that accesses Business Central APIs should authenticate through OAuth tokens. True or false?

   Answer: True

8. Business Central is limited to any two languages at a time, which can be defined in the General Ledger setup. True or false?

   Answer: False

9. API type objects cannot contain AL code: all data manipulation must occur outside of the API object. True or false?

   Answer: False

Index

A

packtpub.com

Subscribe to our online digital library for full access to over 7,000 books and videos, as well as industry leading tools to help you plan your personal development and advance your career. For more information, please visit our website.

Why subscribe?

- Spend less time learning and more time coding with practical eBooks and Videos from over 4,000 industry professionals

- Improve your learning with Skill Plans built especially for you

- Get a free eBook or video every month

- Fully searchable for easy access to vital information

- Copy and paste, print, and bookmark content

Did you know that Packt offers eBook versions of every book published, with PDF and ePub files available? You can upgrade to the eBook version at packtpub.com and as a print book customer, you are entitled to a discount on the eBook copy. Get in touch with us at customercare@packtpub.com for more details.

At www.packtpub.com, you can also read a collection of free technical articles, sign up for a range of free newsletters, and receive exclusive discounts and offers on Packt books and eBooks.

Other Books You May Enjoy

If you enjoyed this book, you may be interested in these other books by Packt:

Extending Dynamics 365 Finance and Operations Apps with Power Platform

Adrià Ariste Santacreu

ISBN: 978-1-80181-159-0

- Get to grips with integrating Dynamics 365 F&O with Dataverse

- Discover the benefits of using Power Automate with Dynamics 365 F&O

- Understand Power Apps as a means to extend the functionality of Dynamics 365 F&O

- Build your skills to implement Azure Data Lake Storage for Power BI reporting

- Explore AI Builder and its integration with Power Automate Flows and Power Apps

- Gain insights into environment management, governance, and application lifecycle management (ALM) for Dataverse and the Power Platform

Becoming a Dynamics 365 Supply Chain Management Functional Consultant Associate

Juan Bravo Vargas, Mariano Martínez Melo

ISBN: 978-1-80461-800-4

- Understand the scope of the Dynamics 365 Supply Chain Management platform
- Find out how to define an effective strategy to set up and control products and inventory
- Implement core supply chain flows such as procure to pay and order to cash successfully
- Discover how to comply with quality assurance controls
- Define and optimize warehouse management flows and transport management shipping
- Plan and schedule all your replenishments with master planning

Packt is searching for authors like you

If you're interested in becoming an author for Packt, please visit `authors.packtpub.com` and apply today. We have worked with thousands of developers and tech professionals, just like you, to help them share their insight with the global tech community. You can make a general application, apply for a specific hot topic that we are recruiting an author for, or submit your own idea.

Share Your Thoughts

Now you've finished *Programming Microsoft Dynamics 365 Business Central*, we'd love to hear your thoughts! Scan the QR code below to go straight to the Amazon review page for this book and share your feedback or leave a review on the site that you purchased it from.

`https://packt.link/r/1803236418`

Your review is important to us and the tech community and will help us make sure we're delivering excellent quality content.

Download a free PDF copy of this book

Thanks for purchasing this book!

Do you like to read on the go but are unable to carry your print books everywhere?

Is your eBook purchase not compatible with the device of your choice?

Don't worry, now with every Packt book you get a DRM-free PDF version of that book at no cost.

Read anywhere, any place, on any device. Search, copy, and paste code from your favorite technical books directly into your application.

The perks don't stop there, you can get exclusive access to discounts, newsletters, and great free content in your inbox daily

Follow these simple steps to get the benefits:

1. Scan the QR code or visit the link below

https://packt.link/free-ebook/978-1-80323-641-4

2. Submit your proof of purchase
3. That's it! We'll send your free PDF and other benefits to your email directly

www.ingramcontent.com/pod-product-compliance
Lightning Source LLC
Chambersburg PA
CBHW060644060326
40690CB00020B/4515